HARVARD ECONOMIC STUDIES

Out of print.

HARVARD ECONOMIC STUDIES

VOLUME LXXVIII

LONDON : GEOFFREY CUMBERLEGE

OXFORD UNIVERSITY PRESS

THE ECONOMIC ASPECTS
OF
ARGENTINE FEDERALISM

1820-1852

BY

MIRON BURGIN

CAMBRIDGE, MASSACHUSETTS
HARVARD UNIVERSITY PRESS
1946

To my wife
Janet Harriet

PREFACE

THE POLITICAL struggles in Argentina during the first decades of her independence centered primarily around the constitutional issue. As soon as the danger of Spain's return to the shores of La Plata had passed the problem of national organization and of the nature and authority of central government became the burning question of the day. The conflict between those who advocated a strong central government and those who desired to safeguard local autonomy was not an academic problem to be resolved solely by persuasion and by reference to recognized authorities. On the contrary, the problem was intensely practical; it was rooted in the economic pattern of the country, and its solution deeply affected the economic interests of all classes of Argentine society and of every province of the Confederation.

It was inevitable that economic issues should have been injected into the political struggles of the day. It was inevitable, too, that economic considerations should have at all times influenced the doctrinal position and the tactics of the political parties in their struggle for power. Had the economy of the country been more homogeneous, or had regional interdependence been more evenly balanced, the question of local autonomy, whether political or economic, might have been solved within the precincts of the constitutional assembly. But the economic structure which Argentina inherited from the colonial era was neither homogeneous nor well balanced. It lacked the necessary resiliency to enable the country to adapt itself to the new political and geographic environment. Independence did not reconcile the divergent economic trends latent within the viceroyalty. On the contrary, under the brilliant sun of political freedom the conflicts engendered by economic emancipation grew in scope and intensity. It was not possible to isolate the economic aspects of the constitutional issue and to deal with them without reference to the problem of state organization, and it was for this reason mainly that the political struggles of the period were so bitter and so protracted.

The political history of the period covered in this study has been the subject of intensive research by distinguished scholars, and the main outline of the struggles and of the issues involved is well known. The purpose of this study is to direct attention to the economic factor which formed the background for and was at the same time an important ingredient of the historical process that guided the Argentine nation from the stormy days of the Constituent Assembly through *suma del poder público* to Caseros.

It is a pleasant duty for the author to record his gratitude to all those who have been helpful in preparing this study. He is deeply indebted to Professor C. H. Haring, of Harvard University, who suggested and encouraged this study and who followed its development through all stages. During his stay in Argentina the author enjoyed the privilege of having at his disposal the erudition and experience of Professor Emilio Ravignani, director of the Instituto de Investigaciones Históricas.

The preparation of the study would not have been possible without the unstinting coöperation of many institutions in Argentina. The author would express his gratitude to the directors and personnel of the Archivo General de la Nación, of the Museo Mitre, of the Archivo Histórico de Tucumán, of the Archivo de Gobierno of Córdoba, and of the Archivo de la Provincia of Entre Ríos. Thanks are also due to the Director and personnel of the library of the Banco Tornquist, and to the firm Martínez de Hoz whose business files the author was permitted to examine.

It is not possible to mention all those in Argentina whose friendliness and hospitality enabled the author to gain a more intimate knowledge of the country. He would, however, pay special tribute to Sr. Ricardo Frondizi, Dr. Manuel Lizondo Borda, Sr. Julio Irazusta, Sr. Guillermo Saraví, Dr. Francisco J. V. Silva, Dr. José María Funes, Dr. Arturo Frondizi, Sr. Alfredo J. Weiss, Sr. Víctor Díaz, and Señorita Eileen Tynan.

In conclusion the author wishes to acknowledge his debt to his wife, Janet H. Burgin, who cheerfully undertook the thankless task of preparing the manuscript for the press.

M. B.

Washington, D. C.
December 1945

CONTENTS

TABLES

THE ECONOMIC ASPECTS OF ARGENTINE
FEDERALISM

ABBREVIATIONS OF REFERENCES

Archivo Americano

Pedro de Angelis (ed.). *Archivo Americano y Espíritu de la Prensa del Mundo.*

Archivo General

Archivo General de la Nación.

Asambleas Constituyentes

Emilio Ravignani (ed.). *Asambleas constituyentes argentinas, seguidas de las textos constitucionales, legislativos y pactos interprovinciales que organizaron políticamente la nación.*

Compilación

Compilación de leyes, decretos, acuerdos de la Excelentísima Cámara de Justicia y demás disposiciones de carácter público dictadas en la provincia de Córdoba desde 1810 á 1870.

Diario de Sesiones

Diario de Sesiones de la Junta de Representantes de la Provincia de Buenos Aires.

Mabragaña

Heraclio Mabragaña (ed.). *Los mensajes. Historia del desenvolvimiento de la nación argentina, redactada cronológicamente por sus gobernantes, 1810–1910.*

Recopilación

Recopilación de leyes, decretos y acuerdos de la Provincia de Entré Ríos, desde 1821 á 1873.

Recopilación de leyes y decretos

Recopilación de leyes y decretos promulgades en Buenos Aires desde el 25 de mayo de 1810 hasta fin de diciembre de 1835.

RO

Registro Oficial de la Provincia de Buenos Aires.

CHAPTER I

THE ECONOMICS OF INDEPENDENCE

El corifeo de la independencia no es un soldado. Fué un economista, el doctor Moreno.—JUAN BAUTISTA ALBERDI.

Nuestra economía había sido por la España substancialmente pervertida.—LUCAS AYARRAGARAY.

AMONG the many and varied forces which caused the decline and finally the fall of the Spanish Colonial Empire in America none stand out so saliently as the economic. Just as the growth of the colonial system was determined primarily by the economic needs of the mother country, so its disintegration was conditioned by the inability of Spain to adapt the system to the changing economic relationships within and without the Empire. The forces making for maladjustment were at work on both sides of the Atlantic: on the one side was the economic decline of the mother country, on the other the expansion of colonial economy. Each of the two processes was in its way instrumental in undermining the very foundation on which the economic structure of the Empire rested, for the growing disparity in the rate of economic development between the various parts of the Empire was accompanied by a weakening of the bonds that held them together. The political and social unity of the metropolis and the colonies, on the one hand, and of the several colonial administrative areas, on the other, became increasingly tenuous.

In subjecting the economic intercourse between the mother country and the overseas colonies to strict supervision the Spanish government pursued a double aim. First it was determined to keep foreigners away from the natural resources of the newly discovered territories; secondly it was anxious to secure all commerce with the colonies to Spanish nationals. While it was comparatively easy to enforce prohibition of immigration to Spanish America from countries other than Spain, the task of keeping colonial commerce in Spanish hands proved to be much more difficult. All trade with the colonies was limited to two fleets. One of these made annual voyages to Portobello, and the other sailed to Vera Cruz once every two or three years. Only the former fleet was permitted to carry on trade with Peru, Chile, and the River Plate.

The limitation of shipping, together with other restrictions on overseas commerce, led to the growth of monopolies. From the time of Charles V, in Spain, and of Philip II, in Mexico and Lima, the merchants engaged in colonial trade banded into privileged corporations. These corporations, since they were assured of large profits, did not resist too strongly the elaborate regulations and numerous taxes by means of which the government attempted to increase its revenues. It was realized in the mercantile community that if the markets in both the colonies and the mother country were kept free from foreign interference, the cost of regulation and taxation could be easily shifted to the consumer.

The consistent application of this policy of scarcity produced far reaching consequences of an economic and political nature. To make the policy effective it was not enough to exclude foreign participation in the traffic from and to Spain's overseas possessions. For as the colonies grew in population, as their economy became more differentiated, and their productive capacity expanded, they endeavored by means of intercolonial trade to free themselves from the economic tutelage of the Spanish merchants. So, in order to safeguard the colonial markets for domestic industry and commerce, the Spanish government was forced to adopt a restrictive policy with respect to the internal economic life of the colonies. Not only was intercolonial trade kept at a minimum, but even within each colony the establishment of industries which competed with the manufactures of the mother country was consistently discouraged and often entirely forbidden. Consequently, the pattern of colonial economic development was, at least in its broad outlines, determined by Spain's commercial and fiscal interests. The limits set by Spain to the economic expansion of the colonies were seldom relaxed, for her primary interest lay in preserving intact the economic position she had achieved during the reign of Charles V.

The economic system established by Spain in her far-flung Empire was fully developed during the reigns of Charles V, and his successor Philip II. Its basic principle was the development of a tightly closed economy, with Spain as the center. This vast territory with its great variety of climates and its seemingly inexhaustible resources, among them the most prized commodities of the time, gold and silver, appeared to provide a solid foundation for a strong and well-knit economic structure. Overseas commerce, based partly upon geographic division of labor and partly also upon the industrial superiority of the mother country, seemed to assure a continuous expansion of the component parts of the economy, and therefore of the Empire as a whole. And when by the middle of the sixteenth century a rich and powerful Spain enforced respect for her mercantilist policies and protected her nationals both on the high seas and in the colonies, the economic structure appeared to have become indestructible.

Yet, towards the end of the sixteenth century the system began to show unmistakable signs of decay. At first gradually, and then in the second half of the seventeenth century at an accelerated rate, the system, from being an effective instrument of economic policy, became instead a serious obstacle to the development and continued expansion of colonial society. And the final breakdown was the more disastrous, since the Spanish government, oblivious of the basic shortcomings of its policies, failed to adjust these policies to the changing conditions in Spain and abroad.

Even under the most favorable conditions Spain would have had difficulties in maintaining the colonial system intact. As long as the colonies were sparsely populated and economically weak the problem of keeping them within the orbit of Spain's economic influence was comparatively simple. Without undue strain upon her economic resources and productive capacity, Spain could supply all the needs of her colonies in exchange for precious metals and such commodities as had a ready market. In the final analysis, therefore, the system rested upon a geographical division of labor, so that with the inevitable growth and diversification of colonial economy its stability depended primarily upon a parallel development of the mother country. But by the middle of the sixteenth century Spain had entered upon a period of sharp economic decline. So far from matching the economic expansion of her overseas dominions, Spain was experiencing a rapid deterioration of her mining and manufacturing industries. Not only was the country unable to absorb the produce and manufacture of the colonies, but it was frequently obliged to curtail exports in order to safeguard the stability of domestic prices, already inordinately high.

Paradoxically enough the very success of the mercantilist policy in the period of colonial expansion was one of the principal causes of its failure in the ensuing period of stabilization and economic differentiation in the overseas possessions. For the unprecedented rise of prices in the mother country was the result of the rigid application of mercantilist policy to transatlantic trade. Owing to the influx of specie to Spain, prices there rose much faster than in other European countries. Smuggling across Spanish frontiers in Europe and in America became extremely profitable and threatened to supplant legitimate trade. Spain was powerless to emforce respect for the law, partly because she lacked the necessary military and financial resources, but largely because she was no longer able to fulfill her economic obligations to the colonies. Under the later Habsburgs Seville depended upon foreign manufactures for five-sixths of her overseas exports, while in the colonies contraband trade carried on by Portuguese, French, Dutch, British, and other merchants, tolerated and even encouraged by the authorities, exceeded legal commerce in volume and value. Thus Spain's transatlantic commerce all but disappeared, and mercantilism as the fundamental principle of colonial policy became an empty shell devoid of all economic and political content.

Not until the accession of the Bourbons to the throne did the Spanish government acknowledge the failure of mercantilism as an instrument of economic and colonial policy. In a series of economic and administrative reforms it endeavored to broaden the basis of Spain's relations with the colonies. The Seville merchants were deprived of their monopoly; in 1718 the Casa de Contratación was removed from Seville to Cadiz; the fleet system was abolished in 1748; the privilege of overseas trade was extended to nine Spanish ports in 1764; and to thirteen additional ports in 1778. In the dominions, too, overseas and to some extent international trade was permitted in a number of ports, including Buenos Aires, Montevideo, Valparaiso, and Guayaquil. Furthermore, in 1797, while Spain was involved in the Napoleonic wars, neutral vessels were given the right to engage in trade with the colonies. But the commercial liberalism of the Bourbons did not extend to commerce between the colonies and foreign countries, although in 1791 France obtained the privilege of importing annually a fixed number of slaves, and of calling at colonial ports for the purchase of supplies. Twelve years later this concession, somewhat liberalized, was transferred to England. Yet if these concessions had important political implications, their immediate economic significance was negligible.

The Bourbon reforms provided no adequate basis for a solution of the many problems which confronted the colonies. The opening of ports in Spanish America and in the mother country did, of course, stimulate transatlantic commerce, but the increase in the volume of traffic was far from sufficient to meet the growing requirements of the colonies. In fact, to the colonies the legalization of commercial relations with the mother country was no longer a problem of major importance. What the colonies needed above all was direct contact with world markets, for the interposition of Spain in the flow of commerce between Spanish America and the outside world necessarily worked to the disadvantage of the colonies. The reforms were bound to remain an empty gesture so long as Spain's economic advance continued to lag behind that of Western Europe and North America and so long as her treasury continued to rely heavily upon overseas commerce. Stimulated by the industrial revolution in Western Europe the economic development of the colonies had far outgrown the half-hearted liberalism of the Bourbons. Spanish America could no longer be satisfied with mere trading privileges. What it needed and demanded were economic freedom and autonomy, which alone were capable of assuring the expansion of its productive capacity and a more national utilization of its vast natural resources. Under the existing system, however modified by the liberalistic tendencies of the Bourbon policies, the productive forces of Spanish America were chained to the backward economy of the metropolis. In order to free these forces from the fetters of the economic and fiscal interests of the mother country the old social and political ties had to be abolished. Accordingly, the struggle for economic freedom was at the same time a political struggle, the struggle for independence and for control of the state power without which the reorganization of colonial society was impossible. The social and political conditions for such a reorganization were already ripe towards the end of the eighteenth century, but it was not until news of a revolt in Spain had reached the continent that the "cry of liberty" raised in Buenos Aires resounded to the farthest corners of the Spanish Overseas Empire.

2

Of all the Spanish colonies in the New World none was less adapted to the commercial and economic policies, which formed the backbone of the Spanish colonial system, than the provinces (later the viceroyalty) of La Plata. Among the last territories to be added to the co-

lonial Empire, removed from the already established highways of transatlantic commerce, poor in readily exploitable mineral wealth, the vast
territories of the River Plate region were from the very beginning neglected by the mother country. Nor could it be otherwise. For not
only were the newly established colonies insignificant as a source of
revenue, but owing to their geographical position they presented a
constant threat to the integrity of Spanish colonial policy.

It was precisely in order to preserve the mercantilist system intact
that the Spanish government sacrificed, and thought itself justified in
sacrificing, the most fundamental economic interests of the River Plate
territory. Almost immediately after the second founding of Buenos
Aires in 1580 the province was confronted with serious difficulties in
establishing direct commercial contact with either Spain or the outside world. Buenos Aires and the whole River Plate region were subject to the law of 1561, which prohibited all overseas commerce through
ports other than those expressly designated for the purpose. Any legal
infraction of this law required a specific dispensation from the crown.
True, such dispensations were granted from time to time, but they were
always limited and never sufficient to satisfy even the most immediate
needs of the province. So, for example, in 1602 the crown allowed the
export to Brazil of a fixed amount of flour, meat, and tallow per year
(valued at about 12,500 pesos) in exchange for clothing, shoes, iron
wares, and other necessities. This arrangement, which remained in
force for six years, was extended for a similar period in 1608, and for
five more years in 1614. But when in 1620 the *Procurador general* of
the provinces of La Plata, don Manuel de Frías, petitioned the king to
allow the colony to continue commercial relations with Brazil and
Spain, the petition was rejected on the ground that existing laws banned
commerce with Peru by way of Buenos Aires, and that the opening of
the Buenos Aires port would jeopardize the prosperity of the provinces
of Tierra Firme. Throughout the remainder of the century these restrictions were not only upheld but even intensified on occasion.

Regard for the interests of the Lima merchants, as well as fiscal considerations, determined Spain's policy in the River Plate provinces.
An open port on the shores of La Plata could have only one result: to
make the whole territory east of the Andes commercially tributary to
Buenos Aires. Hence, if the markets of Córdoba, Tucumán, Salta,
and Jujuy were to be preserved for the commerce of Lima, it was
essential that Buenos Aires be prevented from developing into a

transit point for imports from Europe. Moreover, because the proximity of Portuguese ports made control of contraband trade at Buenos Aires extremely difficult, and because also the balance of trade of La Plata was necessarily adverse, the concession of trading privileges to Buenos Aires had to result in loss of treasure. Here, again, sound policy seemed to demand the total prohibition of commerce.

Thus the interest of Peruvian commerce and the interest of the Spanish treasury blended nicely. The crown lent a ready ear to Peruvian merchants, and was more than willing to be persuaded that Buenos Aires ought to be closed to all overseas traffic. And when it was found that foreign goods were brought to the markets of Córdoba and Tucumán in spite of legal prohibitions fortified by harsh penalties, measures were taken to stop contraband trade by imposing surtaxes on goods moving westward, and by severely restricting the flow of specie from the Interior to Buenos Aires.

In 1622 the so-called "dry customs" (*aduana seca*) was established in Córdoba. A tax of 50 per cent *ad valorem* was imposed upon all goods passing the city, which was situated halfway between Buenos Aires and Tucumán. The object of this tariff wall was to isolate Buenos Aires from internal markets. And in order to fight the menace of Buenos Aires competition at its source, importation of precious metals in any form into the River Plate region was prohibited by law in 1623. It was not until 1661 that the law of 1623 was somewhat modified, in order to relieve the acute shortage of circulatnig media in the Litoral. But the "dry customs" in Córdoba was maintained until 1695, when it was moved to Jujuy.

Spain's solicitude for the welfare of Peruvian commerce at the expense of Buenos Aires, her rigid adherence to mercantilist doctrine, all but strangled the economic development of the River Plate region. Enclosed within the colonial system, but separated from its markets by distance and special regulations, restricted by law and nature to agriculture and grazing, the colony remained "as poor as it was remote." In order to survive, the colony was forced to wage a constant if surreptitious struggle against the stifling effects of the economic policies of the mother country. Defeated in the Council of the Indies, where it sought to obtain modification of the stringent laws of commerce, it resorted to subterfuge, aided and abetted by both local authorities and foreign merchantmen. Contraband trade began to flourish on the shores of La Plata in defiance of all the efforts of the Spanish crown. Foreign goods not only surmounted the outer walls of the port of Buenos Aires but crossed the Paraná and La Plata. They escaped the "dry customs" of Córdoba and penetrated into the interior markets where they successfully competed with the merchandise of Lima. In spite of all prohibitions gold and silver continued to flow eastward towards Buenos Aires.

So the River Plate colony, and particularly Buenos Aires, came to occupy a special place in the imperial system. An integral part of that system, Buenos Aires was yet one of the most persistent forces making for its disintegration. So long as the colony remained economically weak and underpopulated the threat to the integrity of the colonial system was slight. Spain could well afford the risk, not only because of her vastly superior strength, but also because the colony performed the important function of safeguarding the Empire against Portuguese expansion. Contact with Brazil, and through Brazil with foreign countries was, of course, unavoidable, but the mother country hoped to neutralize this danger by isolating Buenos Aires from the West. However, economic isolation could never be wholly successful, nor could it be maintained indefinitely. As the population and wealth of the colony grew, pressure against the legal barriers surrounding the River Plate region gathered momentum, and since direct attack upon the system was impracticable, wholesale evasion of the laws supporting that system was resorted to. Thus, while still standing guard over the territorial integrity of the Empire, Buenos Aires was at the same time undermining the Empire's economic exclusiveness.

The prohibitions by means of which Spain attempted to enforce the economic isolation of Buenos Aires were rescinded in the course of the eighteenth century. The liberalization of Spain's economic policies in the River Plate region began with the transfer of the *aduana seca* from Córdoba to Jujuy, in 1695. Early in the eighteenth century Spain adopted the practice of granting special permits to ships scheduled to call at the port of Buenos Aires. One Andrés Martínez de Arurbua obtained such a permit as early as 1716. At first these permits were few and far between; however their number grew in the second half of the century. Thus, in 1752 twelve ships entered the port of Buenos Aires. After 1742 Spanish vessels were permitted to travel to Callao by way of Cape Horn, and were authorized to make stops at Buenos Aires, although cargo destined for the Interior provinces could not be unloaded there. In 1768 direct mail service was established between

Buenos Aires and Spain, and in order to cover the resulting deficit the boats were permitted to load cargo to and from Buenos Aires. Eight years later, in 1776, the royal decree of 1774 which legalized commercial intercourse between Peru, New Spain, New Granada, and Guatemala was extended to Buenos Aires. In that same year the River Plate provinces obtained administrative autonomy through the establishment of the viceroyalty of Rio de la Plata, with Pedro de Cevallos as the first viceroy. By a decree of November 6, 1777, confirmed by the Spanish government in 1778, imports to the interior provinces (Tucumán, Salta, etc.) through Buenos Aires were legalized in the face of strenuous opposition of Peruvian merchants. That decree completed the series of measures which brought about the economic autonomy of Buenos Aires and the territories comprising the new viceroyalty.

The administrative and commercial reforms of the Bourbons provided a powerful stimulus to the economic development of the River Plate, and especially of Buenos Aires. Freed from the economic and administrative jurisdiction of Lima, the country was at last in a position to utilize the advantages of the more direct route to markets through the port of Buenos Aires. Abrogation of laws prohibiting interprovincial trade resulted in a rapid increase of commerce based upon territorial division of labor. There was a considerable decrease in import prices and a simultaneous appreciation in the value of commodities destined for overseas markets. For the first time the country was in a position to make full and open use of the vast cattle resources which had accumulated in the past two centuries.

In this process of economic expansion Buenos Aires, province as well as city, was far in the lead. The province, and generally the pampa, was the most important producer of the country's exportable commodities, so that the city now became the port, the only important one, of a vast territory, the terminus and transit point of a large and constantly growing interprovincial and overseas commerce. From an overgrown village of "four hundred houses" in the second half of the seventeenth century, when Azcarate du Biscay visited the country, Buenos Aires grew into a city of more than 25,000 inhabitants in 1779, and of about 40,000 in 1801. It was now the capital of the viceroyalty and also the financial and commercial center of the country. It had become a "new city devoted since the advent of free trade to the cares and peaceful pursuits of business, its warlike habits having been transformed into the habits which usually characterize a mercantile community."

However, towards the end of the century the economy of Buenos Aires was again threatened with stagnation. It soon became evident that prohibition of direct intercourse with foreign countries was a most serious obstacle to the economic development of the colony. The problem which now confronted the viceroyalty of La Plata once more revolved around Spain's capacity to absorb all of the colony's produce, and to satisfy the growing demand for manufactures at a reasonable price. The mother country was in no position to fulfill either of the two conditions. Great as her economic resurgence was in the second half of the eighteenth century it was not great enough to satisfy the requirements of the colony. The only function Spain served was as an intermediary between the River Plate and foreign countries, a function as costly as it was superfluous, in view of the facility with which direct contact with international markets could be established. To Buenos Aires the necessity of trading through Spain appeared the more iniquitous since it was not Spain but England which was the largest consumer of the colony's produce, and also the most important source of the commodities it needed. To force Buenos Aires to trade with England via Spain meant, in fact, to rob the colony of nearly all the benefits flowing from international commerce. The dominion traded in international markets, but the prices it received or paid were determined largely by Spanish and domestic monopolists. This abnormal situation was brought to the attention of the colony almost daily, for even under the regime of the *Reglamento de comercio libre* contraband trade continued to be extremely profitable to both the native merchants and the foreigners.

Considered from a purely economic point of view the problem was relatively simple. Given the high cost of Spain's services as the intermediary in the colony's overseas commerce, prohibition of direct trading with foreign countries of necessity handicapped a more complete utilization of the country's natural resources. So long as exploitation of the vast cattle resources, accumulated in the period of economic isolation, required a minimum amount of labor and practically no capital investments, the country could without undue difficulty bear the cost of reaching European markets by way of Spain. But as the surplus of cattle stock diminished, as land became relatively scarce, and production more costly, the colony could no longer afford to part with a substantial share of its profits. It became essential that the prices received for commodities exported, and those paid for imports, should be brought into closer correspondence, for upon this depended the continued expansion of the grazing industry, the backbone of the colonial economy. And this in turn implied the elimination of the metropolis as the intermediary in the commercial intercourse between the colony and foreign countries; it implied the opening of the port of Buenos Aires to all commerce, the abolition of the outer ring which held the imperial economy together.

Had it been possible to confine the problem to its economic aspects alone the solution might have been attained without seriously impairing the political unity of the Empire. In reality, however, the social and political aspects of the movement for "free trade" were inseparable from the economic aspects. And they were as important. For one thing, the opening of the port, and therefore of the colony, to all commerce was a direct threat to the economic and social security of those who had already occupied a privileged position with respect to overseas trade. The merchants-monopolists, who together with the crown officials formed the upper strata of colonial society, saw in "free trade" the end of their economic and political power. For not only would "free trade" wipe out monopolistic gains, but it was certain to promote the economic welfare, and therefore also the social and political prestige of those who were to be the direct beneficiaries of the expansion of commerce, namely, the non-monopolist merchants and the landowners-cattlebreeders. Nor were the monopolists in Buenos Aires alone in opposing "free trade." For the opening of the port of Buenos Aires was bound to affect the industries of Córdoba, Tucumán, and the provinces of Cuyo. Furthermore, it spelt the doom of Peruvian commerce in the northwestern markets of the viceroyalty. Consequently, what the advocates of "free trade" at first conceived as a mere change of economic policy, an extension of the *Reglamento del comercio libre*, was gradually transformed into the problem of economic autonomy, and from this it was a short step to the problem of emancipation. "Free trade" became synonymous with freedom in general; its preservation—with political independence.

3

The proclamation of the *Cabildo abierto* on the 25th of May 1810 was unmistakably a revolutionary act. Not only was this act of self-government the first step towards independence, but it was also the beginning of a series of profound changes in the economic and social structure of the viceroyalty. Some of these changes were the result of the revolution itself. Confined largely to Buenos Aires and the provinces of the Litoral they were accomplished with comparative ease. But in the interior provinces which were more intimately related to the Spanish Colonial Empire adjustment to the new economic environment was difficult and complicated. It involved the destruction of many things which prior to the Revolution had a purpose and justification; it required adaptation to a new set of geo-political factors, which might or might not be favorable to the economic potentialities of the region.

If the area comprising the viceroyalty of La Plata had been less extensive, or its economy more uniformly pastoral, the transition from colonial status to independence might have taken place without undue strain. For it would have been relatively easy to weather the maladjustments which a sudden abolition of restrictions upon trade was likely to occasion. But the economy of the viceroyalty was neither uniform nor simple. The viceroyalty was divided into several unequal regions, each having its own pattern of development; a development conditioned on the one hand by physical environment and available labor power and skill, and, on the other, by the exigencies of Spain's colonial policies. Whatever unity the economy of the viceroyalty possessed was based primarily upon the territorial division of labor. Hence the abolition of trade restrictions resulted in maladjustments which were unavoidable and more than merely temporary. In fact the immediate effect of the Revolution was to nullify in some sections of the country much of what had been achieved in the preceding years.

The sectors of the economy of the viceroyalty which benefited most from the Revolution of 1810 were the grazing industry, overseas commerce, and that portion of inter-regional trade which emanated from or passed through Buenos Aires. The grazing industry in every form quickly responded to the opening of the country to foreign trade. There was a broadening of the market for hides and other by-products of the industry. Land appreciated in value, and cattle owners and meat producers flourished. Commerce followed in the wake of grazing. The fact that the country was now able to obtain better prices for its exports, and that it was free to buy in the cheapest markets, increased the volume of trade and on terms more advantageous than hitherto. Although a portion of these benefits accrued to the ultimate consumer a good deal remained in the hands of the merchant class. Thus so far as the litoral provinces and the city of Buenos Aires were concerned the hopes of the protagonists of the Revolution of 1810 were amply justified. Here, more than in any other part of Argentina, political emancipation not only consolidated the achievements of the preceding decades, but also cleared the ground for further progress.

The interior provinces presented a different picture. In these regions grazing, although important, was not the only source of subsistence. Partly because of a greater variety of natural resources, and partly because of the highly protective features of Spain's commercial and administrative policies, the provinces of the Interior managed to achieve a higher degree of economic integration and self-sufficiency. Backward as these provinces were, they yet succeeded in developing certain industries which, in addition to supplying local needs, produced surpluses for exports to other parts of the Spanish Colonial Empire. Coarse textiles were produced in considerable quantities in the Jesuit missions, in the province of Córdoba as well as in other provinces; linen of fair quality was manufactured in Catamarca; Corrientes supplied the viceroyalty with girths; the production of wine and brandy reached a high degree of development in Mendoza, San Juan, La Rioja, and Catamarca; in Tucumán and Mendoza local timber was utilized in the production of wagons; and in Tucumán sugar was manufactured. All these provinces were in close commercial relations with Buenos Aires as well as with Lima both as termini and as transit points for the considerable mule trade between the River Plate region and Peru.

Precisely because the colonial system was mercantilist and protectionist, the interior provinces achieved a certain measure of economic prosperity. Remoteness from the main ports of overseas commerce, the presence of abundant labor owing to the incorporation of the Indian tribes into the colonial economic system, and the plentiful supply of raw material (cotton, vine, timber, etc.), plus the availability of internal markets—all were factors making for the emergence of a fairly integrated economy. It should be noted, however, that, given the primitive methods of production, the industry had little power of survival. In spite of the cheapness of labor, native industry was unable to withstand foreign competition either with regard to cost or quality of production. The decline of the Spanish Colonial system was, therefore, bound to have a particularly damaging effect on the economic stability of this region in the River Plate viceroyalty.

The process of economic dislocation, always a threat because of the constant inflow of contraband goods, had already begun in the last quarter of the eighteenth century, after Buenos Aires was designated as a port of call for Spanish ships. As a result of the *Reglamento del comercio libre* the interior provinces were forced to withdraw from the Buenos Aires markets. Spanish and foreign goods were easy victors in the competition against domestic products in the River Plate area, and threatened to invade the interior provinces. The expansion of interprovincial commerce, which followed the opening of Buenos Aires, was only a partial compensation for the loss of markets. Thus the economy of the Interior entered upon a period of gradual deterioration. And the Revolution of 1810 accelerated the process. It opened the gates to a flood of commodities which soon swamped the country. Sugar and rice from Brazil, wine and brandy from Spain and Portugal, textiles and other manufactures from England and Europe, poured in increasing quantities into Buenos Aires, where they were distributed to the farthest corners of the country. Some of the worst predictions of those who before 1810 opposed "free trade" began to materialize. Domestic industry was faced with ruin. The economic difficulties of the Interior were further aggravated by the circumstance that shortly after the Revolution commercial relations with Peru, as well as with the contiguous territories of Bolivia and Chile, were either entirely interrupted during the wars of independence or seriously hampered afterwards. There was little consolation in the fact that foreign commodities could now be obtained at prices considerably below those prevailing before 1810; for the Interior was rapidly approaching a position in which even the lowest prices were too high. To these provinces of the young Republic the Revolution was therefore of little immediate economic value. So it is all the more remarkable that they were willing to sacrifice men and money in the cause of independence.

The political aspects of the process of disintegration of the national economy were clear enough. Faced with a declining trade and industry the cities of the Interior and their tributary territories tried to preserve the *status quo* by achieving as high a degree of economic self-sufficiency as possible. Anxious, on the one hand, to maintain and to increase their share of national commerce, and, on the other, to protect their industries and agriculture against the encroachments from abroad, the provinces resorted to special tariffs, transit duties, differential taxation, and direct economic legislation. But it soon became evident that an economic policy so reminiscent of mercantilism and so injurious to the commercial interests of Buenos Aires could not survive except under conditions of a fairly broad political autonomy for each of the provinces. Hence the tendency of the provinces to circumscribe the political power of Buenos Aires; hence also their opposition to all such attempts at state organization as would place Buenos Aires in a position of political and economic leadership. In this way economic self-defense became one of the most important factors in the emergence of that political particularism whose programmatic expression was the federalist conception of state organization. Thus the economic problem became a political issue in which states' rights were pitted against centralization. Around this issue centered the political and social struggles of the first four decades of Argentina's independence. Nor were the struggles confined to interprovincial relationships. Just as the changes in the national economy cut across administrative divisions, so also the question of the form of state organization obliterated provincial boundaries. Therefore, it was only as the doctrines of federalism and unitarism reflected economic interests and tendencies that the political conflict assumed substance and meaning.

In Buenos Aires the rise of economic particularism was conditioned by a different set of circumstances. Here federalism derived its strength and vitality from the desire to monopolize the economic gains of the Revolution. The nationalization of the port of Buenos Aires and of the revenues derived from foreign commerce could have no other effect but to deprive the province of economic and financial supremacy, and to place a heavy burden in the form of taxes upon the rural population as well as upon the small traders and artisans in the city. On the other hand, the program of centralization, in so far as it promised to do away with interprovincial tariffs, and to make the internal markets more accessible to foreign goods, expressed in political terms the interests of all those who were concerned with the expansion of overseas and domestic commerce. Thus within the province of Buenos Aires the problem of state organization revolved around the struggle of two tendencies: the one emphasized commerce as the source of national wealth and the basis of economic prosperity; the other envisaged the expansion of the cattle breeding industry within the province, and relegated commerce to a subordinate position.

CHAPTER II

THE ECONOMIC PATTERN OF BUENOS AIRES, 1821–1829

Las repúblicas del Plata . . . deben en gran parte su nacimiento a las necesidades del comercio libre.—JUAN BAUTISTA ALBERDI.

Buenos Aires nació, creció y floreció al calor del comercio externo.—EMILIO HANSEN.

WHILE IN THE far off Andes the armies of the Republic were fighting the last battles of independence; while within the country the problem of political organization was being debated by word and sword; while the provinces of the Interior were making strenuous efforts to regain and even to extend the relative prosperity they enjoyed before 1810;— Buenos Aires was rapidly growing in wealth and importance. Neither the wars against Spain and Brazil nor the political and social struggles within the province and country could stem the tide of economic expansion. As if anxious to make up for the opportunities lost under Spanish domination the province entered a race against time in availing itself of all the advantages which its geographical position, its natural resources, and the new political order afforded. Having abolished the system of economic restrictions the province proceeded to replace the old by a new economic order, more appropriate to its economic needs and potentialities. The first among the provinces to break away from Spain, Buenos Aires was also the first to join Europe—that Europe the representatives of which were England in the field of economic endeavor and France in the field of political and social thought. And as the province drew closer to Europe, the gulf between it and the rest of the country became wider. Indeed, economically and culturally England and France seemed nearer to Buenos Aires than Tucumán, Mendoza, or even Córdoba.

In the economic configuration of the young Republic Buenos Aires occupied a position that was in more than one respect unique. Vast natural resources, a relatively large internal market, free and direct access to the sea, were all advantages which none of the sister provinces enjoyed to any comparable extent. Exploitation of natural resources required comparatively small investments of capital. Hides, meat, tallow, and other by-products of the grazing industry found ready markets in Europe, Brazil, Cuba, and North America. It was also in these markets that the province procured manufactured goods and foodstuffs that could not be grown at home. Thus Buenos Aires was in some measure economically independent of the rest of the country.

Moreover, whatever intercourse developed between the Interior and Buenos Aires, its terms were necessarily more advantageous to the latter. Both as a consumer of the produce and manufactures of the Interior, and as an intermediary in the flow of commerce between the Interior and foreign countries, Buenos Aires enjoyed a semi-monopolistic position. Far from being dependent upon the Interior for the supply of commodities such as wine, coarse textiles, hard leather, sugar, etc., Buenos Aires could easily obtain these goods in European and American markets, and at prices that compared favorably with those demanded by domestic producers. And on the other hand, the Interior had no direct commercial contact with foreign countries, except through the port of Buenos Aires.[1] Thus, as exporters of commodities consumed in the Buenos Aires market the producers in the Interior were subject to severe competition from abroad. And as a consumer of foreign manufactures the Interior was obliged to pay for the services of Buenos Aires merchants whose sole restraint was what the traffic would bear.

So the uniqueness of the position of Buenos Aires depended upon the extent to which the post-revolutionary development of the province did, or did not, conform to the economic needs of the country as a whole. Freed from the restrictions of the Spanish colonial system the province was rapidly adapting itself to the requirements of European economy. This process of economic reorganization associated with and based upon commercial and industrial expansion was not confined solely to Buenos Aires; yet in no part of the Republic was the problem of economic readjustment solved as easily and naturally as it was in this province. And as the difference between the rate of expansion of Buenos Aires and the Interior widened, both the basis and scope of the economic development of the former transcended the immediate potentialities of the country as a whole. Buenos Aires formed an in-

---

[1] Foreign trade, it is true, could be carried on through Chile and Peru, and in fact some provinces (Mendoza, Tucumán) did occasionally use these routes. High costs of transportation, however, seriously hampered the development of trade through these channels.

tegral part of the Republic; yet the interests of the province did not always coincide with, and were sometimes opposed to, those of the nation. In an attempt to maintain its superior position the province tended to keep aloof from the problems which beset the country during the troubled years of political and economic readjustment. But this aloofness was one-sided, for Buenos Aires seldom hesitated to utilize its economic supremacy to further its own interests. It is true, of course, that the Interior derived substantial benefits from the economic growth of Buenos Aires. But it is equally true that these gains were indirect and tenuous, dependent upon and conditioned by the day to day policies of Buenos Aires.

From the point of view of the Interior, therefore, the economic expansion of Buenos Aires was not an unmixed blessing; for it depended largely upon the province and the policies its government pursued whether the Interior was to become an active participant in the economic resurgence of the country, or merely a passive recipient of whatever economic opportunities Buenos Aires was willing or able to accord to it. It is not surprising, therefore, that the Interior came to be profoundly concerned with the economic affairs and policies of Buenos Aires, and that the province and its relation to the country became a national question almost immediately after the Revolution of 1810. Nor is it surprising that this problem finally became the central issue around which the struggle between unitarism and federalism in its early stages revolved. The problem was unavoidable. It was inherent in the very process of economic development, a development whose unevenness engendered frictions and maladjustments, and gave rise to conflicting group and regional interests.

2

At the time of the administration of Rodríguez (1821–1824) the territory of the province of Buenos Aires extended south and west from the shores of La Plata and the seacoast as far as the resistance of the Indian tribes would permit. However, the boundaries of the province were not defined with any degree of exactitude. The pampa was primarily a frontier country, and the movement southward and westward, though frequently retarded because of scarcity of men and resources, was nevertheless sustained. By 1823 the territory of the province extended considerably beyond the Salado river, reaching out southward as far as Tandil.[2] The whole territory between the sea-coast and a line drawn from the fort of 25 de Mayo to Patagones was brought under control of the provincial government.[3] In 1821 the newly established Departamento Topográfico estimated the area of the province at 1,518 square leagues, or about 41,000 square kilometers. But, as the *Registro Estadístico* states, cattle breeding establishments were fairly frequent south of the thirty-sixth parallel.[4] By 1826, according to Ramos Mejía,[5] cattle *estancias* extended over an area of about 102,688 square kilometers, within a line running from Mar del Plata, through Tandil, Azul, Alvear, 25 de Mayo, Bragado, Junín, Rojas, Pergamino, and north of San Nicolás de los Arroyos.[6] At the conclusion of the 1827–28 expedition the area available for exploitation was still further extended. A direct overland contact was established with Bahía Blanca and Carmen de Patagones, both situated at the southern extremity of the province.

Detailed examination of the process of territorial expansion is not within the scope of this investigation. Yet it is important to indicate the manner in which this expansion took place, not only because it reflects the nature of the economy of the province, but also because it reveals some aspects of the economic and social background of the political struggles of the period. The frontier movement in Buenos Aires was not primarily a movement of individual pioneers driven by economic pressure. Though this circumstance did play a part in the process of territorial expansion, the real causes were intimately related to changes which had occurred in the social and economic structure of the province. With the opening of the country to foreign trade cattle breeding became the mainstay of the economic life of the province, so that as the overseas markets for hides and meat broadened, the problem of an adequate supply of land became more urgent. In a very real sense acquisition of new territory at the expense of the Indians was a problem of increasing the capital equipment of the country, of bringing land into the system of capitalist productive relations. Such ac-

[2] The frontier ran along the line from Melincué southeast to Federación (now Junín), to Independencia (now Tandil), and then northwest to the Atlantic.

[3] The new frontier ran from Melincué, to Federación (Junín), to 25 de Mayo, to Bahía Blanca, and to Patagones.

[4] *Registro Estadístico*, No. 1 (February 15, 1822).

[5] J. M. Ramos Mejía, *Rosas y su tiempo* (Buenos Aires: 1907), pp. 158–159.

[6] Ramos Mejía states that his calculations are based on trustworthy sources; he fails, however, to indicate the nature of these sources, or the manner in which he arrived at the above figure.

quisition, moreover, could not be accomplished except by way of large scale military operations against the Indians.   Gradual penetration of pioneer settlers, even if it could be sustained, would hamper rather than stimulate the expansion of grazing, which was essentially a large scale enterprise.

The government, too, was vitally interested in extending the territory of the province.   Of first importance was the problem of safeguarding interprovincial commerce from Indian attacks.   Constant incursions of warring Indian tribes, accompanied by widespread plunder, was a serious threat to the economic interests of the province.   Defense against these attacks required mobilization of men and resources on a scale which no one save the government could undertake with any hope of success.   Indeed, protection against Indian attacks came to be considered an essential task of the government.[7]   Government action was the more urgent since other provinces served as markets for cattle robbed from the *estancias* in Buenos Aires.[8]

Financial difficulties together with the economic losses of the Brazilian war provided yet other motives that induced the provincial government to organize and finance expeditions against the Indians.   The war against Brazil, which in spite of military successes ended in a diplomatic and political compromise, was from the point of view of the country's economic interests an outright defeat.   The confederation lost a rich province and an important port; it acquired instead a formidable industrial and commercial competitor.   For as a capital of an independent republic Montevideo was a much more dangerous rival of Buenos Aires than as a capital of one of the provinces of the Argentine Republic.   Moreover, from the three year long conflict the

[7] "Entre los deberes sagrados que se ha impuesto el Gobierno, considera que el poner a cubierto las fronteras de la provincia de la incursión de los bárbaros, es de los mas urgentes y privilegiados.   Las medidas ordinarias son inaplicables mientras no vuelven a organizarse regimientos de línea, y los puntos fortificados se rehabilitan de medios de conservación y de defensa, aniquilados durante la guerra civil."   From preamble to the decree of September 19, 1829 (RO–118; L–8; no. –8).

[8] In 1824 the government of Buenos Aires instructed its representative in Córdoba to demand that the latter province take measures against merchants and landowners who bought cattle robbed by Indians in Buenos Aires and Santa Fe.   The protest was based on reports from the various districts of the province.   One of these reports, dated April 21, 1824, reads in part: "Demasiado constante y notorio es el pillage que los bárbaros han hecho en Santa Fe y esta Provincia de inmenso número de ganados; y es voz pública que van a efectuar su venta en la de Córdoba y que entre esta y la de Buenos Aires hay tráfico de cueros del ganado robado." (*Archivo General de la Nación*, Ant. C. 20–A. 3–no. 3.)

province emerged with an empty treasury, its credit strained to the breaking point, its economy badly shaken. Financial and economic rehabilitation had become one of the major problems confronting the government. And the solution, as the government envisaged it, was to consist not only in better management of public finances, but also in broadening the very basis upon which the economic prosperity of the province was to rest. Acquisition of new territories was, therefore, considered to be the best, if not the only way out of the difficulties besetting the province. New land was to provide an important source of immediate revenue, a stimulus to further development of the grazing industry, and a basis for the expansion of commerce. Governor Manuel Dorrego was merely voicing the opinion of his constituents when in a message to the legislative assembly of the province he referred to the newly established frontier in the following terms:

The new frontier has already been established. This undertaking as desirable as it is important was begun under the best auspices. The barbarians towards whom the government continues with great success to apply measures of peace and conciliation will no longer commit depredations with impunity, and the immense territory acquired recently will provide additional security for public debt, so that this obligation of the government could be discharged on short notice, were such action advisable. But much more important is the circumstance that by establishing the new frontier we have come into possession of Bahía Blanca, which is surrounded by convenient ports, fertile forests. Abundance of fish and good ports along the coast will make it possible to develop a vigorous navy ready at all times to defend the Republic. Overland communication with Chile is from that point the shortest and most convenient, and navigation on the Colorado river might provide an easy and convenient outlet for the produce of some of the provinces of the Interior.[9]

Few, if any, of these hopes ever materialized. They reveal, however, the spirit in which the government of the province approached the problem of territorial expansion. And if the legislature, composed largely of *estancieros* and businessmen, was somewhat less extravagant in praising the initiative of the government, that was not because it failed to appreciate the importance of the undertaking, but rather because it was much more conscious of the magnitude of the task and the tremendous sacrifices its fulfillment required. The *estancieros*, whether in or out of the legislative assembly, fully realized the economic implications of the operations against the Indians; they knew

[9] Heraclio Mabragaña, *Los mensajes. Historia del desenvolvimiento de la nación argentina, redactada cronológicamente por sus gobernantes, 1810–1910. Publicación autorizada por la Comisión Nacional del Centenario* (Buenos Aires, Talleres gráficos de la Compañía Gral. de Fósforos: 1910. 6 vols.), I, 238–239. Message of June 13, 1828.

also that they were to be the most important beneficiaries of these campaigns.[10] Hence the readiness with which the legislature voted appropriations for the financing of expeditions; hence also the willingness to vote special taxes upon cattle.[11] In few other instances was the government supported so unanimously by all classes of the population, and particularly by the cattle breeders and meat producers.

The fact that during the period under consideration agriculture was not an important factor in the economic life of the province was mainly responsible for the insignificant role which the farmer played in the process of territorial expansion. This was also in no small part due to the attitude of the cattle breeders. The *hacendados* were well aware that a strong and prosperous agriculture might, because of an increased demand for land, adversely affect prices. Expansion of agriculture threatened to undermine the monopolistic position of the *hacendados*, who until then were the only important buyers or tenants of the public domain. No wonder, then, that the provincial legislature gave only grudging support to measures designed to foster large scale agricultural and pastoral colonization from abroad.[12]

3

Territorial expansion was not accompanied by a proportionate growth of population. Since the abolition of restrictions on immigration the number of inhabitants in the province increased considerably, but on the whole the flow of immigrants was insufficient to keep pace with the constantly growing demand for man power. Exact data on the growth of population in the province of Buenos Aires are not available. Whatever figures have been published are hardly more than estimates based upon more or less incomplete and almost certainly inexact censuses (*padrones*) taken from time to time in various districts of the province.

[10] Cf. *Diario de Sesiones de la Junta de Representantes de la Provincia de Buenos Aires,* Session 37 (November 7, 1827), ff.

[11] Law of November 13, 1827. The law authorized the government to levy a tax of 1 real per head on cattle and horses. The tax was to remain in force during 1828 and 1829 (RN–2232).

[12] Cf. *Diario de Sesiones,* Sessions 68–76, and particularly Sessions 74, 75, and 76 (February 14, 15, and 16, 1828). Also, Law of February 16, 1828. Characteristic in this connection was the attitude of Tomás Anchorena, parliamentary leader of the cattle breeders, who demanded that foreigners be denied the right to receive lands in tenancy directly from the government.

According to a report submitted in 1779 by Gregorio Ramos Mejía to Juan José de Vertiz y Salcedo the total population of the city of Buenos Aires and the territory under its jurisdiction amounted to 37,130 inhabitants, of which number 24,205 resided in the city and the remaining 12,925 in the country districts.[13]   In 1801 Félix de Azara estimated the population of Buenos Aires (city) at 40,000 inhabitants,[14] and nine years later Mariano Moreno gave 35,000 as the number of residents in the city, excluding suburbs.[15]   Two later estimates are to be found in a report prepared by the United States commissioners Caesar Augustus Rodney and John Graham.[16]   One of these estimates refers to 1815 and puts the number of inhabitants of the province at about 96,000 "excluding troops and transient persons, and Indians." The above figure, according to Graham, is based upon an "imperfect census, taken, it is believed, in 1815."   A somewhat later estimate quoted by Graham put the population of the province at 120,000, "excluding Indians."   The Commissioner does not state to what year this later estimate refers; nor does he express any opinion as to which of the two estimates is more exact.   Graham's estimate is somewhat below the figure published by the *Registro Estadístico*.   Basing its cal-

[13] "Estado general que manifiesta el número de habitantes que hay en esta ciudad, capital del Virreinato del Río de la Plata y su jurisdicción, de que es dignísimo Virrey, Gobernador y Capitán General el Exmo. Sr. D. Juan José de Vertiz y Salcedo, Caballero Comendador de Puerto Llano en el Orden de la Calatraba, y Teniente General de los Reales Ejércitos, y de orden de S.M. comunicada por S. E. a este Ilustre Cabildo, y se ha formado individualizando los casados, viudos, solteros, párvulos de ambos sexos, así de Españoles, como de las demas castas, incluyendo igualmente los forasteros habitantes, sacados todos de los padrones particulares, que se han hecho en el año pasado de mil setecientos setenta y ocho y de comisión de dicho Ilustre Cabildo, lo ha hecho su Regidor más antiguo, arreglandose en cuanto le ha sido posible a la orden de S.M. según lo ha permitido la variación de los citados padrones." Cf. *Revista del Plata*, no. 2.

[14] Félix de Azara, *Viajes por la América meridional . . . comisario y comandante de los límites españoles en el Paraguay desde 1781 hasta 1801 . . . Publicados con arreglo a los manuscritos del autor, con una noticia sobre su vida y sus escritos, por C. A. Walckenaer, enriquecidos con notas por G. Cuvier. Traducida del francés por Francisco de las Barras de Aragón* (Madrid, Calpe: 1923). Vol. 2, ch. 17, table following p. 204, entitled "Cuadro de población del gobierno de Buenos Aires."

[15] *Revista del Plata, loc. cit.* It is difficult to gauge the trustworthiness of Moreno's figure; nor is it possible to say how much Moreno was influenced by Azara. That it does not differ appreciably from Azara's estimate makes it acceptable as a fair approximation.

[16] Caesar Augustus Rodney and John Graham, *The Reports on the present state of the United Provinces of South America; drawn up by . . . commissioners sent to Buenos Aires by the government of North America and laid before the Congress of the United States; with their accompanying documents; occasional notes by the editor and an introductory discourse. . . .* (London: 1819.)

culations upon the rate of mortality the *Registro* arrived at the figure of 143,496 inhabitants. Of these 68,896 resided in the city and 74,600 in the country.[17] This estimate was generally accepted by contemporaries as authoritative. It is quite possible, however, that the *Registro's* estimate was too optimistic, especially when it is considered that the death rate must have been above the average in those troublesome years.[18] However, if the *Registro Estadístico* tended to exaggerate, the error was not too excessive. The *Registro's* data are also more differentiated, the figures for the city and country districts being given separately.

The preceding review would be incomplete without mention being made of the calculations prepared by Diego de la Fuente, published in the *Primer Censo de la República Argentina, 1869.*[19] There can be little doubt that Diego de la Fuente used contemporary estimates as the basis for his own calculations. This explains why his figures agree so closely with the estimates quoted above. The figure given by de la

TABLE 1

GROWTH OF POPULATION IN THE PROVINCE OF BUENOS AIRES, 1779–1829

Year	City	Country	Province	Estimate by
1779	24,205	12,925	37,130	Gregorio Ramos Mejía [a]
1801	40,000			Félix de Azara
1809			92,000	Diego de la Fuente [b]
1810	35,000 [c]			Mariano Moreno
1815			98,000 [d]	Rodney and Graham [e]
18—			120,000 [f]	Graham
1819			125,000	Diego de la Fuente
1823	68,896	74,600	143,496	*Registro Estadístico*
1824	96,000 [g]			*Revista del Plata*
1829			153,000	Diego de la Fuente

(a) Quoted from *Revista del Plata*, no. 2 (October, 1853); (b) *Primer Censo de la República Argentina*, 1869 (Buenos Aires: 1872); (c) Excluding suburbs; (d) Excluding troops; (e) Calculation based upon incomplete returns of a census supposed to have been taken in 1815; (f) Excluding Indians; (g) The *Revista* does not state whether the estimate pertains to the province or only to the city of Buenos Aires.

Fuente are included in Table 1, in which the various estimates are arranged in chronological order.

[17] No. 12 (March, 1823).

[18] Thus the *Revista del Plata* (October 1853), basing its calculations on the statistics of births and deaths as published in the same *Registro* for 1824, arrived at a figure of 96,000. Unfortunately the *Revista* does not state whether the above estimate refers to the province as a whole, or only to the city.

[19] Buenos Aires: 1872, p. 23.

It will appear from the various estimates that the province was seriously underpopulated. Of course, relatively low density of population is normal in a preponderantly grazing economy, but it should be noted that more than 50 per cent of the population resided in the capital and other towns. It is true that in the period from 1779 to 1823 population in the country districts grew much faster than in the capital (from 12,295 to 74,600 in the former as against an increase from 24,205 to 68,896 in the latter), but this discrepancy in the rate of growth diminished rapidly after 1810, and probably disappeared entirely in the third decade of the nineteenth century. In fact, the failure of the government's colonization policy is ascribable, at least in part, to the tendency of the immigrants to settle in the city of Buenos Aires. The country districts and the city were competing against each other for the available supply of labor. And because the city was able to offer better wages and a higher standard of living it is not surprising that having once reached the shores of La Plata immigrants tended to remain in the capital.

Relative scarcity of population and the simultaneous expansion of economic activity in the city and country districts gave rise to the problem of labor shortage. In the early twenties the problem was sufficiently serious to warrant government intervention. Laws regulating the employment of apprentices and peons were passed in 1821 and 1823 respectively.[20] They were designed to prevent laborers from leaving employment before the expiration of their contracts and they were also intended to reduce competition among employers. An attempt was also made to increase the supply of labor by indirect means. In 1822 the government decreed that laborers entering Buenos Aires from other provinces were not to be pressed into military service as long as they were employed.[21] On the other hand, begging was subjected to strict regulation by a decree (February 28, 1823) which denied begging permits to all persons able to maintain themselves by work.[22]

The above exhausts the list of measures which directly affected labor. The years following the administration of Rodríguez were years of political and social unrest, and there was neither time nor opportunity for a broad and consistent labor policy. It is probable that even the few

[20] Law of November 17, 1821 (RO–82); Decree of July 17, 1823 (RO–516).
[21] Decree, December 7, 1822 (RO–426).
[22] RO–465 (Article 9).

measures mentioned above were not enforced,[23] and that in so far as they were intended to relieve the shortage of labor their efficacy was rather dubious.[24] Nor could it be otherwise; for the factors responsible for scarcity of labor lay beyond the reach of legislation. Some were external to the economic system altogether. The wars in which the province had been involved almost uninterruptedly since the day of the Revolution were a constant drain upon the available labor resources. The effect of this factor was the more impressive because at no time did the country possess a surplus of population. But more important, though perhaps less evident, were the causes inherent in and arising out of the kind of economic expansion Buenos Aires was experiencing. The significant fact about the economic development of Buenos Aires, like that of any new country, consisted in that territorial expansion and the rapid growth of the cattle breeding industry were not accompanied by a simultaneous increase in the supply of labor. Acquisition of new pasture lands was accomplished at the expense of the Indians, who remained outside the provincial economy.

[23] So, for example, deputy Benites complained in 1828 that it was not possible to hire laborers from other provinces, because employers were unable to give satisfactory assurances that laborers would not be pressed into military service. Cf. *Diario de Sesiones,* Session 21 (February 6, 1828).

[24] Throughout the period complaints were frequent against high wages demanded by laborers (*peones*) in rural establishments. It is not possible to determine the extent to which these complaints, voiced mainly by landowners (*hacendados*), were justified. That in the latter twenties wages should have risen in terms of paper pesos was to be expected, in view of the depreciation of paper money. The question is whether this rise in money wages more than compensated the increase in the cost of living. That it did so is very doubtful. The following wage rates obtained from various sources are quoted here in order to provide a point of reference. From a list of wages paid in a government-owned arms factory: *Peones,* 4 reales per diem; foremen, 10 reales per diem; gunsmiths, 8 to 10 reales per diem; filers, 5½ reales per diem. These rates were in effect in 1818 and 1819. The lowest monthly wage paid to *peones* on an *estancia* was 12 pesos (Statement by Rosas, Terrero y Cía.—quoted by Saldías, *Confederación,* I, 45, footnote 4). In 1823 the government fixed the remuneration of stevedores (*cargadores*) at 2 reales per hour (Decree of January 7, 1822). The budget of the legislative assembly of the province of Buenos Aires for 1828 contains the following items: "Un portero—35 pesos mensuales: un sirviente—16 pesos mensuales; un ordenanza con caballo—35 pesos mensuales" (*Diario de Sesiones,* Session 17, September 1827). In that same year (December 1827) master carpenters were paid 3 pesos per day; master masons, 3 pesos; masons (*peones*), 2 pesos (Relación de los carpinteros, albañiles y peones empleados en la obra de la Catedral—*Archivo General de la Nación,* Ant. C. 29–A.1–no. 3). In rural establishments, protested deputy Obligado, foremen were paid 2,000 pesos a year, "sueldo que equivale a uno de los empleos que hacen la subsistencia de cualquiera indivíduo decente." (*Diario de Sesiones,* Session 40, November 13, 1827.)

And since economic expansion was fairly evenly distributed over all sectors of provincial economy, labor shortage was general. The problem, then, could not be solved by transferring labor from employments where it abounded to those where it was scarce (though such redistribution was unquestionably taking place) but rather by increasing the total supply of labor. And no measure short of mass immigration provided a satisfactory solution of the problem.[25]

4

The process of transformation of the economy of Buenos Aires preceded by many years the Revolution of 1810. The events of 1810 and the subsequent declaration of independence gave political sanction to economic changes which had already taken place, and provided a powerful stimulus for further modernization of the economic life of the province. Within the confines of the provincial economy this process of growth and readjustment was fairly general. It affected the city and the country, commerce and industry, capital and labor. It evolved a new pattern of economic and social relationships. The economy itself became more complex, more differentiated; its institutions more numerous, their functions more varied. And at the same time interdependence between the various parts of the economic structure was becoming more intimate, though not at all more harmonious.

In the country districts (*campaña*) economic development found expression not only in territorial expansion and increase in the number of cattle breeding establishments but also in the transformation of the *estancia* into a capitalist enterprise. Grazing came under industrial control and management. Land and cattle and meat were no longer to be had for the taking. Though enclosures were still unknown, largely because of the expense involved, enforcement of property rights in land and cattle was becoming progressively stricter. Increase in the size of the *estancia*[26] implied larger investments of capital; cattle began to be bred not only for their hides but also for their meat and horns, tallow and hoofs. It was becoming more profitable to pay the

[25] That the various governments of the province conceived the problem in terms similar to those stated above is evident from the repeated efforts to stimulate mass immigration.

[26] The law of emphyteusis of February 16, 1828 permitted holdings of government-owned land up to 12 square leagues. There was, of course, no limit to outright holdings. *Estancias* of 40 leagues were not uncommon.

peons a fixed wage, and to charge them for the meat they consumed.[27] Spurred by rising prices and growing demand for hides and meat the cattle breeders became economically more active than at any time before. Landownership was no longer mainly a matter of social prestige. The *estancia* had become a commercial and industrial enterprise with the *estanciero* in control of the means and methods of production.

It is easy to see why the *estancieros* as a class should have assumed a leading role in the economic and political affairs of the province. In the years following the Revolution of 1810, as the country opened its ports to foreign trade, cattle breeding and allied industries entered upon a period of unprecedented expansion. Already in the first decade after the Revolution cattle prices rose almost threefold, from 3.3 pesos per head in 1809 to 9.6 pesos in 1819 (cf. Table 2). High prices were

TABLE 2

ACCOUNT OF TRANSACTIONS OF AN ESTANCIA IN THE PROVINCE OF
BUENOS AIRES, 1803/08–1819 [a]

Year	No. of cattle sold	Total value (gold pesos)	Average price per head
1803/08	474	1,431$ 0	3.0
1809	315	1,041$ 0	3.3
1810	447	1,257$ 0	2.8
1811	520	1,934$ 6	3.7
1812	608	2,387$ 5	3.9
1813	936	4,211$ 2	4.5
1814	427	1,196$ 2	2.8
1815	885	3,166$ 7	3.6
1816	775	4,084$ 2	5.3
1817	709	4,934$ 3	6.9
1818	1,000	11,213$ 7	11.2
1819	791	7,546$ 2	9.6

[a] Cf. *Registro Estadístico*, no. 3 (April 1822), p. 55, Sección 3, Tabla 8. "Es curioso," remarks the *Registro*, "y por lo tanto lo publicamos, observar la siguiente progresión de una de nuestras estancias, fundada en 1803, y cuyo dueño ha tenido la proligidad de llevar y conservar una cuenta anual exacta."

maintained during the twenties, assuring thus continued prosperity to the industry. "Our rural industry," announced the government in

[27] Juan Álvarez, *Estudio sobre las guerras civiles argentinas* (Buenos Aires: 1914), *passim*. Speaking of post-revolutionary changes in the economy of Argentina Álvarez writes: "Occurió entonces (to the cattle breeders) que lo mas importante del novillo fué la carne, y hubo que discutir si la seguirán comiendo los gauchos del litoral, o si debía ser vendida en provecho de los hacendados a los propietarios de esclavos del Brasil, Africa y las Antillas. El sistema de cazar vacas sin otro cargo que el entregar los cueros al propietario de la estancia iba a ser sustituido por el de trabajar algunos meses en el saladero y comprar con el jornal la carne que se pudiese al precio marcado por los consumidores del extranjero" (p. 98).

1823, "is growing rapidly, and the flow of capital to the country (*campaña*) is so great that it promises an incalculable growth of wealth." [28] Not even the war of 1825–1828, with its blockade of Buenos Aires, caused serious dislocations in the industry, and consequently in the economy of the country. Early in 1828 deputy Anchorena pointed out in the provincial legislature that nearly all lands suitable for cattle breeding which the government offered for lease (emphyteusis) had been taken; and deputy Viamonte admitted, however grudgingly, the prosperous condition of the *estancieros*.[29]

Indicative of the kind of economic development Buenos Aires was experiencing was the introduction of sheep breeding, an industry almost unknown before the Revolution. The first merino sheep were imported from abroad as early as 1813, and in the twenties sheep breeding and production of wool had passed the experimental stage.[30] It is true that at no time during the period under discussion did sheep breeding become an important source of national income. As late as 1829 exports of wool amounted to about 30,000 arrobas (about 750,000 pounds) valued at 91,000 pesos. It does reveal, however, a tendency toward greater differentiation of the agro-industrial structure of the country.[31]

In contrast to grazing, agriculture showed little progress during the first decades after the Revolution. There was, of course, some increase in the number of farms as well as in the total area under cultivation, but on the whole this increase lagged behind the general rate of expansion. The province lacked the most essential elements for making agriculture a profitable field for the investment of capital and labor. The absence of roads and the generally prohibitive cost of transportation prevented the extension of agricultural activity beyond a comparatively narrow circle around cities and towns, where land was fairly expensive.[32] But even in the vicinity of Buenos Aires the eco-

---

[28] Mabragaña, *op. cit.*, I, 179–180 (Message, May 5, 1823).

[29] *Diario de Sesiones,* Sessions 68 and 69 (January 28 and 30, 1828).

[30] Cf. *Revista del Plata,* no. 1 (1853).

[31] For a detailed discussion of the Argentine sheep breeding industry see E. Gibson, *The history and the present day sheep breeding industry in the Argentine Republic* (Buenos Aires: 1893).

[32] Cf. P. Schmidtmeyer, *Travels into Chile, over the Andes in the years 1820 and 1821* (London: 1824); E. A. Coni, *La verdad sobre la enfiteusis de Rivadavia* (Buenos Aires: 1927). In the vicinity of Buenos Aires public land for farming was officially valued at 20 pesos per cuadra, or 75,000 pesos per square league (Law of emphyteusis, July 16, 1828). This compares with a valuation of 3,000 pesos per square league of pasture land.

nomic position of the farmers was precarious. Exposed to foreign competition in a market that was highly sensitive even to relatively slight fluctuations in the supply of wheat and flour, the *porteño* farmer was frequently forced to sell his grain at prices which barely covered costs of production. Anxious to keep these costs at the lowest possible level the farmer hesitated to make additional investments in more efficient tools, or to improve his method of cultivation.[33] Lacking the incentive of profit, agriculture alone among the various fields of economic endeavor remained stagnant and was barely able to hold its own in the changing economic environment.

Not even the government succeeded in overcoming the difficulties that stood in the path of agriculture. Realizing the importance of agriculture, and eager to populate the country districts, the government launched an ambitious program of colonization. In fact, the program was much too ambitious. The government contracted with numerous promoters for the transportation and settlement of hundreds of immigrants and their families, taking upon itself to pay for transportation, to set aside suitable land, and to equip the immigrant with cattle, agricultural implements, and food.[34] The realization of these plans involved expenditures that went far beyond the financial and economic resources of the provincial government. While in the early twenties, that is, in a period of economic expansion and consolidation, the government might have had some reason to believe in the financial feasibility of its colonization program, such illusions could no longer be entertained after the war of 1825–1828. As the government itself admitted later (1829) "the cost of transportation of immigrants alone exceeded the ordinary revenues of the province." [35] Moreover, as experience

---

[33] Arsène Isabelle, *Voyage à Buenos Aires et à Porto Alegre, par la Banda Oriental, les Misiones d'Uruguay et la province de Rio Grande do Sul* (Havre: 1835). "Faites moi de plaisir de me dire," exclaims the author, "si au temps de Janus, à l'époque de cet heureux âge d'ôr dont nous parlent les poëtes, . . . dites moi, je vous prie, si les instruments étaient plus imparfaits, plus barbares?"

[34] Cf. J. A. B. Beaumont, *Travels in Buenos Ayres and the adjacent provinces of the Rio de la Plata* (London: 1838).

[35] Transportation costs included also profits of the promoters. The contracts usually stipulated payments per immigrant. Thus the contract of one Francisco Morales, who undertook to bring settlers from the Canary Islands, stipulated payment of 100 pesos in gold or silver for each immigrant over 15 years, and 50 pesos for every immigrant below that age. It is worth noting that the promoter had no other obligation except to bring the immigrants to the western bank of the Rio de la Plata (*Archivo General*, Ant. C.29–A.10–no. 5).

had shown, it was not at all certain that having once reached Buenos Aires the immigrants would take up farming. The future of agriculture in these years was not particularly enticing, and it was only natural that the immigrants should have tended to settle in cities and towns, where economic opportunities were more numerous and the standard of living higher. These considerations, together with the hostile attitude of the *estancieros,* who saw in colonization a menace to their privileged position with respect to land distribution, led the government to abandon the program altogether. By a decree of January 2, 1829 the government terminated all existing contracts with colonizers.[36]

It would be erroneous to ascribe the failure of the government's colonization program solely to lack of financial resources. Important as this factor undoubtedly was, its decisive influence was conditioned by the inability of the government to formulate a consistent agricultural policy. It was not enough to encourage immigration: farming had to be made profitable. And this in turn depended to a large extent upon the existence of a broad and stable internal market. Thus, protection of domestic grain markets against foreign competition became an integral part of agricultural policy. The government was no doubt aware of the importance of a proper tariff policy with respect to agriculture. Already in the first general tariff schedule provision was made for a sliding scale of duties upon foreign grain and flour.[37] Wheat was to pay 4 pesos per fanega when the internal price was 6 pesos, but no tax was imposed upon foreign wheat when the price in the internal market exceeded 9 pesos. In the case of flour, free import was permitted when the domestic price exceeded 10 pesos per fanega. The principle of sliding scale duties was maintained with slight exceptions throughout the decade, though beginning with the tariff of 1822 the tax was somewhat higher.[38] These rates were sufficiently high to provide adequate protection of the domestic grain and flour markets, but their effect was nullified by frequent changes and outright revocations of the established rates. The fact is that in the political struggles of the period the price of bread had become a political issue, and the long range view of agricultural protection was lost in the maze of immediate political problems.

[36] RO–1076; L–8, no. –1.
[37] Law, December 15, 1821 (RO–114, L–1).
[38] Decree of November 28, 1822 (RO–420); Law of November 25, 1822 (RO–423). For a detailed discussion of tariff legislation in Buenos Aires see chap. iii.

5

The development of the rural sector of the provincial economy was accompanied by a parallel movement in the city and port of Buenos Aires. The expansion of the cattle breeding industry found its counterpart in the growth of foreign and interprovincial trade, increase of population, in greater specialization and in the rise of handicraft industries. The last two stimulated the development of the city of Buenos Aires and hastened its transformation into the financial and commercial center of the nation.

Several factors combined to elevate the city of Buenos Aires to a position of economic preëminence among all the cities of the Republic, not excluding Montevideo with its superior harbor. To begin with, no city of comparable size, except Montevideo, was better equipped to serve foreign trade. The very circumstances which under Spanish domination stunted the growth of the Viceregal capital were now responsible for its rapid expansion. From a city farthest removed from world markets Buenos Aires was transformed almost overnight into a port with a vast tributary territory in direct contact with the outside world. The commercial growth of the provincial capital was further stimulated by the fact that Buenos Aires became the designated port of entry for all foreign vessels. This policy, somewhat reminiscent of Spanish commercial practices, and only rarely modified by the various provincial and national governments, gave Buenos Aires what amounted to a monopoly of foreign trade. The expansion of cattle breeding in Buenos Aires and adjacent provinces provided the material basis for the growth of the city in wealth and importance. It was from the pampa that the vast quantities of exportable goods flowed continually towards the port for shipment abroad; and it was the pampa, too, which provided ready markets for a large portion of imported manufactures. Hence there developed in the city a demand for warehouses, for credit facilities, for skilled and unskilled labor, for many and manifold services required to handle the growing volume of trade. The city's population formed a sizable market in its own right for foreign as well as domestic produce. The monoproductive nature of the economy of the province necessitated importations not only of manufactures but also of foodstuffs, part of which were produced or grown in the Interior. This demand provided a basis for commercial intercourse between Buenos Aires and the Interior provinces—a relationship in which the city of Buenos Aires came to play a paramount role. In this way a large part of the Republic came under the commercial hegemony of the country's largest port, and the city's interests, in turn, tended to transcend the comparatively narrow limits of the province of which it was the capital. Merchants, financiers, and all those whose welfare was more or less closely linked with commerce very soon learned to think in terms of national economy. To this extent their interests conflicted with those of the cattle breeders, whose economic activities seldom penetrated beyond provincial boundaries.

A thorough analysis of the overseas commerce of Buenos Aires is handicapped by the lack of detailed data. Figures relating to foreign trade where they are at all available are incomplete and not always exact. Of the secondary sources of information the most reliable is Woodbine Parish, whose description of the Argentine Confederation is one of the standard works in the field.[39] As British consul in Buenos Aires, Parish had access to officially compiled statistics. It should be noted, however, that Parish's presentation of his material differs somewhat from that to be found in government publications. Parish separates specie exports from commodity exports (a distinction unknown in official trade statistics), though he later adds the two to obtain the grand total of the value of exports. The latter operation is misleading, since specie remittances in any given year do not necessarily indicate the deficit in the balance of trade for that year. With respect to Buenos Aires there is the additional consideration that, because gold and silver were subject to export duties, a good portion of specie was leaving the country clandestinely. More serious is Parish's use of gold prices in order to arrive at the value of exports for 1829. After 1826 currency in Buenos Aires was depreciated, and with very few exceptions prices were quoted in paper pesos the gold value of which fluctuated rather widely from month to month.[40] Trade figures for 1829 compiled by the government and based on returns of the Collector General of customs revenues are stated in terms of paper cur-

[39] Woodbine Parish, *Buenos Ayres and the Provinces of the Rio de la Plata, from their discovery and conquest by the Spaniards to the establishment of their political independence. With some account of their present state, trade, debt, etc.; an appendix of historical and statistical documents; and a description of the geology and fossil monsters of the pampas* (London: 1852).

[40] Thus in 1829 the value of paper peso fluctuated between 26.72 per cent of par (January, monthly average) and 16.58 per cent of par (October, monthly average). See chap. iii, Table 14.

rency. They differ substantially from the estimate given by Parish, whose list of gold prices (apparently yearly average prices) is hardly better than guesswork.

In spite of its shortcomings the material assembled by Parish is sufficiently accurate and detailed to allow of significant conclusions with respect to the export trade of Buenos Aires during the twenties. The total value of exports increased from 3,641,814 gold pesos in 1822 to 3,999,079 gold pesos in 1825 and to 4,477,045 gold pesos in 1829. At the same time specie remittances, in so far as these have been recorded, decreased from 1,358,814 pesos in 1822 to 722,965 gold pesos in 1829.[41] Hides, beef, horns, horsehair, tallow, etc.—all products of the grazing industry—formed the bulk of exports. Ox hides alone accounted for nearly 65 per cent of the total value of exports in 1822; in 1829 the proportion rose to more than 75 per cent (see Table 3). Because of price fluctuations export values do not always fully reveal significant changes in the economic development over a period of years. Volume of trade is in such cases a better index. For example, beef exports decreased from 350,652 gold pesos in 1822 to 329,638 gold pesos in 1829. This decrease in total values was due entirely to a decline of prices, for in 1829 the province exported nearly twice as much beef as in 1822. The same is true of horns. The increase in value is less than 100 per cent, while volume of exports rose nearly 150 per cent.

Information concerning imports is so scarce that only very broad generalizations are possible on the basis of available data. Woodbine Parish calculated the value of imports for 1825 at 1,550,000 pounds sterling or about 7,825,000 gold pesos. This total was divided among the various exporting regions in the manner shown in Table 4. In 1829 imports were valued at 36,836,601 paper pesos, according to the report of the Collector General. At the average rate of exchange for that year this would indicate a total of approximately 8,900,000 gold pesos. More than half of the imports, about 55 per cent, consisted of woolen and cotton goods, shoes, and wearing apparel. Foodstuffs and liquors made up 30 per cent of the total, while the remaining 15 per cent consisted of manufactured goods, machinery, military and naval stores, and semi-manufactures, such as iron, lead, and copper.

---

[41] These are Parish's data. In official reports for 1829 the value of exports including specie exports is given in paper pesos. Total exports excluding specie amounted to 21,426,588 paper pesos. Specie exports for that year were officially calculated at 4,135,352 paper pesos, of which more than half (2,762,691 paper pesos) was in gold coins.

TABLE 3

EXPORTS FROM BUENOS AIRES IN THE YEARS 1822, 1825, AND 1829

Commodity	1822 Volume	1822 Value gold $	1822 % of total	1825 Volume	1825 Value gold $	1825 % of total	1829 Volume	1829 Value gold $	1829 % of total
Ox Hides	590,372	2,361,488	64.86	655,255	2,621,020	65.56	854,799	3,419,196	76.37
Horsehides	421,566	421,566	11.58	339,703	339,703	8.60	64,563	96,844	2.15
Chinchilla Skins (doz.)	9,077	36,308	1.00				6,625	33,125	0.74
Nutria Skins "	9,914	29,742	0.82	36,670	170,350	4.46	59,756	179,268	4.00
Sheepskins "									
Jerked Beef ql.	87,663	350,652	9.65	130,361	521,444	13.04	164,818	329,638	7.36
Horns mil.	673,000	47,110	1.29	1,553,880	93,228	2.33	1,500,905	90,000	2.02
Horsehair arr.	38,137	114,411	3.24	44,776	134,028	3.56	26,682	110,046	2.46
Tallow "	62,400	124,800	3.44	12,167	18,250	0.46	21,757	65,271	1.45
Wool "	33,417	33,417	0.94				30,334	30,334	0.69
Bark lbs.	5,824	2,912	0.08	5,879	2,939	0.08			
Flour "									
Corn fan.									
Miscellaneous		118,780	3.10		84,117	2.11		123,333	2.75
Total Value		3,641,186	100.00		3,998,079	100.00		4,477,045	100.00
Export of Specie		1,358,814			1,551,921			722,955	

Source: Woodbine Parish, *Buenos Ayres and the Provinces of the Rio de la Plata* (London: 1852). Chap. xxi, p. 353.

TABLE 4

VALUE OF ARGENTINE IMPORTS FOR 1825 [a]

Importing Region	Pound Sterling	Gold Pesos
Great Britain......................	800,000	4,000,000
France...........................	110,000	550,000
Gibraltar, Spain...................	115,000	575,000
Northern Europe..................	85,000	425,000
United States.....................	180,000	900,000
Brazil............................	190,000	950,000
Havana and other regions...........	85,000	425,000
Total........................	1,565,000	7,825,000

[a] W. Parish, *op. cit.*, p. 361.

The available trade figures and other evidence indicate that during the decade under discussion the province was an importer on balance. The surplus of imports was paid for with exports of gold and silver. In the years for which export statistics are available gold and silver exports were considerable. But these figures do not in all probability reflect the real situation. Large sums were continually shipped abroad unrecorded. The fact that in the latter half of the decade the province was almost completely drained of specie, in spite of the constant influx from the Interior, is a strong presumption that the outward movement of precious metals was fairly consistent. A part of the surplus of imports over exports was covered from the proceeds of the London loan. The loan which netted the province about 3,500,000 gold pesos was consummated in 1826, so that its influence upon the country's balance of payments was not felt until the second half of the decade.

It has already been pointed out that the foreign trade of Buenos Aires was not wholly confined to the province. Just as a portion of the exports originated in the Interior and the Litoral, so only a small portion of the total trade between the Interior and foreign countries was direct. Most of the provinces produced little that was exportable, and very few had gold and silver. For the provinces the problem was to find internal markets where their produce could be sold in exchange for either specie or exportable commodities. Buenos Aires, precisely because its economic structure was geared up to the requirements of foreign markets, was in a position to solve this problem. The province imported for internal consumption the produce and manufactures of the Interior, remitting in payment foreign goods, which in turn it obtained in exchange for hides, meat, and other by-products of the grazing industry. This portion of the trade was, therefore, triangular with Buenos Aires, city and province, occupying a central position.

The pattern of interprovincial trade with Buenos Aires was determined by the geographical division of labor. From Córdoba Buenos Aires imported hides, textiles, nutria skins, alfalfa, cotton, fruits; Mendoza sent wines, *aguardiente,* dried fruits; from Tucumán and San Juan came hides, hard sole leather, cotton, timber, cheese, sweets, dried fruits, starch, sugar, wines, and *aguardiente.*[42] In exchange Buenos Aires shipped to these and other provinces textiles, wearing apparel, machinery, and other foreign manufactures. Some commodities, such as hides, sole leather, etc., were destined for foreign markets; but the bulk of the imports were consumed in Buenos Aires and adjacent provinces.

It is not possible to determine the extent of commerce between Buenos Aires and the Interior. Unlike the data on foreign trade the reports on overland traffic do not indicate the value of goods entering or leaving the city. The various measures used in recording this trade were the number of wagons (*carretas*) and mule trains (*arrias*), the total volume in terms of weight, the number of men employed in each shipment or train, and the number of beasts used—all very tenuous standards. Besides, the gathering of statistics of this kind was sporadic, and much of the data has since been lost.

The earliest statistical reference to the interprovincial trade of Buenos Aires is to be found in the *Registro Estadístico* for March 1823 (no. 12). According to the *Registro,* imports for the last nine months of 1822 amounted to 75,942 quintals, for which 1,259 wagons and 190 mule trains were employed. Exports for the same period reached 34,684 quintals, with 1,042 wagons and 82 mule trains. In 1825, according to the same source, Buenos Aires imported from the Interior 178,827 arrobas, but exports amounted to 61,316 arrobas.[43] For 1828 trade statistics are incomplete. The Collector's report gives import figures for the first eleven months of the year, while export data are so sketchy as to be entirely useless. On the other hand, the report lists imports from each province separately, a procedure unknown in previ-

---

[42] From a report of the Collector General for 1828 (*Archivo General,* Ant. 6–A. 7–no. 2). Since other provinces of the Interior traded with Buenos Aires either through Córdoba or Tucumán they are not specifically mentioned in the Collector's report.

[43] *Registro Estadístico,* nos. 18, 19 (1826). Arroba equals 25 pounds.

ous compilations. The total volume of imports was estimated by the Collector at 180,627 arrobas, of which 49,587 came from Córdoba, 74,474 from Mendoza, 32,550 arrobas from Tucumán, and 24,016 arrobas from San Juan.[44]

Commercial relations with the Litoral provinces were of a somewhat different nature. Geographical division of labor, although it was the basis of commerce between Buenos Aires and the Interior, played a secondary role in the relations with the Litoral. With respect to Buenos Aires the economy of the provinces on the Paraná river was competitive as well as complementary, and their dependence upon Buenos Aires was conditioned by the necessity of using the port of Buenos Aires as a point of contact with markets abroad. It is important, however, to note that from the viewpoint of the Litoral the utilization of Buenos Aires as a gateway to and from overseas markets was economically superfluous, since the Paraná river was accessible to ocean-going vessels. But given the commercial policies of the Buenos Aires government (national and provincial) and the fact that Buenos Aires controlled the entrance to the Paraná, the Litoral provinces became commercially and financially dependent upon Buenos Aires. Exportable goods from these provinces were shipped to Buenos Aires for reshipment to foreign markets. The same procedure was adopted for goods moving inland. The Paraná river served as the best and cheapest means of communication, and most of the trade was carried on by means of vessels seldom exceeding 100 tons displacement.

It is impossible to estimate even approximately the trade between Buenos Aires and the Litoral. No official records were kept of either the value or the volume of commodities moving between Buenos Aires and the Paraná ports. For several reasons statistics of small tonnage or national vessels entering or leaving Buenos Aires cannot be used as an index of interprovincial trade. In the first place, the reports of the port authorities or the Collector General make no distinction between vessels engaged in interprovincial commerce, those serving the various ports within the province of Buenos Aires, and those plying between Montevideo and Buenos Aires. Secondly, it is extremely difficult to gauge the volume of trade by the number of vessels, even assuming that every ship was fully loaded, because of wide variations in the size of ships. And finally, there is strong evidence that some of the early reports did not include certain classes of vessels.

[44] Report of the Collector General for 1828, *Archivo General, loc. cit.*

6

Unquestionably, expansion of trade was the most important single factor in the growth of the provincial capital after the Revolution. Yet it would be erroneous to define the economic structure of the city solely in terms of foreign and interprovincial commerce. Other factors besides the one mentioned above contributed to make Buenos Aires the most populous and economically the most integrated city in the Republic. The increase in wealth and the growth of population lay back of the division of labor in the field of industrial activity. Commerce itself as it grew in volume and variety created a demand for specialized services and opened new fields for the investment of capital. The development was two-sided. On the one hand, there was an increase in the number of industrial enterprises, and on the other, new enterprises grew up in response to a constantly expanding internal market. Again, while in many cases industrial technique and organization never passed the handicraft stage of development, in other instances the factory method of production began to make its appearance.

That industry should have developed at a much slower pace than commerce or grazing is not surprising. The very nature of the economy of the province, the scarcity of skilled labor and of capital, were all factors that imposed severe limitations upon industrial expansion. Succeeding governments, anxious to obtain immediate returns, were apt to neglect the industrial sector, whose contribution to the national dividend was necessarily limited. It was only towards the end of the decade that protection of domestic industries against competition from abroad was thought to be compatible with the economic interests of the province.

The available data bearing upon the industrial structure of the province are obviously incomplete and inaccurate. There is, for example, no indication whatever as to the number of laborers or apprentices employed; nor is there any way of determining even approximately the value or volume of industrial output. Both the *Registro Estadístico* and Blondel's *Almanaque*,[45] the only sources of information, refer solely to the city of Buenos Aires, and as a result industrial enterprises operating outside the city limits (a large portion of jerked beef and

---

[45] *Registro Estadístico*, no. 11 (December 1822); J. J. Blondel, *Almanaque de Comercio de la Ciudad de Buenos Ayres para el año de 1830* (Buenos Aires).

tallow production) are entirely omitted. And, finally, the yearly lists of business establishments compiled by Blondel lack uniform classification; firms classified as commercial enterprises in one year are listed as industrial establishments the next year. This lack of uniformity makes it difficult to follow the development of industry from year to year.

Of the two lists compiled by the *Registro* and the *Almanaque* the former is more clearly aware of the distinction between commercial and industrial enterprises. Partly in order to give as full a description of industrial Buenos Aires as possible, and partly also in order to provide a basis for comparison, it was thought advisable to reproduce the *Registro's* list in full. (See Table 5.) Blondel's compilation for 1830

TABLE 5

NUMBER OF SHOPS AND FACTORIES IN BUENOS AIRES IN 1822 [a]

Kind of business	No.	Kind of business	No.
Fan shops	2	Knife shops	5
Starch factories	2	Barber shops	65
Trunk shops	1	Beverage factories	1
Drugstores	17	Brass shops	1
Chocolate factories	7	Lime kilns	2
Lace makers	6	Boiler shops	2
Carpenter shops	104	Mattress shops	7
Confectionary shops	7	Tanneries	5
Cigar shops	37	Spaghetti factories	4
Inns	12	Tinner shops	26
Guitar shops	3	Blacksmith's shops	4
Brick kilns	67	Printing shops	3
Soap factories	8	Harness shops	22
Windmills	1	Silversmiths' shops	7
Comb shops	7	Bakeries	26
Fur shops	1	Powder factories	1
Reins shops	1	Tailors' shops	47
Hat factories	17	Furniture shops	21
Meat plants	16	Cooper shops	13
Lathe shops	2	Tallow chandlers	8
Shoemakers' shops	110		

[a] *Registro Estadístico*, no. 11 (pp. 203–204), *Ligera noticia del número de casas y variedad de artes que hay en las tres secciones de esta ciudad que comprenden su centro y arrabales.*

differs substantially from that of the *Registro*. In the first place the *Almanaque* enumerates all occupations, and is, therefore, more extensive than the *Registro*. Secondly, the *Almanaque* omits certain enterprises altogether, and to this extent its scope is narrower. And, finally, the two compilations differ in their method of classification. Thus the *Registro* lists 104 carpenters' shops, while Blondel lists only 68. The difference with respect to shoemakers is even greater, for as against 110 recorded in the *Registro* there are only 35 noted in the *Almanaque*. If both compilations are correct, though this is not at all certain, the discrepancies should be attributed at least in part to Blondel's classification of a number of carpenters as merchants. The basis of comparison is, therefore, narrowed to the extent to which the two compilations overlap. Taking the *Registro* as a basis for comparison we obtain the following figures from Blondel's list for 1830:

TABLE 6

NUMBER OF SHOPS AND FACTORIES IN BUENOS AIRES IN 1830

Kind of business	No.	Kind of business	No.
Carpenters	68	Bakers	39
Tailors	33	Shoemakers	35
Hatters	33	Druggists	32
Tinsmiths	16	Tanners	17
Harness makers	16	Cabinetmakers	14
Brick makers	14	Candy makers	14
Candle makers	11	Mattress makers	14
Chocolate makers	8	Lathe mechanics	8
Comb makers	5	Lime manufacturers	3
Carriage manufacturers	3	Spaghetti manufacturers	6

More important than the numerical growth of industrial and handicraft establishments was the process of social stratification, which the development of manufactures fostered. The artisans formed the backbone of a middle class whose economic interests and political ideology were beginning to crystallize towards the end of the decade. As yet economically too weak to play an independent role in the political life of the province, these groups were nevertheless forced to take sides in the struggle between the two major political parties. In return for their participation in the political and economic struggles these groups demanded recognition of their specific interests, and in many instances were able to make this demand effective.

CHAPTER III

FINANCIAL REFORM IN BUENOS AIRES, 1821–1829

Sabido es que sin el dinero no hay poder, no hay fuerza pública, no hay estado.— U. S. FRÍAS, I, 418 Session, July 30, 1819.

THE PROBLEM of financial reorganization which confronted the province of Buenos Aires was not purely economic, as it might have been under stable conditions. The economy of Buenos Aires was not stable. Its very basis was as yet in process of formation, so that the problem of financial organization outran the relatively narrow limits of a stabilized economy. In the absence of such stability, fiscal and commercial policies were more than mere reflections of established social-economic relationships; they acted also as factors of change in their own right, capable of influencing not only the rate but the direction of economic development.

In Buenos Aires financial reconstruction lagged behind economic development. Uncertainty as to the political future of the viceroyalty, wars against the mother country, and civil strife within the country and province engaged the attention and monopolized the resources of the government. For its normal needs the province was content for the time being to rely upon the financial system it had inherited from the viceregal administration. And to meet the extraordinary requirements arising out of war the government resorted to special measures which sometimes supplemented, but more frequently contradicted, the principles and practices of the old administration. The result was a complex system of imposts and administrative regulations, a system that was becoming increasingly inefficient in a rapidly changing economic and political environment.

Both the economy and the state came to be vitally interested in financial reform. The old system of taxation and fiscal administration, with its deeply entrenched mercantilist traditions, its privileges and prerogatives, its numerous offices and officials, was unwieldy and costly. The old forms no longer fitted into the new pattern of social-economic reality. They were adjusted to activities that had all but disappeared from the economic scheme of things in the province, and so failed to conform to new situations and to open up new sources of revenues. The state, too, had reason to be dissatisfied. During the ten years of foreign and civil wars it became evident that the colonial system of taxation and fiscal administration was no match for the new and complex problems facing the treasury. And as forced loans, voluntary and semi-voluntary contributions, special taxes, and other extraordinary measures—nearly always arbitrary and excessively burdensome—found increasing resistance among the population, the task of financial reorganization became more urgent than ever. The task was far from simple; it involved not only the overhauling of the whole system of taxation, but the establishment of a new and simplified administration of revenues and expenditures as well as of the public indebtedness of the province. Anything short of a thorough recasting of the whole framework of provincial finances would perpetuate rather than do away with the financial confusion of the first ten years of independence.

It was not until the administration of Rodríguez (1821–1824) that the problem of financial reform received serious attention. Two names are of the first importance here: Bernardino Rivadavia, Minister of Government and Foreign Affairs, and José Manuel García, Minister of Finance. Rivadavia and García formulated a series of measures whose object was not only to lay the foundation for an adequate and well-functioning fiscal system, but to bring about the financial rehabilitation of the province.

The problem of the collection and administration of revenues, together with the control of expenditures, was met by the establishment of corresponding central offices under the direct supervision of the Minister of Finance. Three such central offices were established and their functions defined in decrees of August 28 and September 1, 1821.[1] The next step introduced the practice of budgeting the province's revenues and expenditures. The legislative assembly reserved to itself the

---

[1] RO–16, L–1, p. 36; RO–19, L–1, p. 37. Article 1 of the decree is fundamental in this connection. It reads: "Habrá tres oficinas generales para la administración, recaudación y conservación de las rentas públicas en la provincia de Buenos Aires, a saber: una contaduría, que liquide todas las acciones activas y pasivas, que intervenga en todas las recetas y pagos del tesoro; que arregle y metodice el establecimiento y cobranza de los impuestos directos y indirectos. Una tesorería, en que se inviertan todos los caudales públicos que se recibirán y entregarán por ella en virtud de libramientos del secretario de hacienda, intervenidos por la contaduría. Una receptoría general por la que se recauden todos los impuestos directos y indirectos de la provincia."

right of imposing taxes and authorizing expenditures, while it obliged the government to present at the end of each year an estimate of revenues and expenditures for the following budgetary period.[2]   The diversion of funds for purposes other than those specified by the legislature was forbidden.   Nor could the government legally exceed the budget except by special permission of the parliament.[3]

The introduction of budgeting led to a more or less detailed examination of the existing sources of income.   It was found that some of the taxes had become obsolete and that others were burdensome, causing wholesale evasion and expense in enforcement.   On the other hand, several sources of income were found to be intact.   In the course of two years, as revenues from customs became stabilized and as the success of the financial reforms became more certain, the government abolished some of the more objectionable imposts such as the *contribución de comercio*, the *alcabala de venta*,[4] the *sisa*, the *media annata de oficios*, the extraordinary tax imposed upon certain business establishments,[5] and various extraordinary contributions decreed in the previous decade and still in force.[6]   This action greatly simplified the tax pattern of the province.   Customs and port duties, stamp duty, license tax, and a moderate tax upon property and capital (*contribución directa*) were the sources from which the government derived the bulk of its income.   As a rule the taxes were administered directly by the government, but in cases where the government lacked experience they were farmed out either for a fixed payment, or on a percentage basis.[7]   In all cases, however, the tax schedules were made public and the principle of equality was strictly enforced.

[2] Law of September 5, 1821.

[3] Law of December 19, 1822 (RO, L–2, no. –26); Law of December 24, 1821 (RO, L–1, p. 2).   The first budget was presented to the legislative assembly of the province in 1823.   For 1822 the provincial legislature authorized expenditures up to 600,000 pesos, but directed the government to present a detailed account of all revenues for that year, as well as the manner in which they were disposed of.

[4] Law of September 24, 1821 (RO–50, L–1, p. 80); also law of December 19, 1821 (RO–119, L–1, p. 195).

[5] Law of December 2, 1822 (RO–431, L–2, no. –24).

[6] Law of November 22, 1821 (RO–91, L–1, pp. 156–157).

[7] Farming out was found necessary in the case of the *contribución directa*, for example. In announcing its decision to leave the collection of this tax to private individuals the government admitted that it had been unable to enforce the tax, and that unless the tax was farmed out the law establishing it was likely to remain inoperative.   Cf. Decree of October 6, 1824 (RO–682, L–4, no. –10).

By far the largest portion of the government's revenues was derived from the tariff duties. In 1822 revenues from customs duties accounted for 82.5 per cent, in 1824 the proportion was 78.3 per cent, and in 1829 nearly 82 per cent of total income came from foreign and interprovincial trade.[8] Thus the financial prosperity of the province was directly dependent upon the fluctuating fortunes of foreign and interprovincial commerce. The government as well as the legislature was well aware that such dependence was a constant threat to the financial stability of the province. In 1823 the government spoke of the "hazard of depending almost entirely upon contingent revenues from customs," and promised to give careful consideration to the problem of broadening the basis of provincial finances.[9] It is hardly necessary to emphasize that the government failed to find a substitute for customs duties. Indeed, such a substitute hardly existed. Import and export taxes met with little resistance from the population, so that the collection and administration of these taxes was relatively simple and inexpensive. But the industrial structure was as yet too weak to bear even a small portion of the total tax burden. Even the moderate capital tax found little favor among the property owners, and particularly among the landowners and cattle breeders.

The *contribución directa,* because it was the only direct tax in the whole system of provincial taxation, merits closer analysis. The tax was introduced in 1821. The rate varied according to the nature of property subject to the tax. Commerce paid .08 per cent, manufacture, .06 per cent, grazing, .02 per cent, agriculture, .01 per cent. All enterprises not otherwise specified were subject to a tax of .02 per cent.[10] The schedule for 1823 was slightly modified. The tax on capital employed in grazing establishments was raised to .04 per cent, and in the case of agriculture to .02 per cent.[11] However, from 1823 on, the rates remained unchanged throughout the twenties.

[8] The proportion of revenues from foreign trade was in reality slightly larger, for the percentages above do not include port dues (*derechos de puerto*). From this source the treasury obtained 1.4 per cent of total revenues in 1822, 1.4 per cent in 1824, and 0.7 per cent in 1829.

[9] Cf. *Mensaje del Gobierno a la Sala de Representantes,* May 5, 1823 (RO, L–3, no. –7).

[10] Decree of December 17, 1821 (RO–120, L–1, pp. 120–121). Capital of 2,000 pesos in the case of married persons, and of 1,000 pesos in the case of single persons was tax exempt.

[11] Law of December 4, 1822; in *Recopilación de las leyes y decretos . . .* (Buenos Aires: 1836), pp. 426–427.

As a source of revenue the capital tax was disappointing. In 1822 the tax produced only one per cent of revenue, and in 1829, after seven years in operation, the proportion of income from this source did not exceed three per cent of the total.[12] Faulty administration was mainly responsible for the failure of the tax to produce appreciable results. In 1824, after the tax had been in force for two years, the government admitted that "experience has demonstrated the necessity of adopting more efficacious measures for the exaction of the moderate capital tax, which was introduced as absolutely indispensable to the maintenance of public order." [13] In that year the government decided to farm out the tax, and it was not until 1828 that direct administration was again attempted.[14]

There is little to be said about the remaining imposts which made up the provincial tax system. Neither the license tax (*derecho de patentes*),[15] nor the stamp duty (*papel sellado*) was important as sources of revenue. The license tax was borne by all commercial and industrial establishments, the amount depending upon the nature of business and its location. Farms and grazing establishments paid no license tax. The stamp duty was enacted in connection with the use of government stamped paper. The rates were determined from year to year by the legislative assembly.

Revenue from sources other than taxation was comparatively small. It consisted largely of rentals from lands and buildings leased to private interests, dividends on shares of the Banco Nacional, and proceeds from the sale of public lands. Rentals from land (emphyteusis) probably contributed the largest part of revenue in this group, though at times it may have been exceeded by the proceeds from the sale of the public domain.

The total revenues of the province, together with the relative importance of the various sources of income, are shown in Table 7. Four years for which complete data are available were taken for comparison.

---

[12] Capital invested in grazing and farming was exempted from payment of this tax for 1829 (Decree of September 22, 1829; RO–1206, L–8, no. –9). However, the effect of this decree upon returns for 1829 could not have been great, because the tax for any given year was usually collected in the following fiscal period.

[13] *Mensaje del Gobierno a la Cuarta Legislatura de la Provincia*, May 3, 1824 (RO, L–5, no. –4).

[14] Mabragaña I, 241 (Message, June 23, 1828).

[15] The first license tax schedule was enacted by the Legislature on December 3, 1822 (RO–432, L–2, no. –24).

TABLE 7

REVENUES AND EXPENDITURES OF THE PROVINCE OF BUENOS AIRES IN THE YEARS 1822, 1824, 1829, AND 1830

	1822 Pesos	%	1824 Pesos	%	1829 Paper pesos	%	1830 Paper pesos	%
REVENUES								
Customs	1,987,199$ 3¼	82.5	2,032,945$ 3¾	78.3	6,474,520$ 6¾	81.9	9,131,712$ 5	75.7
Stamp duty	74,789$ 2	3.1	118,907$ 3	4.6	186,373$ 3½	2.3	388,210$ 2	3.2
License tax								
Capital	23,210$ 0	1.0	21,099$ 6	0.8	229,343$ 7	2.9	337,788$ 6¼	3.2
Port dues	35,303$ 5	1.4	36,947$ 4½	1.4	58,235$ 3	0.7	131,749$ 0	1.1
New duties					148,716$ 6½	1.9	1,196,971$ 0½	9.9
Diezmo	51,870$ 3¾	2.1						
Interest			196,843$ 6¾	7.6	578,307$ 5½	7.3	706,140$ 4¾	5.8
Sales			78,582$ 2¼	3.0	129$ 3		56,011$ 2	0.5
Various	235,868$ 7	9.9	140,315$ 5¼	4.3	239,931$ 3	3.0	106,665$ 4	0.8
Total	2,408,242$ 0¾	100.0	2,596,040$ 2½	100.0	7,915,579$ 2½	100.0	12,055,249$ 0½	100.0
EXPENDITURES	1822 Pesos	%	1824 Pesos	%	1829 Paper pesos	%	1830 Paper pesos	%
Government	446,140$ 2½	20.3	679,585$ 2¼	25.8	1,255,749$ 7¾	13.0	1,842,983$ 2⅝	18.0
War	843,935$ 6	38.4	1,111,976$ 3¾	42.2	6,133,095$ 7¾	62.9	5,317,919$ 3⅕	51.7
Foreign affairs					61,763$ 6½	0.6	299,381$ 2¾	2.9
Treasury	264,187$ 2½	12.0	290,696$ 4	11.2	376,189$ 7¾	3.8	588,360$ 6	5.8
Interest	643,701$ 3	29.3	547,107$ 0	20.8	1,925,205$ 0¾	19.8	2,216,624$ 0½	21.6
Total	2,197,964$ 6	100.0	2,648,845$ 3	100.0	9,752,805$ 0½	100.0	10,276,340$ 1⅛	100.0

Source: *Registro Oficial de la Provincia de Buenos Aires* L–3, no. –2; L–5, no. –2; L–9, no. –4; L–2, no. 13.

The first fiscal year under the administration of Rodríguez was 1822. Economically it was a year of sustained prosperity; the province had regained most of the ground lost in the preceding years of civil wars. Politically the province was at peace with the world and itself. But from the point of view of public finances the year was one of transition. The great financial reforms of Rivadavia and of García, though already far advanced, had not yet been completed. The license tax had not yet made its appearance, the capital tax was hardly more than an experiment, and the *diezmo* was still a part of the tax system. The last year of Rodríguez' administration (1824) reflects more fully the financial reforms begun in 1821. The *diezmo* disappears entirely as a source of revenue, and income from sources other than taxation (interest on securities held by the government, rentals, and proceeds from sales of public lands) is accounted for separately.

The period from 1825 to 1828 was in every respect abnormal. To begin with, the province lost a good deal of its former political and financial independence. The city of Buenos Aires was transformed into a federal capital, and customs, the most important source of revenue, were nationalized. The war against Brazil and the blockade of the port of Buenos Aires had an adverse effect upon the economic and financial position of the province. Unable to finance the war out of ordinary revenues, the national government resorted to internal borrowing which in the end undermined the province's monetary stability. The paper peso (notes of the Banco Nacional) began to depreciate early in 1826, and towards the end of 1828 gold was quoted on the Buenos Aires Stock Exchange at 60 pesos per ounce.[16] The so-called "Presidential adventure" was over by the middle of 1827, but the question of peace with Brazil was not settled until September of the following year.[17] Compared with 1822 and 1824 the last two years of the decade were hardly normal. The province, it is true, regained its old status within the Confederation, but it was now burdened with a large debt and a huge deficit accumulated during the Presidency and the Brazilian war. Politically the situation was highly precarious. The struggle for supremacy between the unitaries and the federalists became more intense than ever before, culminating in an open rebellion

---

[16] At par the peso was worth $\frac{1}{17}$ of one ounce of gold.

[17] Bernardino Rivadavia resigned the presidency of the United Provinces on July 3, 1827, and on August 12, 1827 Manuel Dorrego assumed charge as governor of the province of Buenos Aires.

of the unitaries, the execution of Governor Manuel Dorrego, and the assumption of power by Juan Manuel Rosas in December of 1829. Meantime the province was forced to assume responsibility for the notes issued by the Banco Nacional. To counteract the steady process of depreciation the government announced gradual withdrawal of the notes from circulation. This was to be accomplished with funds obtained from a special tax (*impuesto nuevo*) imposed upon imports from overseas.[18] Thus commerce was made to contribute a still greater proportion of the total revenue of the province. And it may be added, in passing, that only a small portion of the new income was used for the purpose for which the "new duties" were established.

The pattern of expenditures requires little comment. All expenditures were grouped under four headings which corresponded to the four administrative departments.[19] Payments on account of interest and amortization of the public debt were charged to the Ministry of Finances. The distinction between ordinary and extraordinary expenditures was unknown, although in practice each Ministry, especially the Department of War, had at its disposal discretional funds.[20] The laws of September 5, 1821 and of December 19, 1822 required specific authorization by the legislature for all expenditures, but this requirement was frequently disregarded. In the latter half of the decade the legislature was satisfied with global appropriations. The distribution of expenditures among the various departments affords an interesting insight into the causes of the financial difficulties in which the province became involved towards the end of the decade. In 1822 the Department of War was responsible for 38.4 per cent of the expenditures of the province. This proportion rose to 42.2 per cent in 1824, and in 1829 nearly two-thirds of the total expenditures (77 per cent of all the revenues) went to the military and naval forces of the province. At the same time the budget of the Ministry of Government, which was in charge of all activities not explicitly assigned to other departments, was considerably curtailed. This department's share of total expenditures decreased from 20 per cent in 1822 and nearly 46 per cent in 1824, to 13 per cent in 1829 and 18 per cent in 1830.

---

[18] Law of October 2, 1829 (RO–1239, L–8, no. –10).

[19] Until 1824 the Minister of Government had charge of the foreign affairs of the province.

[20] So, for example, in 1829 the special expenditures of the Department of War amounted to 2,470,484 pesos out of a total of 6,133,095$ 7¾.

2

The financial reform launched by Rivadavia and García would have been incomplete had it confined itself to the reorganization of the fiscal system. Equally important was the question of the province's public indebtedness. When Rodríguez assumed charge of the provincial government the indebtedness of the province consisted of treasury bills issued in anticipation of revenues, of bonds of the Caja Nacional de Fondos Públicos de Sud América,[21] of obligations arising out of forced loans, and various other claims. The extent of these claims was unknown, and the problem of ascertaining the amount owed by the Treasury was urgent. The task was entrusted to a special commission, which in a report submitted to the government in October 1821 classified the public debt of the province under the following headings: [22]

Treasury bills....................................	192,837$ ¾
Bonds of the Caja Nacional (all coupons)...........	342,151$ 7
Government loans (1813–1821)...................	332,464$ 4¾
Claims for freed slaves..........................	28,922$ 3¼
Receipts issued for supplies......................	569,696$ 0
Unpaid salaries (army and officials)...............	132,052$ 4¾
Total indebtedness.............................	1,598,224$ 4½

The commission was careful to point out that the above statement was not accurate. In the first place, a considerable part of the bonds of the Caja Nacional de Fondos Públicos was no longer outstanding. Nearly 130,000 pesos had been either amortized or accepted by the government in payment of customs duties.[23] Secondly, the amount of Treasury bills was calculated as of July 26, 1821 the date the commission began its investigation. The figure stated in the report should be reduced, therefore, by the amount amortized during the period of the commission's work.[24] Thirdly, at least one of the forced loans listed

[21] The Caja Nacional de Fondos Públicos de Sud América was created in 1819. The Caja was empowered to issue certificates (bonds) against deposits of treasury bills, acknowledged claims against the government, and cash. The certificates carried coupons of 8, 12, and 15 per cent. Cash deposits were entitled to 15 per cent, certificates issued in payment of supplies received 12 per cent, and treasury bills issued on the basis of the decree of March 29, 1817 commanded a rate of 8 per cent. The government guaranteed payment of interest and principal. Proceeds from a surtax of 6 per cent on all imports were to be set aside for the service of these bonds. The certificates of the Caja were negotiable, but the principal could not be withdrawn except with the approval of the government. Cf. RN–1224.

[22] RO, L–1, pp. 114–116.

[23] Loc. cit., Nota segunda.

[24] Loc. cit., Nota tercera.

in the report had been nearly paid off.[25] And, finally, the commission pointed out that it had not succeeded in determining the total amount due on account of supplies and salaries. Accordingly, the last two items in the above statement were in reality larger.[26] Having taken into consideration all these factors the commission estimated the total indebtedness of the province at about 2,000,000 pesos.[27]

The structure of the public debt of the province was highly unsatisfactory. Of the total indebtedness only a very small portion was of the long term variety. The remainder formed a huge mass of negotiable bills, which seriously hampered current credit operations. Moreover, as the bills and other short term obligations were returned to the treasury in payment of customs duties and other taxes, the government was forced to reissue the bills. In this manner the floating debt of the province became virtually a long term debt, without the advantages of the latter form of indebtedness. Government obligations, as they increased in number and variety, became the object of speculation, in which both the government and the original holders sustained considerable losses.[28] To extinguish the short term debt by way of accepting all bills in payment of taxes was, of course, impossible. The amount of bills outstanding was too large, and the government needed all the revenues it could get. The solution lay in the consolidation of the total indebtedness and its conversion into a long term debt. The funding operation was accomplished towards the end of 1821.

The law of October 30, 1821 authorized the government to issue bonds to the amount of 5,000,000 pesos, of which 2,000,000 pesos were in 4 per cent certificates, and 3,000,000 pesos in certificates bearing 6 per cent coupons.[29] The Collector General was directed to make annual transfers of 300,000 pesos to the Caja de Amortización for the service of the loans. These transfers were to be made in preference to

[25] *Loc. cit., Nota cuarta.*

[26] *Loc. cit., Nota quinta.*

[27] *Loc. cit., Nota sexta.*

[28] Speculators would buy government obligations from original holders at a discount as high as 60 per cent, and resell them to merchants who returned the bills to the Treasury in payment of customs duties at face value.

[29] Cf. RO–69, L–1, pp. 118–124. The law consisted of six sections (*capítulos*). Section I established a Register of Public Indebtedness (*Libro de Fondos Públicos*); Section II provided for an immediate issue of 5,000,000 pesos; Section III created the Caja de Amortización for the administration and service of this and future loans; Section IV defined the function of the Caja de Amortización; Section V dealt with the amortization and service of bonds currently issued; Section VI regulated future bond issues.

all other obligations of the Customs Administration.   The actual funding operation was carried out on the basis of the decree of November 19, 1821.[30]   All claims originating before July 1, 1821 were subject to conversion.[31]   Claims which originated before May 25, 1810 were to be exchanged for 4 per cent bonds.   All other creditors received 6 per cent bonds.   Those whose claims were acquired directly from the government were entitled to a 25 per cent bonus in addition to the principal.   In the process of conversion it appeared that the 1821 bond issue was not sufficient to cover all the outstanding claims.   The legislature, therefore, authorized the issue of two more loans, one to the amount of 1,800,000 pesos in 1823, and another of 300,000 pesos in 1824.[32]   With these issues the funding operation was completed.   But before the decade was over the funded debt of the province was further increased by 6,260,000 pesos.   In 1825 the government issued 6 per cent bonds to the amount of 260,000 pesos,[33] and in 1827, soon after the resignation of Rivadavia, the government floated the 6,000,000 peso loan.[34]   Towards the end of the twenties the total funded debt still outstanding amounted to 10,817,541 pesos, as shown in Table 8.

TABLE 8

THE FUNDED DEBT OF THE PROVINCE OF BUENOS AIRES AS OF AUGUST 31, 1829

	Date of issue	Amount of issue	Amortized	
1821	October 30 4% bonds equivalent to..............	1,333,333	Redeemed to	
1821	October 30 6% bonds.........	3,000,000	August 31, 1829....	1,875,792
1823	December 17.................	1,800,000		
1824	November 10	300,000		
1825	December 14................	260,000		
1827	September 29..............	6,000,000	Outstanding.........	10,817,541
Total............................		12,693,333		12,693,333

Source: *The British Packet and Argentine News*, September 26, 1829, vol. 4, no. 162.

Analysis of the long term indebtedness of the province would not be complete without mention of the so-called London loan.   At first the government intended to obtain three or four million gold pesos to be

---

[30] RO-85, L-1, pp. 85–86.

[31] The date was changed to September 1, 1821.   Decree of November 28, 1821.

[32] Law of December 17, 1823 (RO-574, L-3, no. -18); Law of November 10, 1824 (RO-707, L-4, no. -12).

[33] Law of December 14, 1825 (*Registro Oficial de la Provincia de Buenos Aires*, Año de 1825, Buenos Aires, 1874, p. 58).

[34] Law of September 17, 1827 (RO-850, L-6, no. -3).

used for the construction of a port in Buenos Aires, the establishment of new settlements along the Indian frontier, and the construction of waterworks in the capital.[35] The principal of the loan was later increased to 5,000,000 gold pesos, and the government was authorized to conclude arrangements with Baring Brothers of London on condition that the province receive not less than 70 per cent of the par value of the bonds, that the interest rate would not exceed 6 per cent per annum, and that amortization be set at the rate of ½ per cent a year.[36] The loan was consummated in 1824, and the province received 3,000,000 gold pesos after interest and amortization up to January 12, 1827 had been deducted.[37] The subsequent history of the loan, interesting though it is, need not detain us here. Suffice it to say that the progressive deterioration of the province's financial condition in the second half of the decade forced the government to suspend payment of interest and amortization service. In 1827 an effort was made to avoid outright default, but to no avail.[38] It was not until 1844 that service of the loan was partially resumed, only to be suspended in 1845, and again resumed in 1849. It is not surprising, therefore, that the price of Argentine bonds on the London Stock Exchange declined from 93⅞ in January 1825 to 20 per cent of par in October 1829. In this concise language the City expressed its hopes and disappointments over the financial and economic prospects of Buenos Aires. (See Table 9.)

3

Fiscal reorganization was not solely a matter of administrative reform. Of much greater importance was the question of the economy's ability to sustain the new financial superstructure. Indeed, the fiscal and economic problems were inseparable. For while economic prosperity was essential to the success of the government's program of fiscal reconstruction, economic expansion itself was at least in part conditioned by the prevailing monetary and credit system. The gov-

[35] Law of August 19, 1822 (RO–403, L–2, no. –22).

[36] Law of November 28, 1822 (RO–430, L–2, no. –22).

[37] Pedro Agote, *Informe del Presidente del Crédito Público don Pedro Agote sobre la Deuda Pública, Bancos y Emisiones de Papel y Acuñación de Monedas de la República Argentina* (Buenos Aires: 1881), I, 12–15.

[38] On August 6, 1827 thirty-one *hacendados* and merchants guaranteed payment of interest and amortization until one year after the termination of the Brazilian war. Nothing, however, came of it. On April 5, 1828 the government authorized the sale of two frigates (*Asia* and *Congreso*), the proceeds to be paid on account of interest due January 12, 1827. Cf. Agote, *loc. cit.*

TABLE 9

AVERAGE MONTHLY QUOTATIONS OF THE LOAN OF 1824
ON THE LONDON STOCK EXCHANGE

(In percentages of par)

	1825	1826	1827	1828	1829	1830
January	93⅞	74	58¼	43	47	30½
February	92	82¼	52½	38½	37¾	29
March	91⅛	59½	54½	34½	29½	31½
April	91	61	58	34¼	23	35
May	91½	60	60¾	38¾	25	38¾
June	92¼	58¾	61	43½	24½	33
July	92¼	50	60½	45½	23	45½
August	88	52	64	43	20	—
September	64½	58	57¾	45	24	25½
October	83	62	45¼	48½	25	24½
November	78	63	48	48	24	22
December	73½	64	49	48	27	—

Source: Pedro Agote, *Informe del Presidente del Crédito Público don Pedro Agote sobre la Deuda Pública, Bancos y Emisiones de Papel Moneda y Acuñación de Monedas de la República Argentina* (Buenos Aires: 1881), IV, 97–98.

ernment, too, was directly interested in the modernization of the financial mechanism. In the first place, the treasury was at all times a heavy borrower of short term funds. Secondly, consolidation and conversion of the floating debt had a better chance of succeeding under conditions of easy money and adequate credit facilities. However, precisely because of commercial and industrial expansion, capital became relatively scarce. The very process of economic development accentuated the lack of credit facilities relative to the requirements of the economy.[39]   It was in order to meet the financial needs of the prov-

[39] Loanable capital was never plentiful in Buenos Aires, but after the Revolution its relative scarcity increased considerably. Interest rates of 4 and 5 per cent per month on private loans, and of 2 to 3 per cent per month on government borrowings were not uncommon. The following monthly averages of discount rates in the Buenos Aires market are based on weekly quotations in the *British Packet and Argentine News:*

	1828	1829	1830
January		2.166	2.640
February		2.250	2.500
March		1.625	2.687
April		1.666	3.375
May		1.750	3.650
June		1.875	3.250
July		1.906	2.650
August		2.000	2.562
September		2.000	2.244
October		2.300	2.525
November	1.821	2.594	2.375
December	1.969	2.500	2.344

ince as well as to facilitate its own credit operations that the government encouraged the establishment of a discount bank.

Conversations with a view to establishing such a bank were begun as early as 1821. Towards the middle of the following year the government introduced in the Legislative Assembly a bill which granted a private company the exclusive right to establish a discount bank. The bill was approved and passed by the legislature on June 22, 1822.[40] The bank, known officially as the Banco de Buenos Aires, began operations on September 6, 1822 and rapidly assumed a central position in the financial and economic system of the province.

The financial structure and activity of the Banco de Buenos Aires were defined in the bylaws. The bank was to have a capital of 1,000,000 pesos divided into 1,000 shares.[41] Shareholders were required to pay only 200 pesos a share at the time of subscription, 200 pesos more within 60 days after the opening of the bank, and the remainder at times designated by the Board of Directors, but always in installments of 200 pesos payable within 60 days. Capital invested in shares of the bank was free from the *contribución directa*. The principal activity of the bank consisted in discounting operations, acceptance of deposits, collection of funds on account of others, dealing in foreign exchange, and so forth. The bank acted also as agent for the provincial treasury. In addition the bank could issue notes in denominations of not less than 20 pesos.[42] These notes were redeemable in gold on demand. Forgers of bank notes and the bank's seals were to be considered as forgers of money, and subject to the penalties provided for such crimes. The bank was governed by an elective Board of Directors, which consisted of nine members before the capital was fully subscribed, and of thirteen members afterwards.

In establishing a bank of issue the government hoped to accomplish two things. First, it believed that the bank would mobilize a substantial amount of specie, and thus provide a sound basis for currency expansion. Secondly, it was expected that currency expansion accom-

---

[40] Cf. RO–735. Monopoly was granted for a period of 20 years.

[41] The bank's capital could be increased by a vote of the General Assembly of Stockholders and with the approval of the Provincial Legislature.

[42] The privilege was later extended to notes of smaller denominations. In 1834 the bank took over from the government the issue of small notes (*vales*). In 1826 the amount of such notes in circulation was 587,186 pesos, as compared with 150,000 pesos in 1824. (Cf. Balance sheet of the Banco de Buenos Aires for February 28, 1826.)

panied by a liberal discount policy would ease considerably the credit situation within the province. These hopes were not unreasonable, and given time they might have been realized. That they were not realized even on a moderate scale, that far from exerting a stabilizing influence in the provincial economy, the bank became instead an object of unbridled speculation and a center of bitter political controversy, was in the final analysis due partly to political developments within the province, and partly to the financial environment of the bank.

The financial position of the bank was weak from the very beginning and contrary to expectations it failed to attract any considerable amount of specie. On February 28, 1825, after the bank had been in existence for more than two years, its holdings of specie barely reached 300,000 pesos. At that time the bank's capital was fully subscribed and paid up, but that was only because a large portion of the bank's shares were paid for with its own funds.[43] The bank, therefore, was never able to assume a commanding position in the financial market, and because of its weak capital structure it was frequently tempted to have recourse to note issues.

With respect to currency and credit the bank's achievements were hardly more reassuring. In the course of three years the note issue rose from 290,000 pesos to 2,694,856, while specie holdings declined from 270,937 pesos to 250,000 pesos. Thus at the end of three years the reserve ratio was less than 10 per cent. This position was highly vulnerable, for even a slight demand for conversion of notes into gold, a demand that might be caused by an unfavorable balance of trade, would force the bank to suspend payments. That depreciation of the bank's notes did not occur long before the bank issued its last semi-annual report was, in all probability, due to the fact that a large portion of the notes filled a genuine demand for currency. But anything in excess of this constant demand could not but adversely affect the value of gold. Apparently such a point was reached early in July in 1826, for in February of that year gold was selling at a premium of 6 per cent. This marked the beginning of a prolonged process of depreciation which

---

[43] Augustín de Vedia believes that nearly half of the capital was paid for in this manner. This is not at all surprising, since it was profitable to borrow from the bank at 9 or even 12 per cent and buy shares which paid in dividends 19 per cent in 1824 and 19½ per cent in 1825. Cf. Agustín de Vedia, *Banco Nacional* (Buenos Aires: 1890), xvii, 513 pp.; "Argos" for December 18, 22, and 25, 1824 (Buenos Aires); *Diario de Sesiones*, Session 210 (September 1, 1830), speech by Nicolás Anchorena.

TABLE 10

FINANCIAL POSITION OF THE BANCO DE BUENOS AIRES AT STATED PERIODS: 1823–1826 [a]

Period	Capital	Notes issued	Specie holdings	Discounts	Dividends pesos	%
1823						
August 31	445,000	291,000	270,937	705,284	53,400	12
1824						
February 28	469,000	910,000	154,192	1,352,464	46,900	10
August 31	1,000,000	1,680,000	204,629	2,565,525	90,000	9
1825						
February 28	1,000,000	1,698,000	285,267	2,457,233	100,000	10
August 31	1,000,000	1,934,000	253,035	2,594,532	95,000	9½
1826						
February 28	1,000,000	2,694,856	255,000	3,280,536	115,000	11½

[a] Pedro Agote, *op. cit.*, I, 90.

towards the end of the decade brought the value of the peso down to 15 per cent of par.[44]

As a dispenser of cheap credit the bank was only partially successful. The increase of discounts from 765,284 pesos in 1823 to 3,280,526 pesos in 1826 would indicate that the bank pursued a liberal discount policy. However, the quality of the bank's discounting operations left much to be desired. In the first place, since the bank could not discount for terms longer than 90 days its activity was necessarily confined to commercial transactions. Thus, for example, the grazing industry with its protracted cycle of production could not freely utilize the credit facilities available at the bank. Secondly, much of the bank's funds were used for speculative purposes or for purely financial operations. Moreover, a large proportion of the loans was in reality of the long term variety, since the bank was frequently forced to make periodic extensions. As a result a large portion of the bank's assets was virtually immobilized. Contraction of credit became extremely difficult, and the activity of the bank was reduced to the collection of interest.

If dividends are taken as a criterion the bank was a highly successful enterprise. The directors and stockholders of the bank had every reason to be confident about its future. But the profit and loss account is not the sole, nor even the most important, criterion of a bank's role in the process of economic development, especially if the bank occupies a

[44] See Table 10.

monopolistic position.   More important is the question whether or not the bank contributed to the improvement of credit conditions in the province.   And in this respect the bank belied the hopes of both the government and the industrial and commercial community.   Far from becoming a stabilizing factor the bank tended to encourage speculation, and by its careless monetary policy it actually weakened the monetary system of the province.   Towards the end of 1825 the financial condition of the bank was rapidly deteriorating.   As the war against Brazil strained the financial resources of the provincial government, large expenditures had to be made outside the boundaries of the province, where notes of the bank were not accepted.[45]   Demand for gold grew apace, and the bank was forced to apply to the government for a suspension of the conversion clause.[46]   The bank was saved from disaster only because at this time plans for the establishment of a new bank had already been completed.   Early in 1826 the Banco de Buenos Aires ceased to exist.

4

The Banco Nacional was a much more ambitious project than its predecessor, the Bank of Buenos Aires.[47]   The new bank's privileges as well as the manner in which it was to operate were also more carefully defined in the enabling act of January 28, 1826.[48]   The bank's capital was to consist of 10 million pesos divided into 50,000 shares of 200 pesos each.   The government undertook to subscribe 15,000 shares, and the Banco Nacional was to take over the capital of the Bank of Buenos Aires through an exchange of shares on the basis of 7 shares of the new stock for each share of the old bank.[49]   The remaining 5,600,000 pesos were to be obtained through public subscription. The government reserved the right to acquire shares in addition to those

[45] Attempts to stimulate circulation of bank notes in other provinces were unsuccessful. Thus, the branch which the bank opened in Entre Ríos (October 1825) had to be liquidated four months later (February 1826).   Bank notes issued in payment for supplies in other provinces were speedily returned to Buenos Aires and presented at the bank.

[46] The bank's specie holdings were placed at the disposal of the government by decree of January 9, 1826.   The bank was ordered to suspend further issues of notes. Bank notes already in circulation were guaranteed by the Banco Nacional. Cf. *Registro Nacional*, vol. 2, no. 1877.

[47] The official name of the bank was: Banco de las Provincias Unidas del Río de la Plata.   Banco Nacional is the term most reguently used in official acts.

[48] *Registro Nacional*, vol. II, no. 1881.

[49] Decree of March 13, 1826 (*Registro Nacional*, vol. II, no. 1911).

already subscribed, as well as to sell part or all of the shares it held. The scope of the bank's activity was defined as follows: discount of commercial paper bearing two endorsements; dealing in foreign exchange and letters of credit; acceptance of deposits in domestic and foreign currency; collection for the account of others; coinage according to specifications and conditions determined by the legislature; issue of bank notes convertible into specie on demand.[50]   In exchange for the franchise the Banco Nacional undertook to act without remuneration as the government's financial agent, to discount notes issued by the treasury, and to open a credit of 2,000,000 pesos in favor of the government.   The bank was exempt from stamp duties, and capital invested in bank shares was to pay the minimum rate of the *contribución directa* schedule.   The bank charter was for ten years, and extension required a special act by the Legislature.

When the Banco Nacional began operations (February 1826) its capital consisted of 1,400,000 pesos taken over from the Bank of Buenos Aires and 3,000,000 pesos subscribed by the government.   Of the latter sum only 20,000 pesos was in cash, the rest in treasury bills.   In other words, the bank began its career without funds.   Public interest was sluggish.   By July 1, 1826 only 1,706 shares of the 38,000 offered to the public were subscribed, and by the end of the year public participation in the bank was still below 500,000 pesos.[51]   In the meantime the bank was obliged to open a credit to the government of 2,000,000 pesos (a statutory provision), and to discount treasury bills.   Indeed, in less than two months after the opening of the bank, discounts and advances to government increased from 3,280,536 pesos to 7,553,226.[52] There can be little doubt that nearly all of this increase consisted of advances to the treasury.

The Banco Nacional thus began its career in circumstances even less auspicious than those attending the opening of the Bank of Buenos Aires.   To all the causes which forced the Bank of Buenos Aires to suspend conversion there was now added a new one.   For the increased expenditures caused by war prevented the government from balancing the budget.   Further, the blockade made serious inroads into the reve-

---

[50] The government reserved the right to determine the amount of notes which the bank could issue in the first year.   Afterwards the issue of notes was to be subject to legislative control.

[51] See Table 11.

[52] See Table 12.

TABLE 11

BANCO NACIONAL: PAID-UP CAPITAL, BANK NOTES ISSUED, NOTES IN CIRCULATION

Date	Paid-up capital	Notes issued	Notes in circulation
1826			
February 11	4,400,000	2,694,856	2,253,011
April 1	4,400,000	3,782,436	2,226,281
May 1	4,400,000	4,514,346	3,582,900
June 1	4,400,000	4,881,846	4,417,483
July 1	4,741,200	5,077,276	4,441,232
August 1	4,810,100	6,700,288	6,344,342
September 1	4,810,100	6,027,788	5,283,349
October 1	4,840,400	7,109,007	6,450,792
November 1	4,840,400	6,979,207	5,978,881
December 1	4,840,400	7,439,766	6,586,066
1827			
January 1	4,840,400	7,881,176	7,000,786
February 1	4,841,400	8,332,776	7,535,906
March 1	4,865,400	8,745,456	7,574,726
April 1	4,867,200	8,761,425	7,657,330
May 1	4,868,600	9,022,899	7,821,823
June 1	5,088,600	9,018,744	7,853,691
July 1	5,098,600	9,658,548	8,274,634
August 1	5,104,800	9,746,148	8,613,465
September 1	5,104,800	10,215,639	8,647,286
October 1	5,104,800	10,492,349	9,329,124
November 1	5,104,800	11,037,039	9,807,265
December 1	5,104,800	10,662,489	10,338,702
1828			
January 1	5,104,800	10,703,984	9,660,372
January 22	5,104,800	10,168,263	9,495,143

Source: Report of Félix I. Frías, Mariano Fragueiro, and Félix Castro on the activity of the Banco Nacional prepared for the Junta de Representantes de la Provincia de Buenos Aires. (Typewritten copy of the original in the Instituto de Investigaciones Históricas.)

nues of the province, and the treasury in search of funds resorted to short term borrowings. These borrowings took the form of advances made by the bank. And since the bank had no resources of its own, such advances to the government were, therefore, immediately translated into an increase of notes in circulation. This in turn raised the question of convertibility. Already in April 1826, i.e., two months after the bank began operations, the question of conversion came up before the Congress. Notes of the Banco Nacional were declared legal tender, and on May 5, 1826 the Congress approved a temporary and partial suspension of gold payments. Conversion was entirely suspended until November 25, 1826, and thereafter redemption of notes

TABLE 12

BANCO NACIONAL: ADVANCES TO COMMERCE AND GOVERNMENT

Date	Total Advances	Advances to Government	Discounts
1826			
February 11	3,280,536		
April 1	7,563,226		
May 1	8,191,276		
June 1	9,112,420		
July 1	9,422,565		
August 1	9,014,466		
September 1	9,440,906		
October 1	9,477,104		
November 1	9,570,797		
December 1	10,025,758		
1827			
January 1		8,970,164	3,269,147
February 1		9,582,446	3,203,459
March 1		9,624,961	2,991,045
April 1		9,624,961	2,928,012
May 1		9,785,363	2,869,726
June 1		9,933,720	3,033,452
July 1		10,327,165	3,156,698
August 1		11,000,314	2,922,584
September 1		11,046,245	2,639,397
October 1		11,509,660	3,125,938
November 1		11,906,716	3,315,062
December 1		12,208,425	3,056,648
1828			
January 1		12,144,376	2,540,647

Source: Report of Félix I. Frías, Mariano Fragueiro, and Félix Castro on the activity of the Banco Nacional prepared for the Junta de Representantes de la Provincia de Buenos Aires. (Typewritten copy of the original in the Instituto de Investigaciones Históricas.)

was to be resumed, but only of sums not less than 1,000 pesos. After May 25, 1828 all restrictions relating to conversion were to cease.[53] But even this partial restoration of the conversion clause remained inoperative. By November 25, 1826 the bank was less prepared than ever before to meet the demand for gold. The redemption clause was, therefore, again repealed and the government took over the bank's specie holdings.[54]

Repeal of the conversion clause marked an important step in the evolution of the National Bank. Earlier in the year the government abolished the treasury (Tesorería General) and utilized the bank as

[53] *Registro Nacional*, vol. II, no. 1972.
[54] Law of December 7, 1826 (*Registro Nacional*, vol. II, no. 2084).

the main collecting and distributing agency for the province.[55]   At the same time bank notes were declared legal tender, so that all contracts which excluded bank notes as means of payment became non-enforceable.   All government offices were directed to receive and make payments in notes of the Banco Nacional at their face value.[56]   Now that the bank was deprived of its specie holdings and the bank notes were transformed into inconvertible paper money in all but name, the bank itself became virtually a government institution.   The role of the bank as a factor in the economic life of the province gradually diminished. While advances to the government grew from 2,000,000 pesos in 1826 to 12,144,376 pesos in January 1828, discounts decreased from 3,280,536 pesos to 2,540,647 pesos in the same period.[57]   Even after the war against Brazil the activity of the bank was confined almost exclusively to credit and currency operations for the account of the government.

The failure of the National Bank to become an organic part of the provincial and national economy was due to a variety of causes.   Some of these were political.   Conceived as a national institution at a time when political unification was as yet a thing of the future, sponsored by a party whose political ideals found little or no response in most of the provinces in the Interior, the bank was opposed by all who saw in it an instrument of economic and financial domination controlled by the central government.   In Buenos Aires where political struggles over the problem of national organization were particularly violent, and where also the financial powers wielded by the Banco Nacional were better appreciated, opposition to the bank was of the bitterest sort.   In this province, more than in any other, the Banco Nacional came to be considered a symbol of unitarism, a stronghold of all those forces which were instrumental in depriving Buenos Aires of home rule.

Of still greater importance were the financial difficulties which confronted the province as a result of the Brazilian war.   Since the burden of financing the war fell upon Buenos Aires it was natural that the bank should have been utilized for this purpose.   The truth is that the National Bank was prevented from playing an important part in the economic life of the province.   From the very beginning its facilities were

[55] Law of May 20, 1826 (Registro Nacional, vol. II, no. 1992).

[56] Decree of May 10, 1826 (Registro Nacional, vol. II, no. 1978); Decree of May 24, 1826 (Registro Nacional, vol. II, no. 1997).

[57] See Table 12.

almost entirely monopolized by the government. It is not surprising, therefore, that the attempt to draw upon commerce and industry for capital met with such indifferent results. And the fact that the bank was at no time capable of mobilizing the financial resources of the country was to a large extent responsible for the transformation of the bank into a government fiscal agency. The government itself could do little to change the course of events, for it was constantly faced with the fact that the normal revenues of the province were entirely inadequate to meet the extraordinary expenditures occasioned by the war of 1825–1828. By far the most important source of income was commerce, and it was precisely this branch of economic activity which was hit hardest by the Brazilian blockade of the nation's largest port. And since it was impossible for political and economic reasons to strengthen the tax system by shifting part of the taxes from foreign trade to industry, the government was forced to resort either to outright inflation, as a special form of taxation, or to borrowing in the internal market. The government chose the second alternative as the easiest and politically the most expedient course to follow. But the effect of this kind of borrowing was distinctly inflationary. Contrary to what one would expect, the government did not resort to loans of the long term variety. Fearing, perhaps, that long term loans would find no response among the industrialists and merchants, and not willing to risk its financial and political prestige, the government preferred to utilize the credit facilities of the National Bank. This method was also cheaper, for the interest charged by the bank was considerably below the open market rate. But the credit resources of the bank were far short of the needs of the treasury. Not even the calling in of all commercial loans could satisfy the requirements of the government. The only way out, therefore, was the issue of bank notes. Thus the growth of bank notes in circulation closely corresponds to the increase of the government's indebtedness to the bank. What was at first merely a temporary expedient became in time one of the most frequently used methods of procuring funds. Even after the Brazilian war the government continued the practice of borrowing from the Banco Nacional. So, while advances to the government in the interval between January 1, 1828 and December 31, 1829 increased by nearly 6,000,000 pesos to 18,-126,826 pesos,[58] the amount of bank notes in circulation rose to 15,-

---

[58] *Estado General de Erario a fin del año de 1829* (RO, L–9, no. –4).

152,726 in July 1830, an increase of nearly 6,500,000 pesos since January 1, 1828.[59]

5

The growth of the government's indebtedness to the National Bank does not fully reveal the financial plight of the province. Nor does it reveal the conditions which forced the government to turn to the bank for accommodations. More significant in this respect are the yearly balance sheets of the provincial treasury. In his first message to the provincial legislature Governor Manuel Dorrego reported that at the end of 1826 the accumulated deficit amounted to more than 4,000,000 pesos.[60] In the first nine months of 1827 only about one-third of expenditures were covered by revenues.[61] And in 1828 the treasury reported an income of 3,659,783 pesos 7 reales as against expenditures of 9,307,357 pesos 4 reales.[62] Thus, for four consecutive years the treasury showed considerable deficits, and it was not until 1830 that the government succeeded in reducing the accumulated deficit by about 1,500,000 pesos. (See Table 13.)

TABLE 13

CUMULATIVE GROWTH OF TREASURY DEFICITS IN BUENOS AIRES: 1826–1830 [a]

	Intervening period	End of period
December 31, 1826		4,203,611$ 6¾
July 31, 1827	4,022,312$ 6¾	8,225,824$ 5½
December 31, 1827	797,597$ 1¼	9,023,421$ 6¾
December 31, 1828	4,354,427$ 5¼	13,377,849$ 4
December 31, 1829	1,731,663$ 1	15,109,512$ 5
December 31, 1830 surplus........	1,366,824$ 0	13,542,688$ 5

[a] Sources: see footnotes 60, 61, 62; also: *Estado General del Erario a fin del año* . . . (RO, L–9, no. –4; RO, L–9, no. –13).

It will be noted that the deficits shown in the above table are not true deficits in that proceeds from the sale of bonds were sometimes recorded as income on the balance sheets of the treasury. However, the difference between the recorded and true deficits is so small as to make correction unnecessary.

[59] *British Packet and Argentine News*, July 17, 1830 (vol. IV, no. 205).

[60] September 14, 1827 (RO–841, L–6, no. –2).

[61] *Bosquejo del Estado General del Erario* (RO, L–6, no. –3).

[62] "General Statement of the Public Treasury to the end of the Year 1828," *British Packet and Argentine News*, September 5, 1829, vol. IV, no. 159.

On only one occasion in the four years between 1826 and 1829 did the government resort to long term borrowing. The loan was frankly a budgetary measure, and the conditions under which it was floated reflect the extremely precarious position of the treasury. The whole issue of 6,000,000 pesos was taken over by a syndicate for public distribution. The treasury received in exchange promissory notes to the amount of 52 per cent of the loan.[63] The government promised also to refrain from new bond issues for a period of six months from the date of the contract (October 1, 1827). Six months later (March 1828) when the government in desperate need of funds planned another bond issue of 2,000,000 pesos the legislature refused authorization, on the ground that in view of the prevailing scarcity of money and declining bond prices the loan was likely to fail. Although it was aware of the inflationary effect of this measure the Junta de Representantes argued that a note issue would act in the same way as a tax levied "upon all classes"; [64] that the government would benefit to the full extent of the debt contracted; and, finally, that the increase of notes in circulation would cause a rise in bond prices.[65] The position of the provincial legislature with respect to the borrowing policies of the government is significant. In deciding upon expansion of currency as against bond issue the legislative assembly was not only solicitous about the interests of the Treasury (the bank was ordered to advance the loan without interest), but it was also anxious to protect the bondholders and to avoid the imposition of new taxes or the more stringent collection of old ones.

[63] The syndicate was formed by José María Esteves, Félix Castro, Juan García Praga, Braulio Costa, Alejandro de Molina, Larrea Hermanos, Ruperto Albarellos, Pedro Alfaro, Félix Ignacio Frías, Miguel Ambrosio Gutiérrez, and Jorge Frank. *Diaria de Sesiones*, Session 20 (September 28, 1827).

[64] *Ibid.*, Report of the Financial Commission of the Provincial Legislature (Felipe Senillosa). The Legislature's concern for the interests of the bondholders and its readiness to resort to note issue is especially interesting in view of the fact that the number of bondholders was relatively insignificant. According to a preliminary report prepared by the Junta Administrativa de Crédito Público (May 5, 1830) there were:

605 individual holders of 6 per cent bonds .... 9,594,897$		
49 corporate " " " " " " .... 473,967$		10,068,864$
244 individual holders of 4 per cent bonds .... 1,541,497$		
24 corporate " " " " " " .... 125,921$		1,667,318$
Total...		11,736,182$

Cf. *Archivo General*, Ant. C.22–A.2–no. 5.

[65] *Diario de Sesiones*, Sessions 91–93 (March 29–April 1, 1828); Law of April 9, 1828.

The process of inflation began in February of 1826 and continued almost uninterruptedly until the middle of 1830. At first depreciation was slow, but it gathered momentum in the second half of 1826, as the financial instability of the National Bank and the Treasury became increasingly evident. In December of that year gold commanded a premium of nearly 200 per cent. After a brief interval the peso resumed its downward course in July 1827. In October of that year the peso was quoted at about 24 per cent of par. In February and March of 1828 the peso regained nearly all of the ground lost in the preceding year. The spectacular come back, as sudden as it was short-lived, was due primarily to Dorrego's deliberate policy of retrenchment and economy. The financial horizon began to look more hopeful once more with the suspension of hostilities against Brazil. But the revolt of Juan Lavalle and the execution of Manuel Dorrego thoroughly undermined the financial position of the province. The price of gold on the Buenos Aires Stock Exchange rose steadily to 102 pesos per ounce in October 1829. At that figure the premium amounted to 500 per cent. The price continued to climb for some time after Juan Manuel Rosas had assumed control of the government, and by April of 1830 the peso depreciated to 12.3 per cent of par. Thereafter, partly as a result of political stability and partly also in response to Rosas' policy of strict economy, the value of the peso rose slowly to 15.2 per cent of par in December of 1830.[66]

Currency depreciation was much more than a symptom of financial maladjustment. What at first appeared to be a temporary disturbance of the monetary mechanism developed finally into a process of readjustment of the whole pattern of economic relationships of the pre-inflation period. This process, which in the final analysis involved changes in the distribution of the national income, was brought about by a series of alterations in commodity prices, wages, and profits. The rise in prices following the decline of the paper peso, though general, was not evenly distributed over the whole range of commodities and services. Commodity prices rose on the whole faster than wages and salaries, with the result that the real income of wage and salary earners decreased, both relatively and absolutely. On the other hand, not all commodity prices were equally sensitive to currency depreciation. Commodities entering foreign trade, whether on the import or the export side, responded quite readily to fluctuations in the price of gold,

[66] See Table 14.

TABLE 14

MONTHLY AND YEARLY AVERAGE PRICES PAID FOR ONE OUNCE OF GOLD
ON THE BUENOS AIRES STOCK EXCHANGE

Month	1826	1827	1828	1829	1830
January...............	17	51	70½	63⅜	104
February.............	18	50	66¾	61⅗	111½
March................	18¼	45	39¼	62	128¼
April.................	18½	40	42½	66½	138
May..................	19¾	50⅔	49½	77½	124½
June.................	22⅜	53½	48	74½	116⅛
July.................	23¼	56¾	48¼	77⅗	115¾
August...............	28¾	60¼	48½	82⅖	117
September............	34¼	67¼	39½	88½	116⅘
October..............	46¹⁄₁₂	70	39⅛	102½	116
November............	48¾	67½	46¼	99⅛	114½
December............	50¾	67½	60	100¾	112¾
Yearly average........	30	56½	50	79⅙	117¾

Source: Pedro Agote, *Informe del Presidente del Crédito Público don Pedro Agote sobre la Deuda Pública Bancos y Emisiones de Papel Moneda y Acuñación de Monedas de la República Argentina* (Buenos Aires: 1881), I, 126–127.

while prices of goods produced and consumed within the province lagged behind the general trend. It would seem, therefore, that the industrial and commercial classes, especially artisans and manufacturers for domestic markets, bore the greater part of the burden of currency depreciation. On the other hand, the cattle breeders were in a more favorable position. Therefore, far from having their real income diminished this class was likely to benefit from the depreciation of the peso. The cattle breeders and meat producers benefited not only as employers of labor but also as tax payers and exporters. In the latter capacity the position of the *hacendados* was especially advantageous, largely because of the manner in which exports of the produce of the grazing industry were taxed. Accordingly cattle breeders were much better situated than merchants, so that the economic position of the one improved not only absolutely but also in relation to the position of the other.

6

Perhaps the best illustration of how currency depreciation tended to shift the burden of taxation from one group to another is the tariff. In it, as in a mirror, were reflected not only the commercial and fiscal policies of the government, but also the manner in which inflation affected the interests of the various economic groups and at the same time vitiated the whole fiscal system of the province.

In its foreign commercial policies Buenos Aires was guided by two kinds of considerations. First, it was necessary to find foreign markets for the produce of the grazing industry. And secondly, since the country suffered from an acute shortage of manufactured goods there was every incentive to open the province to foreign imports. However, this tendency towards free trade was mitigated by fiscal considerations. The country was too weak financially to dispense with foreign commerce as a source of revenue, for of all the available sources it proved to be the most fertile and dependable. Industrial backwardness and the opposition of the cattle breeders excluded the possibility of increasing internal taxes and so of lifting the tax pressure from foreign trade. Consequently the government was forced to reconcile enthusiasm for free trade with the financial exigencies of the moment, with the result that duties were imposed upon both imports and exports.

The first general tariff went into effect on January 1, 1822.[67] It provided for a basic rate of 15 per cent *ad valorem* on all overseas imports. A considerable group of commodities, however, was set apart for special consideration. Mercury, agricultural tools, mining machinery, semi-manufactured wools and furs, plaster, construction materials, coal, silks, watches, books, objects of art, lime, bricks, saltpeter, and jewelry were subject to a sole duty of 5 per cent *ad valorem*. Powder, flints, arms, tar, naval stores, rice, and raw silk paid 10 per cent. On the other hand, a tax of 20 per cent was imposed upon foreign sugar, coffee, cocoa, *yerba mate*, tea, and foodstuffs. Furniture, clocks, carriages, shoes, vinegar, cider, mirrors, saddles, clothing, wines, beer, and tobacco were charged with a duty of 25 per cent. And finally, 30 per cent was imposed on brandy, liquors, and *caña*. Specific duties were applied to four commodities. Hats of foreign manufacture were required to pay an import duty of 3 pesos each. With respect to salt, wheat, and flour the sliding scale principle was applied. The maximum duty on salt was set at 1½ pesos per fanega when the internal price was 2 pesos per fanega. With the increase of the internal market price the duty automatically decreased, so that when salt sold at 5 pesos imports were duty free. Foreign wheat was subject to a tax of

[67] Law of December 15, 1821 (RO–1, no. –114). There were, of course, tariff regulations prior to 1822, but none as comprehensive.

4 pesos when the internal price was 6 pesos. As the price of wheat increased to 9 pesos the duty was lowered to one peso per fanega. Free importation of wheat was permitted when the price rose above 9 pesos per fanega. With respect to flour the scale differed only as to the limit at which imports were free. The maximum duty of four pesos per quintal was imposed when the market price was 6 pesos or less. At the price of 10 pesos flour was subject to a tax of one peso per quintal, but no duty was exacted when the price rose above 10 pesos per quintal.[68]

The above rates referred exclusively to overseas imports. Interprovincial trade was treated separately. The basic rate on imports from other provinces of the Confederation was 4 per cent *ad valorem.* Exceptions to this general rate were few. Thus, *yerba mate* from Corrientes, Misiones, and Paraguay, and tobacco were subject to a duty of 10 per cent, and cigars paid 20 per cent while several commodities such as wood, salted meat, rice, wool, cotton, horsehair, brandy, wines paid no import duty.[69]

The schedule of export duties was much simpler. Overseas exports were subject to a general *ad valorem* tax of 4 per cent. Exceptions affected hides, precious metals, and certain other commodities. Hides were taxed at the rate of 1 real (cattle) and ½ real (horses) each; silver and gold were subject to an export duty of 2 per cent and 1 per cent respectively; and grain, salted meat, flour biscuits, and manufactured furs paid no duty. Nor was a tax imposed upon exports to other provinces of the Confederation.[70]

The tariff of 1822 was framed to meet the actual and potential needs of the province as well as of the country. And because the immediate interests of Buenos Aires did not always coincide with those of other provinces the tariff was necessarily a compromise. So, for example, protection was accorded to the wine and brandy industries of Mendoza and San Juan, and to the sugar industry of Tucumán at the expense of the consumers in Buenos Aires. Domestic tobacco and *yerba mate* (Paraguay was still considered an Argentine province) which was grown outside of Buenos Aires (in Corrientes, Misiones, and Paraguay) received preferential treatment. Mercury and machinery for the mining industry in Córdoba and the northwestern provinces were

[68] *Loc. cit.,* Section I, articles 1–7.
[69] *Loc. cit.,* Section III, articles 1–4.
[70] *Loc. cit.,* Sections II and IV.

permitted to enter the country upon payment of one-third of the normal duty.

As an instrument of economic policy the tariff reflected not only the actual needs of the economy of the province but the hopes and aspirations of those who directed the country's economic and political destinies. The vastness of the country, the unknown extent of its natural resources, and the feeling, therefore, that they were unlimited stimulated idealization of the economic potentialities of the province. Exaggeration in this direction led to a more or less serious undervaluation of the immediate interests of domestic industries. The tariff envisaged a large and continued inflow of foreign capital; it encouraged large scale heavy industry, such as mining; at the same time it failed to provide adequate protection for domestic industries, or to assure a stable market for domestic grain and manufactures. However, there were important exceptions. For example, the hat and shoe industries were given a modicum of protection and the cattle industry, especially, was given every possible consideration. Export duties on hides were moderate, and meat paid no duty whatever. At the same time the duty on salt imports was maintained at a relatively low level.

With certain modifications, confined largely to the import tax schedule, the 1822 tariff was retained throughout the remainder of the decade. For 1823 the sliding scale duty on grain and flour was revised in order to meet the needs of agriculture more effectively. The new schedule contained a minimum duty of 2 pesos per fanega of wheat and per quintal of flour, and the price at which the minimum became applicable was lowered to 7 pesos in the case of wheat and to 8 pesos in the case of flour. Especially significant was the change in the duty on salt. The sliding scale was entirely abolished and a flat rate of ½ peso per fanega imposed.[71]

Further revisions were made in the tariff for 1824. In the import schedule the 5 per cent class was broadened to include timber, which previously paid 15 per cent, and *caña,* which until then was subject to a duty of 30 per cent. The duty on liquor and brandies was reduced from 30 per cent to 25 per cent. In the overseas export schedule the basic rate of 4 per cent was retained, but the list of duty free exports was enlarged to include wool and all commodities of domestic manufacture. On the other hand, salted meat was to pay an export tax un-

[71] Law of November 28, 1822 (RO–420).

less shipped in national bottoms. The export duty on gold was reduced to 1 per cent. A sweeping change was introduced into the tax schedule on overland imports. With the exception of *yerba mate,* tobacco, and cigars, imports from other provinces were declared free of duty. The duty on *yerba mate* and tobacco was retained, and with respect to cigars the tax was reduced from 20 per cent to 10 per cent, provided that the value did not exceed 20 pesos per arroba.[72]

Changes in the 1825 tariff were slight. According to the new schedule all commodities which in 1824 paid a duty of 25 per cent were now subject to a tax of 30 per cent, and the sliding scale duty on flour imports was replaced by a flat rate of 3 pesos per quintal. The remaining provisions of the 1824 tariff remained unchanged.[73] Thereafter the tariff schedule was renewed from year to year until 1829, when several important modifications were made.[74]

The changes introduced during the years from 1823 to 1825 were nearly all dictated by the desire to adapt the tariff more closely to the economic requirements of the province. So, for example, the increase of duty by 5 per cent on a number of commodities such as saddles, shoes, and furniture was designed to protect handicraft industry against foreign competition, while the reduction of duty on *caña* from 25 per cent to 5 per cent was fully justified since *caña* was produced exclusively within the Confederation (San Juan and Tucumán), and therefore was not threatened by importations from abroad. Abolition of duties on overland imports was a move in the right direction, in so far as it made the port of Buenos Aires more easily accessible to the provinces of the Interior and at the same time stimulated the expansion of commerce in the provincial capital. The change in the duty on salt was in all probability beneficial to the cattle and meat industry, although it would be difficult to determine the precise extent of the gain.

During the three years from 1825 to 1828 the tariff remained unchanged. Yet, its effectiveness was in several respects substantially altered owing to the progressive decline in the gold value of the peso and the parallel rise in prices. In the case of specific duties the effect of currency depreciation was to nullify the tariff both as a measure of protection and a source of revenue. So, for example, the duty of 3

---

[72] Law of November 25, 1822 (RO–423).

[73] Law of August 16, 1824 (RO–662, L–4, no. –8).

[74] Certain tariff regulations because of their temporary character are left out of consideration.

pesos per quintal on foreign flour became little less than nominal in the face of a threefold increase of flour prices. The same fate befell the duty on hides. Before inflation a tax of 1 real on ox hides amounted to an *ad valorem* duty of 2 to 3 per cent, corresponding to a price of 4 to 6 pesos per hide. But in November of 1828 the average price of ox hides was 11.5 pesos and in December of that year hides of best quality sold as high as 14.3 pesos. At these prices the duty was equivalent to slightly more than 1 per cent in November and to 0.87 per cent in December.

With respect to *ad valorem* duties the influence of currency depreciation was less direct. These duties, since they were calculated in terms of a fixed proportion of the value of the commodity, rose with the increase of prices. But the rise of prices, though general, did not affect all commodities equally. And duties, precisely because they were proportionate, tended to emphasize this inequality. Currency depreciation is itself a barrier against importation of goods which compete with domestic manufactures, due to the fact that domestic prices rise more slowly than international prices. And since *ad valorem* duties were in reality gold duties their effect was to widen the gap between domestic and international prices. Moreover, the extent of this difference was largely determined by the height of the duty. From the point of view, therefore, of domestic industry, currency depreciation, since it tended to bring out more fully the protective features of the 1825 tariff, was not without its merits.

It was not until late in 1829 that an attempt was made to meet the situation created by the depreciation of the peso. In its decision to introduce changes into the tariff schedule the government was motivated by two considerations. In the first place the treasury was in desperate need of funds and, secondly, it became increasingly clear that specific duties in force since 1825 were no longer tenable. The revision was largely confined to specific duties. The export tax on hides was raised from 1 real to 1 peso per hide (an increase of 700 per cent), and the distinction between cattle hides and horse hides was abolished. Import duty on foreign hats was raised to 9 pesos, which in comparison with the previous rate represented an increase of 200 per cent. Foreign salt was to pay 2 pesos, as compared with ½ peso in the preceding years. The tax on cigars was increased to 20 per cent *ad valorem*.[75]

[75] Decree of September 8, 1829 (RO–1200, L–8, no. –9); Decree of September 18, 1829 (RO–1201, L–8, no. –9).

Of greater importance from the point of view of both the treasury and the economy was the decree of October 2, 1829 which imposed additional duties upon certain classes of imports. The basic duty was increased from 15 to 17 per cent, a 4 per cent tax was added to the 20 per cent classification, and, finally, imports which prior to the decree paid 30 per cent were now charged with an additional duty of 10 per cent.[76]

The decree of October 2, 1829 was primarily a financial measure. Revenue from the additional duties was reserved for the retirement of bank notes from circulation, and the surtax was to cease as soon as the currency situation improved.[77] But whatever the financial plans of the government the economic effect of the duties was to accentuate the protective aspects of the tariff as a whole. It will be noticed that commodities in the lower brackets of the tariff schedule were not subject to the surtax. Among them were certain raw materials and semi-manufactured commodities, machinery, construction materials, etc. At the same time, foreign manufactures such as shoes, clothing, saddles, wines, etc., were now subject to a duty of 40 per cent. In this manner domestic handicraft industries obtained a further advantage against foreign manufactures.

[76] Law of October 2, 1829 (RO–1239, L–8, no. –10).

[77] The additional duties were, in fact, never revoked, and of the proceeds only a small portion was used for the retirement of currency.

CHAPTER IV

THE UNITARY EXPERIMENT

La muerte de la provincia! Si, señores, la muerte de la provincia, cuya resurrección será la entrada triunfal de su territorio en la marcha nacional, y que ocupará un lugar en la historia que será grabado con caracteres de una luz inmortal.—VASQUEZ, *Asambleas Constituyentes*, Sesiôn, Febrero 24, 1826.

ALTHOUGH ten years had elapsed since the colony challenged the authority of Spain, it was still in the throes of profound political and economic unrest. The Congress of Tucumán proclaimed the country's independence, without however solving the vitally important problem of national organization. So far from facilitating the process of political reorganization, the constitution of 1819 imposed upon the country a political system which, though republican in form, closely resembled the colonial regime. The constitution reaffirmed the supremacy of Buenos Aires; it curtailed the political and fiscal autonomy of the provinces; it excluded the masses from the political life of the nation; it assured political control to a group of men whose monarchical convictions and inclinations were widely known.

The provinces of the Litoral, where autonomist tendencies were strongest and distrust of Buenos Aires most deeply rooted, were the first to challenge the authority of the Congress of Tucumán and the leadership of Buenos Aires. There was no doubt in the minds of the opposition leaders (Estanislao López of Santa Fe and Francisco Ramírez of Entre Ríos) that so long as the authors of the constitution of 1819 continued in political control of Buenos Aires the democratization of the Revolution and the fulfillment of the political and economic demands of the provinces were impossible. No further steps towards national organization could be taken till the government renounced all claims to authority beyond the boundaries of the province. Absolute equality among provincial governments was an essential prerequisite for any interprovincial agreement concerning the political future of the country. Nor was it any less essential as a guarantee of the integrity of provincial political institutions. It was precisely because the constitution of 1819 failed to recognize the right of the provinces to self-determination that Ramírez defied the authority of the Congress and of the central government.

In Buenos Aires the defeat at Cepedá marked the beginning of a period of political confusion. During the eight months following the battle of Cepedá no less than thirteen governments were established and overthrown. On at least three occasions government reverted to the municipal council (*Cabildo*), and at one time two governors claimed the right to preside over the destinies of the province.[1] The only restraint upon factionalism, which was rampant, was the ever-present threat of invasion of the victorious troops of Ramírez and López. Not until the election of Martín Rodríguez,[2] who succeeded in securing the support of the landowner class and the benevolent neutrality of Estanislao López, did the political situation in Buenos Aires begin to show signs of stability.[3]

There were several reasons why the crisis of 1820 failed to solve the pressing problems of the country. To begin with, neither the problem of national organization nor the problem of economic adjustment to the new political environment was as yet clearly defined. It was impossible for this reason to determine the new pattern of social economic relationships and to anticipate an appropriate political structure. Moreover, in time the process of transformation of the colonial society broadened; the lower strata of the population, which in the early stages of the Revolution had been hardly more than mere spectators, were now demanding a larger share in molding the new political and economic order. This movement injected a new element into the unfolding revolutionary process. It prevented the revolution from degenerating into a mere political and economic reform, and it brought to the surface forces which upset the calculations of the protagonists of 1810. To this extent the crisis of 1820, far from solving the question of national organization, made it more complex. In one respect, however, it clarified the situation. It put an end to the futile and costly attempts to reconcile the social structure of the colonial regime with the new political and economic environment. It was now clear

---

[1] Antonio Zinny, *Historia de los gobernadores de las provincias argentinas* (Buenos Aires: 1920–21). *Edición reordenada, con un prólogo de Pedro Bonastre*, II, 21–40.

[2] September 26, 1820.

[3] For a detailed discussion of the events òf 1820 see V. F. López, *Historia de la República Argentina* (Buenos Aires: 1883), vol. II; Adolfo Saldías, *Historia de la Confederación Argentina* (Buenos Aires: 1911), I, 33–127; Ricardo Levene, *Lecciones de historia argentina* (Buenos Aires: 1920), vol. II, chap. xiii, ed. 5.

that the problem of national organization could not even be formulated, let alone solved, until the economy had achieved a certain degree of stability; that whatever the solution, it would have to take into account the interests of those classes which until then had been excluded from the nation's political life.   In this respect the crisis opened a new phase in the history of the young republic.   For the first time the rural population, the gauchos and the farmers, as well as the middle and lower classes in the cities, entered the political arena.   Guided by instinct rather than by conscious evaluation of political doctrines, above all suspicious of the new intellectual and commercial aristocracy, these classes gave ready support to leaders like Ramírez, López, Quiroga, and others whose political ideals and economic programs were close to the soil.

Once the crisis subsided, the political situation of the country assumed a more orderly aspect.   Though considerably simplified, the issue which was the basis of the political struggles of the preceding decade remained, of course, the same.   Discussion no longer centered round fundamental principles.   That a national government should be established at the earliest opportunity was recognized by all the provinces.[4]   Further, it was generally agreed that the country was to remain a republic.[5]   However, there was still the task of defining more closely the specific forms which the national government was to take. It was obvious that the question was of more than academic interest; that the most vital interests of the nation were involved; and that,

---

[4] The treaty of Pilar (February 23, 1820) between Francisco Ramírez, chief of the army of the Litoral provinces, and M. Sarratea, governor of Buenos Aires, stipulated, among other things, that within sixty days after ratification a meeting of provincial representatives be held in San Lorenzo, Santa Fe, for the purpose of convoking a constitutional convention at some future date.   This treaty was the first interprovincial pact dealing with constitutional problems.   Article 7 guaranteed, however indirectly, the republican form of government.   For a detailed analysis of this as well as subsequent interprovincial treaties bearing upon the question of national organization, see Emilio Ravignani, *Historia constitucional de la República Argentina* (Buenos Aires: 1926, 3 vols.), vol. I, chaps. 15, 16, *et seq.*

[5] It may be noted here that monarchical tendencies so much in evidence in the years of the Tucumán Congress had not disappeared altogether after 1820.   Adolfo Saldías seems to believe that on the occasion of the arrival in Buenos Aires of the royal commissioners from Spain on December 4, 1820, plans were afoot among some members of the provincial legislature to restore under certain conditions the authority of the Spanish throne.   Cf. Adolfo Saldías, *La evolución republicana durante la revolución argentina* (Madrid: 1919), chap. xii.   Saldías suggests also that monarchical tendencies were latent in the Constituent Congress.   *Ibid.*, chap. xiii, pp. 178–179.

whatever the solution, it would profoundly affect the economic interests and the political status of the various social groups as well as of whole regions. The intricacy and complexity of the problem was not lessened by the fact that the economic interests of the social groups and of the province did not always coincide. Political alignments on the question of national organization sometimes coincided with, and at other times cut across interprovincial boundaries.[6] However, this circumstance did not mitigate the intensity of the political struggles. If anything, it aggravated intraparty conflicts and so destroyed the possibility of compromise between parties. And as the parties grew more intransigent discussion became worse than useless. The nation was once more plunged into a series of civil wars.

2

By the time Bernardino Rivadavia invited the provinces to send representatives to a constituent assembly the political aspects of the problem of national organization were sufficiently crystallized to permit the emergence of political parties based upon doctrine rather than personal influence. In its main outlines the issue was relatively simple, for within the republican framework the question of organizational forms was reducible to two alternatives: one was the establishment of a centralized system of state organization (the unitary doctrine); the other was a union of provinces headed by a federal government (the federalist doctrine).

The unitaries contended that, if the country were to achieve political stability and the various regional groups were to be welded into one political system, it was essential to establish a national government invested with broad political and economic powers. In this view the centralized system of state organization was alone capable of assuring an equitable distribution of the benefits arising out of the political consolidation of the country. Economically backward countries, especially those without experience in self-government, and in which political education and ability were at a premium, stood to benefit by a centralized system, though such a system implied either the total abolition or

---

[6] So, for example, it was not uncommon in the Constitutional Congress for representatives of a province whose legislature favored a federalist constitution to take a strong unitarist position. In many cases the attitude of the representatives in the Congress towards various measures was determined solely by the interests of the province they represented, rather than by the circumstance that the measure was either federalist or unitary.

a considerable emasculation of provincial autonomy. The provinces would be reduced to a position of administrative districts in which home rule, if at all permitted, would be closely supervised or controlled by the central government. On the unitarian theory the sacrifice of provincial autonomy was justified not only on the ground of economy of effort and resources, but also on the ground that centralization effectively eliminated internal political friction. Regionalism, whether economic or political, was dangerous, both because it embodied interests opposed to those of the nation and because it impaired the efficiency and smooth functioning of the national administration.[7]

Although the federalist doctrine denied neither the necessity nor the usefulness of a central political authority, it stood for the widest economic, fiscal, and political autonomy for each of the provinces. Self-government, the federalists claimed, was rooted in the very traditions of the Argentine people. It was, therefore, erroneous to believe that the nation's political integrity could be preserved without at the same time leaving intact the principle of political self-determination within the provinces. While it is true that provincial autonomy sets definite limits to the powers and authority of the central government, it does not follow that within its own designated field the national government must necessarily be ineffective. Far from engendering anarchy a federal system of state organization would consolidate the nation politically, for federalism reflected, as unitarism did not, the democratic ideals of the revolutionary movement. The federalists rejected the argument frequently voiced by the unitaries that the nation had neither the necessary resources nor the experience for an elaborate system of overlapping authorities. While not denying the greater complexity of the federalist system, they nevertheless insisted that in view of the country's vast territory with its consequent economic and political regionalism, it was adaptable to Argentine conditions. Moreover, the provinces had already shown their ability to establish and maintain local governments, so it could not be argued that they were politically inexperienced.

---

[7] These views were embodied in Section 7 of the final draft of the constitution of 1826, which was rejected by the provinces. The full text of the constitution may be found in *Registro Nacional*, vol. II, no. 2104. For a detailed analysis see E. Ravignani, *op. cit.*, vol. 3, *passim.* For a verbatim report of the constitutional debates in the Constituent congress see E. Ravignani, ed., *Asambleas constituyentes argentinas, seguidas de los textos constitucionales, legislativos y pactos interprovinciales que organizaron políticamente la nación* (Buenos Aires: 1937–38, 6 vols.), vol. 3.

Neither unitarism nor federalism evolved a clearly defined and consistent body of economic doctrine. But this was not a fatal shortcoming, for the more important economic implications of the two political systems were clear enough. Preference for one system as against the other was determined less by abstract principles of economic theory than by the immediate needs and aspirations of those who made the decision. This was natural since the fundamental conditions of the country's economic development were firmly established by the Revolution itself. Given the general direction of economic development the issue became primarily a matter of determining to what extent this or that economic policy reflected the specific needs as well as the economic potentialities of the country. Accordingly the appropriateness of one or the other political system of state organization depended in the final analysis upon the nature of Argentina's economic structure. Economic contradictions conditioned and nurtured political conflicts, and as these contridictions grew more intense the struggle for control of the state tended to become more violent.

The change in the political status of the viceroyalty was accompanied by serious economic disturbances and, although the Revolution of 1810 greatly stimulated the economic development of the country as a whole, progress was uneven and contradictory. The eastern part of the country, especially Buenos Aires, and to a lesser extent the riparian provinces, benefited most from the change. Here the overthrow of Spain's domination was the beginning of an era of economic expansion. But in the Interior the advantages of direct overseas trade were far outweighed by the loss of domestic and foreign markets upon which the welfare of the provinces largely depended. In this area, where national emancipation was attained at the price of economic decline, the process of adjustment to the new political geographic environment was difficult and costly. So the economic development of post-revolutionary Argentina was characterized by a shift of the economic center of gravity from the Interior towards the seacoast, brought about by the rapid expansion of the latter and the simultaneous retrogression of the former.

The uneven character of economic development resulted in what was to some extent a self-perpetuating inequality. The country became divided into poor and rich provinces. The Interior provinces were forced to relinquish ever larger portions of the national income to Buenos Aires and other provinces in the East, which were quick to utilize the advantages of their geographical position and superior capital means. And in an effort to stem the flow of wealth towards the seacoast and to conserve whatever resources were still in their possession the provinces entered upon a course of economic isolation. At the same time they demanded a more equitable distribution of that part of the national income which Buenos Aires monopolized in the form of customs revenues.

It was in the light of these circumstances that the provinces viewed the problem of political organization. In so far as unitarism proposed to nationalize revenues derived from foreign and domestic commerce the attitude of the provinces was uniformly pro-unitarian.[8]   The provinces felt that since they contributed to the total volume of commerce passing through Buenos Aires they were entitled to a share in the revenues derived from that source, especially when no other ports could be used for overseas trade.   But while agreeing to nationalization of customs revenues the provinces nevertheless opposed any move designed to curtail their fiscal autonomy.   And that was precisely what the unitary party proposed to do.   The Constitution of 1826 denied the provinces the right to derive revenues from indirect taxation.[9]

It was with a good deal of misgiving that the provinces viewed the tendency of foreign and *porteño* capital to finance exploitation of whatever natural resources they possessed.   The provinces were loath to relinquish any revenues derived from these sources or to grant monopolistic privileges to outsiders.   If this tendency to defend local economic interests against intrusion from abroad were confined solely to large scale industry, such as mining in La Rioja, Catamarca, or Córdoba, the question might have been solved with relatively little friction.   Actually, economic regionalism and interprovincial rivalry were too intense to admit of an easy solution.   Ever since the opening of the country to foreign commerce and the virtual cessation of commercial intercourse

---

[8] The law of nationalization of customs revenues (*Registro Nacional*—1912, March 13, 1826) was passed by the Constituent Congress with a majority of thirty votes against one. Cf. *Asambleas Constituyentes*, II, 901–911.

[9] Cf. Text of the Constitution (*Registro Nacional*), Section 7. The position of the provinces on the question of national finances was not stated very clearly in the Constituent Congress, undoubtedly because the deputies were in the majority unitaries. However, it is reasonable to suppose that the proper solution of the problem was to divide the revenues among the provinces on a pro-rata basis. This view was clearly stated five years later in the course of discussions about the interprovincial congress of 1831 in Santa Fe. Cf. *Relaciones interprovinciales. La Liga Litoral*. This phase of the unitarist-federalist struggle will be analyzed in the following chapters.

with Peru, the provinces were anxious to protect their industries and trade against outside competition. And from the point of view of each province outside competition implied not only foreign capital and trade, but also those of the other provinces. Each province endeavored to attain as high a degree of economic self-sufficiency as possible, hoping thereby to make itself politically and financially independent of other provinces and especially of the government of Buenos Aires. True, this policy of economic isolation was never pushed to its ultimate conclusion, if for no other reason than that the provinces lacked the necessary means to become economically self-sustaining. Nevertheless, the policy did succeed in creating vested interests which fed upon isolation. The farmers, the artisans, and local merchants were all vitally interested in the successful continuation of the policy of economic exclusiveness. These groups, when faced with the choice between unitarism and federalism, leaned towards the latter, since it offered greater economic security, and was most likely to ward off the dangers of foreign and extraprovincial competition. To these groups unitarism signified abolition of protective tariffs, further expansion of foreign trade at the expense of domestic industries, neglect of agriculture, and heavier financial burdens upon the cattle breeding industry.

Although in its general outlines the struggle between unitarism and federalism bore the same character throughout the country, the precise terms of the conflict varied from province to province, and from region to region. Accordingly, the organizational forms as well as the tactical moves of the unitary and the federalist parties differed in many essentials. The unitary party which emphasized national issues at the expense of local problems achieved a high degree of homogeneity, both organizationally and doctrinally. It was small numerically, but what it lacked in this respect was more than made up by the quality of its leadership. Many of the leaders were excellent orators, most of them were skilled parliamentarians, and nearly all were deeply convinced that the unitary party was alone capable of leading the country to a better economic and political future. The unitaries were in the minority, but a very compact and homogeneous minority, highly articulate, conscious of its aims, and occupying a strategic position in society and economy. The federalist party lacked all these characteristics. Political and economic particularism effectively prevented the emergence of a permanent organization on a national scale. The party was hardly more than a loose federation of sectional organizations, united in opposition to the unitaries, but at the same time free to pursue their own aims within the provinces. Uniting under its banners a large portion of the population the party represented a conglomerate of divergent social and regional interests, highly unstable politically and organizationally. The party's political and economic doctrine was, therefore, confined to the more general aspects of the problem of national organization, for within each province or group of provinces federalism pursued aims adjusted to local conditions. However, neither the heterogeneity of social composition nor the divergence of economic aims was fatal to the success of the party in its struggle for power. On the contrary, the very lack of an elaborate doctrine gave the federalist party freedom of action and flexibility, which proved to be invaluable in the crucial period during and immediately after the Constituent Congress. Thus, able to adapt itself to local conditions and to broaden its social base, the federalist party became the spokesman of the most vital forces in Argentine society.

3

In Buenos Aires the effects of the battle of Cepedá and the ensuing series of violent political changes which culminated in the election of Martín Rodríguez were not entirely adverse to the prestige and welfare of the province. The government was divested of its national character, but the curtailment of its political and administrative powers was more than compensated for by the political stabilization of the country and the province. Economically and financially the province lost none of the advantages it held prior to the interprovincial agreement. For to the extent that the treaty of Pilar left the government of Buenos Aires in control of the country's largest overseas port, that is, of the nation's most important source of revenue, the province, far from sacrificing any of its vital economic interests, was in reality getting the best of the bargin. Hence political and military defeat was converted into an economic and financial victory, which in turn encouraged the provincial government to bid once more for the political leadership of the nation.

The provision of the treaty of Pilar calling for the convocation of a national convention within 60 days from the date of ratification was allowed to lapse, the reason being that at this early date many of the provinces, and especially Buenos Aires, were totally unprepared to tackle the serious and complicated question of national organization.

It was generally realized that so long as political conditions remained uncertain no national assembly truly representative of the country could be organized, and that it was preferable to postpone consideration of the problem of national organization, rather than to risk an almost certain failure. Buenos Aires did not achieve political stability until after the election of Rodríguez in September 1820; in other provinces the process of autonomous organization was even slower. Santiago del Estero separated from Tucumán early in 1820, but Catamarca remained under the jurisdiction of the latter province until August 1821. The provinces of Salta and Jujuy declared their independence of the central government in August 1821. San Juan severed its ties with Mendoza in March 1820, but it was not until January of the following year that a constitutional administration under Urdinarrea was established. In the Litoral the Republic of Entre Ríos dissolved into its component parts after the death of Francisco Ramírez, the *Jefe Supremo* of the Republic. Entre Ríos became an autonomous province in December of 1821; Corrientes followed suit when on December 11, 1821 it adopted its first provisional constitution.

More important than political instability within the various provinces was the attitude of Buenos Aires, at first lukewarm, and later altogether hostile to the immediate convocation of a constituent congress. A serious effort to organize a national congress was made by Governor Bustos of Córdoba, who in November of 1820 requested the provinces to send representatives to the provincial capital. The proposed congress was scheduled to begin sessions on March 24, 1821, yet by that date the provinces of Tucumán, Salta, Santiago del Estero, and Catamarca had not even designated their representatives. The assembled deputies decided to postpone the inauguration of the congress until the arrival of the missing delegations, but in the meantime Buenos Aires, never an enthusiastic supporter of the congress, forbade its representatives to discuss or commit themselves on any but non-constitutional questions. Shortly thereafter (September 24, 1821), and against the strenuous opposition of the province of Córdoba, the government of Buenos Aires recalled its delegation altogether. The withdrawal of the Buenos Aires delegation broke the backbone of the Córdoba congress even before it began to function. Córdoba's frantic efforts to save the congress from complete failure were of no avail. The final blow to the congress came early in 1822 with the signing of the quadrilateral treaty, which in article 13 enjoined the signatory provinces from any participation in the "diminutive Congress assembled in Córdoba." [10]

There were several reasons why the province of Buenos Aires pursued an obstructionist policy with respect to the Congress of Córdoba. To begin with, it was realized in Buenos Aires that such a congress would be entirely dominated by Córdoba.   It was realized, also, that the government of Córdoba would do everything in its power to insure a federalist solution of the constitutional problem and that in view of the prevailing distrust of the intentions of Buenos Aires Córdoba would have no difficulty in achieving this result.   Furthermore, if the congress intended to adopt the federalist political program it would in all probability do so without regard to the peculiar position of Buenos Aires in the national economy.   The economic and financial policy which a federalist congress would be likely to pursue would inevitably weaken Buenos Aires politically, and such a result would in turn threaten the very existence of the unitary party.   For it was clear that once the country constituted itself on a federalist basis the unitary party would be unable to regain political control except by open rebellion.   It was precisely in order to avoid this eventuality that the government of Buenos Aires actively opposed the convocation of the Córdoba Congress.

The opposition of Buenos Aires to the Congress of Córdoba was a matter of expediency rather than principle.   The unitaries, who directed and controlled the provincial government, considered convocation of the congress by Bustos premature, not so much because they believed that the country was unable to cope with the problem of political organization as because the party itself was in no position as yet to assure the victory of its economic and political program.   What the government of Buenos Aires wanted was not only postponement; it wanted the national congress to convene in the city of Buenos Aires. Leaders of the Buenos Aires administration believed, not without reason, that one or two years of preparatory work would greatly enhance their chances of obtaining a substantial unitary majority in the forthcoming congress.   They were anxious to continue the *status quo* created by the treaty of Pilar, hoping in the meantime to strengthen their

---

[10] The treaty was signed on January 25, 1822.   The signatory provinces were: Buenos Aires, Santa Fe, Corrientes, and Entre Ríos.   For a detailed analysis of the treaty see E. Ravignani, *Historia constitucional de la República Argentina* (Buenos Aires: 1927), II, 209 ff.

hold upon Buenos Aires and to place the province once more in a position of political and economic leadership. They counted upon their ability to accomplish the economic and financial reorganization of Buenos Aires, and in this way to demonstrate the practicability and the advantages of the unitary economic program and policies. They reasoned that if the administration of Rodríguez, and his ministers Rivadavia and García, were successful, other provinces of the Confederation would more readily accept the leadership of Buenos Aires, and that a National Congress convened in Buenos Aires could thus be induced to approve a unitary constitution. From the unitary point of view, therefore, the quadrilateral treaty in so far as it tended to nullify the Córdoba Congress was an outstanding political victory.

The years of the Rodríguez administration are frequently referred to as the most remarkable in the nation's history. Never before, and only rarely afterwards, was Buenos Aires the scene of such varied and far-reaching legislative and administrative activity. Hardly a sector of the provincial economy escaped reform. In some sectors it was confined to recognizing and sanctioning changes already effected by the Revolution; in other fields serious efforts were made to replace old institutions by new; and in still others future development was anticipated. These reforms and innovations were not haphazard; they were all closely interrelated; each formed an integral part of a social economic system fashioned after the pattern of Western Europe. Its creators were the spiritual sons of the social and economic philosophers of England and France. They accepted the fundamental principles of classical economics as universal, convinced that economic policy based upon these principles was alone capable of assuring continued progress and prosperity. From the unitary point of view the economic and social backwardness of Argentina was owing not so much to her lack of material resources as to the economic and fiscal policies of the Spanish regime. Restrictions upon production and distribution, minute regulation of economic activities, oppressive taxation, all of which characterized Spain's economic policies, were contrary to the best interests not only of the colony but of the mother country as well. The policy of restriction was based upon the notion that the interests of the state (treasury) were opposed to those of the individual. The notion was mistaken and harmful, for in reality no such antagonism existed. The welfare of the state was dependent upon and conditioned by that of the individual. Individual prosperity was the foundation of the economic and political strength of the state. Hence the latter should interfere as little as possible with the economic activities of the individual. Instead, it should give free rein to natural laws whose unimpeded operation must result in a harmonious development of the national economy as a whole. Thus economic freedom in Argentina came to mean not only national emancipation, but also a radical reorientation of internal economic policy. Mercantilism was giving way to laissez faire.

It was upon these general premises that the government of Martín Rodríguez built its economic program and policy. Taking the revolutionary program of 1810 as its starting point the government expanded this program into a general reconstruction of the provincial economy. The plan of reconstruction called for the transplantation of Western European economic institutions and norms to Argentinian soil at the same time that it called for the abolition of the colonial economic structure. It was a program for the Europeanization in the shortest possible time of a backward and semi-feudal economy. To hasten the process of reconstruction the government actively intervened in determining the rate and direction of economic development. In many instances changes in the economic structure of the province were introduced by government *fiat*. The government, with an eye to the future, imposed upon the economy reforms for which there was no immediate need and which necessarily caused a good deal of dislocation in the existing pattern of economic and social relationships.

It was precisely this paternalistic attitude of the government toward the problem of economic reconstruction that made the position of the unitary party contradictory. Theoretically unitarism was liberal and democratic, yet in practice it became authoritarian and aristocratic; authoritarian—because the unitary party enforced its economic program in spite of mounting popular resistance in Buenos Aires and other provinces; aristocratic—because unitarism addressed itself primarily to the upper strata of Argentine society, above all to merchants and intellectuals, and made no attempt to create a broad popular following. Nevertheless, the liberal conscience of the unitaries was clear. Confident that their system was alone capable of securing an integrated national economy, convinced also that whatever sacrifices the population might be called upon to endure were justified by the ultimate advantages which would accrue to the country, the unitaries attributed popular disapproval of their doctrine and policies to ignorance. The unitaries argued that if the nation rejected their economic and political philosophy it was not because the doctrine or the policies were either harmful or impracticable, but rather because the gaucho, the farmer, and the artisan were simply unable to think in terms of national welfare. So the unitaries felt it incumbent upon themselves to enlighten the nation, by force, if necessary, just as it is the duty of parents to force reluctant children to attend school. To accusations that such an attitude engendered a pecuniary aristocracy the unitaries replied that this sort of aristocracy was both inevitable and useful.[11]

Although the unitaries were confident that the country possessed all the resources necessary for the ultimate development of a well balanced economy, they were nevertheless acutely aware of the immediate difficulties facing them. They realized that no real advance towards economic integration was possible so long as the country lacked abundant capital resources, labor, and the necessary technical skill. The program of economic reconstruction could be accomplished only by removing "the obstacles which retard the realization of the country's destiny, by stimulating a much more rapid growth of population, by increasing consumption and production, and enlarging profits which would intensify exchange and accelerate the circulation of wealth." [12] And since neither capital nor technical skill was available in sufficient quantities from native sources, these had to be procured from abroad. It was argued, therefore, that the country should be thrown open to foreign commerce and foreign investments, that colonization and immigration should be encouraged by every means at the disposal of the

[11] This position was quite unequivocally stated by José Antonio Castro, an influential member of the Constitutional Commission in the Constituent Congress. "Se dice," spoke Castro, "que de este modo se introduce insensiblemente una aristocracia la mas perjudicial que es la aristocracia del dinero. Antes he dicho, y ahora repito, y siempre repetiré una verdad, que no puedo dejar de ser mientras haya hombres y gobiernos, y mientras haya leyes, y es de que, si no se inmuta la naturaleza de las cosas, nunca puede dejar de haber esa aristocracia, que se quiere aparecer como un mónstruo tan perjudicial a la sociedad, que es la que hace conservar la sociedad y el orden según ella esté establecida. Hay ciertas aristocracias, que son de las que debemos huir; pero hay otras a las que debemos dar valor y dejarlas correr como un torrente, y el atajarlas sería perjudicial. La aristocracia de sangre, hereditaria, monárquica, esas si son peligrosas, porque se oponen a las leyes y a un sistema libre; pero aquellas aristocracias que nacen de la naturaleza de las cosas, no hay poder en la tierra que puede vencerlas. Quien podrá hacer que el ignorante sea igual al que tiene talento, ó al hombre sábio? Dios no lo puede hacer, porque Dios ha puesto esa misma desigualdad en las cosas, y no puede obrar con implicancia." *Asambleas Constituyentes*, III, 738–739 (Session, September 25, 1826).

[12] Cf. Preamble to decree of November 24, 1823 announcing the formation of a mining company for the exploitation of gold mines in La Rioja. *Registro Nacional*, II, 46.

government.   And if for various reasons these measures should prove inadequate or their effect too gradual, the government must itself undertake such economic and financial activities as were beyond the capacities of the community.

Such were the major premises of the unitary economic doctrine. The reasoning was no doubt consistent and in accord with the most advanced postulates of contemporary economic theory; but the reasoning was too abstract and the economic policy based upon it shrank at the first contact with Argentine reality.   Even with respect to foreign commerce the unitaries were forced to compromise almost from the start.   The issue of foreign trade was the spark which set off the movement for economic and political emancipation, and it would seem that the question of commercial policy was easily soluble.   In reality, however, the mapping out of an appropriate commercial policy presented grave problems.   For while in 1810 opinion was unanimous that the country must have freedom to trade with states other than Spain, there was much less unanimity with regard to how much freedom should be given to foreign commerce.   On the unitary theory foreign trade was to be given as much freedom as possible, for was not free trade in the classical meaning of the term the ideal policy?   Free trade would increase consumption, accelerate the circulation of wealth, and attract foreign merchants-capitalists to the shores of La Plata. However, free trade was not immediately realizable.   The new state was in constant financial difficulties and therefore unable to dispense with revenues from customs duties.   Until other sources of revenue were developed, taxes upon imports and exports were unavoidable. But such duties should have no other purpose than that of providing revenues, and above all must not hamper the flow of goods to and from the country.   Nevertheless, not even modified free trade was wholly practicable.   The interests of domestic industries had to be taken into account, and to that extent protection rather than revenue was the underlying principle of tariff making.   Even the first general tariff schedule contained protective features, not because the Rodríguez administration considered protection desirable, but rather because it wished to avoid political complications in its dealings with other provinces.   Yet, if political considerations forced the unitaries to retreat from their theoretical position they did not conceal their impatience with demands for thoroughgoing protection.   And it was precisely this refusal of the unitaries to recognize the limitations of the national economy that turned the question of tariffs into a political issue. At the stage of economic development then prevailing the country at large was simply not prepared to accept free trade. Nor were the provinces ready to abolish interprovincial tariffs, at least not until the problem of distribution of revenues from overseas commerce was satisfactorily solved.

The impracticability of the unitary economic program was especially evident in their policies of industrialization and colonization. In spite of official optimism the country offered little opportunity for investment in industrial enterprises, for it lacked all the elements essential to industrialization, such as coal, iron ore, and building materials. In addition the domestic market was much too small to warrant capital outlays and manufacturing on a large scale. The extractive industries were somewhat more promising, and it was to this field that foreign capital investments were first attracted. With the encouragement of the Buenos Aires government a company was formed in London for the exploitation of mines in La Rioja and the neighboring provinces. However, the venture did not go beyond preliminary surveys, largely because of the opposition of native capitalists in both the Interior and Buenos Aires.[13] Both economically and politically the undertaking was unsound. The government of Buenos Aires, by conceding important economic privileges in territories beyond its jurisdiction, caused resentment in the provinces. The argument of the unitaries that such action was dictated by purely economic considerations carried no weight, since in the eyes of the provinces the political and economic aspects of the constitutional problem were inseparable.

The colonization policy of the unitaries was hardly more successful. Here as elsewhere the unitaries seemed unable to bridge the gap between theory and practice. It was one thing to establish a colonization commission and to encourage the formation of colonization companies, and quite another to finance the transportation of prospective

[13] The Compañía de Minas de las Provincias Unidas del Río de la Plata was organized in England on December 24, 1824. After the project had been abandoned the company's promoters claimed from the government of Buenos Aires the sum of 52,520 pounds sterling, presumably spent on preliminary surveys of the mines. Cf. Decree of November 24, 1823 (*Registro Nacional*—1704, II, 46–47); Message of Governor Manuel Dorrego to the Junta de Representantes, September 14, 1827 (Mabragaña I, 231); and also, Joseph Andrews, *Journey from Buenos Ayres through the provinces of Cordova, Tucumán and Salta to Potosí, thence by the deserts of Coronja to Arica, and subsequently, to Santiago de Chili and Coquimbo, undertaken on behalf of the Chilean and Peruvian Mining Association in the years 1825–1826* (London: 1827).

colonists and to provide land for their settlement.[14]   The fact is that the government was unable to meet the cost of transporting and settling immigrants, nor was the country prepared to absorb them either economically or socially.   The policy of government-financed colonization, far from strengthening the national economy, immobilized much-needed capital on which no immediate returns could be expected.   Furthermore, it is doubtful whether under the prevailing conditions colonization on a large scale was economically justifiable.   For to the extent that the expansion of farming tended to raise land prices, it tended at the same time to increase the cost of production in the cattle industries. It is not surprising, therefore, that the majority of cattle breeders displayed so little enthusiasm for the colonization plans of the Rodríguez administration and the National Government of Rivadavia.

The tendency of the unitary leaders to overestimate the economic capacity of Argentine economy was brought to light once more in their financial policies, especially in the establishment of a central provincial, and later national, bank.   The theoretical considerations which prompted the unitaries to foster the organization of a bank of issue were clear enough.   In a rapidly expanding economy in which commerce and industry were to play an increasingly important role, the financial mechanism of the colonial regime was no longer adequate. In commerce more than in any other field of economic activity credit was essential.   And while credit operations were no doubt common in Buenos Aires in the pre-revolutionary period, they were based largely upon personal debtor-creditor relations and consequently lacked the stability and continuity which only a public institution such as a bank could provide.   The bank would not only place the credit structure of the country on a more secure footing, but would also create new credit facilities for commerce and industry.   It would mobilize loanable funds hitherto scattered in the province and the country, and relieve the chronic shortage of capital, and force a decrease in the usually high interest rates.   The success of the program of fiscal reorganization and of consolidation of the province's public debt depended to a large extent upon the degree of liquidity of the capital market in Buenos Aires. If it had done nothing more than enable the government to complete its fiscal reform, the creation of the bank would have been fully justified.   During the war against Brazil when the blockade of Buenos

---

[14] The financial aspects of colonization have already been indicated and need not be gone into any further (see chap. ii, pp. 47–49).

Aires deprived the treasury of much of its normal revenues the services of a central credit institution were particularly in demand.   The Minister of Government urged approval of the Banco Nacional charter, saying:

It is impossible to meet all payments under such circumstances, unless we begin by stimulating the growth and development of the country's productive forces; in this way we shall be able not only to increase the needed revenue, but obtain the credit without which it will be impossible to raise funds required to meet the exigencies of war and the expenses of administration; unless we do this, we shall have to raise taxes to an insupportable level.[15]

To the Minister of Government then, the alternatives were increased taxes, or increased production by means of credit expansion.   And it is characteristic of the unitary approach that the third and most obvious alternative was not considered at all: that was the extension to the government of credits based upon bank note issues.   There was yet another consideration which in the unitary view strongly favored the establishment of a central bank, namely, that such a bank with branches in every province would become a powerful factor in the political unification of the country.   Community of economic interests would clear the path to political understanding among the provinces, and no agency would accomplish this more easily or more thoroughly than the Banco Nacional.   The bank, according to one prominent unitary,

will be the strongest of all ties uniting the provinces and their inhabitants; it will consolidate individual interests and neutralize all claims.   From the very moment that these advantages will begin to be appreciated, the Congress will have little or nothing left to do in order to accomplish the nationalization of the provinces.[16]

Thus the bank was conceived not only as an instrument of economic and financial stabilization but of political control as well.   And for this reason the unitaries did not hesitate to advocate close governmental supervision of the bank's activities.[17]

---

[15] *Asambleas Constituyentes* II, 407 (Session, January 7, 1826).

[16] Julián S. de Agüero, Session of January 19, 1826 (*Asambleas Constituyentes* II, 431).

[17] In support of Article 7 of the bank charter which gave the government the final authority on questions concerning dividend payments, Julián S. de Agüero stated: "Se dice que es un asunto puramente económico.   Y quien ha dicho que en un establecimiento de esta naturaleza, de la primera entidad, no debe tener intervención la primera autoridad?   Si, Señor, debe tenerla; porque un establecimiento de esta clase tiene una trascedencia tal que solo de él dependa la prosperidad de todo el país, su quietud, su sosiego y la estabilidad del Gobierno mismo." "El (the bank) tiene la clave, y el es el resorte por donde se mueven todas las ruedas de la sociedad; todo está a su disposición." (*Asambleas Constituyentes* II, 449; Session, January 20, 1826.)

It will be noticed that the unitaries who argued for the Banco Nacional never posed the question whether the state of the provincial or national economy rendered the establishment of such a bank superfluous or premature. From the unitary point of view the question was irrelevant. For the bank's usefulness was determined not only by present needs but above all by what it could contribute to the economic development of the country in the future. To doubt the utility of a central bank of issue amounted therefore to doubting the possibility of further expansion of the country's economy. For in the unitary conception of economic development, the bank was to become the motive power of the country's industrial growth. Whether this contention of the unitaries was valid, and to what extent, is a question that cannot be readily answered. Neither the Banco de Buenos Aires nor the Banco Nacional was given the opportunity to prove or disprove the unitary thesis. Yet it is important to note that most of the unitary hopes and predictions concerning the banks were belied by reality. Neither of the two banks succeeded in mobilizing any considerable portion of the country's capital resources. The specie holdings of the Banco de Buenos Aires never amounted to more than 28½ per cent of the capital,[18] and the Banco Nacional was even less successful than its predecessor. Of the 5,600,000 pesos which were offered for public subscription only 704,800 pesos were taken up. The attempts of the bank to increase its gold reserves by purchases in the Interior and in Chile failed, with the result that the Banco Nacional was forced to suspend conversion almost immediately after opening its doors.[19] At no time was the Banco Nacional an important factor in the economic life of the province, except perhaps as it provided a convenient mechanism for the realization of the monetary policies of the government. This bank from the moment of its birth was "subjected to the exactions of the government and the country." [20]

The government's domination over the Banco Nacional was unavoidable; certainly it was justifiable by the exigencies of the Brazilian war. Nevertheless, the fact that the bank served no purpose other

[18] For a more detailed analysis of the capital structure of the Banco de Buenos Aires and the Banco Nacional, see *supra*, chap. iii.

[19] Letter of the Board of Directors (March 30, 1826) to the Minister of Finance (*Archivo General*, Ant. C.20–A.9–no. 2, *Legajo* 2).

[20] Andrés Lamas, *Estudio histórico y científico del Banco de la Provincia de Buenos Aires* (Buenos Aires: 1886), p. 17.

than that of supplying the treasury with funds made its usefulness as a factor of economic development negligible. The extent to which the government monopolized the credit facilities of the Banco Nacional becomes apparent in the light of the bank's advances during the first two years of its operation, the most active years in its history. The portfolio of discounts which the bank took over from its predecessor amounted to over 3,250,000 pesos. On January 1, 1827 the bank's advances to both the treasury and business amounted to more than 12,000,000 pesos of which 3,270,000 pesos were commercial loans. Six months later private discounts decreased to 3,156,000 pesos, while advances to the government rose to 10,300,000. On January 1, 1828 the bank's commercial loans were reduced to 2,540,000 pesos, and in August of that year these loans dropped to slightly under 2,200,000 pesos.[21] Not all of the bank's advances were bona fide commercial loans. In many cases funds borrowed from the bank were used for speculation. On the other hand, the bank's credit operations were limited by law to 90 days' commercial paper. It could offer no credit accommodations to industries in which the period of production exceeded three months, such as the cattle industry and agriculture. Hence the bank's activities were confined to a relatively small but highly concentrated sector of the provincial economy.[22] It was therefore natural that among the farmers as well as cattle breeders the Banco Nacional should have been considered not only superfluous but politically dangerous; superfluous—because it failed to improve to any marked extent the credit conditions in the province; and dangerous—because in the hands of the national government the bank became an instrument of political oppression. It was the symbol and the source of power of the money aristocracy and of the unitary party.

The fact that in defining the functions of the bank no recognition was accorded to the needs and interests of agriculture and cattle breeding was not due to oversight. Clear and detailed on questions of com-

---

[21] See *supra,* chap. iii, Table 12; also *Archivo General,* Ant. C.21–A.6–no. 3.

[22] In its report of January 28, 1828 the Board of Directors of the Banco Nacional stated that loans to private persons and enterprises totaling 2,229,815 pesos numbered 371. The largest loan amounted to 32,221 pesos. A large portion of these loans were secured by shares of the bank. In 1830 more than a third of the bank's stock was used as security for such loans. These shares represented a nominal value of 625,000 pesos. Cf. Statement of the Banco Nacional of February 4, 1830, *Archivo General* (Ant. C.22–A.2–no. 5).

merce, industry, and finance, the unitary economic doctrine was singularly fragmentary and uncertain on problems concerning agriculture, cattle breeding, and land distribution. In this field, more than in any other, the unitaries failed to appraise the situation correctly and to formulate a policy consistent with the prevailing trends of Argentina's economic development. This lack of understanding of the agricultural sector of the provincial economy, although curious, is not inexplicable. In the unitary conception of economic development, commerce and not agriculture played the dominant role. The cattle breeding industry was taken for granted, while grain growing was too insignificant to deserve more than passing consideration. The economic greatness of Argentina rested not upon agriculture but rather upon the development of industry and, above all, upon commerce.

In the unitary program relating to agriculture and grazing no measure was as far reaching as the introduction of the system of emphyteusis.[23] This system rested upon the principle of public ownership of all land not already in private possession; so that the sale of public lands was prohibited except by special permission of the legislature. Such lands could be rented to individuals and corporations for a stated number of years and at fixed rentals. The rent on land used for pasture was fixed at 8 per cent of its value, while in the case of agricultural land the rent was only 4 per cent. Special commissions (juries) were charged with the task of determining the market value of land in each district. The period of tenancy was 20 years, though the government reserved the right to change rentals after 10 years. Tenants could not be evicted except for non-payment of rental, and had the right of priority if the land was offered for sale. Too, they were permitted to sell their rights to third persons, or to parcel out their lots to subtenants.[24]

It is the contention of many Argentine historians that the system of emphyteusis, for which Bernardino Rivadavia was mainly responsible, was intended to provide a permanent framework for the development of the national economy. The theory is that what Rivadavia and the

---

[23] The system of emphyteusis was introduced in the province of Buenos Aires under the administration of Rodríguez. In 1826 the Constituent Congress extended the system to other provinces.

[24] Law of May 18, 1826, *Recopilación de las leyes y decretos promulgados en Buenos Aires desde el 25 de mayo hasta fin de diciembre de 1835, con un índice general de materias* (Buenos Aires: 1886), part 2, p. 797; see also decree of June 27, 1826, *ibid.*, pp. 798–801.

unitaries had in mind was the institution of a single tax system of public finances based upon rentals and the increment in the value of land. Some writers went so far as to assert that by means of emphyteusis Rivadavia and his collaborators hoped to prevent the growth of large landed estates (*latifundia*).

It is very doubtful whether Rivadavia and the unitary party intended the emphyteusis to become the basis of a single tax system of public finances. If that had been their object they would not have advocated the adoption of the *contribución directa*. Actually all that the proponents of emphyteusis hoped for was that land rents would in time form a substantial source of revenue. In other words they believed that land rent together with the *contribución directa* would make the treasury less dependent upon customs duties, and so insure greater financial stability. The hopes entertained in this regard did not materialize. Till 1827 revenues from this source barely exceeded 5,000 pesos! [25] Nor was this pitiable result owing merely to laxity in collecting the rentals; there was also the circumstance that the rent was assessed on the basis of values determined by commissions composed of landowners rather than government officials. Further, there is no reason to believe that the unitaries ascribed to emphyteusis as profound a social significance as is usually associated with the single tax ideology. Not once throughout the five-day discussion of the law of May 18, 1826 [26] did the advocates of emphyteusis refer to it as a measure designed to bring about a more equitable distribution of the national dividend. The arguments of the Constitutional Commission as well as of the most prominent unitary leaders, who defended the measure, centered mainly around the economic and financial-juridical aspects of the law. Economic necessity rather than social justice ex-

---

[25] Emilio A. Coni, *La verdad sobre la enfiteusis de Rivadavia* (Buenos Aires: 1927), p. 36. It follows from a report prepared by the Contaduría General (September 1, 1827) that up to the end of August of that year the majority of tenants had not paid the emphyteusis rent since 1825, that one tenant had not paid since 1823, and another since 1822. Cf. *Archivo General*, Ant. C.21–A.6–no. 3. In a report submitted to the Governor of Buenos Aires (February 14, 1828) the Collector General stated that no rentals could be claimed from 11 tenants out of a total number of 45, because it was impossible to determine the exact location and area of land held in emphyteusis. The other 34 tenants owed in rents 4,076 pesos per year, but actually nearly twice that sum remained unpaid (7,602 pesos 5¼ reales). Cf. *Archivo General*, Ant. C.21–A.9–no. 2.

[26] Cf. *Asambleas Constituyentes* II, 1196–1268, Sessions, May 10, 11, 12, 16, 17, 18, 1826.

plains the law of emphyteusis. The fact is that the government was not allowed by law to sell public land pledged as security against foreign and internal loans. The result was that vast areas of land which had accumulated in the hands of the government remained unproductive. It was precisely in order to solve this problem of the accumulation of unproductive land that the law of emphyteusis was devised. The government retained ownership of the land, thus complying with the letter of the law, and at the same time vast areas were given over to economic exploitation. Hence to read into the law of emphyteusis a social ideology of the type and complexity which underlies the single tax movement is to romanticize not only the leaders of the unitary party but also the economic reality of early-nineteenth-century Argentina. If the intention of the authors of emphyteusis was to prevent or to curtail the growth of large landed estates the measure was singularly ineffective. Neither as introduced by the Minister of Government, Julián Segundo de Agüero, nor in its final form did the law contain provisions limiting the area that might be held in emphyteusis. Nor did the law prohibit the sale of tenancy rights to third persons. The government was not unmindful of the possibility that the law of emphyteusis might stimulate the development of *latifundia,* but had no objections to large landed estates so long as these were being exploited. The aim of the government was to prevent large accumulations of land from becoming an object of speculation. And it was convinced that the rental requirement would effectively check whatever tendencies might develop towards land monopoly.[27] That was perhaps the main reason why the government in administering the law showed so little concern about the danger of land monopoly. In the two and a half years, from 1824 to May, 1827, individual land grants of over 10 square leagues (66,710 acres) were not uncommon.[28] In the preamble to the

[27] "Si el canon que se les imponga," argued Agüero in defense of the proposed 8 per cent rent rate, "es regular, ellos tendrán que dejar una parte que no pueden poblar, y solo retendrán aquella que esté en proporción con su fortuna para poderla poblar. Si el canon es muy módico, ellos la conservarán porque es poco lo que les cuesta, y con la esperanza de que mañana aumentándose la demanda en proporción que la población se aumente, y según que suba el valor de las tierras podrán enagenar su derecho con grandes ventajas, o subarrendar á un canon y á una renta enorme." ". . . si se adopta el 4 porciento . . . el canon viene a quedar reducido a cero, y de aquí resultará el monopolio y la ocupación de las tierras en grandes porciones." Cf. *Asambleas Constituyentes* II, 1231–1232; Session May 12, 1826.

[28] The following table computed from the *Relación de los terrenos concedidos en enfiteusis desde el 27 de septiembre 1824 hasta 1° de mayo 1827* shows the distribution of

decree of May 10, 1828, the government expressed concern about the manner in which the emphyteusis law operated.

Until now (states the government), public lands, regardless of the area solicited, have been conceded in emphyteusis without any restrictions whatever, and this has given rise to abuses whose consequences are already beginning to be felt. Immense territories are claimed without any intention or possibility of settling them, but with the certainty of making a profit out of the right that has been acquired at such a low cost. As a result all the public lands within the new frontier, although still largely unsettled, are already almost wholly distributed. The accumulation of such vast territories in a very few hands will necessarily retard their settlement and cultivation. It is unjust that only a few should benefit from advantages which the law accords to all. The government has been anxious to establish rules which would facilitate the distribution of land in a more equitable manner, and thus avoid the drawbacks stated above; hence it has ordered the Departamento Topográfico to supply all the necessary data. So far it has not been possible to devise the proper methods, and until this is done the government feels obliged to proceed with greater economy in the distribution of the public domain, for the government is determined not to allow public lands to become the property of few at the expense of the general public and to the detriment of the welfare of the most numerous classes of the population.[29]

This pronouncement was well justified but somewhat belated, for the major portion of the public domain had already been disposed of. Nearly one thousand square leagues, i.e., over 6,500,000 acres, had been given out in emphyteusis, so there was not much left that needed to be guarded against the greed of land monopolists and land speculators.[30]

---

land through emphyteusis for the period indicated. The *Relación* is transcribed by E. A. Coni, *op. cit.*, pp. 171–175.

Size of Grants	No. of Grants	Total Area
1.5000– 2.9999 sq. l.................. 42		83.5022 sq. l.
3.0000– 5.9999 sq. l.................. 22		90.2853 sq. l.
6.0000– 9.9999 sq. l.................. 22		159.2918 sq. l.
10.0000–19.9999 sq. l.................. 16		213.9959 sq. l.
20.0000 and over..................... 10		368.7833 sq. l.
112		915.8565 sq. l.

It will be noted that grants of less than 1.5 square leagues were not included in the above table. It is assumed that such grants were given to farmers rather than cattle breeders. Coni estimates that in the period under consideration there were 86 such grants with a total area of about 85 square leagues. It should be emphasized also that the number of grants is higher than the actual number of beneficiaries, since two or more grants were accorded to one individual if he so desired. According to Coni the number of persons who received land in emphyteusis during this period was 85. Cf. Coni, *ibid.*

[29] *Recopilación*, etc., part II, pp. 859–860.

[30] The new policy of restriction was initiated by two decrees. The first (May 5, 1827; *Registro Nacional*—2154, II, 187) dealt with frontier areas. It limited grants to actual

The unitary economic program was national in scope. Although the unitaries confined themselves at first to Buenos Aires they never abandoned the idea of extending their policies to the other provinces. Political unification as it was embodied in the constitution of 1826 meant the establishment of a central government, and simultaneously the curtailment of provincial political and financial autonomy. It was hoped that by these means the economic system instituted in Buenos Aires might be extended to the whole country. Even before the Congress of 1826 had resolved the constitutional problem the unitary party initiated the process of economic and financial unification of the country. The provincial Bank of Buenos Aires was forced to make room for the Banco Nacional which with its branches in every province of the Republic was to become the central unifying factor in the national economy. So, too, the provincial law of emphyteusis was extended to the public domain of other provinces. The nationalization of customs revenues in the province of Buenos Aires presaged similar action with respect to Mendoza, Tucumán, Catamarca, and elsewhere. And, finally, with the passage of the law of federalization of the city and port of Buenos Aires the process of unification was practically complete.

4

Federalist opposition to the unitary program crystallized rapidly as that program assumed the proportions of a national economic and political system. For the first time the economic aspects of the question of national organization came into full view. The government enacted a number of concrete measures in which the economic program and policies of the unitary party stood revealed in their full scope. Unitarism could no longer be opposed on merely general grounds, such as democracy and provincial autonomy. Whether in the Constituent Congress or in the provinces, the federalists were now obliged to ex-

---

settlers. The latter were entitled to grants of 2,500 varas and a *quinta,* if the settler took up farming, or 0.75 square league of pastoral land, if the tenant wished to set up a cattle breeding establishment. The settlers were not required to pay rent for a period of 8 years, but they were obliged to construct a house, and to cultivate the land or to procure at least 200 heads of cattle. They were not allowed to sell their emphyteusis rights, or to sublet their tenancies during the first 8 years. The second decree (May 10, 1827) made the granting of tenure rights in any part of the country contingent upon previous investigation by the Departamento Topográfico, and the government reserved the right to reject any petition.

amine the main postulates of the unitary program and to formulate specific objections.

The approach of the federalists to the economic and political problems of the day differed substantially from that of the unitaries. In the first place, the federalist party was an opposition party. While firm in its demand for provincial autonomy the party was content to leave the solution of economic problems to the Constituent Congress. The constitutional question dominated all others, and it was therefore futile, the federalists reasoned, to define more closely the pattern of interprovincial economic relations before the fundamental political issues had been settled. For, once the constitution was recognized, the principle of provincial autonomy would *ipso facto* determine the country's economic structure. This reasoning would have been correct had the Congress devoted itself exclusively to the drawing up of a constitution. But as a matter of fact the Congress postponed the constitutional problem for nearly two years. Instead it set up a national government which proceeded to carry out a distinctly unitary program. Hence the federalist minority was obliged to define its position with respect to specific issues before the more general question of national organization was even formulated. In the second place, federalism unlike unitarism viewed the problem of national organization from the standpoint of provincial and regional interests. Provincial autonomy implied non-interference in the economic policies of the provincial governments. Accordingly the federalist party refused to consider problems which were not of national concern. The party recognized the existence of divergent economic interests in the several provinces and groups of provinces, and so abstained from advocating economic policies which presupposed a uniformity of economic development throughout the country. Strictly speaking there was not one, but several federalist parties in Argentina, all of them united in their opposition to the unitary system of economic organization, but opposed to each other with respect to matters of economic policy. Different federalist groups represented different economic interests. This did not preclude their agreement on the question of political organization. On the contrary, in view of the uneven development of the national economy, political federalism seemed alone capable of providing an adequate basis for the solution of inter-regional differences. Beyond this very general postulate the federalist doctrine did not venture. So there was no questioning of either the motives or aims of all those who in the name of federalism opposed the unitary solution.

In Buenos Aires opposition to the economic and financial program of the unitaries was especially strong in the rural districts, among the cattle breeders and farmers, as well as among the gauchos. The cattle breeders had good reason for being distrustful of unitary policies. Above all they disliked the comparatively high import duty on salt. This duty was the more burdensome as the industry was already subjected to internal and export taxes. But dissatisfaction was rife also in the city among the lower and the middle classes. The commercial policies of the Rodríguez and Rivadavia administrations showed no regard for the economic interests of a considerable portion of the provincial population. The tariff of 1821 as well as the tariffs of later years did little to provide adequate protection to domestic agriculture. Further, the duties on manufactures such as furniture, shoes, candles, clothing, etc., were insufficient to exclude foreign competition. On the other hand, the imposition of import duties ranging from 20 to 30 per cent on wines and a variety of foodstuffs tended to raise the cost of living in the city of Buenos Aires. The argument that the duties on foreign wines and foodstuffs were necessary in order to protect important industries in the Interior was of doubtful validity from the point of view of the consumer. Nothing could be plainer than the divergence of economic interests between Buenos Aires and the Interior provinces; nor was it any less plain that the unitary party was prepared to sacrifice the immediate interests of the province for political purposes. But the political program of the unitaries was not of the kind to arouse enthusiasm either in the Interior or in Buenos Aires. To Buenos Aires it signified renunciation of the economic and financial advantages attained since the Revolution; and to the provinces it meant abandonment of all hope of improving their economic status. The hiatus between the economic program of unitarism and the actual potentialities of the national economy forced the party to resort to compromises, a policy which satisfied no one, and antagonized the majority of the population.

Nor were the financial and banking policies of the unitaries popular among *porteño* cattle breeders. These were willing supporters of the Banco de Buenos Aires so long as they believed that the bank was capable of improving the credit situation in the Buenos Aires money market. But when the Bank of Buenos Aires was superseded by the

Banco Nacional, the attitude of the cattle breeders changed radically. It became clear that the new bank would extend little if any help to the cattle breeding industry, and that far from serving the interests of the province of Buenos Aires it endangered the economic autonomy of that as well as other provinces.   Moreover, the federalist leaders knew that the Banco Nacional financed the unitary administration, and that after the fall of Rivadavia in July 1827 it lent support to the unitary cause. The federalists accused the bank of clandestine and illegal issues of bank notes, of speculating upon the fall in the value of the peso, and of having caused the economic difficulties of the post-presidential period. While blaming the bank (unjustly, it may be added) for all the evils of inflation, the federalists were opposed to the policy of deflation advocated by the bank and by those who held government bonds and other financial obligations of the Treasury.   To the federalists and generally to the popular masses the Banco Nacional symbolized the money aristocracy, a group of "bankrupts and money jobbers," who abused the confidence of the people and who constantly plotted against the legally constituted authorities.[31]   Hence the demand for a thorough investigation of the bank's activities during the years of the "presidency"; hence also the suggestion that in the future the bank be subjected to strict governmental control.   The high-handedness with which the provincial legislature ordered the bank to extend further credits to the Dorrego administration is, therefore, not surprising.[32]   The middle classes, i.e., the merchants, the artisans, and the farmers, as well as government employees, supported the federalist attacks upon the bank. To these strata of the population the bank bore the responsibility for that inflation from which they were the first to suffer.

The unitary policy of colonization and land distribution, which was liberal to the point of wastefulness, aroused a good deal of dissatisfaction among landowners and cattle breeders.   The hacendados demanded greater caution and circumspection in administering the law of emphyteusis.   They insisted that the beneficiaries of emphyteusis grants be required to introduce a stated number of cattle upon the land.

[31] See Rosas' letter to Estanislao López, dated December 12, 1828.   British Packet and Argentine News, January 17, 1829; also Manuel Bilbao, Historia de Rosas (Buenos Aires: 1868).

[32] The attitude of the federalist party toward the Banco Nacional was stated quite unmistakably in the course of a discussion of a bill introduced by deputy Grela.   See Diario de Sesiones, vol. 4, nos. 62, 79–85 (Sessions, January 14, 1828, February 25, 26, 27, 28, 29, and March 1, 5, 1828).

Some of the cattle breeders went so far as to demand that foreigners be denied the right to receive land in emphyteusis directly from the state. This demand was made in the form of an amendment to a new emphyteusis bill submitted to the provincial legislature by Manuel Dorrego. Its sponsor was Tomás Anchorena who was warmly supported by prominent federalists, such as Felipe Arana, Juan José Viamonte, and Grela. The government had to use the whole weight of its authority in order to defeat a motion so little in accord with the democratic traditions of Argentina.[33]

In general, the cattle breeders and farmers felt that under the unitary administrations of Rodríguez and Rivadavia the rural districts had not received their due share of attention. They believed that the burden of taxation was unequally distributed between the city and the country districts, and that the unitaries tended to favor the city, and especially foreign commerce. Thus deputy Obligado in the provincial legislature complained

that the rural districts carry a large burden, for there seems to be a conspiracy to make these districts bear the entire brunt of taxation, while what is needed is consideration not only for the hardships suffered by the country side, but also for the fact that this (tax) falls upon wretched people who have always lived in poverty, and who only now are beginning to improve their lot; so it is particularly unjust that at this moment, when they have hardly begun to acquire property of their own, they should be deprived of their good fortune, and the profits now accruing to the rural districts be turned over to the capitalists of Buenos Aires.[34]

Whether the grievances voiced by deputy Obligado were real or imaginary is not easy to determine. The charge that the provincial and national governments were disposed to favor the city as against the country in matters of taxation may have been well founded, but it is doubtful that the burden of taxation was really oppressive. The large landowners, who of all the rural classes complained most, were in all probability least entitled to demand relief. Nevertheless the fact that this group thought it advisable to champion the cause of the rural population indicates that there was in the rural districts a good deal of resentment against the policies of the unitary regime.

Nor did the *hacendados* agree with the broader aims of the unitary

[33] Cf. *Diario de Sesiones,* vol. IV, nos. 74–76 (Sessions, February 14, 15, 16, 1828). The motion was presented in the form of article 8 to be added to the bill submitted by the government.

[34] Cf. *Diario de Sesiones,* vol. IV, no. 69 (Session, January 30, 1828). Discussion of article 6 of the bill of emphyteusis submitted by Dorrego. The article, rejected by the Legislature, provided for a tax upon land at the rate of 15 or 20 pesos per square league.

party. The unitary solution of the constitutional problem was distinctly disadvantageous to the interests of the grazing and meat industries. For political centralization meant the nationalization of customs revenues, and this in turn meant that the provincial government, deprived of its most important source of income, would be forced to impose new taxes and to increase the old ones. Nationalization of the port of Buenos Aires and the opening of other overseas ports on the Paraná river was almost certain to nullify the advantages which the *porteño* hide and meat producers had over their competitors of Santa Fe, Córdoba, and Entre Ríos. Moreover, it was probable that in a unitary regime the central government was likely to devote all its time and resources to the development of the interior rather than continue the program of territorial expansion towards the south. This fear of the federalists was not unfounded. As the spokesmen for the commercial interests of the capital, the unitaries saw little advantage in the acquisition of unpopulated and therefore commercially valueless lands beyond the Indian frontier. The chief interest of the unitaries lay rather in expanding the internal markets and linking them to Buenos Aires and other ports. So the government of Rivadavia, too busy to consider the recommendations of Juan Manuel de Rosas on the subject of protecting the Buenos Aires frontier against Indian attacks, gave much thought to the project of a canal linking Bermejo and the Paraná rivers.[35] It was clear to the cattle breeders and to the population in general that the province of Buenos Aires, far from gaining as a result of political consolidation on a unitary basis, would be called upon to relinquish the privileged position it had until then occupied within the Confederation. And if any doubts existed as to what the province could expect from the unitary regime they were dispelled soon after the election of Bernardino Rivadavia to the presidency, when the government submitted to the Congress the bill of federalization of the provincial capital. Whatever the reasons which led the national government to demand the federalization of the city of Buenos Aires, and the reasons adduced in the Constituent Congress were hardly con-

---

[35] The memorandum of Rosas was published by Adolfo Saldías in an appendix to the first volume of his *Rosas y su época*. In this memorandum Rosas indicated that it would be advisable to appoint a special commissioner for the Indian frontier. The government did not even acknowledge receipt of the memorandum. Cf. Carlos Ibarguren, *Juan Manuel de Rosas* (Buenos Aires: 1930), pp. 134–136. On the plan for the construction of the Bermejo canal see Aurelio Prado y Rojas, *Leyes y decretos promulgados en la provincia de Buenos Aires desde 1810 á 1876* (Buenos Aires: 1877), t. 3, pp. 192–193.

vincing,[36] the measure sounded the death knell of the province. As Gregorio Funes, deputy from Córdoba stated, "This bill now before the Congress at one stroke cuts off the head of the province of Buenos Aires, leaving it in an impossible position, despoiled of the institutions which form the basis of its strength and integrity." [37]   Gregorio Funes was not exaggerating, for as Juan José Paso, deputy from Buenos Aires, put it, the province thus dismembered stood to lose more than three-quarters of its wealth.[38]   Indeed, the federalization of the city of Buenos Aires meant to the province the loss, first, of a considerable part of its territory (commercially the most important part); secondly, the loss of about 50 per cent of its population and a much higher proportion of its wealth; and thirdly, the loss of nearly all revenues.   Such was the price which the province was asked to pay for the unitary solution of the problem of national organization.   At the time the price seemed particularly exorbitant since of all the provinces of the Confederation Buenos Aires was economically as well as financially the strongest, and also the best equipped to maintain its economic position of the pre-congressional period.   It was therefore natural that even the unitary deputies from Buenos Aires were reluctant to approve the bill.[39] Nor is it surprising that in the eyes of the population the federalist party, which strenuously opposed the bill, became the champion par excellence of the economic and political integrity of the province. Moreover, since the law of federalization of Buenos Aires was passed in patent contravention of the law of January 23, 1825 which guaranteed the political and institutional integrity of the provinces until the

---

[36] Among the reasons given by the Minister of Government the following were the most important: first, the President was without authority in the province; second, Provincial authorities were inclined to obstruct the activities of the national government; third, the province refused to cede its veteran army to the national government; and fourth, the national government was without revenues. Cf. *Asambleas Constituyentes* II, 697, *et seq.* (Session, February 22, 1826). That the argumentation of the unitaries was not convincing was admitted by Vicente Gómez, a prominent member of the unitary party and one of the chief supporters of the bill. "Yo no me extenderé a decir," said Gómez, "que las demostraciones que se han aducido en favor del proyecto, hayan sido completamente victoriosos pero lo que si es verdad, es que la materia está agotada, y que a este respecto al congreso ya no le queda mas que pronunciarse." *Ibid.*, II, 772 (Session, February 27, 1826).

[37] *Ibid.*, II, 769 (Session, February 27, 1826).

[38] *Ibid.*, II, 778 (Session, February 27, 1826).

[39] So, for example, Mariano Sarratea, Juan José Paso, Vicente López, Félix Castro, all unitaries or unitary sympathizers, voted against the bill. See *Asambleas Constituyentes* II, 815, *et seq.* (Session, March 1, 1826).

adoption of the constitution, the onus of illegal procedure was placed squarely upon the shoulders of the unitary party.

5

The partition of the province of Buenos Aires was indeed short-lived. Sixteen months after the enactment of the law of federalization, the Constituent Congress was facing a hostile country. Most of the provinces refused to accept the constitution drafted by the Congress. Confronted with an impossible political situation Barnardino Rivadavia resigned the presidency, and the Congress, after placing presidential authority in the hands of Vicente López, declared its own dissolution. Vicente López stayed in office for four days, and then, convinced of the collapse of the unitary regime, called upon Manuel Dorrego, the parliamentary leader of the federalist party, to assume the duties of governor of the reconstituted province of Buenos Aires. This was the first major victory of *porteño* federalism.

The political isolation of the national government of Rivadavia was brought about by its own mistakes quite as much as it was brought about by the accuracy of the federalist party in gauging the economic and social trends in the province. In their bid for political power the federalists appealed primarily to the immediate interests of the population. Unfettered by abstract doctrine, intensely practical in their aims and methods, they kept in close touch with the economic and social realities of the moment. The party had few ideological preconceptions and so subscribed to no set system of dogmas. It envisaged no radical transformation of the social economic structure of the province or the country; it advocated no revolutionary changes in the existing system of economic relationships; it offered no far-reaching plans of institutional reconstruction according to the European pattern. Within the province of Buenos Aires the federalist party had no designs on the economic *status quo,* but looked simply to the continued expansion of the cattle breeding industries. The federalist program of economic development, although far less spectacular than that formulated by the unitary party, was none the less sufficiently serious to engage the resources and the attention of the government and the population of the province. It also had the advantage that its benefits could be realized immediately. It was a program understood by all and in which all were vitally interested. It called for territorial expansion southward, for the incorporation of newly acquired lands into the economy of the province, for the defense against Indian attacks by means of internal colonization in the vicinity of forts constructed along the frontier. Further, it promised expansion of overseas exports the profits of which were to remain within the province rather than go to the national economy. Nor was the party unmindful of the condition of domestic agriculture and industry. Although the federalist program concerning this sector of the provincial economy was somewhat vague and uncertain, the party was pledged to serious consideration of the question of the protection of domestic markets. So, in the realm of economic values the federalist struggle against unitarism in Buenos Aires appeared to the population as a struggle in defense of the province's economic birthright. The inhabitants of the province were asked to choose between the probability of a strong and prosperous provincial economy, with or without the nation, on the one hand, and a series of economic and financial sacrifices for the sake of a possible national prosperity in the more or less distant future, on the other. There can be little doubt as to the preference of the majority, for just as the economic and social ideals of the unitaries appeared to the average *porteño* as visionary and even anarchical, so the program of the federalist party seemed concrete, practical, and rooted in the traditions of the period.

The party's attitude to the problem of national organization was determined primarily by the immediate interests of the provincial economy. In this connection it is important to remember that Buenos Aires wanted no change in the economic position it had attained in the post-revolutionary era. On the contrary, what the province wanted was stabilization of the political pattern evolved after the crisis of 1820. In sole control of the country's foreign trade policies the province was also the recipient of all the revenues derived from the overseas traffic. This is to say that Buenos Aires was economically and financially independent of the rest of the country. Any change, therefore, which involved the nationalization of customs revenues or the port was to the disadvantage of the provincial economy. Yet just this change was implied in the unitary solution of the constitutional problem; although it should be added that even under a federalist system of state organization Buenos Aires could not be certain that it would not have to relinquish its privileged position. The *porteño* federalists had no illusions about the attitude of the provinces in the Interior and the Litoral on the question of national finances. Nor were they unaware that any concessions on this point would cripple the whole program of the province's territorial expansion. Hence the refusal of Buenos Aires to sanction the nationalization of customs revenues; hence, also, the demand that the national government be prohibited from borrowing against the security of provincial revenues.[40] Herein lay the peculiarity of *porteño* federalism; not only did Buenos Aires desire political and economic autonomy, but it could also afford to practice it. In this Buenos Aires was far ahead of its sister provinces.

Although the representatives primarily of the interests and aspirations of the cattle breeding industry, the federalists addressed themselves at the same time to the lower classes in the rural districts as well as in the city. In the country districts the *estanciero* was the dispenser of employment and the guarantor of economic security. He spoke the language of the gaucho and the peon, knew intimately their customs and habits, and shared their traditional distrust of the city. Economically dependent upon the landowner, the rural population accepted his political leadership, the more readily since the unitary party made no serious effort to enlist rural support. In the capital the federalist party raised the standard of democracy, and by its demand for a popular government based upon universal male suffrage was able to enlist a large following among the lower classes, which until then had been excluded almost entirely from political life. The federalists capitalized, too, on the unpopularity of the unitary attempt at forced Europeanization, and on the population's fear of the growing influence of foreign capital.

During the years of the Constituent Congress the democratic tendencies of *porteño* federalism were genuine enough. Manuel Dorrego and Manuel Moreno, the two outstanding leaders of the federalist wing in the Congress, conceived the issue between federalism and unitarism as one between democracy as it was exemplified in the United States, on the one hand, and a centralized constitutional republic governed and controlled by representatives of the so-called "money aristocracy," on the other. In Dorrego's view the federalist system of state organization was alone capable of insuring the full development of the country's economic potentialities under conditions of the fullest political de-

40 In drawing up instructions for its delegates to the forthcoming national convention the provincial *Junta* was careful to emphasize that it considered customs revenues to be the property of the province. When deputy Aguirre argued that the claims of the provinces to revenues from customs duties were not entirely unfounded he was promptly rebuked by Felipe Arana and the majority of the legislature. Cf. *Diario de Sesiones* (Session, November 22, 1827).

mocracy. No other system, however well intentioned, could succeed, for the sufficient reason that federalism alone was acceptable to the majority of the population. "The federal system," Dorrego declared in the Congress, "can bring us happiness because it expresses most faithfully the feelings of the people, because it lies closest to their hearts." [41] Dorrego and other federalist leaders indignantly rejected the unitary argument that the provinces were incapable of self-government either because of lack of political education and experience, or because of lack of resources. In his congressional speeches as well as in numerous articles in the *Tribuno,* Dorrego never tired of emphasizing that the provinces, and among them Buenos Aires, were fully prepared for the exercise of economic and political autonomy and that the population was overwhelmingly in favor of the federalist system of national organization.[42] So that unless the demand for democracy and provincial autonomy were heeded another period of sanguinary civil wars was inevitable.

Dorrego remained in power for only seventeen months in which period economic and financial problems as well as the Brazilian war pushed the question of national organization into the background. Peace with Brazil was not concluded until August of 1828, and in the face of a desperate financial situation aggravated by a developing economic crisis there was little that the government could do in behalf of political appeasement. The provincial legislature, although friendly to Dorrego's administration, was much more conservative and also less inclined towards reconciliation with the unitary party. The position of the right wing of the federalist party became clear in the course of the deliberations on a series of bills submitted by Dorrego dealing with the Banco Nacional and emphyteusis. It was Nicolás Anchorena who accused the Banco Nacional of clandestine issues of bank notes, and who supported Grela's demand for a strict governmental supervision of the bank's activities. It was Anchorena, too, who by his bitter denuciation of foreign capitalists and landowners injected into the federalist ideology a nationalist note which under Rosas was destined to develop into xenophobia. Dorrego succeeded in perfecting the law of emphyteusis of pastoral lands and in placing agricultural lands under a similar system. He succeeded also in overcoming some of the finan-

[41] Cf. *Asambleas Constituyentes,* III (Session, October 2, 1826).

[42] *Dorrego y el federalismo argentino, documentos históricos.* Con introducción del Dr. Antonio Dellepiane (Buenos Aires, n.d., pp. 113–181).

cial difficulties facing the treasury, though not without strenuous opposition from both sides of the legislature. But he had neither the opportunity nor the means to put his plans of political and economic reconstruction to the test of practical politics. The successful revolt of the unitaries under the leadership of Juan Lavalle, followed by the execution of Dorrego on December 13, 1828, made conciliation and cooperation between the two parties impossible.

The rebellion of December 1 was a clear demonstration of the political and social isolation of the unitary party. Besides this it undermined the position of the moderate *dorreguista* wing of the federalist party. Within the party, leadership after the execution of Dorrego passed into the hands of Juan Manuel Rosas, who, as chief of the rural militia, directed the military and political operations against the unitaries. The Civil war terminated in the agreement between Lavalle and Rosas (June 24 and August 24, 1829) according to which both chiefs agreed to support a provisional government until elections could be held. In reality the Lavalle-Rosas agreement was clearly a federalist victory, for the provisional government was obviously anti-unitary. It merely paved the way for federalist administration under the leadership of Juan Manuel Rosas. So the federalist party won its second major victory. But this time political power passed into the hands of extremists who felt that their policy of irreconcilability towards the unitaries was now vindicated. Accordingly the solution of the problem of national organization became even more difficult, for as *porteño* federalism grew in power it was less inclined to come to an understanding with the other provinces of the Confederation.

CHAPTER V

THE PROVINCES

. . . la envidia que excitaba una ciudad poderosa y rica entre sus vecinos pobres y atrasadas, hablaba de federación. Los intereses materiales gritaban contra el comercio libre; la presidencia parecía una dominación extranjera.
—D. F. SARMIENTO, *Los caudillos. El general fray Félix Aldao* (Buenos Aires: 1928).

El federalismo argentino no ha sido una invención, ha sido una evolución.
—ERNESTO QUESADA, *La época de Rosas* (Buenos Aires: 1898).

ARGENTINE historians usually ascribe the rise of federalism to factors whose effect supposedly was to intensify the economic isolation of the provinces of the Confederation. The factors most frequently mentioned were the sparseness of population, the lack of transportation and communication facilities, and, accounting for the self-sufficiency of the provinces, the relatively low standard of living. According to the argument economic self-sufficiency bred political isolation. And the ideological expression of this isolation was federalism. In this view Argentine federalism, rooted in the poverty and ignorance of the masses, was neither a system nor a program, but rather an instrument of political oppression for the benefit of the *caudillo* and his satellites. Hardly distinguishable from factionalism, federalism was a smoke screen for the political and economic aggrandizement of the *caudillo*. So the struggles and civil wars of the whole period from the early twenties until the fall of Rosas are deprived of any social significance, except as indicating the degeneration of the nascent state into a conglomerate of feudal fiefs. To one school of historians, then, the federalism of the Rosas period was the Argentine counterpart of European feudalism, or better still of the French Restoration; to still another, federalism was a system in which the spontaneous lawlessness of the *gaucho* was matched only by the limitless authority of the ruler. Hence the years of federalism's supremacy are referred to as the middle ages of Argentina's history, as a barbarous interlude between an earlier and later epoch of civilization and progress.[1]

[1] For studies in which the above aspects of Argentine federalism are stressed, see Domingo F. Sarmiento, *Facundo* (first published, Santiago: 1845; Buenos Aires: 1916);

It cannot, of course, be denied that the disintegration of the national economy into more or less self-sufficient provincial areas was to a large extent responsible for the emergence of federalism as an economic program and political doctrine. Yet there were other factors at work. For while the federalist program demanded economic and political autonomy for the provinces, it stood also for the political integrity of the nation and country. The provinces were clearly aware that isolation was neither desirable nor possible. And the very fact that they were neither willing nor able to become, like Paraguay, economically self-sufficient was a cogent argument in favor of federalism. It was precisely in order to avoid the economic consequences of isolation that the provinces turned to the federalist solution of the constitutional problem. The federalists rejected centralization, without losing sight of the economic and political interdependence of the provinces. At the same time that it affirmed the necessity for national unity, federalist doctrine acknowledged the existence of specific provincial interests, complementary to and compatible with the interests of the nation as a whole. In this respect federalism was much closer to Argentine reality than unitarism, for it showed a clearer insight into the complex fabric of Argentina's economy as well as into the processes of the country's economic development.

What was this country? Neither the population nor even the area of the thirteen provinces which together with Buenos Aires composed the United Provinces of the River Plate are exactly determinable.[2] The available data on population are hardly more than estimates, often grossly exaggerated. United States Commissioner Rodney, who visited the United Provinces in 1819, estimated the population at 1,300,000. This figure did not include 700,000 civilized Indians, so that the total population on this estimate was about 2,000,000 inhabitants.[3] Commissioner Graham, who submitted a separate report, was much more

---

Andrés Lamas, *La época de Rosas* (Buenos Aires: 1910); José Ingenieros, *La evolución de las ideas argentinas* (Buenos Aires: 1918–20), 2 vols.; Lucas Ayarragaray, *La anarquía argentina y el caudillismo* (Buenos Aires: 1904).

[2] The territory of the Argentine Confederation underwent considerable modifications after the Revolution. At the time of the Constitutional Congress the Confederation included the province, later the republic, of Uruguay, the province of Tarija, and claimed sovereignty over Paraguay. The territory of Misiones was given the status of a province.

[3] C. A. Rodney and J. Graham, *The reports on the present state of the United Provinces of South America; laid before the Congress of the United States with accompanying notes by the editor; and an introductory discourse* (London: 1819), p. 19.

modest in his calculations. He estimated the population of eleven of the fourteen provinces at 523,000 inhabitants distributed as follows: [4]

TABLE 15

ESTIMATE OF THE POPULATION OF BUENOS AIRES AND THE PROVINCES
OF THE INTERIOR FOR 1819 [a]

Province	No. of Inhabitants
Buenos Aires	120,000
Córdova	75,000
Tucumán	45,000
Santiago del Estero	60,000
Catamarca	40,000
La Rioja	20,000
San Juan	34,000
Mendoza	38,000
San Luis	16,000
Jujuy	25,000
Salta	50,000
Total	523,000

[a] In Graham's report the table is entitled: "Estimate of the Population of the provinces of Buenos Aires, Córdova, Tucumán, Mendoza or Cuyo and Salta, under the names of the different towns or districts which send representatives to the Congress." In a note which accompanies the table Graham calls attention to the fact that Corrientes, Santa Fe, and Entre Ríos as well as "some districts of some of the other provinces" are not included in the estimate. Graham does not indicate to what year the above estimate refers. Source: C. A. Rodney and J. Graham, *op. cit.*

Graham's table may be supplemented by estimates for the Litoral provinces. So Ignacio Benito Núñez, whose *Account* was published in 1825, claimed 20,000–30,000 inhabitants for Entre Ríos,[5] and J. P. Robertson, writing in 1821, estimated the population of Corrientes at 50,000.[6] For the country Núñez calculated the population at 527,000, a figure far below Graham's, since Núñez' estimate included the provinces of the Litoral.[7] The latter's figure was accepted by Diego de la Fuente, director of the first census in Argentina (1869). According to de la Fuente's calculations Argentina had a population of 634,000 inhabitants in 1829 and 768,000 in 1839.[8] Apart from Buenos Aires we obtain the following survey of the growth of population in the thirteen provinces for the period from 1809 to 1839:

[4] *Ibid.*

[5] Ignacio Benito Núñez, *Account historical, political and statistical of the United Provinces of Rio de la Plata* (London: 1825), p. 246.

[6] J. P. Robertson and William P. Robertson, *Letters on South America, comprising travels on the banks of the Paraná and Rio de la Plata* (London: 1843).

[7] Ignacio Benito Núñez, *op. cit.*, p. 248.

[8] Diego de la Fuente, *Primer censo de la República Argentina, 1869* (Buenos Aires: 1872), pp. xx, *et seq.*

TABLE 16

GROWTH OF POPULATION IN ARGENTINA: 1809–1839

Year	Total	Buenos Aires	13 Provinces
1809	406,000	92,000	314,000
1819	527,000	125,000	402,000
1829	634,000	153,000	481,000
1839	768,000	180,000	580,000

Source: Diego de la Fuente, *Primer censo de la República Argentina, 1869* (Buenos Aires: 1872).

There is reason to think that the estimates of Graham and de la Fuente are overoptimistic. The Englishman Andrews, who traveled extensively in the Interior, believed that Graham's figure of 50,000 inhabitants for Salta was grossly exaggerated, and was even inclined to discount Núñez' claim for 40,000 inhabitants for that province.[9] Andrews was also skeptical about the Tucumán government's estimate of the provincial population at 40 to 45 thousand. Nor was this skepticism merely ill natured, for the provincial legislature countered the government's claim with a statement that "the population of the province certainly did not amount to 40,000 souls" and that 30,000 must stand as the official number till a census was taken.[10] The census of 1845 showed a population of 57,876 inhabitants.[11] A similar discrepancy may be noted with respect to Mendoza. Graham's figure for this province is disputed by Schmidtmeyer, who estimated the number of inhabitants at 30,000.[12] It is probably safe to assume that Graham's estimate referring to the ten provinces of the Interior should be reduced by about 10 to 15 per cent. On this basis the total population of the thirteen provinces at the time the second Constituent Congress was in session amounted to about 450,000 inhabitants.

Counting Buenos Aires we have a population of less than 600,000 scattered over a vast area which extended from the Atlantic coast west as far as the Andes and the present southwestern boundary of Bolivia, and south from Paraguay and Bolivia towards what is now the northern border of the territories of Pampa and Neuquén. The extent of this

[9] Joseph Andrews, *op. cit.*, pp. 301–303.
[10] Cf. *Acta de la Sala de Representantes de la Provincia de Tucumán* (Session, July 25, 1825).
[11] Cf. *Noticias oficiales de la estadística del Territorio y productos de la provincia de Tucumán.* Also, Decree of November 26, 1845.
[12] Peter Schmidtmeyer, *Travels into Chile over the Andes in the years 1820 and 1821* (London: 1824), p. 183.

area cannot be exactly determined, for neither the northern nor the southern boundaries of the Republic were clearly defined. Large parts of Buenos Aires, Córdoba, and Cuyo, in the south, and of Santa Fe, Santiago del Estero, and Corrientes, in the north, were occupied by numerous Indian tribes, who often recognized no authority except that of their chiefs (caciques). Hence any estimate of the territorial extension of the United Provinces proper must take into account the territories occupied by hostile Indians. Yet the area of the provinces was such that the density of population was not much over one inhabitant per square mile. The distribution of the population among the provinces, on the one hand, and among the country districts and cities, on the other, was uneven. Over one-third of the total population was concentrated in Buenos Aires and Córdoba. Of the remaining provinces Tucumán and Mendoza had probably the largest populations for their size, while the northwestern provinces were least populated. The disparity between urban and rural population was most pronounced in Buenos Aires, 50 per cent of the inhabitants residing in the capital alone.[13] In other provinces, especially those in which the capital was the only city of importance, urban population was in the minority. Outstanding examples are the western and northwestern provinces, such as San Luis, San Juan, La Rioja, and Catamarca. The case with respect to Litoral provinces was different, for in this region the opening of the country to foreign trade resulted in the expansion of river traffic, which in turn contributed to the growth of river ports. Rosario in Santa Fe, Gualeguaychú and Concepción del Uruguay (Arroyo de la China) in Entre Ríos, had all become important commercial centers within twenty years after emancipation, so that in these provinces the process of urbanization was especially rapid.

The most important cities and towns were situated along the two main commercial routes from Buenos Aires to Chile and Peru. Both routes led through Santa Fe and Córdoba. From Córdoba the route to Chile passed through San Luis and Mendoza, the distance between Córdoba and Mendoza being about 120 leagues (360 miles). Another route from Córdoba led by way of Santiago del Estero to Tucumán (160 leagues, or about 480 miles) and thence to Salta and Jujuy (about 100 leagues or 300 miles). Transportation and communication over these routes was difficult and costly. Traffic across the plains as far as Córdoba and even Mendoza was carried on in wagons drawn

[13] See *supra*, chap. ii.

by four to eight oxen and equipped with huge wheels to permit passing through sloughs (*pantanos*). In the mountainous regions west
of Córdoba, mule trains were used for transportation.[14] The cost of
transportation varied from region to region, depending upon the character of the country traversed. So the cost per ton-league between
Salta and Chuquisaca was 1.200 pesos silver. Between Mendoza and
Chile the charge was 0.300 silver peso. From Buenos Aires to Salta
the average rate was 0.374 silver peso, while from Buenos Aires to
Córdoba transportation charges amounted to 0.259 silver peso. At
the same time the cost of transportation from Buenos Aires to Corrientes by water was 0.060 silver peso per ton-league, and only 0.006
peso silver to European ports.[15] In 1826 the government of Buenos
Aires paid 140 pesos in specie for the transportation of one wagon load
of 150 arrobas from Mendoza to the capital. This indicates a rate of
about 0.300 peso silver per ton-league.[16] It becomes apparent from a
computation published in the *Gaceta Mercantil* of Buenos Aires how
these costs influenced the pattern of interprovincial and foreign commerce. The computation, although limited to a small group of commodities in the Buenos Aires market, typifies conditions throughout
the republic.

For example, the producers of wine in San Luis received less than
half of what it sold for in the Buenos Aires market. Wine producers
in Mendoza, San Juan, and Tucumán were even more seriously handicapped. Indeed if it were not for the duty imposed upon foreign wines
the markets of Buenos Aires and of the Litoral provinces would have
been entirely inaccessible to the domestic wine industry. As it was
even the duty of 25 per cent *ad valorem* imposed by Buenos Aires upon
foreign wine was considered insufficient to assure the domestic industries adequate profits. With respect to export trade the position of the

[14] For a description of methods of transportation see A. Caldcleugh, *Travels in South
America* (London: 1825); J. Andrews, *op. cit.*; E. E. Vidal, *Picturesque illustrations of
Buenos Aires and Monte Video, consisting of twenty four views: accompanied with descriptions of the scenery and of the costumes, manners, etc., of the inhabitants of those
cities and their environs* (London: 1820).

[15] These rates are quoted from an article *Vías públicas* published anonymously in the
Gaceta Mercantil, no. 3236 (March 11, 1834). See also, *Revista del Plata*, no. 4 (December 1853).

[16] Order for payment issued by the Minister of Finance to the Contaduría General
(*Archivo General*, Ant. C.28–A.10–no. 5). The article in *Gaceta Mercantil* quoted a rate
of 0.182 silver peso for the Mendoza-Buenos Aires haul. This quotation, unusually low
in comparison with the rates on other overland routes, is in all probability a typographical
error. The article should doubtless have quoted 0.282 peso per ton-league.

TABLE 17

DISTANCES FOR WHICH COST OF TRANSPORTATION EQUALS HALF THE PRICE OF STATED
COMMODITIES IN THE BUENOS AIRES MARKET [a]

Commodity	Distance
Bricks...................................	6 leagues
Maize....................................	60 leagues
Wheat....................................	75 leagues
Jerked beef..............................	95 leagues
Domestic wines...........................	200 leagues
Tallow...................................	226 leagues
Caña de Mendoza..........................	320 leagues
Salted hides.............................	240 leagues
Wool.....................................	400 leagues
Horsehair (mixed)........................	426 leagues
Dry hides................................	515 leagues

[a] The table bears the title: "Distancia á que los productos de campaña con destino á Buenos Aires no pueden tener en el lugar de su extracción, sinó la mitad del valor en esta capital por causa de los gastos de conducción."

Source: *Gaceta Mercantil*, no. 3235.

interior provinces was equally disadvantageous. Of exportable commodities, such as jerked beef, hides (salted and dry), tallow, wool, and horsehair, only dry hides, wool, and horsehair could bear the cost of long overland hauls. The interior provinces had no share at all in the export of jerked beef or even tallow. And the prices which these provinces obtained for dry hides, wool, or horsehair were about 20 to 30 per cent below those received by Buenos Aires producers. The Litoral provinces were in a better position. Although they, too, were forced to trade with foreign countries through Buenos Aires, the cost of shipping by river was not excessive. Nevertheless, the cattle breeders and exporters in the Litoral provinces realized that their competitive position would improve considerably were the Paraná and the Uruguay rivers opened to foreign shipping. The establishment of overseas ports on the Paraná would not only make the services of the Buenos Aires port superfluous, but would also divert a part of the Interior's foreign trade from Buenos Aires to the Litoral provinces.[17]

The rapid progress of political emancipation had little effect on the economy of the Interior. The mode and forms of production and distribution evolved under the colonial system continued, practically without change, to dominate the economic life of the provinces. What the Revolution of 1810 did was to transform the political and geographic

[17] For example, the opening of Rosario or Santa Fe to foreign trade would cut the overland haul of exports from Córdoba by about 50 leagues and reduce transportation costs by nearly 20 per cent.

environment which conditioned the rise and development of the Interior economy. The Revolution abolished mercantilism as an instrument of economic policy; it substituted competition for paternalistic regulation and protection; it linked the economy of the country to overseas markets, at the same time that it separated the Interior from areas of which in the colonial era it formed an integral part. While these changes were in accord with the fundamental line of development of the eastern portion of the River Plate viceroyalty, they ran contrary to the needs and interests of the western provinces. For the growth and development of the economy of the Interior depended precisely upon keeping the pre-revolutionary political and administrative system intact. Given the natural resources and the geographical position of the Interior, its economy depended less upon foreign commerce than upon the preservation of political unity with contiguous areas. The interior provinces were interested in the opening of the country to foreign trade only in so far as it resulted in a more plentiful supply of manufactures at reasonable prices. But to the extent that direct commerce between the River Plate and Europe jeopardized the security of domestic industries, political emancipation in the interior provinces entailed economic and financial hardships. These hardships were further intensified by the circumstance that territories, which prior to the Revolution were economically complementary to the Interior, remained outside the Argentine Confederation. So the economy of the Interior was not only exposed to the devastating competition of overseas industries in the Eastern markets, but was also deprived of those markets in which European competition was least effective, namely, Bolivia and Peru. Adjustment to the new political environment might have been less difficult had the Interior been able to match the industry of Western Europe. But this was far from being the case. In methods of production and industrial organization the Interior remained rigidly colonial. To the Interior, therefore, emancipation and unrestricted commercial intercourse with Europe meant a considerable curtailment of production in some of its most important industries, the annihilation of its transandine commerce, and the contraction of its interprovincial trade.

The economic problem confronting the provinces of the Interior was fundamentally different from that confronting Buenos Aires. In Buenos Aires the solution of the problem entailed nothing more than the setting up of an appropriate administrative and fiscal structure. For the abolition of the colonial system was in itself a step forward in the economic development of the province. In the Interior the problem was to conserve the pre-revolutionary *status quo*, or as much of it as possible. It was a problem of devising the proper means of defense against the encroachments of foreign industry and commerce, and of limiting the rate and scope of economic and financial decline. The Revolution and political emancipation had resulted in irreparable loss to the Interior. For example, it was impossible to revive the mule trade between the Litoral and Peru, or to restore commerce with Bolivia, Chile, or Peru to its pre-revolutionary level. The provinces could exercise some measure of control over internal markets. They could minimize the impact of foreign imports upon domestic industries and in this way effect a more orderly adjustment in the economic structure. The wine and brandy industries of Tucumán and the provinces of Cuyo, the manufacture of leather goods in Santiago del Estero and Córdoba, the cloth industry of Córdoba, and finally the handicraft-industry—in all these sectors of the national economy a policy of protection might at least mitigate the process of economic decline. Such a policy, provided it were national in scope, might not only save the native industry from ruin, but allow of a gradual modernization of the Interior's industrial plant. For it was reasonable to assume that with profits assured, domestic industries would be in a position to bid successfully for the capital resources and technical skill necessary to raise the standard of industrial production. Protection would undoubtedly raise the prices of consumers' goods, but it would also cause a shift in the distribution of the national income in favor of the Interior and so make for a better balanced national economy.

But a protective commercial policy on a national scale was unrealizable, and for the very reasons which led the Interior to demand such a policy. The control by Buenos Aires of the country's overseas port was the decisive factor here. Buenos Aires would accept protection only on one condition, that she gain as much from it as the Interior. But this was out of the question. Of all the provinces of the Confederation, Buenos Aires was least interested in fostering a restrictive commercial policy. In so far as a policy of high duties would result in a lower volume of overseas trade and higher prices on consumers' goods it was politically inexpedient and economically harmful. To the extent that an increase in the cost of living would result in higher money wages the burden of higher duties would fall upon the employers, that is, the cattle breeders, hide and meat producers, and merchants. Nor were these classes in the least inclined to submit to such an eventuality, the more so as it was highly improbable that the fall in the rate of profit had any chance of being compensated for by an increase in the volume of production or overseas trade. On the contrary, there was every reason to anticipate a reduction in both exports and imports, and hence in the volume of industrial production. The argument that the loss sustained by Buenos Aires would be more than offset by the revival of industrial activity in the Interior, and that ultimately the national dividend would gain on balance failed to convince the *porteños*. For it was not at all certain that a more stringent commercial policy would stimulate industrial expansion on a scale sufficient to counterbalance contraction of economic activity in Buenos Aires. Whether or not these doubts were well founded, one thing was clear: Buenos Aires had nothing to offer except the services of the middleman, and these under protection would become in large part superfluous. The economic future of Buenos Aires depended then upon strengthening its commercial relations with Europe rather than upon the expansion of the provinces in the Interior. The adoption of a policy of protection, such as the Interior demanded, held out the prospect for Buenos Aires of a restoration of pre-revolutionary conditions. Buenos Aires, therefore, had no other choice but to keep the port wide open.

Unable to secure the coöperation of Buenos Aires the provinces of the Interior attacked the problem of protection on the basis of provincial and sectional rather than national interests. Provincial tariffs and special regulations designed to protect local markets and native industries were introduced as a substitute for a national commercial policy. At the same time the provinces endeavored to encourage interprovincial trade by means of commercial treaties. By these methods the provinces of the Interior hoped to offset the commercial liberalism of Buenos Aires and to arrest the process of economic disintegration. In no condition to undergo a thorough social and economic reorganization, the provinces sought relief in economic isolation. However, they were not prepared to follow this policy consistently, for none could hope to attain self-sufficiency. Isolation, far from strengthening the economic position of the provinces, only intensified their dependence upon Buenos Aires. For this reason more perhaps than any other the provinces were anxious to finish with the task of political organization in a way that would guarantee their economic and political autonomy and at the same time stabilize interprovincial economic relations.

In the Litoral the process of adjustment to the post-revolutionary environment had a pattern of its own. With respect to resources and economic potentialities the provinces of the Litoral, especially Santa Fe and Entre Ríos, resembled Buenos Aires. Like Buenos Aires the riparian provinces were large producers of hides, meat, and other by-products of the cattle breeding industry. Like Buenos Aires, too, these provinces depended upon foreign markets for a considerable part of their income. It would seem, therefore, that the economic prospects opened up by the Revolution of 1810 were as bright for the Litoral as they were for Buenos Aires. Actually, however, economic progress in the riparian provinces was disappointing when compared with the progress of Buenos Aires. Nor can the difference in the rate of economic development between Buenos Aires and the Litoral be ascribed to the inability of the Litoral to adjust itself to the post-revolutionary environment. The Litoral had no industrial structure comparable to that of the central and western provinces. Hence its problems were of a different order from those confronting the Interior. These problems all had their origin in the maladjustments created by the Revolution itself. For the Interior the Revolution of 1810 went too far; for the Litoral it did not go far enough. Since economic reform did not go beyond the opening of Buenos Aires to foreign commerce the Revolution failed to satisfy the basic demand of the Litoral provinces, that is, the demand for "free trade." The restriction of foreign commerce to the port of Buenos Aires could have no other result than to subordinate the commercial and financial interests of the Litoral provinces to those of Buenos Aires.

From the point of view of the Litoral, Buenos Aires had monopolized the economic gains of the Revolution. Although the province controlled the nation's foreign trade its commercial policies were determined by considerations of provincial rather than national welfare. This sectionalism of Buenos Aires was keenly resented in the riparian provinces, partly because the latter competed against Buenos Aires in foreign markets, but mainly because unlike the Interior they could easily dispense with the services of the Buenos Aires port. Indeed, both the Paraná and Uruguay rivers were accessible to ocean-going vessels, so that direct commercial relations between overseas markets and the provinces of Santa Fe and Entre Ríos were quite practicable. Buenos Aires was no less aware than the Litoral of the economic and financial consequences of opening the Paraná and Uruguay to foreign navigation. For one thing direct contact with foreign markets would eliminate the transportation costs and other charges of the Buenos Aires market. Nor were these costs inconsiderable. They included the difference between small and large tonnage transportation charges from the river ports to Buenos Aires, the cost of reloading, transit duties, and commissions of the *porteño* wholesale merchants. Likewise the import side of the Litoral's foreign trade stood to benefit by river navigation. Furthermore, ports like Rosario and Paraná could easily extend their tributary territories beyond the provincial boundaries to areas which, owing to the high cost of transportation, were practically cut off from foreign markets. In general, the opening of the Paraná and Uruguay rivers to foreign navigation promised advantages to the producers as well as to the consumers of the riparian provinces. That is why for the Litoral the economic program of the Revolution was much broader than that actually realized under the aegis of Buenos Aires. The most important economic postulate of the Revolution was "free trade," but the extremely narrow interpretation placed upon free trade by Buenos Aires reduced the Litoral to much the same position as that occupied by Buenos Aires prior to 1810. Under the colonial regime Buenos Aires had had to fight against the merchants-monopolists of the Interior and Lima; so likewise in independent Argentina the riparian provinces were rebelling against the stifling monopoly of Buenos Aires. The issue was now more complex, and the struggle, having become a civil war, more bitter.[18]

[18] For more detailed discussion of economic life in the provinces in the first and second decades after the Revolution the reader is referred to contemporary descriptions by foreign visitors to the country. Without exhausting the list of such descriptions the following works may be mentioned: J. Andrews, *op. cit.;* Schmidtmeyer, *op. cit.;* Rodney and Graham, *op. cit;* A. B. Beaumont, *op. cit.;* S. B. Head, *Reports relating to the failure of the Rio Plata Mining Association, formed under an authority signed by his excellency Don B. Rivadavia* (London: 1827); A. Caldcleugh, *Travels in South America, during the years 1819–20–21, containing an account of the present state of Brazil, Buenos Ayres, and Chile* (London: 1825); S. Haigh, *Sketches of Buenos Ayres and Chile* (London: 1829); E. E. Vidal, *op. cit.* A more complete bibliography of the relevant literature will be found in *Economic Literature of Latin America,* prepared by the Harvard Bureau for Economic Research in Latin America (Cambridge: 1935), I, 39–87. Practically nothing is available in the way of monographic studies of the economic history of the provinces. Vast materials in the provincial archives remain untouched by Argentine historians who until now have been preoccupied mainly with the political and military history of the country. It is indeed unfortunate that Juan Álvarez, whose excellent study of Santa Fe appeared in 1914, should have found no followers among Argentine historians.

2

Fully as important as protection and river navigation was the question of finances. Here, too, both the Interior and the Litoral faced a situation whose urgency as well as complexity placed a severe drain upon the economic and political resources of these provinces. Broadly, the problem was two-sided. On the one hand, there was the necessity for a more or less extensive revision of the very principles of the pre-revolutionary fiscal system. On the other hand, each of the provinces tried to establish an autonomous fiscal system appropriate to its economic needs. The two aspects of the problem were, of course, inseparable. For by the time reorganization of the financial system was no longer postponable, the process of political differentiation of the country into autonomous provinces had already been completed. Therefore the establishment of provincial treasuries was intimately related to the reorganization of the financial mechanism inherited from the viceroyalty. Such reorganization went beyond mere administrative reform, for it involved a definite point of view towards the central economic problem of the provinces. It was a causal factor in its own right, capable of influencing the rate and direction of economic development.

The need for financial reform was generally recognized in all the provinces. It was realized that the colonial system of taxation no longer corresponded to the economic realities of post-revolutionary Argentina.[19] But how far reform needed to go was less clearly understood. The example of the Buenos Aires government inspired the belief that legislative action alone would suffice. But this belief rested upon a tendency to overestimate the efficacy of the fiscal policies adopted in Buenos Aires and to disregard the peculiarly favorable conditions in which the economy of the province of Buenos Aires found itself after the Revolution.[20] What was possible in Buenos Aires, with

[19] "Los legisladores antiguos," states the report of the Córdoba Legislative Commission submitted to the provincial legislature, "no tuvieron otro objeto que el engrosamiento de sus arcas, y este es el orígen de tanto impuesto, bajo diferentes nombres, y por diferentes y las mas veces especiosos pretextos. Pero la ignorancia les hacía adoptar unos medios del todo opuesto al fin que se proponían y aquí está la causa de la confusión complicada del sistema de rentas, por lo mismo opresivo y con el que no puede existir por tiempo la provincia." Cf. *Archivo de la Honorable Cámara de Diputados de la Provincia de Córdoba* (Córdoba: 1912–1914), I, 261 (Session, October 14, 1824).

[20] The case of the province of San Juan is instructive in this respect. In 1829 the governor in a message to the provincial legislature suggested a series of reforms, designed

its growing overseas commerce and general economic expansion, provided no clue to what was practicable in the economically stagnant provinces. And in the provinces whose resources were relatively abundant, plans for financial reform were always being upset by civil wars and other emergencies.

The financial position of the provinces outside of Buenos Aires was never anything but precarious. It was an exceptional year when a provincial treasury could boast of a surplus. Deficits appeared with monotonous regularity, and empty treasuries were the rule. Scarcity of funds often forced the provincial governments to suspend the servicing of public debts, to reduce the salaries of civil and military officials, and to curtail the activity of the administration to the barest essentials. The annual financial reports of the provincial governments and the preambles to decrees dealing with public finances are full of such phrases as "exhausted treasury," "lack of credit," "need for economy." Waste and mismanagement played their part, no doubt, but these things on the whole were too insignificant to account for the financial difficulties of the provincial treasuries. The trouble lay much deeper. It lay in the progressive impoverishment of the provincial population. The cardinal problem in many provinces was not to economize, for expenditures were already reduced to a minimum, but to obtain sufficient revenues to prevent the administrative machinery from collapsing altogether. For example the budget of the province of Jujuy for 1839 called for a total expenditure of 9,040 pesos. Of this sum the department of government was allotted 2,860 pesos, including the governor's salary of 1,500 pesos. The province set aside 480 pesos for public education! [21] It is true that the province of Jujuy was one of the poorest in the Confederation, but conditions in other provinces were only slightly better. Córdoba, one of the largest inland provinces, with a population estimated at 60,000 inhabitants and situated on the most

---

to make direct taxation (*contribución directa*) the basis of the provincial finances. He advocated abolition of tariff duties, "which some call the system of contraband and monopolies," and the adoption of direct taxation, which alone was capable of suppressing "the vexatious routine of taxes and contributions." Free trade in the classical meaning of the phrase, consolidation of public indebtedness, abolition of the *diezmo* tax, publicity in accounting, such were the main features of the plan of financial reform. It was so much at variance with the possibilities offered by the economic development of the province that with the exception of the abolition of the *diezmo*, not one of the suggested innovations ever materialized. Cf. *Registro Oficial de la Provincia de San Juan, año 1829*, Message of July 30, 1829.

[21] *Registro Oficial de la Provincia de Jujuy*, Libro i, p. 112.

important commercial routes between the seacoast and the Andes, possessed an income of slightly over 70,000 pesos in 1824. In that same year the revenues of Buenos Aires amounted to more than 2½ million pesos. Receipts in Buenos Aires from stamp duties and license taxes alone exceeded by more than 50 per cent the total revenues of Córdoba. Even the most prosperous provinces such as Corrientes and Entre Ríos could not compare with Buenos Aires. The average annual revenues of Corrientes for a period of thirteen years, from 1827 to 1839, amounted to about 115,000 pesos, ranging from 68,000 pesos in 1827 to 152,000 pesos in 1835.[22]

The provinces relied upon customs duties for the bulk of their revenues. Taxes were imposed upon imports and exports, as well as upon goods in transit. The proportion of revenues derived from these sources varied from province to province and from year to year. In some provinces, for example, Corrientes and Entre Ríos, customs duties produced at times as much as 70 per cent of the total revenue, and rarely less than 50 per cent. In the interior provinces interprovincial and overseas trade played a less important role as a source of revenue. In San Juan customs revenues made up only 40 per cent of the total, and in Córdoba the proportion was about 60 per cent. Next to the customs duties in importance were the stamp duty and the license tax. In imposing these taxes the provinces followed the lead of Buenos Aires. The schedules of these imposts varied from province to province, provision sometimes being made for preferential treatment of natives as against foreigners and inhabitants of other provinces.[23] In almost all the provinces some of the colonial taxes such as the *diezmo* and the *sisa* were retained. As a source of revenue the *diezmo* was the more important of the two, and the provincial governments were reluctant to abolish this tax. Special and extraordinary imposts under various denominations (*impuesto nuevo, impuesto extraordinario*) were frequently resorted to by the provincial governments in times of emergency. But as often as not these exactions, intended as temporary measures, were allowed to become an integral part of the fiscal system. In every province some revenue was derived from the sale of

[22] The total revenues of the province of Corrientes included incomes from loans, which together with other non-periodic revenues were listed under the rubric *eventuales* (see Table 21). The real revenues of the province were, therefore, smaller than shown above, although it is not possible to state by how much.

[23] Cf. Tariff schedule of the province of Santa Fe for 1821, chapter "Alcabala," *Registro Oficial de la Provincia de Santa Fe*, I, 61 (February 21, 1821).

TABLE 18

REVENUES AND EXPENDITURES OF THE PROVINCE OF SAN JUAN FOR THE YEARS 1823, 1824, 1836, AND 1837

REVENUES

	1823 Pesos	%	1824 Pesos	%	1836 Pesos	%	1837 Pesos	%
Customs duties	4,962$ 1½	28.8	3,798$ 3¼	19.0	3,555$ 6	33.1	3,641$ 4½	32.6
Stamp and license duty	3,410$ 0½	19.8	3,273$ 1½	16.3	2,966$ 1½	27.6	3,484$ 3	31.2
Diezmo	5,305$ 0	30.8	9,070$ 0	45.3			133$ 6	1.1
Hide export tax	815$ 3	4.7	1,495$ 0	7.5	544$ 5½	5.1	459$ 1½	4.1
Other	2,754$ 0⅛	15.9	2,372$ 6¾	11.9	3,667$ 0½	34.2	3,466$ 7½	31.0
Total	17,246$ 5⅛	100.0	20,009$ 3½	100.0	10,733$ 5½	100.0	11,188$ 6½	100.0

EXPENDITURES

	1823 Pesos	%	1824 Pesos	%	1836 Pesos	%	1837 Pesos	%
Government	1,952$ 1	12.3	6,996$ 2¼	36.1	3,685$ 2⅝	30.2	4,354$ 5¼	36.8
Treasury	1,196$ 0	7.5	1,931$ 0	10.0	1,652$ 0	13.5	1,887$ 5¾	16.0
War	8,005$ 0	50.5	7,281$ 2½	37.6	5,539$ 5¾	45.3	4,574$ 2	38.7
Other	4,696$ 0⅝	29.7	3,167$ 7	16.3	1,345$ 3¼	11.0	1,009$ 4¼	8.5
Total	15,849$ 1⅝	100.0	19,376$ 1¾	100.0	12,222$ 3⅜	100.0	11,826$ 1¼	100.0

Source: *Registro Oficial de la Provincia de San Juan.*

TABLE 19

REVENUES AND EXPENDITURES OF THE PROVINCE OF TUCUMÁN FOR THE YEARS 1822, 1824, 1826, 1827, 1829, 1831, 1833, 1835, 1838, 1844, 1845, 1847

Year	Total Revenues	Total Expenditures[b]	Customs revenues (alcabala)	%	Impuesto extraordinario	%	Other revenues[d]	%	War expenditures	%	Loans
1822	14,183$ 2¾	22,957$ 4⅛	8,705$ 2	66.4	1,205$ 0	8.5	4,273$ 0¾	25.1	13,183$ 6⅝	57.4	18,775$ 6
1824	22,115$ 3¾	33,178$ 3¾	5,576$ 3¾	25.2	2,273$ 0½	10.3	14,263$ 7½	64.3	24,753$ 4	74.3	11,063$ 0
1826	38,641$ 6⅞	41,397$ 2⅞	7,168$ 4¼	18.6	3,459$ 7	8.9	28,013$ 3⅝	72.5	27,551$ 7¾	71.3	2,878$ 2
1827[a]	7,560$ 6⅛	72,130$ 0⅛	2,577$ 3⅛	34.1	378$ 6	5.0	4,604$ 5	60.9	56,218$ 1⅛	77.9	74,117$ 7½
1829	21,390$ 2⅜	26,966$ 6	9,678$ 5⅞	45.2			11,711$ 4½	54.8	16,394$ 1½	60.8	5,583$ 4
1831	14,563$ 6½	31,333$ 1¾	4,367$ 0½	29.9	1,322$ 2	9.1	8,874$ 4	61.0	16,620$ 7¼	53.5	16,967$ 5½
1833	24,144$ 6	28,697$ 3½	9,418$ 0½	39.0	6,732$ 7¾	27.9	7,993$ 5¾	33.1	12,458$ 3¼	43.4	4,646$ 0
1835	21,922$ 2	23,403$ 5⅛	7,816$ 0¾	35.6	5,515$ 7⅛	25.2	8,590$ 1¾	39.2	8,125$ 4¾	34.7	1,550$ 5⅛
1838	22,252$ 2⅛	25,526$ 0½	4,266$ 0⅝	19.2	3,290$ 7¾	14.8	14,695$ 1¾	66.0	7,944$ 0	31.1	3,274$ 6⅛
1844[c]	33,417$ 4½	30,109$ 4	25,860$ 2	77.4			7,557$ 2½	22.6			
1845[c]	29,842$ 0	31,865$ 4	20,486$ 5½	69.0			9,355$ 4	31.0			
1847[c]	27,270$ 0½	28,754$ 5	18,970$ 5	69.5			8,299$ 3½	30.5			

Source: *Archivo Histórico de la Provincia de Tucumán*, vols. 66, 67, 71–72, 73–74, 78, 83, 88, 99, 102, 116, 119, 125.

[a] Eleven months only. [b] Including service or repayment of loans.

[c] Customs revenues for these years are listed under the following headings: Entrada de ultramar; Entrada de la República; Extracciones de la provincia; Derecho de tránsito.

[d] The most important items under this heading for the period from 1822 to 1838 are: Impuesto sobre aguardiente; Impuesto del papel sellado; Nuevo impuesto provincial; Patentes (since the early thirties); Diezmo del Estado. In the years 1844 to 1847 the following were the more important sources of revenues in addition to customs: Ramo de patentes; Ramo de proprios; Papel sellado.

TABLE 20

Revenues and Expenditures of the Province of Cordoba for the Years 1824, 1825, 1826, and 1836

	1824		Revenues 1825		1826		1836	
	Pesos	%	Pesos	%	Pesos	%	Pesos	%
Customs duties	33,438$ 6	47.6	32,044$ 0	48.8	31,559$ 3	44.2	39,896$ 2½	58.9
Stamp duties and licenses	5,860$ 7	8.3	6,908$ 3½	10.5	6,334$ 1⅝	8.9	4,955$ 4½	7.4
Sisa y nuevo impuesto	4,023$ 0¼	5.7	5,869$ 0½	8.9	5,022$ 1½	7.1		
Other revenues	26,874$ 0⅞	38.3	20,758$ 4	31.8	28,554$ 7½	39.8	22,840$ 3⅝	33.7
Total	70,196$ 6⅛	100.0	65,579$ 1	100.0	71,470$ 5⅝	100.0	67,692$ 2⅝	100.0
Loans	11,096$ 7		13,359$ 6½		11,544$ 7½		34,074$ 7	

	1824		Expenditures 1825		1826		1836	
	Pesos	%	Pesos	%	Pesos	%	Pesos	%
Government	7,712$ 1¼	9.9	7,406$ 5¾	9.4	9,887$ 0	12.0	10,097$ 6¾	10.0
Treasury	5,769$ 7	7.4	5,759$ 2½	7.4	5,855$ 5½	7.1	5,126$ 5¼	5.0
War	51,497$ 5⅝	64.7	46,682$ 6¾	59.1	40,614$ 4⅞	49.5	57,605$ 2¼	56.7
Other expenditures	13,497$ 3	18.1	19,086$ 0	24.1	25,739$ 1⅛	31.4	28,803$ 2	28.3
Total	78,032$ 0⅞	100.0	78,943$ 7	100.0	82,096$ 3½	100.0	101,633$ 0¼	100.0

Sources: *Archivo del Gobierno de la Provincia de Córdoba:* Libro 89, 91, 149.

TABLE 21

REVENUES OF THE PROVINCE OF CORRIENTES IN THE PERIOD FROM 1827 TO 1839

Year	Total Revenues Pesos	%	Customs and Port Dues Pesos	%	Stamp duties and License tax Pesos	%	Diezmo Pesos	%	Sales of Land, Police, etc. Pesos	%	Eventuales Pesos	%
1827	68,189$ 1¾	100.0	36,942$ 7	54.2	7,476$ 7¼	4.0	3,023$ 7¼	4.5	4,407$ 6¾	6.5	16,337$ 4½	23.8
1828	79,044$ 1	100.0	28,669$ 7¼	36.3	6,280$ 7½	7.9	12,038$ 6¾	15.3	9,827$ 1	12.4	22,227$ 2½	28.2
1829	115,876$ 6	100.0	71,200$ 3¾	61.7	7,872$ 0½	6.7	6,745$ 4	5.8	6,235$ 4¼	5.3	23,825$ 1½	20.5
1830	114,071$ 6½	100.0	73,120$ 6¼	64.1	8,082$ 6	7.1	18,099$ 6½	15.9	9,565$ 0¾	8.4	5,203$ 2	4.5
1831	99,961$ 7¼	100.0	63,658$ 2⅝	63.7	8,750$ 7	8.7	12,877$ 3¼	12.9	8,696$ 5¾	8.7	5,978$ 5½	6.0
1832	108,935$ 0¼	100.0	75,196$ 6¼	69.0	9,509$ 6½	8.8	9,203$ 7½	8.7	7,005$ 1¾	6.4	8,019$ 2¼	7.3
1833	117,240$ 1¼	100.0	81,767$ 5½	69.7	9,204$ 6½	7.9	10,809$ 3½	9.2	6,965$ 4½	5.9	8,501$ 5¼	7.3
1834	149,133$ 4	100.0	84,632$ 3½	56.7	9,162$ 6½	6.1	9,517$ 1	6.4	7,361$ 5	5.0	38,459$ 4	25.8
1835	151,909$ 3⅞	100.0	113,030$ 2⅜	74.4	11,228$ 6	7.3	14,993$ 7¾	9.9	7,864$ 4½	5.2	4,791$ 7¼	3.2
1836	133,608$ 3¼	100.0	86,447$ 7¼	64.7	11,536$ 1¾	8.6	16,558$ 0½	12.4	8,590$ 4½	6.4	10,475$ 5¼	7.8
1837	137,931$ 0¾	100.0	101,186$ 1¼	73.3	10,155$ 1	7.4	13,018$ 5	9.4	8,877$ 5¾	6.5	4,693$ 3¾	3.4
1838	112,691$ 3¾	100.0	72,119$ 4	63.9	9,651$ 1½	8.6	13,769$ 4½	12.2	8,135$ 7½	7.3	9,015$ 2¼	8.0
1839	107,131$ 5½	100.0	14,994$ 7¾	14.0	5,628$ 1	5.3	4,351$ 4	4.1	3,995$ 1½	3.7	78,161$ 7¼	72.9

Sources: *Registro Oficial de la Provincia de Corrientes.*

TABLE 22

Expenditures of the Province of Corrientes in the Period from 1827 to 1839

Year	Total Expenditures Pesos	%	Government Pesos	%	Treasury Pesos	%	War Pesos	%	Extraordinary exp. Pesos	%
1827	88,755$ 5⅜	100.0	6,845$ 5¾	7.7	5,330$ 1¼	6.0	50,795$ 6¼	57.3	25,784$ 1½	29.0
1828	80,352$ 2½	100.0	7,888$ 2½	9.8	6,115$ 4½	7.6	45,008$ 2½	56.0	21,341$ 1	26.0
1829	99,693$ 6	100.0	6,041$ 4¼	6.1	7,273$ 2½	7.3	49,859$ 7¼	50.0	36,519$ 0	36.6
1830	122,201$ 4¼	100.0	8,345$ 7½	6.8	7,295$ 5¼	5.9	55,377$ 5	45.3	51,182$ 2½	41.0
1831	100,431$ 7¾	100.0	6,713$ 6	6.7	7,163$ 4¼	7.1	51,200$ 3¼	51.0	35,354$ 2¼	35.0
1832	97,489$ 5⅞	100.0	7,570$ 0	7.7	7,247$ 4	7.6	44,313$ 0¾	45.4	38,359$ 1⅛	39.3
1833	111,953$ 0½	100.0	6,844$ 1½	6.1	8,058$ 3¼	7.2	53,561$ 2	47.8	43,489$ 1¼	38.9
1834	152,998$ 2⅛	100.0	6,870$ 5	4.5	9,722$ 0½	6.4	52,603$ 7¼	34.4	83,801$ 5⅛	54.7
1835	154,114$ 2⅝	100.0	7,504$ 3½	4.9	11,167$ 5½	7.3	53,977$ 2¾	35.0	81,364$ 6⅞	52.8
1836	125,420$ 7¼	100.0	9,927$ 2¼	7.9	12,124$ 7¾	9.7	55,267$ 0¼	44.1	48,101$ 5	38.3
1837	147,762$ 3¼	100.0	10,106$ 0	6.8	10,805$ 5	7.2	64,063$ 1	43.4	62,788$ 5¼	42.6
1838	116,293$ 3	100.0	12,767$ 7½	11.0	10,048$ 5	8.6	51,245$ 2¼	44.1	42,231$ 4¼	36.3
1839	120,681$ 7¼	100.0	7,621$ 4½	6.3	5,655$ 7¾	4.7	32,334$ 1	26.8	75,070$ 2	62.2

Sources: *Registro Oficial de la Provincia de Corrientes.*

public land, from penalties for transgression of police regulations, from rental of government property, etc. However, income from these sources was relatively insignificant.[24]

It has already been pointed out that as a rule revenues from taxation and other sources were insufficient to cover expenditures. Civil and interprovincial wars, which had become a routine part of the political life of the nation, exhausted the provincial treasuries. Financial crises followed each other in rapid succession and in order to meet these emergencies the governments resorted to extraordinary measures. One of the commonest methods was to exact loans or contributions from the population. The loans were almost always forced loans, even those which were supposed to be voluntary. Distributed among the merchants and landowners these loans were usually short term loans, and their size and frequency were determined by considerations of expediency and the immediate needs of the treasury. Thus, in the province of Córdoba not less than twelve such loans, ranging from 5,000 to 80,000 pesos, were launched by the government in the eighteen years

TABLE 23

INTERNAL LOANS IN THE PROVINCE OF CÓRDOBA: 1827–1844

Year	Date	Amount	Remarks
1827	Jan. 25	15,000	
1828	May 5	10,000	
1829	Apr. 28	15,405	Only 1,475 p. was subscribed voluntarily
1829	Sept. 1	80,000	Interest bearing notes
1829	Nov. 17	15,000	
1833	Jan. 17	40,000	
1837	July 28	17,000	
1837	Nov. 20	8,000	
1838	Nov. 20	5,500	To replace contributions in kind
1840	June 6	10,000	
1842	Jan. 21	6,000	
1844		12,000	Voluntary loan. Only 3,862 subscribed by 46 individuals.

Sources: *Archivo de la H. Cámara de Diputados de la Provincia de Córdoba; Compilación de leyes, decretos, acuerdos de la Excma. Cámara de Justicia, y demas disposiciones de caracter público, dictadas en la provincai de Córdoba, desde 1810 á 1870* (Córboda: 1870); *Archivo de Gobierno de la Provincia de Córdoba.*

from 1827 to 1844 (see Table 23). In Entre Ríos the provincial government had recourse to loans, forced and voluntary, on twelve different

[24] See Tables 18, 19, 20, 21, and 22. It has not been possible to obtain data for each province of the Confederation. However, the compilations for Córdoba, San Juan, Tucumán, and Corrientes are thought to be sufficiently representative for the country as a whole.

occasions in the course of the thirteen years between 1821 and 1832. It should be noted, however, that two of these loans were obtained from Buenos Aires, and that at least one loan (for 100,000 or 150,000 pesos) never advanced beyond the stage of authorization by the provincial legislature. Some of the remaining loans were only partially realized (see Table 24). As already mentioned, government borrowings were

TABLE 24

GOVERNMENT BORROWINGS IN ENTRE RÍOS: 1821–1832

Year	Date	Amount		Remarks
1821	Dec. 16	3,000		Secured by 50% of revenues
1822	Nov. 5	6,000		6 mo. treasury notes, interest coupon 1%.
1823	Apr. 22	18,000		Borrowed from Buenos Aires. Due in 1825.
1823	June 3	10,000		
1823	Dec. 22	1,336		
1824	July 10	28,000		Borrowed from Buenos Aires
1824	Dec. 16	100,000	or	150,000 Authorized but not realized.
1824	Dec. 22	500		
1827	Oct. 4	4,500		
1828	Oct. 7	4,000		
1828	Nov. 30	5,000		Only 3,665 obtained
1832	Aug. 25	1,200		

Source: *Recopilación de leyes, decretos y acuerdos de la Provincia de Entre Ríos, desde 1821 á 1873* (Uruguay: 1875–1890).

almost invariably of the short term variety, and the obligations issued against these loans were accepted by the treasuries in payment of customs duties.[25] Córdoba and Entre Ríos were not exceptional in this respect. Financing by means of forced loans was as common in other provinces, and long after the practice had been discontinued in Buenos Aires.[26]

In the provinces the task of devising an adequate and consistent fiscal policy was difficult and complicated. On the one hand the provincial governments realized that financial stability depended in the final

[25] When, however, the supply of treasury certificates was especially plentiful their acceptance in payment of duties was restricted to a certain proportion of the total. So in Entre Ríos at least one third of sums owed the treasury had to be paid in specie. Cf. *Recopilación* I, 382–383 (Decree, March 22, 1823).

[26] This phase, like so many others of the economic history of the provinces, has yet to be studied. Very little is known about the number or size of these loans. The following data for Tucumán were obtained from the *Actas de la Sala de Representantes de la Provincia de Tucumán* (unpublished typewritten copy of manuscript): Two loans authorized in 1831, one for 6,000 pesos (February 22), and another for 10,000 pesos (March 17); in 1834 a loan of 3,000 pesos was authorized on June 25; in 1840 the legislature authorized a loan of 5,000 pesos (April 19). Cf. Table 19.

analysis upon the continued growth of taxable wealth; hence their efforts to stimulate production and trade, and to defend the local industries against the disintegrating influence of foreign competition. On the other hand, the governments were harried by the immediate and ever-growing needs for funds, and so were forced continually to increase the burden of taxation. This contradictory position was clearly reflected in tariff policies. To a greater extent than in Buenos Aires the tariff in the provinces was an instrument of internal and interprovincial economic policy, by means of which the provinces hoped not only to solve their financial problems but to stem the tide of economic retrogression.

In general the provincial tariffs were patterned after those of Buenos Aires. Duties were imposed upon both exports and imports, and the schedules of import duties were usually composed of maximum and minimum rates, the former being applied to overseas countries and the latter to imports from provinces of the Confederation. Sometimes intermediate rates were introduced which were applicable to South American countries. Import taxes were as a rule determined on the basis of current market prices (*ad valorem* duties), while the duties on exports were almost always specific. With respect to imports the practice was to establish a general *ad valorem* duty to which all commodities were subject, except those specifically included in other categories. This was the normal rate, and varying from province to province it ranged from 4 to 13 per cent. In certain cases higher taxes were imposed either in order to increase revenues, or in order to protect domestic industries. So, for example, the Córdoba tariff of 1822 called for an import duty of 16 per cent, as against a normal tax of 8 per cent, on all goods which competed with domestic production.[27] In the tariff of October 25, 1829 and October 29, 1830 the normal tax was set at 10 per cent *ad valorem*. At the same time a duty of 16 per cent was imposed upon silk, thread, fine wool, porcelain and crystal wares, sugar, *yerba mate*. Hats, ready-made clothing, shoes and boots, saddles, furniture, arms, powder, munitions, flour, tea, coffee, and foodstuffs were subject to a tax of 20 per cent. Tobacco, cigars, wine, beer, vinegar, cider, paid 25 per cent, and brandy, gin, and other alcoholic beverages were dutiable to the extent of 40 per cent.[28]

The Entre Ríos tariff of October 3, 1821 called for a normal im-

[27] *Compilación*, p. 14.
[28] *Ibid.*, p. 49. Capítulo I.

port duty of 13 per cent. Shoes and wearing apparel were required to pay 20 per cent, but naval stores only 8 per cent. Specific duties were imposed upon tobacco, sugar, brandy, and paper. These rates applied to overseas imports; the normal duty upon imports from other provinces of the Confederation was 4 per cent.[29] The tariff of October 9, 1829 reduced the normal import duty to 8 per cent, and the tax on naval stores to 6 per cent, at the same time that it increased the duty on shoes and clothing to 25 per cent. According to the Provincial government high rates encouraged smuggling and evasion, and accordingly the government demanded a reduction of import duties.[30] The tariff schedule of February 1836, much more elaborate than any previously devised, retained the normal duty of 8 per cent. A considerable number of commodities were subjected to higher duties, ranging from 12 to 24 per cent. The schedule also contained a fairly long list of manufactures whose import was entirely prohibited. This list included certain textile goods, hardware, maize, butter, footwear, certain leather goods, etc. Imports of Argentine origin were also subject to a duty of 8 per cent, but wine, brandy, and sugar paid higher duties.[31]

In Tucumán the normal import tax established by the tariff of October 24, 1826 was 4 per cent. However, jewelry, coffee, and tea, furniture, saddles, clothing, and footwear were subject to a duty of 6 per cent; sugar and *yerba mate* paid 8 per cent, hats 12 per cent, brandies, foreign or domestic, 16 per cent.[32] In 1834 the duty on furniture, shoes, clothing, hats, saddles, and other manufactured goods produced within the province was raised to 30 per cent.[33] Similar, if less extensive, exceptions to the normal duty of 4 per cent were included in the Catamarca tariff of July 18, 1828.[34]

In Corrientes the tariff of January 6, 1825 established a normal duty of 9 per cent, which was raised to 12 per cent in the tariff of January 1831. Importation of footwear, clothing, certain textile and cotton goods, was entirely prohibited.[35] In 1831 sugar was added to the list

[29] *Recopilación de leyes . . . de Entre Ríos*, I, 13 and I, 83.

[30] *Ibid.*, III, 88. Also, message of the provincial government of August 29, 1829 (*Recopilación*, III, 64).

[31] *Recopilación*, IV, 201.

[32] *Actas de la Sala de Representantes de la Provincia de Tucumán*, Acta 55.

[33] *Ibid.*, Sessions, 54 and 57.

[34] *Archivo General*, S.5–C.31–A.6, no. 7; Record of the Sessions of the Junta de Representantes, Sessions of May 29, June 19, 20, 27, July 11, 18, 1829.

[35] *Registro Oficial de la Provincia de Corrientes*, III, 9 (January 4, 1831).

of prohibited commodities,[36] and the list was further extended by the law of October 29, 1832 to include all commodities manufactured in any of the provinces of the Confederation. Liquors were excluded from this general prohibition, because it was extremely difficult to determine whether they were of foreign or domestic manufacture.[37]

In some provinces provision was made for the free entry of certain commodities. So the tariff of Córdoba for 1829 and 1830 permitted the free entry of machines and agricultural and mining instruments. The free list of the Catamarca tariff of 1828 was fairly extensive. It included timber, cattle, grease, tallow, maize, munitions, drugs, books, etc. However, such free lists were rare, and the provinces which inaugurated them were soon forced by financial difficulties to abandon the practice.

All tariffs contained more or less extensive schedules of export duties. The general practice was to establish a normal export duty, which seldom exceeded 4 per cent *ad valorem,* and to list separately those commodities which did not come under the general export tax. Although the number of such commodities was small, they usually formed the bulk of provincial exports. For example, in Corrientes specific duties were imposed upon the export of hides, leather sole, carts, tobacco, timber, mules, and horses.[38] In Entre Ríos the tariffs of October 3, 1821 and October 3, 1822 singled out hides, tallow, horns, soap, wool, horsehair, lime, and leather sole.[39] In 1829 this list was extended to include cattle, horses, and mules.[40] However, in Córdoba, export with few exceptions was free. Commodities subject to export duties included hides, horsehair, and precious metals.[41] Likewise the Catamarca tariff of 1828 imposed no duty upon the majority of exports. In most cases export duties were imposed with a view to providing revenues. These taxes worked to the disadvantage of the domestic producer, for they could not, at least ordinarily, be shifted forward to the ultimate consumer or the middleman. Sometimes export duties were imposed in order to encourage domestic industry or to prevent depletion of natural resources. Thus a relatively high export

---

[36] *Ibid.,* III, 31 (July 19, 1831). In 1834 the law of July 19, 1831 was suspended in view of the impending scarcity of domestic sugar. (*Ibid.,* III, 223.)

[37] *Ibid.,* III, 105 (October 29, 1832).

[38] *Registro Oficial de la Provincia de Corrientes,* L–1, no. 1 (January 6, 1825).

[39] *Recopilación,* I, 13 and I, 83.

[40] *Ibid.,* III, 8.

[41] *Compilación,* pp. 49 and 67.

duty upon horsehides was intended to prevent large scale slaughter of horses. At times the export of live cattle or horses was entirely prohibited.

Many provincial governments imposed taxes upon commodities which passed through their territories. These transit duties were generally determined without regard to the kind or value of the commodity in question. Weight or size of the load, rather than the value of the commodity, was the basis of assessment. So the Córdoba tariff of 1829 provided for a tax of 2 reales upon all parcels, of whatever origin, passing through the province. The transit duty upon wagons was 4 reales, and loads carried by mules paid 1 real per load.[42] In Catamarca transit duties varied in accordance with the origin and kind of commodity. Brandy was subject to a tax of 6 reales per load, wine 4 reales, and dried fruit 2 reales. But all foreign goods were required to pay a transit duty of 1 peso (8 reales) per load.[43] Entre Ríos had a transit duty of 2 per cent on all commodities, except tobacco, wine, and brandy.[44] Similar provisions were inserted in the tariff schedules of other provinces.[45]

Tariff schedules as well as other taxes were often revised and amended in response to the needs of the treasuries, and in accord with changes in the economic policies of the provincial governments. In the absence of national legislation, adjustments of interprovincial economic relations were largely a hit and miss affair. Economic wars were frequent, and they were mitigated rather than settled by bilateral and multilateral commercial treaties. As political and economic differentiation of the country became more pronounced, interprovincial rivalry grew more acute. Pending a general interprovincial agreement each province endeavored to secure the most advantageous bargaining position possible. And when the first serious attempt to settle the question of provincial autonomy failed with the dissolution of the Constituent Congress the struggle among the provinces became more virulent than ever. The expansion of provincial administrations demanded increased economic and financial sacrifices, and it was only natural that each province should try to shift the burden to other prov-

---

[42] Ibid., p. 67, cap. iv, art. 10, 11.

[43] Archivo General, loc. cit., Session, June 7, 1830.

[44] Recopilación, Entre Ríos, loc. cit.

[45] Cf. Registro Oficial de la Provincia de Jujuy, I, 14 (April 14, 1835); I, 18–21 (June 13, 1835); I, 44 (August 4, 1836). Also, Actas de la Sala de Representantes de la Provincia de Tucumán, Session 54 (September 5, 1834).

inces. Hence the tendency towards economic isolation, hence, also, the policy of discrimination against all extra-provincial commerce and industry. When the legislative assembly of Córdoba decided to increase the transit duty from 2 to 3 reales per package, it did so not only because the provincial treasury was exhausted, but also because other provinces had reverted to the same practice. So the legislature complained that

in La Rioja merchants from other provinces are required to sell their wares at retail, while in Santiago del Estero merchants are forced to pay 10 pesos in transit duties per wagon. Not only this, but the commerce of Córdoba suffers at present from the fact that merchants, who had previously traded in the province, leaving thirty to forty thousand pesos (in profits), have now transferred their activities to Buenos Aires.[46]

This declaration of the Córdoba legislature was not a sudden display of bad temper; it was rather a recognition of the deepening of interprovincial economic rivalries. It was a protest against the policies of economic exclusion as well as against the monopolization of national commerce by Buenos Aires. It reflected the intensification of the process of economic disintegration after the failure of the Santa Fe convention. And it served notice that the economic problem of which discriminatory taxation was a part was inseparable from the much broader problem of the political organization of the country.

3

The issues raised by the legislative assembly of Córdoba in its declaration of August 10, 1832 were not new. Ever since the rejection of the Constitution of 1819 the provinces had become increasingly aware that the constitutional question was as much an economic as a political question. The Constitution of 1819 made no attempt to deal with the economic and financial organization of the country, which was simply another way of sanctioning the post-revolutionary *status quo*. It had shown that so long as the central government remained under the influence of Buenos Aires the economic postulates of the Interior would in all probability be disregarded. It had shown, further, that in any central government the influence of Buenos Aires, given its superior eco-

---

[46] Cf. *Compilación*, p. 72, also, *Archivo de la H. Cámara de Diputados*, Session, August 10, 1832. Preamble to law of August 10, 1832 which raised the transit duty to 3 reales per package.

nomic and financial resources, was bound to predominate. If the provinces, therefore, were to escape the economic dominion of Buenos Aires it was essential that they retain some degree of economic and fiscal autonomy, and that the powers and authority of the central government should be more or less clearly defined. The rise of provincial governments during and after the crisis of 1820 was not only a reflection of social and economic disintegration; it was also a spontaneous protest against the complete subordination of local interests to those of Buenos Aires. By assuming control in matters of economic and fiscal policies the provincial governments laid down the fundamental principles of state organization. For whatever the ultimate form which the central government might take the provinces were determined to preserve their autonomy.[47] Home rule was for the provinces a defense against further encroachments upon their economic *status quo*. At the same time it was indispensable, if the cost of economic adaptation was to be reduced to a minimum.

It was, indeed, immaterial to the provinces whether the solution of the constitutional question was along unitary or federalist lines. One solution was as capable as the other of satisfying the more fundamental demands of the provinces. Whether a province favored the federalist or the unitary form of state organization depended upon the extent to which the policies of the central government could be expected to meet the needs of that province, rather than upon the philosophical principles underlying the two ideologies. Thus, while the provinces had secured from the Congress recognition of their autonomous status, which was clearly a step in the federalist direction, they yet supported most of the unitary political program. That unitarism was not compatible with provincial autonomy nor capable of meeting the economic demands of the provinces became clear only later, when the unitary party assumed full control of the national government.

Within the provinces political division resembled that of Buenos Aires. As in Buenos Aires so in the provinces the unitary party addressed itself primarily to the small but highly articulate groups of wealthy merchants and intellectuals, whose economic interests and cultural inclinations blended nicely with the liberal and progressive tendencies of the unitary ideology. Contact between provincial and

---

[47] One of the first acts of the Second Constituent Congress was to guarantee the political and institutional integrity of the provinces. *Asambleas,* vol. II, Law, January 21, 1825.

porteño unitaries was direct, unencumbered by interprovincial rivalries. For the unitaries the problem of specific provincial interests did not exist. Fully prepared to sacrifice the economic and financial integrity of Buenos Aires they were no less prepared to reject the demand for economic and fiscal autonomy in the provinces. Nor did the unitaries in the provinces insist upon home rule beyond what the Constitution of 1826 was willing to grant. On the contrary, their economic and political future depended precisely upon the abolition of interprovincial boundaries and upon the extension of the authority of the national government. They agreed, therefore, with the unitaries of Buenos Aires on the necessity of nationalization of land as well as of the most important sources of revenue, such as customs, stamp duties, license taxes, and other imposts.

The federalist parties lacked the unity of purpose so characteristic of their opponents. Concerned primarily with local problems, and with national problems only in so far as these affected provincial interests, the federalists of one province acted independently, and sometimes in opposition to the federalists of another. But while the various federalist parties differed among themselves on many important points of intra-provincial and national policy, they were nevertheless united on several fundamental issues. First, the federalists in every province recognized the importance of the constitutional problem, and were as anxious as the unitaries to see the country stabilized politically. Secondly, they were agreed that the political organization of the country must not be accomplished at the expense of provincial home rule. Finally, they held that the authority of the central government should be limited to matters of national concern, such as foreign affairs, peace and war, the collection and management of national revenues. The nationalization of customs revenues and their distribution on a pro rata basis among the provinces found enthusiastic supporters everywhere, except in Buenos Aires whose control over such revenue dated from the Revolution.[48] The issue of protection vs. free trade aroused a good deal of controversy, and here, too, Buenos Aires differed from the ma-

---

[48] So, for example, the legislative assembly of the province of Córdoba instructed its deputies to demand the nationalization of customs revenues. "Sera de forzosa obligación de los diputados promover que todos los derechos de importación y exportación marítima, se declaren nacionales, y en caso de presentarse proyectos para la habilitación de algunos otros puertos, cooperen del mismo modo." Cf. *Archivo de la H. Cámara de Diputados de la Provincia de Córdoba* (Córdoba: 1912–1914), vol. II, 419, *et passim*. Session, October 22, 1827.

jority.[49] Again, contrary to the wishes of Buenos Aires, the federalists in the Litoral provinces insisted upon having the Paraná river open to foreign navigation. Frequently the provinces which suffered most from economic dislocation clamored for a national solution of their problems.

At no time during the Constituent Congress did the federalists succeed in formulating a consistent political and economic program. When the Congress convened towards the end of 1824 in Buenos Aires neither the principles nor the implications of federalism as a political and economic doctrine were at all clear. The provinces came to the Congress hoping for such a settlement of the constitutional question as would not only confirm the political *status quo* evolved in 1820, but mark out the basic lines of future development. The question of political stabilization was uppermost in the minds of the deputies, but problems of an economic and financial nature were equally urgent. In the few intervening years between 1820 and the opening of the Congress economic conditions in many provinces had gone from bad to worse. The picture painted by Manuel Antonio Acevedo, deputy from Catamarca, applied not only to his own province but to others as well.

Fate [said the deputy], has brought about in Catamarca an ominous change. . . . Whether it is because of the extremely adulterated currency, which has burdened these regions ever since the deplorable dissolution of the state, or because of foreign competition in all markets . . . Catamarca has had to stand by helplessly, while its agriculture is primitive and costly, its industry without consumers . . . and its commerce by now almost non-existent.[50]

Catamarca was not even able to pay the living expenses of its representatives in Buenos Aires. Misiones, Santiago del Estero, and other provinces in the Interior were in a similar position.[51] The Constitutional Committee of the Congress to which the question of the representatives' salaries was referred argued that the provinces should be

---

[49] Article 4 of the instructions issued to the deputies from Tucumán reads: "Se hará presente al Ejecutivo Nacional por los diputados de la Provincia los perjuicios y ruinas que ocasiona a los pueblos interiores la libre e ilimitada introducción de toda clase de efectos extrangeros; se solicitan en consecuencia la prohibición al menos indirecta de aquellos artículos o frutos comerciales que producen las provincias del interior al fin de animar por ese medio la industria agricultora y la de otros ramos que en ellas se cultivan." Cf. *Acta de la Sala de Representantes de la Provincia de Tucumán* (Acta 33, Session, January 9, 1826).

[50] Cf. *Asambleas,* II, 5 (Session 40, June 7, 1825).

[51] Cf. *loc. cit.,* II, 105–116, 118–132, 168–171 (Sessions 51, 52, 57, August 8, 20, and September 19, 1825).

able to bear the expense, first, because the prospects of economic revival had improved considerably with the termination of the war
against Spain, and second, because the provinces had appropriated
revenues once belonging to the state.[52]   To the provinces these arguments must have sounded hollow (the representative of Misiones considered them insulting) for the prospects of economic expansion were
not as bright as the Committee liked to believe, nor were the provinces receiving their full share of the Confederation's revenue.   The
reasoning of the Constitutional Committee consisted in generalizing the
experience of Buenos Aires, and the reasoning was therefore specious.
It revealed how profoundly the unitary leaders misunderstood both the
nature and scope of the problem facing the provinces.   The war of
emancipation was neither the only nor even the most important cause
of the economic ills of the Interior.   The real cause was emancipation
itself, and the consequent separation of Buenos Aires from the rest of
the country.   The Constitutional Committee's faith in the economic
resurgence of the Interior following the termination of the war against
Spain was baseless, as the economic situation of the provinces amply
proved.   There the struggle was not against the ravages of war nor
against a wasteful administration, but against the strangling effects of
foreign and *porteño* competition.   The provinces believed, not without
reason, that Buenos Aires gained much of its wealth at the expense of
the country.   Were they not entitled to a share in this wealth? [53]   Indeed, the basic task of the Constituent Congress was to set up a political system which would assure a more equitable distribution of the
national dividend.   The very life of the Constituent Congress as well
as of the regime it endeavored to establish depended upon carrying
out this task.

That the Congress failed to carry it out was perhaps to be expected.
The majority of the Congress followed the leadership of the national

---

[52] Cf. *loc. cit.*, II, 168–171 (Session 57, September 19, 1825).

[53] These sentiments were quite unequivocally expressed by Lucio Mansilla, deputy from
Entre Ríos, in a speech defending the bill of nationalization of Buenos Aires.   Mansilla,
later one of the most devoted supporters of Rosas, said: "La provincia de Buenos Aires,
en los cinco años en que los pueblos han estado divididos perteneciendo a si mismos, ha
disfrutado de un derecho exclusivo sobre todos ellos, que es preciso que hoy se le quite
para dividirlo entre todos los pueblos.   La provincia del Entre Ríos ha tenido y tiene que
pagar respecto de la provincia de Buenos Aires todos sus efectos de alimento.   Y porque?
Será justo que Buenos Aires sostenga exclusivamente unos derechos que en realidad
pertenecen a todos los pueblos?   Esto no es justo. . . ."   Cf. *Asambleas*, II, 732–734 (Session, February 23, 1826).

government rather than the instructions of their constituents. And the political and economic program of the national government practically ignored the demands of the provinces. Nor is this surprising. The demands of the provinces not only ran counter to some of the major principles of the unitary doctrine, but threatened to undermine the economic position of those classes whose interests the unitary party championed.

For one thing the unitary party was traditionally opposed to protectionism. So far from heeding the demand of the provinces for higher duties on commodities which could be produced at home, the unitaries leaned towards further liberalization of the commercial policies of Buenos Aires. At the same time the Congress and the national government assumed sole authority in the formulation of foreign commercial policies. So the revenues derived from customs duties were brought under the national government's control. But the nationalization of customs duties was only the first step towards the solution advocated by the provinces. That solution called for the distribution of the proceeds among the provinces. The unitary party refused to take this next step. For it was clear that the distribution of customs revenues among the provinces was incompatible with the unitarian doctrine of centralization. A national government financially dependent upon the generosity of the provinces would of necessity remain politically impotent. On the other hand, the unitary solution which would place all revenues recognized as national under the unconditional control of the central government could not but arouse strong opposition in the provinces. Together with the nationalization of the city of Buenos Aires such an arrangement would not only enormously increase the political power of the national government, but would leave the economic supremacy of Buenos Aires intact. In an effort to placate the provinces the unitaries argued that the establishment of a national capital in Buenos Aires would destroy the economic and political power of the province of Buenos Aires.[54] Whether deliberately or not what the unitaries failed to see was that the country was less afraid of the province than of the city of Buenos Aires. This was made clear by Salta's representative, Juan Ignacio Gorritti, who opposed the federalization of Buenos Aires on the ground that as the center of the nation's resources the city would attract wealth from the provinces.[55] Gorritti was only

[54] Cf. *Asambleas*, II, 697–715 (Session, February 22, 1826). Speech by J. S. Agüero.
[55] Cf. *Asambleas*, II, 801–822 (Session, March 1, 1826). Speech by J. I. Gorritti.

voicing the attitude of the provinces, for the provinces had been complaining of the concentration of wealth in Buenos Aires ever since the establishment of the viceroyalty. Had the national government been willing to open the Paraná river to foreign navigation thereby deflecting a portion of the nation's overseas commerce to the provinces it would have probably allayed a good deal of the suspicion and fear of the provincial governments. But on this question as on so many others the unitary party was unwilling and unable to make concessions. Lacking the political support of the majority of the population it was essential for the unitary regime, still in process of organization, to exercise as rigid a control as possible over the economic and financial resources of the country. It was mainly for this reason that the unitary leaders in the Constituent Congress remained deaf to the protests and entreaties of the few representatives who took the instructions of their constituents seriously.

The Congress of Buenos Aires was a constituent assembly. Its primary task was the drawing up of a constitution, subject to the approval of the provincial legislatures. Yet, for nearly two years, the Congress postponed consideration of this fundamental problem. Early in April of 1826, i.e., after the Congress had been in session for fifteen months, President Rivadavia demanded immediate consideration of the constitution, for "nothing disturbed the provinces so much as the lack of a law which would delimit the powers and authority of the (central) government, and would at the same time guarantee their most valued rights. Such is the uniform demand of the people, and there is no reason why the representatives should disregard this demand." [56] Nevertheless, it was not until September of 1826 that the constitutional debate got under way, and by that time the question lost much of its poignancy. For in the intervening twenty months of legislative activity the Congress had shown unmistakably its preference for the unitary political system. In nearly all its measures dealing with national problems the Congress had anticipated the outcome of the constitutional discussion. With the outcome well known in advance the interest of the provinces in the discussion could have been hardly more than academic.

President Rivadavia was not mistaken when in his letter of April 4 he called the Constituent Assembly's attention to the growing restlessness of the population. But he was mistaken in ascribing this restless-

[56] Cf. *Asambleas*, II, 929 (Session, April 5, 1826).

ness to the Assembly's procrastination with respect to the constitutional question. Ever since the partition of Buenos Aires and the nationalization of the provincial capital, an act which was in patent contravention of the law of January 21, 1825, the provinces regarded the Congress with suspicion. They were anxious to do away with the Congress which far from reflecting the sentiments of the majority of the population had become instead an instrument of political oppression in the service of the unitary party. And when at last the constitution was submitted to the provinces, early in 1827, province after province refused to approve it. The unitary party acknowledged the defeat. The president resigned and the Constituent Congress voted its own dissolution. The provinces reverted to their pre-congressional status, eager to begin anew the task of the political organization of the country. But taught by bitter experience they were no longer willing to leave the question of the system of government to the discretion of a national congress. Acceptance of federalism as the basis of political organization became the *conditio sine qua non* of all interprovincial discussion. Argentina was a confederation of provinces *de facto*, and such it had to remain *de iure*. And the solution of the economic and financial problems facing the provinces had to be sought within the federalist framework.

CHAPTER VI

THE FIRST FEDERALIST ADMINISTRATION IN BUENOS AIRES

La federación era una palabra sin sentido. La realidad era el poder tiránico de la aduana de Buenos Aires que, con los recursos de toda la nación, tenía humilladas a las provincias.—CARLOS PEREYRA, *El pensamiento político de Alberdi* (Madrid: 1919).

Porque el caudillaje porteño aspiró tambien al aislamiento como su congénere provinciano, cuando dicho fenómeno lo engendro a su vez, relegando indefinitamente la constitución del país. . . ."—LEOPOLDO LUGONES, *Historia de Sarmiento* (Buenos Aires: 1931).

DON JUAN MANUEL ROSAS faced a difficult and complicated task when on December 6, 1829 he assumed the office of governor of the province of Buenos Aires. Ever since the resignation of Rivadavia the province and the country had been in a state of turmoil. The Lavalle-Rosas pact of June 24, 1829 and the additional agreement of August 24 of the same year, both of which paved the way to ultimate federalist control of the province, by no means ended the struggle between the two contending parties.[1] In spite of their defeat in Buenos Aires the unitaries were still powerful and, far from conceding victory to Rosas, they feverishly prepared for a political and military campaign designed to dislodge the federalist party from its newly won position of supremacy in Buenos Aires and the Litoral. Juan Lavalle, temporarily inactive, was ready at a moment's notice to lead the anti-federalist forces in the Litoral, and José María Paz consolidated his position in Córdoba and the Interior, emerging finally as the supreme

[1] The Lavalle-Rosas pact of June 24, 1829, signed by Lavalle in the name of the government of the city (*gobierno de la ciudad*) and by Rosas in the name of the armed people of the country (*pueblo armado de la campaña*), provided for cessation of hostilities, re-establishment of peaceful relations between the capital and the country, and immediate elections of representatives, who in turn were to designate the governor of the province. It was agreed also that one list of candidates be presented to the electors, each party being equally represented. The agreement of August 24 nullified the provision of the June pact referring to the election of governor. Lavalle and Rosas agreed upon Juan José Viamonte as provisional governor. See Adolfo Saldías, *Rosas y su época* (Buenos Aires: 1892), II, 9 ff.

commander of the military forces of the short-lived unitary league.[2] Civil war was imminent.

Had political stability of the Rosas regime depended solely upon a decisive military victory over the unitary forces the outlook, however uncertain, would not have been serious. The Unitary League while formidable was not invincible, and Buenos Aires in alliance with Santa Fe could accept the challenge with some degree of confidence. But the military struggle was merely one phase of the problem facing the federalist party. The war over,[3] there remained the much more difficult task of economic and political reorganization of the country. It may be well to recall that the great and fundamental problems which had agitated the country since the convocation of the Constituent Congress in 1824 were still awaiting solution. In the years immediately following the resignation of Rivadavia there was neither time nor opportunity to re-examine the constitutional question. But when, after the capture of Paz and the breakdown of the Unitary League, federalist victory seemed assured, the question of state organization became once more pressing. To the provinces in the Litoral as well as in the Interior the issue was of paramount importance. The federalist parties in the provinces were anxious to consolidate their position of local preëminence by obtaining constitutional sanction to the political pattern evolved since the dissolution of the Constituent Congress. A federalist constitution, such as the provinces envisaged, would not only insure local autonomy, but would also provide an adequate basis for normal economic and political intercourse between provinces. Without a federal government to stand guard over the rights and privileges of the provinces, political autonomy was almost meaningless. Regional hegemony of stronger provinces, such as Santa Fe in the Litoral or Córdoba in the Interior, was inevitable, just as it was unavoidable that Buenos Aires should once more constitute itself as the arbiter of the country's destinies.

It was precisely this eventuality that the provinces feared most. They realized that political hegemony of Buenos Aires meant continuation of the economic *status quo*. It meant that Buenos Aires would

---

[2] On the formation of the Unitary League (an alliance of Córdoba, Mendoza, San Luis, San Juan, Salta, Tucumán, Santiago del Estero, Catamarca, and Jujuy) see Antonio Zinny, *Historia de los gobernadores de las provincias argentinas. Edición reordenada, con un prólogo de Pedro Bonastre* (Buenos Aires: 1920–21), II, 245 ff.

[3] Civil war came to an abrupt end when José María Paz was accidentally taken prisoner by the *gauchos* of Estanislao López, March 10, 1831. With the imprisonment of Paz the Liga del Norte dissolved. See A. Saldías, *op. cit.*, II, 77 ff.

continue to exercise sole control over the country's economic policies; that it would continue to keep the internal ports closed to overseas trade; and that it would appropriate the nation's customs revenues. Unless, therefore, Buenos Aires was brought under federal control the provinces had no hope of ever improving their economic and financial condition. Coöperation of Buenos Aires, whether voluntary or enforced, was essential to the provinces. Without it the economic program of federalism was unrealizable, and the political doctrine of federalism lost all meaning and significance.

But the reasons which compelled the provinces to seek an early solution of the constitutional problem were of the kind which appealed least to the *porteños*. To relinquish control of the country's commercial policies, and to turn over customs revenues to a federal treasury was to surrender the political as well as economic integrity of the province. Had the economy of Buenos Aires formed an integral part of the national economy the sacrifice would have been relatively small, and at any rate temporary. But the economic interests of Buenos Aires, on the one hand, and those of the provinces, on the other, were not identical. Far from being identical they were frequently contradictory. The economy of Buenos Aires rested solidly upon large scale cattle breeding and foreign commerce. Abundance of cheap land and a free access to foreign markets were essential to the economic development of the province. Any policy, therefore, which tended to subvert these postulates aimed at the most vital interests of the province.

That the constitutional question was not purely a political problem but an economic one as well became evident as early as 1830 at the Santa Fe conference of representatives of Buenos Aires and the provinces of the Litoral. It was at this conference that Pedro Ferré raised in the name of Corrientes the question of nationalization of customs revenues, and demanded that the provinces be given a voice in the formulation of the country's commercial policies.[4] At the insistence of Buenos Aires these demands were rejected and Corrientes withdrew from the conference. But the issues raised by Ferré were by no means eliminated.

In a somewhat different form they came again to the surface early in 1832 when the Comisión Representativa invited the provinces to adhere

---

[4] Cf. *Memoria del brigadier general Pedro Ferré* (Buenos Aires: 1921); also *infra*, chaps. vii and viii.

to the Litoral pact, and to send representatives to Santa Fe.[5] The program of the projected Federal Congress was defined in section 5 of article 16 of the pact, and embraced some of the most fundamental problems facing the country, such as regulation of foreign and domestic commerce, collection and distribution of national revenues, river navigation, and the national debt. These were precisely the questions which Pedro Ferré, as the representative of Corrientes, wanted to have settled some two years before, during the preliminary discussions of the treaty of January 4, 1831.[6] But now the scope of discussion was much broader. In 1830 when Ferré demanded recognition of the economic interests of the provinces, the question of establishing a national government capable of assuming the functions performed until then by Buenos Aires was not a matter of practical politics. The situation was radically different in 1832. The military forces of the unitary party were all but annihilated, civil war as an instrument of political action seemed to have been discarded, and the provinces were gradually accepting the Litoral pact and the authority of the Comisión Representativa. One year after the signing of the Federal Pact six provinces out of thirteen were represented on the Comisión in Santa Fe, and when the call for a Federal Congress was sent out in March of 1832, two more

[5] Article 15 of the treaty of January 4, 1831 called for the establishment of a Comisión Representativa de los Gobiernos de las Provincias Litorales de la República Argentina, composed of representatives of the three signatory provinces. Provinces which joined the pact later were each entitled to one representative in the Comisión. At the time the Commission sent out the invitation it consisted of six representatives. The Comisión was to reside in Santa Fe. Its attributes were defined in article 16 of the pact, as follows: to conclude peace treaties in the name of the signatory provinces; to declare war; to order mobilization and designate the commander-in-chief; to determine the quota of armed forces for each of the contracting provinces; to invite other provinces to adhere to the pact and to send delegates to a General Congress (Congreso General Federativo) for the purpose of regulating the country's foreign and domestic commerce, of organizing the collection and distribution of revenues, navigation of rivers, etc. See Carlos Alberto Silva, *El poder legislativo de la nación Argentina* (Buenos Aires: 1938), vol. II, segunda parte, pp. 256–260; also Emilio Ravignani, *Historia constitucional de la República Argentina* (Buenos Aires: 1926), vol. III; also E. Ravignani (ed.), *Asambleas constituyentes argentinas, seguidas de los textos constitucionales legislativos y pactos interprovinciales que organizaron políticamente la nación* (Buenos Aires: 1937–1939), vol. IV and vol. VI, part 2, p. lxvii.

[6] It is of interest to note that the convocation of a Federal Congress was decided upon at the suggestion of Manuel Leiva, the delegate of Corrientes, which joined the *Pacto Federal* in September of 1831. See Carlos Alberto Silva, *op. cit.*, pp. 260 ff.; Emilio Ravignani, ed., *Asambleas constituyentes*, VI, 213, *Nota dirijida á la Comisiún Representativa de los Gobiernos de las provincias del litoral (por el comisionado de Corrientes don Manuel Leiva).*

provinces promptly accepted the invitation. Thus the economic problems outlined in section 5 of article 16 of the Litoral pact became the concern of the whole country, rather than of one region only. Moreover, official recognition was given to the fact that the economic problem and the problem of state organization were inseparable.

The projected Congress was to be composed of representatives of provinces which had accepted the pact of 1831. Consequently federalism was no longer an issue, and differences of opinion on this point were not expected. But no such unanimity was possible on the economic problems of the day. Indications of the forthcoming conflict appeared even before the Congress convened, and the issues were clearly drawn by Manuel Leiva, the representative of Corrientes, and Juan Bautista Marín, the delegate of Córdoba. In a letter to Tadeo Acuña, governor of Catamarca, Manuel Leiva expressed his views in the following manner:

The only province which will resist the formation of the Congress is Buenos Aires, because it will lose control of national revenues, which it utilizes to make war upon us, and because the Congress will endeavor to curtail foreign commerce, which is the most important source of revenues: but for these same reasons we, from the provinces, must work together in opposition to Buenos Aires in order to obtain control of our treasury and in order also to curb that commerce which wastes our wealth, has destroyed our industry, and has brought upon us frightful poverty. . . . You will readily understand that unless the problems defined in section 5 mentioned above are solved, our fatherland will continue to remain in a state of chaos; the condition of our country will continue to be precarious and inadequate, because it will lack a solid foundation; our commerce more and more ruinous; our industries destroyed by foreign competition; our rivers—unused by the commonwealth; our revenues monopolized by one province; and the whole country—poor and miserable.[7]

That Manuel Leiva was not merely stating personal views, but representing the position of Corrientes and other provinces, appears clearly from the letters written by Juan Bautista Marín, the delegate of Córdoba, to Tadeo Acuña and Paulino Orihuela, governors of Catamarca and La Rioja, respectively. In these letters Marín urged that the provincial delegates be instructed to act in accord with Santa Fe, Corrientes, Entre Ríos, and Córdoba, in order to make Buenos Aires respect the wishes of the country.[8]

The decision of the Comisión Representativa to convoke a national congress was a serious blow to Buenos Aires. There could be no

[7] Carlos Alberto Silva, *loc. cit.*, p. 276.
[8] *Ibid.*, p. 277.

doubt that the congress, dominated by the provinces, would disregard the special position of Buenos Aires. If the congress succeeded in establishing a national government it would have to nationalize customs revenues and to assume sole authority over the commercial and economic policies of the nation. It was clear, furthermore, that the congress would lend a ready ear to demands for more stringent protection of domestic industries, and that in an attempt to break the commercial monopoly of Buenos Aires it would be prepared to throw the river ports open to overseas commerce. Such solution of the problem Buenos Aires could not accept. The *porteño* federalists were not opposed to political unification of the country, but they insisted that such unification must not be accomplished at the sole expense of Buenos Aires. The federalist party of Buenos Aires rose to its position of political leadership on a program of defense of the economic and financial integrity of the province, and submission to the congress meant not only the destruction of the provincial economy but also the political death of the party.

Determined to thwart the initiative of the Comisión Representativa, Rosas decided to recall the *porteño* delegate José Ignacio Olavarrieta. The discovery of Leiva's and Marín's anti-*porteño* agitation provided merely an additional excuse for a step decided upon long before.[9] The *porteño* delegate withdrew from the Comisión on June 7, 1832. Consideration of Olavarrieta's withdrawal was postponed until the next session which took place on June 18. Leiva suggested that the Comisión issue a manifesto censuring Buenos Aires for infraction of the Litoral pact, but the Comisión took no action at this meeting. On July 13 the Comisión met again to consider a communication from Estanislao López. The governor of Santa Fe pointed out that the Comisión had accomplished all it could, and that the time had come to consider whether the Comisión had not outlived its usefulness. After a brief and perfunctory discussion the Comisión voted its own dissolution.

[9] The letters of Leiva and Marín were intercepted by Facundo Quiroga who transmitted them to Rosas. The latter demanded that Córdoba and Corrientes repudiate their delegates. José Vicente Reinafé, governor of Córdoba, promptly complied and recalled Marín from Santa Fe, but Pedro Ferré refused to heed Rosas' demand. In a letter to José Vicente Reinafé Rosas wrote: "Antes de llegar a noticia del infrascripto el desagradable suceso que ha dado lugar a la presente nota, había ordenado a su diputado en la Comisión Representativa se retirase, por haber ya cumplido el último deber para que le faculta el tratado de la liga en la atribución 5ª del artículo 16. Hoy, en el poder irresistible que ministran las revelaciones de la siniestra intriga de los enunciados diputados, reitera la orden para que se despida." See Carlos Alberto Silva, *op. cit.*, p. 280.

Olavarrieta accompanied his resignation from the Comisión Representativa with a declaration to the effect that the withdrawal of Buenos Aires did not in any way imply renunciation of the federal pact of 1831. On the contrary, Buenos Aires was prepared to participate in a federal congress whenever the political situation in the country became stabilized to a degree which would insure free and peaceful elections.[10] Rosas insisted that immediate convocation of a national congress would be worse than useless. The provinces, argued Rosas, lacked the political experience and the financial resources to tackle successfully the problem of national organization. Buenos Aires refused to take upon itself the burden of organizing and financing such a congress. In the past such efforts failed as they should have failed; for the very fact that the *porteño* government appeared to lead the movement was in itself sufficient to arouse suspicion among the provinces. Time must elapse before the provinces would attain political and economic maturity. Once the provinces are free to decide for themselves, the solution of the constitutional problem within the framework outlined in the treaty of January 4, 1831 should encounter no insurmountable difficulties.[11] And until such congress could be convoked Rosas was willing to respect provincial autonomy in the field of political and fiscal administration as well as in the field of commercial and economic policies.[12]

Rosas' argument against immediate convocation of a national congress carried no conviction outside of Buenos Aires. It was true, of course, that some provinces found it impossible to defray the cost of sending representatives to a federal congress, let alone to support a central government, but it was also true that the provinces were not receiving their share of national revenues. To argue, therefore, that a national assembly should not be convoked until the provinces prove their financial responsibility was to put the cart before the horse. For it was precisely from the congress that the provinces expected financial and economic relief. Nor did Rosas' reference to the political immaturity of the provinces appear very convincing. The argument was

10 This referred to the opening clause of section 5, article 16 of the Federal pact, which read: "Invitar a todas las demas provincias cuando estén EN PLENA LIBERTAD Y TRANQUILIDAD. . . ." See also Carlos Alberto Silva, *op. cit.*, p. 273.

11 Cf. Carlos Alberto Silva, *op. cit.*, pp. 308–312. Rosas' letter to Juan Facundo Quiroga (December 20, 1834).

12 By common consent the Buenos Aires government took over the conduct of the country's military and foreign affairs.

not new. It was used by the unitaries in the Second Constituent Assembly to demonstrate the need for a strong central government. At that time the federalists indignantly rejected the argument as specious. They pointed out that ever since 1820, and in some instances before then, the provinces had shown a remarkable ability to establish well-functioning regional administrations. If the federalist position was valid in Rivadavia's time it was certainly valid now, after the provinces had had eight more years of experience in self-government.

However, the provinces had no alternative but to accept Rosas' interpretation of the Federal pact. To defy Buenos Aires meant to plunge the country into a civil war for which the provinces were economically and politically unprepared. Nor were the provinces unanimous as to the advisability of concerted action against Rosas. In fact, the two most prominent federalist leaders outside of Buenos Aires, Estanislao López in the Litoral, and Juan Facundo Quiroga in the Interior, refused to support Pedro Ferré's anti-*porteño* campaign.

The policies of López and Quiroga may at first glance appear contrary to the interests of the provinces they represented, and of the Interior generally. But a closer examination of the political conditions in the country will reveal that under the circumstances no other policy was feasible. Both *caudillos* were, no doubt, aware that Buenos Aires could not be induced to participate in a national congress. They realized, also, that the Rosas administration was extremely popular in Buenos Aires, and that a war against the *porteño* government meant in fact a war against the population of the province. The outcome of such a war was at best uncertain, since the provinces had neither the resources nor the man power to insure a speedy and decisive victory. But even were the provinces victorious it was not at all certain that Buenos Aires could be forced to coöperate in solving the constitutional problem. Defeat of Rosas would mean also the defeat of the *porteño* federalist party, and in all probability the return of the unitaries to power. This latter eventually was much less acceptable than continuation of the Rosas regime, however selfish and domineering this regime was. Unlike the unitaries, Rosas formally recognized the principle of political and economic autonomy of the provinces, and he was also careful to leave the door open to settlement of the constitutional question at some future time. He declared, furthermore, that such settlement would have to rest upon federalist principles, and this in itself was a step toward the ultimate goal. The provinces had also reasons to believe that in return for political support Rosas might be willing to make economic concessions. In this the provinces were disappointed. Rosas could accomplish very little without impairing the economic and financial integrity of Buenos Aires, and this integrity Rosas and his party were determined to preserve at all costs.

2

The constitutional issue was not the only problem which Rosas and his party were called upon to solve. Equally important and even more immediate was the problem of consolidating the federalist regime and of reshaping the economic and financial policies of the province. The task of political stabilization was accomplished with relative speed and effectiveness. Five days after the election of Rosas the provincial legislature granted him extraordinary powers "to regulate, in conformity with the exigencies of present circumstances, the interior administration of the provinces in all their branches, preserving intact their liberty and independence; to minister to their necessities in the most efficacious manner; to thwart the attacks that the anarchists design against them; and to insure order and public tranquility." [13] In giving Rosas extraordinary powers the provincial legislature responded to the quite general demand for a strong government, capable of swift and decisive action, and unhampered by the requirements and procrastination of parliamentary procedure. The province needed peace, it needed a breathing spell in order to restore its economy shattered by war, revolutions, and drought. Temporary suspension of political liberties seemed a relatively small sacrifice, if it insured order and prevented political disturbances.[14]

[13] Law of December 6, 1829. Quoted from Ricardo Levene, A History of Argentina (Chapel Hill, North Carolina: 1937), p. 404. The full text of the law may be found in Recopilación de las leyes y decretos promulgados en Buenos Aires desde el 25 de mayo de 1810 hasta fin de diciembre de 1835 (Buenos Aires: 1836), part 2, pp. 1025–1026. In federalist terminology the term "anarchist" referred to unitaries.

[14] This attitude was voiced by "El Clasificador o El Nuevo Tribuno" in an editorial of November 30, 1831 (no. 61). Said the editorial: "Es tanta la devastación que ha sufrido nuestra provincia y tan copiosas las lágrimas que han derramado sus habitantes, de resueltas de las sangrientes escenas, de que los parricidas de diciembre han hecho a nuestro país, teatro y víctima, que todos los hombres buenos están justamente alarmados por el temor de la repetición de días tan calamitosos. Lo que han padecido les autoriza para no perdonar medida, ni escusar compromiso que los liberta de padecer segunda vez. De el mal ojo con que generalmente se mira la lenidad del gobierno para con los que pueblo cree cómplices, o coadjutores de la sedición parricida de diciembre. De aquí el

There was yet another reason which induced Rosas and his supporters to demand extraordinary powers. This was the circumstance that the federalist party was not unanimous on many political and economic issues which agitated the province. Differences within the federalist party appeared even before the election of Rosas to the governorship of the province,[15] and in the succeeding years the differences grew sufficiently wide to cause a split within the party. The moderates, known in contemporary political parlance as "lomos negros," desired a return to the liberal traditions of the twenties. They opposed the semi-dictatorial regime of the Rosas administration, and leaned toward reconciliation with the moderate elements in the unitary party. This tendency became especially pronounced under Juan Ramón Balcarce who succeeded Rosas as governor of the province. The Balcarce administration tried persistently to curb Rosas' influence in the political life of the province, but not without determined opposition of the extremists. In October of 1833, less than a year after he took office, Balcarce was forced to resign.[16]

Balcarce's resignation placed Rosas once more in a position of unquestioned leadership. Rosas' return to power was now merely a question of time. In an attempt to forestall dictatorship the provincial legislature designated Juan José Viamonte as provisional governor. But Viamonte was unable to cope with the political situation and tendered his resignation on June 27, 1834. The legislature turned to Rosas, who, however, refused the office (August 9, 1834). In a desperate effort to save its prestige the legislature sought gubernatorial candidates from among Rosas' closest collaborators. The governorship of the province was offered successively to Tomás M. Anchorena (August 14), Nicolás Anchorena (August 31), Juan Nepomuceno Terrero (September 22), and Ángel Pacheco (September 25).[17] It

---

deseo común (que puede ser vehemente, pero que es discreto) de que la autoridad se precaucione mas contra otras nuevas tentativas de los verdugos del estado Argentino. De aquí el clamor público, que es el sentimiento dominante de nuestra provincia, para que se adopten medidas mas eficaces, a fin que no zozobre el baguel del Estado."

[15] For a brief account of early dissensions in the federalist party see Emilio Ravignani, "Primeras disidencias entre los federales triunfantes, elección de Juan Manuel de Rosas, 1829" (*Boletín de la Junta de Historia y Numismática Americana*, IX, 5–23).

[16] Balcarce resigned under the pressure of the so-called *Revolución de los Restauradores* (October 11, 1833).

[17] See RO–681, L–13, no. –8; RO–683, L–13, no. –8; RO–684, L–13, no. –8; RO–689, L–13, no. –9; RO–691, L–13, no. –9; RO–692, L–13, no. –9; RO–693, L–13, no. –9; RO–702, L–13, no. –10.

was only when the federalist leaders refused to heed the call that the assembly turned again to Rosas. After protracted negotiations Rosas agreed to accept the office on condition that the legislature grant him dictatorial powers (*suma del poder público*). The legislature submitted and on March 7, 1835 passed the enabling act.[18]

The act of March 7, 1835 marked the definitive victory of the *porteño* federalists in their long struggle for power. From now on their main concern was to assure the continuance of the *status quo*. The task proved to be even easier since within the province Rosas encountered little opposition. In fact, the province had never had a government more popular than that headed by Rosas. Not only the landowners and the *gauchos* in the countryside, but also the meat producers, the artisans, and the small merchants in the city hailed Rosas and his administration as the only way of restoring peace and order to the war-torn province. Against the enthusiasm of the vast majority the dissident elements, exhausted and disillusioned, were powerless.

The progressive deterioration of the province's economic and financial condition was yet another consideration which induced the Junta de Representantes to strengthen the authority of the executive branch of the government. Contrary to expectations the conclusion of hostilities against Brazil was not followed by economic recovery. Hampered by political dissension and currency depreciation, foreign trade failed to regain the ground lost during the war. And toward the end of the decade, when depreciation seemed to have run its course, the province was hit by a prolonged drought which decimated the country's livestock and nearly destroyed agriculture. The province's foreign trade which in 1829 was valued at 36,836,704 paper pesos in imports, and at 25,561,940 paper pesos in exports,[19] decreased in 1831 to 26,144,545 pesos and 17,203,280 pesos respectively.[20] At the same time the volume of exportable produce brought from the country to Buenos Aires considerably declined. The number of hides brought to

---

[18] See RO–802, L–14, no. –3.

[19] *British Packet and Argentine News,* April 30, 1830 (vol. 6, no. 190), quoted from *Lucero,* April 1, 1830. The *British Packet* notes that the above figures, which are Customs House valuations, should be corrected for duties. The real value of foreign trade was estimated by the *British Packet* at 29,000,000 p. pesos for imports, and about 28,000,000 p. pesos for exports. A similar correction would, of course, apply to figures for 1831.

[20] *Archivo General,* Ant. C.30–A.5, no. 1. *Resumen de los valores de entrada y salida marítima puestos en los estados pasados a el Ministerio de Hacienda.*

Buenos Aires in 1830 was about 39 per cent less than in 1824, the last pre-war year. The decline in sheepskin deliveries was about 19 per cent, in wool about 23 per cent, in grease nearly 27 per cent, and in tallow as much as 70 per cent. The increase in the deliveries of horse hides, nutria skins, horsehair and horns was altogether insufficient to compensate for the losses in other commodities. It was not until 1831 that deliveries of cattle hides rose above the level of 1824. But whether the increase in volume was accompanied by a proportional increase in value is very doubtful, for export prices failed to keep pace with the price of gold.

TABLE 25

VOLUME OF EXPORTABLE COMMODITIES BROUGHT TO THE BUENOS AIRES MARKET
IN 1824, 1825, 1827, 1830, AND 1831

	1824	1825	1827 (9 mo.)	1830	1831
Cattle hides..........	155,963	126,608	65,321	94,516	205,136
Horse hides..........	2,678	1,666	1,268	6,925	6,359
Sheepskins..........	26,616	42,516	11,564	21,684	23,925
Nutria skins.........	26,832	32,592	9,300	34,666	58,610
Grease (arr.).........	5,355	4,174	5,043	3,917	2,347
Tallow (arr.).........	18,354	14,916	12,868	5,631	7,355
Wool (arr.)..........	10,086	16,725	4,362	7,802	30,683
Horsehair (arr.)......	4,129	6,048	4,140	5,942	8,414
Horns..............	142,960	102,763	109,739	250,359	572,045

Sources: *Gaceta Mercantil*, March 29, 1834 (no. 3248), Registro Estadístico, Sección 4, tablas 8, 7, Archivo General, Ant. C. 29–A.10–no. 5, Archivo General, S. 7–C. 9–A. 10–no. 7, Archivo General, Ant. C. 29–A. 3–no. 3.

Early in 1832 the *British Packet and Argentine News* described economic conditions in Buenos Aires in the following terms:

The country is now suffering from the calamity of a long drought and the stagnation of trade occasioned in great part by the late contentions amongst its citizens. It would be folly to disguise the fact that these disputes have not only paralyzed commerce, but they have struck a severe blow against that which is always its main support, viz.:—credit; and nothing but a continuance of internal peace can restore confidence, and renovate the nearly despairing hopes of the merchant and trader.[21]

The *Packet's* concern about conditions in the province was only too well founded. The war of 1825–1828 had placed a heavy burden upon the treasury and had also disorganized the monetary system of the province. The process of financial disintegration continued throughout Dorrego's term, and became especially rapid during the crucial months of the unitary revolt.

[21] January 7, 1832; vol. 6, no. 281.

That deficits were at the root of financial difficulties was recognized by everyone. It was also generally agreed that so long as the political situation remained unsettled deficits were unavoidable. Restoration of financial stability presupposed long-range planning on the part of the government. Such planning entailed drastic changes in the pattern of both expenditures and revenues. It implied, on the one hand, a permanent reduction of military expenses and curtailment of many services hitherto financed by the government, and, on the other, a revision of the existing revenue system and the creation of new sources of income. Of necessity, realization of such a program required time; it presupposed also a united and determined administration, reasonably certain of its tenure of office and willing to bear the burden of responsibility. The experience of the provisional administration of Juan José Viamonte was not wasted upon the provincial legislature and the population at large. It had demonstrated that a long-range fiscal policy, no matter how sound or well intentioned, was doomed in advance precisely because the government lacked the means and the authority to enforce it. It supplied one more reason and additional justification for conceding Rosas dictatorial powers.

In the three years of his first administration Rosas did not succeed in bringing about complete economic and financial recovery. He failed to reduce the province's public indebtedness or to balance the budget. But he was successful in arresting the process of financial deterioration. He had demonstrated that expenditures could be considerably curtailed, that the system of accounting of public funds could be improved, and that public credit could be rehabilitated. Moreover, by abstaining from new currency issues Rosas succeeded in stabilizing the value of paper money. These accomplishments, however modest, could not fail to create a profound impression. They stood out even more clearly in the months following the retirement of Rosas, when with the revival of internal political dissension the province found itself once more upon the brink of financial bankruptcy. Rosas and most of his collaborators became convinced that nothing short of dictatorship could save the province from disaster.

So the act of March 7, 1835, investing Rosas with dictatorial powers, was not only a weapon of political warfare but was also an instrument of economic and financial policy. The economic implications of the measure were as important as its political consequences. For Rosas personified both, the political doctrine as well as the economic program of *porteño* federalism. It was a program of economic isolation from, and political domination over, the rest of the country; a program as selfish as it was injurious to the most vital interests of the Interior and the Litoral. In order to realize this program Rosas needed the undivided support of the whole province, and, lacking that, unlimited authority and power to use and dispose of the province's political and financial resources. Rosas' demand for dictatorial powers was admittedly contrary to tradition of independent Argentina, but it was in accord with the practices of the times, with that difference that while in other countries dictatorship paraded under the cloak of parliamentary democracy, here it was open and explicit, based upon and sanctioned by an act of parliament. The *porteño* legislature simply bowed to the inevitable. It administered the coup de grâce to a system which, transplanted from foreign soil, could never thrive in the stormy climate of the River Plate. And as the last vestiges of democracy were disappearing from the *porteño* political scene the federalist organ, *Gaceta Mercantil,* was writing its obituary, which was at the same time an apologia of the new regime.

The condition of the country, its fundamental interests, its imperative and urgent needs, have molded the principles of a singular policy to fit the most unusual, not to say unique, circumstances . . . a policy based upon experience acquired during twenty-six years of violent social change; a policy founded upon exact knowledge of events and men; a policy based upon strict and careful observance not of dreamy idealism of an absolute theory, ever inapplicable to the special circumstances of each society, but of those rules which a discerning and practical study of the totality of causes, effects and events constituting the mode of existence of the State derives from the very core of the revolutions, and which therefore supply the measure of its needs and requirements.[22]

[22] July 25, 1836; no. 3937.

CHAPTER VII

FEDERALIST FINANCES IN BUENOS AIRES, 1829–1835

No hay proyectos bastantes, no hay plan ninguno que pueda salvar al país del estado en que se halla. No bastaría que el gobierno digese hoy: a nadie debo nada, olvidense los acreedores de lo que los debo. No por esto el gobierno marcharía desembarazado en adelante; no habiendo economía volverían a aglomerarse las dificultades que se aumentarían por las consequencias de aquella negativa.—From a speech by deputy NICOLÁS ANCHORENA, Junta de Representantes, Session 466, November 5, 1834.

WHEN in August of 1829 Juan José Viamonte assumed the governorship of Buenos Aires the province was rapidly heading toward bankruptcy. Symptoms of impending collapse were visible everywhere. In the twenty-nine months, from July 31, 1827 to November 31, 1829, the treasury accumulated a deficit of nearly seven million pesos.[1] The province's indebtedness to the Banco Nacional grew from 11 million to 18 million pesos, and the amount of paper money in circulation increased from 9,495,143 pesos in January 31, 1828 to 15,289,076 pesos in October of the following year.[2] Yet money was scarce; short term obligations of excellent security, such as treasury bills, commanded a rate of about 2 per cent per month and, for commercial paper, rates of 4 per cent per month were not uncommon.[3] The treasury's credit position was so weak that although the government did no long term borrowing after September of 1827, bonds of the Fondo Público were selling at an average discount of about 43 per cent.[4] At the same time the value of the paper peso depreciated from about 30 per cent of par in January of 1828 to less than 17 per cent of par in October of 1829.[5]

Viamonte took a long range view of the problem facing the provincial treasury. He rejected, therefore, measures which offered only

[1] On July 31, 1827 the accumulated deficit amounted to 8,225,000 pesos. It stood at over 15,000,000 pesos in December 1829. Cf. *supra*, chap. iii, p. 66, Table 13.

[2] *Estado de la emisión del Banco hasta la fecha de oy, a saver* (Report of Larrea, President of the Banco Nacional, dated October 1829). Cf. *Archivo General*, Ant. C.21–A.–no. 7.

[3] Cf. *infra*, chap. x, p. 266.

[4] See *infra*, Table 32.

[5] See *supra*, chap. iii, Table 14.

temporary relief. In his opinion the chaotic condition of provincial finances was due primarily to inflation, which undermined public credit and rendered illusory all efforts to balance the budget. Stabilization of currency was an essential condition of recovery. But this alone was not sufficient, for inflation had so reduced the value of money that the province's revenues no longer sufficed to cover expenditures. And since the government was not prepared to advocate increased taxes it suggested the alternative of restoring the value of the paper peso to parity. Viamonte, no doubt, understood the difficulties which his program implied, but he was convinced that nothing short of complete restoration of the gold value of the peso could save the treasury from disaster.

The manner in which Viamonte proposed to realize his program was outlined in several decrees. One of these established the Caja de Amortización de Billetes de Banco, to which was entrusted the task of directing the currency policy.[6] The decree assigned to the Caja the following funds: first, revenues from special taxes upon cattle slaughtered in Buenos Aires; secondly, additional duties on imports; thirdly, half the income from license taxes and stamp duties; and finally, the proceeds from the *derecho de pregonería*.[7] The government undertook also to transfer to the Caja whatever dividends it received from the Banco Nacional[8] and, finally, the Banco Nacional was permitted to raise the discount rate to 12 per cent, on condition that the additional income be turned over to the Caja de Amortización.[9] The Caja was explicitly prohibited from using its funds for purposes other than retirement of bank notes.[10] Currency earmarked for retirement was to be destroyed publicly at monthly intervals.[11]

The Caja de Amortización began operations on November 16, 1829, and two months later it announced the withdrawal from circulation of 131,460 pesos. However, the Caja did nothing thereafter. It continued to accumulate funds until the end of 1832, nearly four million pesos in all, but remained otherwise inactive. The failure to accom-

---

[6] Decree, October 3, 1829 (*Recopilación*, part 2, pp. 998–1000). The provincial legislature approved all the decrees relating to the organization of the Caja de Amortización on October 18, 1830 (RO–127, L–9, no. –11).

[7] Decree, September 18, 1829 (RO–122, L–8, no. –9). Decree, October 2, 1829 (RO–125, L–8, no. –10).

[8] Decree, October 6, 1829 (*Registro Nacional*, no. 2350, II, 248).

[9] *Recopilación*, part 2, p. 1002.

[10] Article 7 of the decree of October 3, 1829.

[11] Article 8, *ibid*.

plish anything more tangible than the retirement of some 130,000 pesos was due partly to the critical condition of the treasury, and partly also to the fact that neither Rosas nor the legislature was prepared to continue Viamonte's policy of deflation. For one thing the Caja proved to be too successful as a collecting agency. The government could not afford to sacrifice the funds which flowed into the Caja at the rate of over one million pesos a year.[12] By November 1831 the Amortization Office had accumulated over 2,000,000 pesos, while the government's short term debt reached the unprecedented total of nearly 3,000,000 pesos, on which interest charges alone amounted to about 150,000 pesos per month.[13] Rather than convert the treasury bills into long term bonds, an operation which would necessitate the issue of nearly 5,000,000 pesos in Fondos Públicos,[14] the government proposed to utilize the funds accumulated in the Caja de Amortización.[15] The legislature fearing that a new issue of Fondos would adversely affect the bond market readily approved the government's plan. It insisted, however, upon repayment of the funds taken from the Caja. Repayment was to be accomplished in monthly installments of 50,000 pesos, the first installment to begin in January 1833.[16] However, when this provision of the law was due to go into effect, the legislature revoked the obligation of repayment and suspended the operation of the Amortization Office for one year.[17] The suspension proved to be permanent, for the Caja was never revived.

From the very outset Viamonte's program of financial rehabilitation by way of deflation was doomed to failure. Had Rosas been able to take a long range view of the province's financial problems he might

[12] On the operations of the Caja de Amortización, see Tables 26 and 27.

[13] See Letter of Manuel José García, Minister of Finance, to the Junta de Representantes (*Diario de Sesiones,* Session of November 5, 1831).

[14] Provided, of course, that these bonds could be floated at about 60 per cent of par, which in view of the state of the money market was very doubtful. The bonds of the Fondo Público were quoted at 57.50 in November, as compared with 79.50 in January and 63.50 in May. It was only reasonable to assume that additional issues would depress bond prices still further.

[15] The operation was a complicated one. Much of the Caja's funds was already invested in government securities the issue of which was authorized by law of February 21, 1830. The government planned either to sell these bonds in the open market or to use them for the redemption of treasury bills. Either operation was certain to depress bond prices.

[16] Law, December 12, 1831 (*Recopilación,* part 2, p. 1106), also *Diario de Sesiones,* Sessions of December 7 and 9, 1831.

[17] Law, January 30, 1833 (*Registro Oficial*).

have been inclined to accept Viamonte's plan. But long range planning was at this stage a luxury which the government could not afford. The treasury needed immediate relief, and that was precisely what Viamonte's plan could not offer. On the contrary, if carried out, the program would in its initial stages impose a heavy burden upon the provincial treasury. The government would have to plan a substantial increase in taxes, or else force the creditors to accept a more or less drastic revision of their claims. Such were the alternatives, and rather than choose between them Rosas preferred to abandon Viamonte's program altogether and to meet each financial emergency as it arose.

TABLE 26

Funds Collected by the Caja de Amortización de Billetes de Banco

Period	Funds Collected	Total Funds Collected
Nov. 16, 1829–Dec. 31, 1829	131,460$ 0	
Jan. 1, 1830–Jan. 31, 1831	1,109,733$ 7½	1,241,193$ 7½
Feb. 1, 1831–Mar. 31, 1831	259,648$ 0	1,500,841$ 7½
Apr. 1, 1831–Nov. 15, 1831	750,411$ 6	2,251,253$ 5½
Nov. 16, 1831–June 30, 1832	880,070$ 0	3,131,323$ 5½
July 1, 1832–Dec. 31, 1832	710,050$ 0	3,841,373$ 5½

Sources: Archivo General, Ant. C. 22—A. 1—no. 8; *British Packet and Argentine News*: v. 5, no. 233; v. 5, no. 242; v. 6, no. 274; *Registro Oficial*: L–11, no. 6; L–11, no. 12.

TABLE 27

Revenues and Disbursements of the Caja de Amortización, November 16, 1829–December 31, 1832

Revenues		Disbursements	
Stamp duty...........	252,565$ 5	Notes burned (Jan. 16, 1830)	131,460$ 0
License tax...........	315,533$ 4	Transferred to the Treasury:	
Cattle tax............	661,445$ 3½	May 28, 1832.............	2,849,509$ 5½
Tariff duties..........	2,447,845$ 1	June 30, 1832	150,000$ 0
Bank discount........	109,508$ 7½	July 31, 1832	100,000$ 0
Pregonería tax........	54,071$ 0½	Aug. 31, 1832	120,000$ 0
Confiscation..........	70$ 0	Sept. 30, 1832	130,000$ 0
Cash................	284$ 0	Oct. 31, 1832	120,000$ 0
		Nov. 30, 1832	120,000$ 0
		Dec. 31, 1832	120,000$ 0
		Cash	354$ 0
Total.............. 3,841,323$ 5½		Total .... 3,841,323$ 5½	

Source: *Registro Oficial:* L–11, no. 12.

On purely economic grounds, too, deflation appeared to be ill advised. It was launched at a time when the province was in the throes of a severe depression. In such circumstances deflation, with its aftermath of falling prices, rising real wages, and scarce money, was dangerous. It was not abundance but scarcity of money that the provincial economy feared most. Any policy whose immediate effect was to restrict whatever credit was still available would serve to intensify the process of deterioration of production and commerce. Buenos Aires was especially sensitive to price changes, in as much as its economy was closely dependent upon foreign markets. Currency depreciation had greatly stimulated all productive activity linked with the export trade, and a reversal of the process would tend to weaken the competitive position of *porteño* producers. Of all the economic groups in Buenos Aires the *hacendados* and the *saladeristas* stood to lose most from deflation, and were therefore least interested in seeing Viamonte's program realized. As property owners, as employers of labor, and as exporters they had derived considerable advantages from currency depreciation. It was only when the money and credit situation threatened to become completely demoralized that the federalist leaders raised the question of monetary stabilization.[18] But they did not wish to go beyond mere stabilization.

There was yet another consideration which made deflation unacceptable to the federalist party. It was obvious that deflation would materially strengthen the position of the Banco Nacional. This institution had always been considered sympathetic to the unitary cause, and was even now reputed to be the center of unitary opposition. A deflationary policy would play into the hands of the unitaries. It would, in fact, provide the opponents of the newly established regime with the sinews of war. Therefore, in the federalist view, continuation of a policy designed to restore the gold value of the peso was not only inexpedient but even dangerous.

Repudiation of Viamonte's program of monetary deflation did not imply the return to the practice of financing government expenditures by means of bank note issues. For political as well as economic reasons Rosas and the federalist party were as much opposed to inflation as they were averse to deflation. To begin with, any financial plan based upon currency expansion implied the coöperation of the Banco Nacional. The government could hardly expect the bank to coöperate except on the basis of reciprocity. This the federalist party wished to avoid. Rosas could, of course, compel the bank to coöperate with the

---

[18] Cf. Mabragaña, I, 248. Message of May 1830, signed by Anchorena, Balcarce, and García.

treasury by means of legislative action, but this was certain to provoke bitter opposition in the Junta de Representantes, where the bank had several able and influential defenders. Rosas was still more reluctant to turn for help to the bank since it was doubtful whether currency expansion served any useful purpose. Depreciation of the peso was particularly damaging to government credit, creating an almost insuperable obstacle to long term borrowing operations. Nor could the government disregard the effect of inflationary policies upon the economic life of the province, as well as upon the various economic groups. It was generally realized that currency depreciation bred speculation and immoderate spending, and the government was anxious to arrest this tendency. It hoped that "the example of frugality and economy will exercise a powerful influence upon the population's habits which are now threatened by the dreadful effects of unjustified luxury and of unchastened, haughty and exacting idleness." [19] Then, too, it was neces-

TABLE 28

MONTHLY AND YEARLY AVERAGE PRICES PAID FOR ONE OUNCE OF GOLD ON THE BUENOS AIRES STOCK EXCHANGE

Months	1830	1831	1832	1833	1834	1835
January	104	114⅜	106⅞	110⅓	120⅓	118⅜
February	111½	124⅔	108⅖	117½	119½	119½[20]
March	128¼	124⅛	109⅓	119⅔	119	120½
April	138	123⅝	112½	119⅘	118⅞	119¾
May	124½	117	113¼	119	118⅛	119
June	116⅛	107⅔	113⅛	120¼	177⅞	118
July	115¾	106¾	112⅝	123	117¾	117¾
August	117	106	112⅞	123⅜	118	118
September	116⅘	104⅜	113	123½	117⅝	—
October	116	100¾	113¾	127⅜	118	117¾
November	114½	104¾	113	122⅓	118	118
December	112¾	104⅞	112¾	118½	—	118⅝
Average	118	111½	117⅞	120⅜	118½	118⅝

Source: Pedro Agote, *Informe del Presidente del Crédito Público . . . sobre la Deuda Pública , Bancos y Emisiones de Papel Moneda y acuñación de Monedas de la República Argentina* (Buenos Aires: 1881), I, 126–127.

sary to consider the incidence of inflation. The classes which suffered most from inflation (wage earners, shopkeepers, artisans, and salaried officials) were those least able to bear the burden. Continued deterioration of the economic position of these classes was politically dangerous, so that unless the government succeeded in stabilizing the peso it was certain to lose all popular support.

[19] Mabragaña, I, 248 (Message of May 1830).

At no time during his first administration did Rosas or his Minister of Finance, Manuel José García, issue a detailed statement on monetary policy. Nor did the legislature express any opinion in this matter. If, therefore, the monetary policy is described here as one of stabilization it is because the value of the paper peso remained actually relatively stable throughout the first half of the thirties. In the five years from 1830 to 1834 gold prices moved within comparatively narrow limits.[20] The price of gold fluctuated more violently in the first two years of Rosas' administration reflecting the extremely difficult position of the provincial treasury. It was generally feared that the government might be forced to have recourse to note issues, but in the early months of 1831 these fears were unfounded. In matters of economic and financial policies Rosas proved himself to be quite orthodox; and also politically the new regime became more secure. The declared policy of Rosas was to "maintain intact the guarantees accorded to the circulating medium," and he carefully refrained from interfering with the "administration in charge of currency," i.e., with the Banco Nacional.[21] Rosas' successors, Balcarce and Viamonte, continued this policy. Nevertheless, as the political outlook became once more uncertain, and the condition of the treasury took a turn for the worse, the price of gold in Buenos Aires rose from an average of about 111 pesos per ounce in 1832 to about 120 pesos in 1833, and 118 pesos in 1834.

2

That Rosas and his successors, Juan Ramón Balcarce and Juan José Viamonte, managed to avoid having recourse to paper money issues should not be taken as evidence of any fundamental improvement in the financial condition of the province. It is true that by dint of strict economy and careful accounting Rosas was able to close the first year of his administration with a surplus of nearly 1,800,000 pesos. However in each of the four following years revenues were short of expenditures. In 1831 the treasury ended the fiscal year with a deficit of over 4,000,000 pesos, and in 1832 and 1833 disbursements exceeded income by about 1,500,000 and 600,000 pesos respectively.[22] In the

[20] See Table 28. Attention is called to the fact that the yearly averages as shown in the table are those calculated by Pedro Agote. They are not quite accurate. These averages should read: 111¾ for 1831, 111¹⁄₁₂ for 1832, 120¹³⁹⁄₃₆₀ for 1833, 118⁵⁄₁₁ for 1834, and 118⁷⁄₁₁ for 1835. The error, it will be noted, is insignificant.

[21] Mabragaña, I, 266. Message to the legislature, May 7, 1832.

[22] See Tables 29 and 30.

TABLE 29

REVENUES AND EXPENDITURES OF THE PROVINCE OF BUENOS AIRES FOR THE YEARS 1830, 1831, 1832, 1833, 1834

	Revenues									
	1830 Paper pesos	%	1831 Paper pesos	%	1832 Paper pesos	%	1833 Paper pesos	%	1834 (6 mo.) Paper pesos	%
Customs	9,131,712$ 5	75.7	6,151,326$ 5½	68.4	7,340,088$ 3½	68.9	9,060,366$ 6¼	74.0	3,084,309$ 3¾	63.5
New duties	1,196,971$ 0½	9.9	1,174,762$ 0½	13.1	1,253,925$ 3¾	11.8	1,497,731$ 5½	12.2	570,550$ 3½	11.7
Stamp duty	388,210$ 2	3.2	387,635$ 0½	4.3	454,029$ 7½	4.3	382,229$ 0	3.1	267,888$ 0	5.5
Property tax	386,413$ 7¼	3.2	359,775$ 5	4.3	316,249$ 7½	3.0	383,209$ 2¾	3.1	132,128$ 0¾	2.7
Port dues	131,749$ 0	1.1	103,426$ 5	1.1	99,310$ 7½	0.9	130,001$ 0	1.1	46,883$ 0	1.0
Cattle tax										
Sales of land	56,011$ 2	0.5	140,490$ 0	1.6	529,762$ 4	4.9	18,053$ 3½	0.2	552,575$ 0	11.4
Interest and rent	706,140$ 4¾	5.9	657,791$ 3	7.3	520,098$ 6¼	4.9	641,717$ 5½	5.3	154,008$ 6¾	3.2
Emphyteusis										
Various	58,040$ 3	0.5	14,026$ 7¾	0.2	143,856$ 3¼	1.3	126,519$ 7¼	1.0	48,743$ 4¾	1.0
Total	12,055,249$ 0½	100.0	8,989,234$ 3¼	100.0	10,657,322$ 3¼	100.0	12,239,819$ 6¾	100.0	4,857,086$ 3½	100.0

	Expenditures									
	1830 Paper pesos	%	1831 Paper pesos	%	1832 Paper pesos	%	1833 Pesos	%	1834 (6 mo.) Pesos	%
Government	1,842,983$ 2⅝	18.0	1,610,203$ 5½	12.1	1,749,281$ 2¼	14.2	1,769,342$ 4½	13.7	1,745,989$ 1¾	17.2
Foreign Aff.	229,381$ 2¾	2.9	93,040$ 7	0.7	171,675$ 7⅜	1.4	162,145$ 4	1.3	130,391$ 7½	1.3
Treasury	2,815,984$ 6½	27.4	3,541,012$ 5½	26.6	399,623$ 1¾	3.2	419,232$ 2½	3.2	572,003$ 0¾	5.6
Int. and amort.					1,232,341$ 7½	10.1	1,035,199$ 3½	10.1	705,099$ 6	6.9
Discounts					986,876$ 3⅛	8.1	804,974$ 0⅝	6.2	940,054$ 6¾	9.3
War	5,317,990$ 3¼	51.7	8,016,886$3 ¼	60.1	7,089,811$ 7⅛	57.9	7,878,694$ 6¼	61.1	6,057,549$ 3¼	59.7
Justice					579,846$ 4¾	4.7	563,717$ 1	4.4		
Various			70,500$ 0	0.5	45,000$ 0	0.4				
Total	10,276,340$ 1⅛	100.0	13,331,643$ 5¼	100.0	12,245,397$ 1⅞	100.0	12,903,305$ 6⅜	100.0	10,151,088$ 2	100.0

Source: *Registro Oficial:* L–9, no. –13; L–10, no. –12; L–11, no. –12; L–12, no. –12; L–13.

TABLE 30

PUBLIC INDEBTEDNESS OF THE PROVINCE OF BUENOS AIRES FOR THE YEARS 1829, 1830, 1831, 1832, AND 1833

	1829	1830	1831	1832	1833
Debts					
Banco Nacional	18,126,026$ 0½	17,465,254$ 7¾	16,848,597$ 1¾	19,346,456$ 7¼	19,346,456$ 7¼
Treasury bills	877,464$ 1¾	199,611$ 7	2,656,018$ 4	1,335,481$ 4⅛	1,725,749$ 3
Deposits	835,666$ 0	831,354$ 7½	836,564$ 2	871,513$ 0½	840,968$ 3¾
Various debts	77,810$ 2¾	90,320$ 5	91,758$ 6	88,026$ 5½	95,394$ 0
Total	19,916,966$ 5	18,586,542$ 3¼	20,432,938$ 5¾	21,641,478$ 1⅜	22,008,568$ 6
Credits					
Bank shares	3,089,166$ 7½	3,084,000$ 0	3,084,000$ 0	3,000,000$ 0	3,000,000$ 0
Collector Gen'l	1,141,690$ 3½	1,225,751$ 6¾	1,620,561$ 2¾	930,497$ 7	672,264$ 5¾
Treasuries	122,979$ 3½	90,104$ 3¾	107,086$ 1¾	54,689$ 5⅝	249,961$ 0
Various credits	455,617$ 1½	634,997$ 4	851,162$ 3¾	850,048$ 3⅛	905,890$ 7¼
Total	4,807,454$ 0	5,043,853$ 6½	5,662,810$ 0¼	4,835,235$ 7¾	4,828,116$ 5
Deficit	15,109,512$ 5	13,542,688$ 4¾	14,770,128$ 5½	16,806,242$ 1⅜	17,180,452$ 1

Source: *The British Packet and Argentine News*, nos. 182, 235, 285, 339.

course of four years, from 1830 to 1833, the treasury had accumulated a deficit of nearly 5,000,000 pesos. About two-thirds of this deficit was covered with proceeds from the sale of Fondos Públicos. The remainder, over 2,000,000 pesos, was met with treasury bills and other short term obligations. Financing by means of treasury bills was particularly heavy in 1831. At the end of that year the short term debt stood at 2,848,597 pesos as compared to a debt of 199,611 pesos at the end of 1830. In the course of 1832 and 1833 the treasury managed to reduce the short term debt by 1,000,000 pesos. Nevertheless at the beginning of 1834 the total deficit exceeded 17,000,000 pesos.

TABLE 31

GROWTH OF TREASURY DEFICIT IN THE PERIOD FROM 1830 TO 1833

Year	Actual yearly deficit	Cumulative deficit	Yearly increase or decrease
1829		15,321,597$ 4¼	
1830	1,778,908$ 7½	13,542,688$ 4¾	1,778,908$ 7½
1831	4,342,409$ 2	14,770,128$ 5½	1,227,440$ 0¾
1832	1,588,074$ 6⅜	16,806,242$ 1⅝	2,036,113$ 4⅛
1833	663,485$ 7⅜	17,180,452$ 6	374,210$ 4⅜

As the amount of treasury bills outstanding grew and the money market showed increasing resistance to new issues, the government turned to long term borrowing. In 1831 the legislature approved the issue of 6,000,000 pesos in bonds of the Fondo Público. These bonds were to be deposited as security against funds withdrawn from the Caja de Amortización de Billetes de Banco.[23] But when the program of currency retirement was abandoned the government utilized the bonds for budgetary purposes. Again, in 1832 the provincial government ordered the Tribunal de Comercio to distribute among merchants, landowners, and cattle breeders 4,000,000 pesos in bonds at 50 per cent of par.[24]

[23] Laws, February 21, 1831 (RO, L–10, no. –2, pp. 37–38, 39–40). For each peso withdrawn from the Amortization Office the government deposited 1½ pesos in bonds.

[24] RO–306, L–11, no. –2 (February 3, 1832). The bonds were fully subscribed, although not without considerable pressure on the part of the government. On February 14, 1832 the *Gaceta Mercantil* claimed in a leading article that the proposed distribution of bonds was neither a loan nor a forced contribution, but rather "a spontaneous private undertaking" (una espontánea empresa particular). Yet ten days earlier the *Gaceta* wrote (February 4, 1832): "Si un sentimiento de patriotismo no impele a los capitalistas a enrolarse en la propuesta subscripción el interés individual se lo aconseja con instancia; pues si fallase este proyecto de desembarazar la tesorería de sus dificultades no es de

In the opinion of the *British Packet and Argentine News* this loan relieved "the Treasury from the 'dead weight' which paralyzed its operations, (enabled) it to discharge all pressing demands, and (threw) a great deal of money into circulation." The editorial went on to say that the loan had made superfluous

all idea of contributions, loans or new issues of bank paper, giving at the same time confidence to the govenment, and additional security to the stockholder, who now need not fear any material depreciation in the prices, certain that those who hold the new stock will not throw it at once upon the market, but will "feed it" (using a London stock exchange phrase) as occasion requires.[25]

This view was altogether too optimistic. In the first place, bond prices depreciated by more than 15 per cent immediately after the loan was launched.[26] And in the second place, the loan brought only temporary relief. Thus far from being able to balance receipts and expenditures the treasury closed the fiscal year (1832) with a deficit of 1,500,000 pesos. And in the following year expenditures exceeded revenues by about 600,000 pesos, only because taxation yielded considerably higher revenues. It is not surprising, therefore, that the provincial government was once more forced to borrow. In March of 1834 the Junta de Representantes authorized a loan of 3,000,000 pesos. And seven months later, as the government came again face to face with bankruptcy, the legislature sanctioned another issue of 5,000,000 pesos in Fondos Públicos.[27]

Unlike the early issues of the Fondos Públicos the loan of 1831 was frankly a budgetary measure. It was used to supplement current revenues, rather than to consolidate the top-heavy short term debt. Such methods of financing deficits could not continue indefinitely. Investment funds, never plentiful in Buenos Aires, were becoming scarcer from year to year, and successive flotations were encountering increasing resistance among prospective investors. In view of the prevailing scarcity of funds and the uncertain monetary situation, the yield of 6 per cent per annum was anything but attractive. It is true that the

---

creerse que el arbitrio que se le subrogue sea tan proficuo a los intereses de los que impiden su realización." It is, perhaps, superfluous to add that most of the prospective subscribers understood quite clearly this thinly veiled threat.

[25] February 25, 1832 (vol. 6, no. 288).

[26] In January 1832 bonds sold at 57 per cent of par, and in March of the same year the average price was 47.50 per cent. Cf. Table 32.

[27] Law, March 14, 1834 (RO–586, L–13, no. –3); Law, November 18, 1834 (RO–749, L–13, no. –11).

bonds were offered for sale at a considerable discount, often amounting to as much as 50 per cent, but even at these prices investors were difficult to find. The financial market of Buenos Aires was rapidly approaching the point of saturation. Moreover, as the public debt grew in volume, interest charges and amortization service consumed an increasing proportion of the province's revenues. It was becoming more and more evident that borrowing could not offer a permanent solution of the financial difficulties of the province. Such solution was to be sought within the limits of the budget, i.e., either in increased revenues, or in reduced expenditures, or in both. Clearly, a reëxamination of the financial position of the province was in order.

The first detailed program of financial reorganization came from Manuel José García, Minister of Finance in Viamonte's second administration. Toward the end of 1833 García submitted to the provincial legislature an extensive report on the financial condition and prospects of the province, and gave an outline of the measures which, in his opinion, could avert certain bankruptcy.[28] García began his report with a brief review of existing conditions. Expenditures exceeded revenues by 7,000 paper pesos per day. The internal long term debt (Fondos Públicos) had increased fourfold since 1821, and the accumulated and unpaid interest and amortization on the London loan of 1824 amounted to 400,000 pounds sterling. The treasury's floating debt stood at 17,000,000 pesos, and interest charges on treasury bills issued in lieu of cash payments equalled principal borrowed over a period of four years. The peso depreciated to about 15 per cent of par. García refused to discuss the forces responsible for this deplorable condition of the provincial treasury. He preferred to confine himself to a discussion of remedies, which, he insisted, must be such as to insure a permanent solution of the difficulties.

The cornerstone of García's reorganization program was monetary deflation. His argument ran along lines similar to those laid down by Viamonte some four years before. Paper money, claimed García, was fatal to commerce and to prosperity in general; it paralyzed credit operations; it discouraged the flow of foreign capital into domestic industries. Inflation was detrimental to both producers and consumers, since its incidence was uncertain and uneven. Moreover, under con-

[28] *Memoria del Sr. Ministro de Hacineda, para la mejor inteligencia de los proyectos elevados a la Honorable Sala de Representantes de la Provincia* (*Gaceta Mercantil*, December 30, 1833, no. 3178).

ditions of depreciating currency the province could never discharge its foreign obligations. Yet foreign credit, reasoned García, was an essential element in any program of financial rehabilitation, and such credit could not, in turn, be secured unless the province succeeded in stabilizing its currency.

What García had in mind was not stabilization of the peso at the level it had attained during the period immediately preceding his report, but rather a return to the metallic standard of the early Rivadavia period. On this basis the plan of financial rehabilitation envisaged the following operations. It implied, first, the payment of back interest and amortization on the London loan, totalling 1,836,000 silver pesos. It involved, secondly, the retirement of bank notes, an operation which would consume about 2,500,000 silver pesos. And, finally, it proposed to extinguish the floating indebtedness of the province. These non-recurring disbursements amounted to 4,500,000 silver pesos. The all-important question was where and how to obtain this relatively large sum. García suggested that a new loan might be negotiated in London, but he realized that unless the government was prepared to pare its expenditures the chances of securing funds from abroad were rather slight. García believed that a balanced budget was not impossible. He thought that normal expenditures of the province could and should be reduced to 1,800,000 silver pesos, and that the servicing of both the foreign and the domestic debts should not amount to more than 550,000 pesos. Interest and amortization of the London loan were fixed in foreign currency and could not be modified. The situation was different with respect to Fondos Públicos. These bonds, and especially those issued after 1828, could be converted into specie bonds on the basis of current exchange rates. Thus, total annual expenditures could be calculated at about 2,400,000 silver pesos, a sum that was not excessive in view of the province's revenues.

García's program failed to arouse enthusiasm in the Junta de Representantes. Return to metallic currency appealed to no one, except perhaps the shareholders of the Banco Nacional and the holders of the London loan bonds. Nor did the plan appear as realistic as García contended. Its success depended upon an initial expenditure of four and a half million silver pesos, at a time when the government was unable to provide for the most urgent needs of the administration. It is true that García did not expect to raise the money in Buenos Aires. He hoped that a loan would be possible in London. But this hope was rather unfounded, in view of the fact that Viamonte's administration was obviously lacking strong political support. It was doubtful, moreover, whether García's estimate of the financial requirements of the province would bear closer scrutiny. It was argued in the legislature that in terms of specie actual expenditures were much higher, and that the limit of 1,800,000 pesos per year set by García was much too low, as experience of recent years amply demonstrated.[29] But even if the government's estimates were correct the plan was unworkable largely because it provided no immediate relief to the harassed treasury. It seemed useless to discuss and draw long range plans when the government was in imminent danger of suspending payments. The task of providing quick relief seemed vastly more important, and it overshadowed the larger problem of financial reconstruction. So the provincial legislature set aside García's bills and approved instead a new issue of 3,000,000 pesos in Fondos Públicos.[30]

The bond issue of March 14, 1834 did not in any way solve the financial problem. It merely postponed for a short period the final crisis. Within two or three months the treasury was once again without funds. Borrowing against treasury bills became impossible except under most onerous conditions. Manuel V. de Maza, who succeeded Viamonte, complained bitterly that immediately before his assumption of office the government was forced to pay 3½ per cent per month on money borrowed against short term bills.[31] The floating debt of the province stood at this time (October 1834) at over 8,000,000 pesos, and in addition the treasury owed nearly 1,500,000 pesos in salaries, unpaid bills, and other obligations.[32] The situation was desperate. The government had no alternative but to ask for additional issues of Fondos Públicos.

Manuel V. de Maza made no attempt to suggest a thorough revision

[29] See articles by "Un estranjero" in *Gaceta Mercantil,* nos. 3181, 3182, 3183, 3187, and 3191 (January 3, 4, 7, 11, 16 of 1834), and especially the article in the *Gaceta* of January 11, 1834. The writer claimed that current expenditures amounted to over 4,500,000 pesos a year, or 1,800,000 silver pesos more than García thought. For other views, see article by "Un gaucho de Luján" (*G. M.,* no. 3183, January 7, 1834), and by "Un comerciante" (*G. M.,* nos. 3218, 3226, January 19, 25, 28, 1834).

[30] Law, March 14, 1834 (RO–586, L–13, no. –3).

[31] Special message of October 28, 1834 (*Diario de Sesiones,* Session 464).

[32] Cf. *Diario de Sesiones,* Session 464. The floating debt consisted of the following items: Pagarés de aduana, 6,154,200 pesos; Treasury bills, 1,909,122 pesos 2 reales; Treasury bills, overdue, 131,588 pesos 2 reales; Unpaid salaries, 1,188,352 pesos; Other obligations, 300,000.

of the financial structure of the province. He confined himself to the more urgent and also much simpler task of reducing the huge floating debt to manageable proportions. The manner in which the government proposed to accomplish this was outlined in three bills. The first bill provided for the issue of 4,000,000 pesos in long term bonds. The second bill, the most important of the three, dealt with several matters. The government proposed to use the proceeds from the loan to retire treasury bills. It undertook, also, to sell the bonds at not less than 50 per cent of par. And it provided for the establishment of a Financial Council (Consejo de Hacienda). The prerogative and duties of the Consejo were defined in article 4 of the bill. The Council was to supervise the sale of bonds as well as the issue of treasury bills and other short term obligations; it was to pass upon all claims against the treasury, even though such claims may have been recognized by previous governments; and, finally, it had the right to approve or reject any transactions involving alienation of public land or real estate. The third bill established the procedure to be followed in retiring the short term indebtedness. Treasury bills and other claims falling due in each of the five months beginning November 1 were to be paid 50 cents on the dollar, the remainder to be paid in installments over a period of 6 months.[33]

The legislature approved the three bills with but slight changes. But it took seven full sessions to accomplish this, in spite of the fact that the Finance Commission of the Junta reported the measures favorably. Opposition to the government's plan rested largely upon the argument that the measures were not sufficiently comprehensive to bring about a fundamental improvement in the financial condition of the province. Deputy Wright, who led the opposition, recalled that ever since 1828 the province had pursued a hand-to-mouth policy in matters of public finance. He contended that the bills introduced by Maza continued the practice of preceding governments, and that the measures were both inadequate and impracticable. The plan, argued Wright, tacitly assumed that the administration could get along on a budget of about 7,000,000 pesos per year. But experience of the past few years

[33] Bills issued on the basis of the decree of November 28, 1833, or those which originated after October 1, 1834 were not subject to this procedure (art. 2). The bill provided, further, that claims falling due between July 31, 1835 and August 31, 1836 must be presented at the treasury for inspection. These claims were to be exchanged when due for notes of the Colecturía payable in 6 to 10 months from the date of approval (art. 3).

had demonstrated that expenditures ran at a rate considerably higher than 600,000 pesos per month. For this reason alone the program presented by Maza could not succeed. Wright also opposed the government's proposal to reduce the interest on certain Treasury bills issued during Viamonte's administration. He claimed that should such reduction be approved it would gravely injure the credit of the province. Nor was Wright enthusiastic about the establishment of the Consejo de Hacienda, on the ground that it set up a dangerous precedent and was contrary to normal constitutional procedure.[34]

TABLE 32

ACTUAL PRICES OF THE 6 PER CENT INTERNAL BONDS QUOTED ON THE BUENOS AIRES STOCK EXCHANGE ON THIRD FRIDAY OF EACH MONTH

	1829	1830	1831	1832	1833	1834	1835
January.......	53.00	60.50	79.50	57.00	45.25	52.25	42.75
February......	55.75	62.00	75.50	53.50	43.75	51.00	40.00
March........	59.50	63.00	57.00	47.50	43.75	51.00	41.00
April.........	62.00	70.00	61.00	46.50	43.00	49.00	43.25
May.........	60.50	72.50	63.50	44.25	42.00	48.00	46.25
June.........	60.00	72.00	55.50	42.25	43.25	46.50	52.50
July.........	56.00	72.50	55.00	42.25	45.50	52.00	56.50
August.......	52.00	77.00	56.00	42.50	44.25	52.00	65.00
September....	55.00	77.50	56.50	42.25	47.00	55.50	59.50
October.......	58.00	78.00	58.00	45.25	51.00	57.50	61.00
November.....	50.00	77.50	57.50	44.50	55.00	52.50	62.25
December.....	61.00	78.00	56.50	44.50	52.50	45.50	62.00
Average......	57.73	71.71	60.93	46.02	46.35	51.06	52.75

Source: *British Packet and Argentine News.*

Wright's contention that the loan proposed by the government was inadequate found support among some members of the Junta. Deputy Lucio Mansilla favored a bond issue of 16,000,000 pesos. Such an issue, Mansilla argued, would enable the government to liquidate the province's short term indebtedness at one stroke. The new issue would bring the province's total debt to 22,000,000 pesos,[35] the servicing of which would require an annual expenditure of 3,000,000 pesos. But in view of the fact that the province's revenues averaged about 12,-000,000 pesos a year the burden of servicing the loan would not be unbearable. Of course, the government would have to enforce strict

[34] *Diario de Sesiones,* Session 467 (November 6, 1834).

[35] Mansilla was obviously mistaken, for at the time of the discussion the long term debt stood at about 15,000,000 pesos. With the issue proposed by Mansilla the debt would amount to about 31,000,000 pesos. See Table 33.

economy, but this in itself was not to be lamented. In fact, the legislature should insist that the government submit a detailed budget within the shortest possible time. This in itself would be an important step toward a speedy solution of the financial difficulties.[36]

TABLE 33

GROWTH OF INTERNAL LOANS OF THE PROVINCE OF BUENOS AIRES AND THEIR AMORTIZATION UP TO DECEMBER 31, 1835

Oct. 30, 1821 .... 4%	2,000,000	Redeemed to Dec. 31, 1835... 7,053,909$ 7½
Oct. 30, 1821 .... 6%	3,000,000	Available for redemption.... 17,835$ 7
Dec. 17, 1823 .... 6%	1,800,000	Outstanding:
		Privately owned..........19,865,942$ 7½
Nov. 10, 1824 .... 6%	300,000	Corporations............ 422,511$ 2
Dec. 10, 1825 .... 6%	260,000	
Sept. 29, 1827 .... 6%	6,000,000	
Feb. 21, 1831 .... 6%	6,000,000	
Mar. 10, 1834 .... 6%	3,000,000	
Nov. 18, 1834 .... 6%	5,000,000	
Total.............. 27,360,000		27,360,000$

Source: *Registro Oficial de la Provincia de Buenos Aires*, Libro 13, no. 6—*Estado General de la Administración de Fondos Públicos y Caja de Amortización de Buenos Aires desde 1° de enero de 1822, en que principió hasta 31 de diciembre de 1835.*

Both demands, i.e., the one formulated by Wright for a more comprehensive program of financial reconstruction, and the other by Mansilla for a complete consolidation and conversion of the short term debt, were rejected by the legislature. Deputies Anchorena and Senillosa, who reported the bills out of the Finance Commission, opposed Wright's motion on the ground that preparation of a comprehensive program would consume too much time. The government could ill afford to wait until a special committee could examine the various aspects of the problem. What the government needed most was immediate relief, and to this extent the proposed measures were sufficient and timely. Besides, the measures under discussion in no way closed the door to more comprehensive plans of financial reorganization. Conversion and consolidation of the short term debt, such as Mansilla proposed, were in reality superfluous. So long as the debt was classified it was, indeed, immaterial whether repayment was accomplished in the form of Treasury bills or Fondos Públicos. As to Mansilla's notion that the bond issue be increased to 16,000,000 pesos Anchorena argued that so large an issue would have a devastating effect upon bond prices. And this in turn might easily bring ruin to innu-

[36] *Diario de Sesiones,* Session 469 (November 10, 1834).

merable private fortunes, the more surely since "in view of the present state of industrial activity numerous individuals had their capital invested in government securities." [37]

The legislature approved the report of the Finance Commission with but one important change. It authorized an issue of 5,000,000 pesos instead of the four million asked by the government.[38] The treasury was thus able to avert suspension of payments and to reduce somewhat the short term debt. But the problem of financial reorganization remained unsolved. This task was left to Rosas, who early in 1835 assumed the governorship of Buenos Aires.

3

Throughout the critical years since the defeat of Juan Lavalle the Banco Nacional played a steadily diminishing role in the financial and economic life of the province. The bank's position had become precarious long before Rosas came to power. Considered by the federalists to be the mainstay of the Rivadavia regime the bank was treated with suspicion by both the Junta and the government of the reconstituted province. Soon after Dorrego assumed office, the provincial legislature forbade further issues of bank notes, except with the express permission of the government, and recognized the bank notes already issued as the direct obligation of the province.[39] In this manner the bank was at one stroke deprived of one of its most important privileges. By far the largest portion of the bank's assets consisted of advances to the government, and since loans to business interests were

[37] *Diario de Sesiones,* Session 469 (November 10, 1834). The part of Anchorena's discourse which referred to Wright's argument is well worth quoting in full, as coming from one who on many occasions had shown considerable knowledge of orthodox economic doctrine. Said Anchorena: "La idea de consolidar la deuda a primera vista es sorprendente: generalmente la han adoptado los Estados, en igual caso en que los particulares se hallan cuando dan punto a sus negocios; y causan las mismas alarmas en aquel caso que en el segundo. Mas en mi opinión la consolidación de la deuda en un Estado no importa sino la clasificación de los diversos créditos que tenga: diversos en el origen y en el modo, para un sistema de pagamento; mas es accidental y es indiferente que sea bajo el sistema de Fondos Públicos u otro. Si bien se considera los proyectos de la Comisión importen una consolidación de la deuda, porque uniformen todas las deudas flotantes del Estado bajo el sistema de letras, y una división periódica que establece, asegurando al mismo tiempo el principal e intereses por una misma ley y un mismo medio, que esto es lo que en realidad significa consolidación de la deuda."

[38] November 18, 1834 (RO–749, L–13, no. –11).

[39] See chap. iii.

not readily recoverable the bank ceased to be a factor in the economic and financial life of the province.

For a brief period the bank's future looked somewhat brighter when late in 1829 Juan José Viamonte launched his drive for a return to the gold standard. And even as the monetary program of Viamonte was being emasculated by the legislature the bank found consolation in what appeared to be a favorable attitude of the Rosas administration. In December of 1830 Rosas called upon the bank to prepare a detailed statement of its financial position. This statement was to serve as a basis for discussion by a commission composed of representatives of the bank and the government. Rosas took this step in order "to dissipate dangerous doubts and to enable the government to take measures which would definitively reconcile the rights and claims of all concerned, and which would once and for all put an end to rumors bred by uncertainty and ignorance of facts."[40] The bank promptly complied with this request, but the government failed to act. In 1831 it became clear that Viamonte's monetary program would be abandoned, and the bank bitterly protested this change. In a letter to the Minister of Finance the bank argued that suspension of the Caja de Amortización jeopardized the most vital interests of the institution, and therefore also of the provincial economy. It accused the government of indifference and pointed out that nothing had been done to put into operation the decree of December 17, 1830.[41] However, the protest made no impression upon the government. The Minister of Finance, it is true, gave assurances that the government would be willing to discuss any reasonable suggestions coming from the bank, but he refused to make any definite promises. The legislature proceded, in the meantime, to nullify the decree of October 3, 1829. In May of 1832 Rosas defined the government's attitude toward the bank in the following terms: first, maintenance of guarantee given with regard to currency; secondly, continued non-interference on the part of the government in

[40] Decree, December 17, 1830 (*Registro Nacional*, no. 2428). The *considerando* read as follows: "No pudiendo tener efecto la Comisión nombrada en 6 de octubre último para investigar el estado del Banco Nacional hasta la reunión de la legislatura del año próximo, y siendo urgente para consultar los intereses públicos y el de accionistas tomar una medida que disipe dudas peligrosas y ponga el Gobierno en aptitud de adoptar de un modo sólido y conciliatorio de los dos derechos, las resoluciones que sean convenientes, cortando de una vez cuestiones que la incertidumbre e ignorancia que los hechos multiplican, y que graves incidentes han acrecentado últimamente hasta un punto que no sería justo ni prudente desatender por más tiempo, ha acordado y decreta:"

[41] *Archivo General*, Ant. C.22–A.4, no. 4.

the administration of currency; and thirdly, careful examination of the just claims of the bank's shareholders.[42]

From the point of view of the Banco Nacional the government's declaration was anything but satisfactory. A hands-off policy was precisely what the bank feared most at this time. It closed the door to further discussions of the bank's problem, and gave notice that the bank should expect no help from the government. It was difficult for the bank to find consolation in assurances of strict neutrality with regard to currency administration. Of vastly greater importance than currency administration was the question of the government's indebtedness to the bank. Indeed, the very existence of the bank depended upon a favorable solution of this problem. In 1830 the bank claimed to have accumulated over 1,500,000 pesos in undistributed profits, but, as the *British Packet and Argentine News* pointed out, these profits were rather illusory. So far from having accumulated any profits, the bank lost a good portion of its capital, and according to the *Packet's* estimate the stockholders' equity in the bank amounted to not much over 50 per cent of their original investment.[43] The balance sheet revealed that the government's debt to the bank amounted to 18,597,562 pesos 7 reales. This debt increased to 19,346,486 pesos in May of 1832,[44] and in January of the following year nearly 89 per cent of the bank's total assets of 23,342,116 pesos consisted of advances to the provincial treasury.[45] As against 20,752,580 pesos loaned to the government the bank had only 1,384,523 pesos in commercial loans, many of which were not readily convertible into cash. The bank was thus transformed into a government agency without, however, deriving any of the benefits which such a relationship normally implied. On the question of the government's bank debt the message of Rosas maintained ominous silence. And Juan Ramón Balcarce, who succeeded Rosas, promised no change in the government's policy. In a message to the provincial legislature Balcarce acknowledged the fact that the

[42] Mabragaña, I, 266 (Message, May 7, 1832).

[43] Cf. Balance sheet in *British Packet and Argentine News*, March 12, 1831 (vol. V, no. 238). The bank claimed to have accumulated 1,616,648 pesos in undistributed profits.

[44] From a report submitted to the government by Santiago Wilde, secretary of the Banco Nacional. Cf. *Archivo General*, Ant. C.22–A.9–no. 3. Actually the government's debt amounted to 20,046,486 pesos, but allowance was made for 700,000 pesos on account of bank notes lost in circulation.

[45] Balance sheet of the Banco Nacional as of January 31, 1833. Cf. *British Packet and Argentine News*, March 16, 1833 (vol. VII, no. 343).

bank's condition remained as precarious as ever. He even recognized "the urgent necessity that the legislature consider the future of the institution," but he asserted at the same time that the government had already defined its position in this matter, and that it did not propose to deviate from the principles outlined by Rosas.[46]

Exasperated by the government's policy of studied aloofness the directors of the bank decided to take drastic steps. At a general meeting (August 1833) the shareholders approved a resolution calling for the dissolution of the bank. The directors were given full authority to make a last attempt to secure help from the government. But in case the government refused to coöperate the directors were empowered to wind up the bank's affairs within three months from the day of the meeting.[47] The directors went further than that. They once again approached the government offering a series of suggestions designed to solve the bank's difficulties. The directors felt that should their plan receive the approval of the government the bank had a fair chance to survive. The plan submitted to the Minister of Finance was simple enough. The government would undertake to amortize its bank debt in yearly installments of 1,200,000 pesos. The bank was to use this sum in the following manner: 150,000 pesos for renovation of bank notes; 120,000 for the repayment of interest to shareholders who subscribed additional capital of 1,000,000; 250,000 pesos for repayment of the loan; and 680,000 pesos for the retirement of bank notes.[48] The directors suggested further that the 1,200,000 pesos might be obtained from additional duties imposed upon both imports and exports.

However practicable, the plan was unacceptable to the government. The treasury was in no position at this time to undertake repayment of the bank loan at the rate of 1,200,000 pesos a year. The suggestion that the funds could be raised by means of additional duties was not feasible on political as well as economic grounds. To impose new duties at a time when the province was just beginning to recover from the effects of a protracted drought and severe depression was to invite economic disaster. Moreover, the political situation being what it was no government dared to sponsor new taxes upon exports. The experiment of Viamonte was still fresh in the memory of the cattle

---

46 Mabragaña I, 278 (Message, May 31, 1833). "El gobierno tiene ya manifestados sus principios á este respecto en el anterior mensaje, y será siempre inalterable en ellos."

47 Cf. *British Packet and Argentine News*, August 24, 1833 (vol. VIII, no. 366).

48 Norberto Piñero, "La disolución del Banco Nacional" (*Revista Argentina de Ciencias Políticas*, vol. XIV).

breeders, and they in fact ruled the province. There was yet another consideration which rendered the reorganization plan untenable. The essential element of the plan was amortization of bank notes. The deflation proposed by the bank was, it is true, much milder than the one advocated by Viamonte or that suggested by García. Nevertheless, the success of the plan hinged upon deflation, and this was precisely what the government wished to avoid. Moreover, the provincial government had long before accepted responsibility for the bank notes in circulation. So long as the fiction was maintained that the circulating medium consisted of bank notes rather than paper money, the treasury was obliged to pay the bank large sums in interest compounded semiannually.[49] Should, however, the bank be liquidated, the government would at once be relieved of this burden, for as paper money the circulating medium would cease to form a part of the province's public debt. In view of this the plan offered by the Banco Nacional was obviously disadvantageous to the government.

The provincial government neither accepted nor rejected the bank's plan. The political situation became at this time rather unsettled. Juan Ramón Balcarce was forced to resign as a result of the *Revolución de los Restauradores,* and the position of his successor, Juan José Viamonte, was too uncertain to permit decisive action in a matter as grave as that of the Banco Nacional. Viamonte remained in office barely eight months, and he, too, failed to solve the problem. The directors of the bank apparently realized that the political situation was not propitious for a calm discussion of the bank's affairs. They decided to abandon plans for the immediate liquidation of the bank, feeling that, since the bank's charter was due to expire in 1836, both the government and the legislature would then be compelled to deal with the problem.

The decision came shortly before the expiration of the bank's charter. In the early months of 1836 Rosas commissioned José María Rojas to prepare a report on the Banco Nacional for submission to the legislature. The report, completed on May 16, 1836, was unequivocally hostile to the bank. Rojas began his exposition by stating that the factors which were mainly responsible for the civil wars still persisted, and he strongly hinted that the few individuals responsible for internal dissension had received financial and moral support from the

---

[49] The government, of course, made no actual payments on account of interest. Every six months interest was added to the principal.

Banco Nacional.   He then proceeded to review the monetary situation emphasizing that the bank was the most important single obstacle to economic and financial recovery of the province.   He recalled that the Banco Nacional was intended as a national institution, but that it had never been able to attain that status.   In the provinces bank notes of the Banco Nacional were not accepted, not only because they failed to inspire confidence, but also because the bank was from its very inception a partisan institution.   Even if it be recognized that the bank could not help giving financial support to the unitary government of Rivadavia, it remained nevertheless true that the bank's political sympathies had never been with those who fought against unitarism.   For this reason alone, Rojas concluded, the continued existence of the bank was incompatible with the best interests of the province.[50]

The report of José María Rojas was hardly more than a formality. It provided justification for an act that had been contemplated and decided upon long before.   The coup de grâce was delivered on May 30, 1836 when by a decree Rosas announced the dissolution of the Banco Nacional.[51]   He thought it necessary, however, to explain his action in the preamble, which cited the following reasons: first, that the charter of the bank had expired; secondly, that currency was guaranteed by the government; thirdly, that the bank merely lent the provincial treasury the imprint on the notes; and, finally, that the government owned nearly three-fifths of the bank's capital.

The dissolution of the Banco Nacional marked the end of an eventful period in the history of Argentine finance.   It marked also the disappearance of one of the last pillars of a financial system which the administration of Rodríguez had so painstakingly erected a decade and a half before.   The Brazilian war had dealt a mortal blow to provincial finances, and the civil wars and internal dissensions speeded up the process of deterioration to a point at which the system was beyond repair.   But, until all hope was given up, repeated efforts had been made by the governments and in the Junta to arrest the process of decay and to restore the system to its erstwhile position of equilibrium. No other problem had received so much public attention, or had been so thoroughly examined, as that of financial rehabilitation.   In the legislature as well as in the press, plans designed to solve the financial problems of the province were discussed at length.   And while these

[50] *Gaceta Mercantil*, May 31, 1836 (no. 3896).
[51] Decree, May 30, 1836 (RO, L–15, no. –4).

plans differed in detail they all had one thing in common, namely, the restoration of the gold standard and the balancing of the budget. With one exception none of these plans ever materialized. And the one plan which had been put to the test of practice soon collapsed and had to be discarded. This was not surprising, for most of these plans were too comprehensive, too far reaching in their effects upon the economic and political life of the province. A return to the monetary and fiscal regime of the early twenties implied also the restoration of the economic pattern of the Rivadavia period and to this extent the financial problem assumed definite political connotations. The extreme wing of the federalist party opposed restoration of the gold standard, and they were supported by all those groups which had risen to the top of the economic and social ladder during the inflationary period. These groups were not inconsiderable. Recruited from all walks of life they were firmly established in the economic pattern of the province as landowners and cattle breeders, meat producers, and entrepreneurs, blending imperceptibly with the older rural aristocracy. Nor did the middle class, such as it was, want to see the return of the gold standard. Exhausted and impoverished by wars, drought, and depression these classes were neither willing nor able to bear the additional burden of financial reconstruction. So it was that the plans for financial regeneration found few friends among the broad strata of the population. And the ruling party preferred naturally enough to forsake the peso, rather than to risk the loss of popularity as well as its position of economic and political preëminence in the province. So long as the Banco Nacional existed, plans for the restoration of the peso were bound to come forth, for the bank served as the rallying center of all those who stood to gain most from deflation. But for this very reason dissolution of the bank became an economic as well as a political necessity. By taking this step Rosas removed the last source of economic and political agitation, and at the same time delivered a staggering blow to the unitary forces within the province. The cattle breeders were now supreme in the economic as well as the political field.

CHAPTER VIII

PORTEÑO FINANCES UNDER ROSAS, 1835–1851

Pero el gobierno tiene en las operaciones de hacienda una divisa escrita que dice ganancia para todos.—From a speech by the Minister of Finance in the Junta de Representantes, March 14, 1837.

WHEN THE DECREE announcing the liquidation of the Banco Nacional appeared in the *Registro Oficial* Rosas had been in power for over a year. From his predecessors he had inherited an enormous deficit, a very much depreciated currency, and a large public debt. The financial problem facing his government was essentially the same as that with which every previous administration had to cope. But, unlike Viamonte, Rosas made no attempt to restore the gold value of the peso. Strict economy in expenditures, efficiency in the administration and collection of revenues—such were the principles upon which Rosas based his program of financial rehabilitation. At no time throughout the seventeen years of his administration did he deviate from these principles.

Rosas' conservatism in matters of public finance was a welcome change. It at once laid at rest all agitation for sweeping changes and radical solutions based upon abstract generalizations rather than upon careful evaluation of economic realities. It insured continuance of the *status quo* in the distribution of the national dividend, and it also permitted a more detailed examination of the existing fiscal pattern and a more dispassionate appraisal of the financial structure of the province.

What, then, was the pattern of the revenue system of the province? In a report to the eleventh legislature the Comisión de Cuentas of the Junta recognized the following main sources of revenue: customs duties (*entrada marítima y terrestre y salida de mar*); port dues (*derechos de puerto*); stamp duties and license taxes (*papel sellado, patentes*); capital tax (*contribución directa*); new tax (*impuesto nuevo*); rentals, including the emphyteusis rent (*arrendamiento, alquileres*), sales of real estate and land, interest, etc.; and sundry taxes usually grouped under the heading Policía.[1] As in previous years customs duties formed the most important source of revenue. In times of normal foreign trade these imposts produced between 85 and 90 per cent of the provincial revenue, and in some years as much as 93 per cent.[2] There were, of course, exceptions. During the seventeen years of Rosas' dictatorship Buenos Aires was twice subjected to blockades by the French and the Anglo-French fleets. So in 1839, the only full year of the French blockade, revenues from customs duties and port dues amounted to 2,258,773 pesos, as compared to 9,136,877 pesos obtained from the same sources in 1837, the last year preceding the blockade. The French blockade was lifted in October 1840, but for some time before that date shipping in Buenos Aires was almost unmolested. In that year income from customs duties rose to 5,448,404 pesos, or 71.7 per cent of total revenues. In 1846, when the port was blockaded by the combined English and French fleets, revenues from tariffs decreased to 6,018,018 pesos from 29,218,637 pesos in 1844 and 32,894,862 pesos in 1843. Yet even in the lean blockade years foreign trade provided the bulk of the treasury's income. With the exceptions just noted revenue from this source rose from slightly over 10,000,000 pesos in 1835 to nearly 60,000,000 pesos in 1850. However, this sixfold increase was in large measure due to the fact that in response to currency depreciation commodity prices rose rather sharply.[3] Duties, it should be remembered, were imposed on an *ad valorem* basis, so that a rise in prices of goods entering foreign trade was automatically reflected in increased revenues.

It was precisely because foreign commerce provided the bulk of the province's revenues that Rosas spared no effort to improve the administration and collection of customs duties. The Comisión de Cuentas appeared to be satisfied with the administration of customs. Nevertheless, Rosas issued elaborate instructions designed to increase still further the efficiency of this service. In 1842 he appointed a commis-

---

[1] Cf. Report of the Comisión de Cuentas, *Diario de Sesiones,* Session 481, December 29, 1834. See also Pedro de Angelis, *Memoria sobre el estado de la hacienda pública escrita por orden del gobierno* (Buenos Aires: 1834), p. 79.

[2] In 1841 customs duties brought in 92.92 per cent of the total revenues of the province, and in the following year the treasury derived 91.46 per cent of its income from this source. It was not until 1849 and 1850 that the proportion of revenues from customs again exceeded 90 per cent. See Table 35.

[3] In 1835 the peso was quoted at 14.2 per cent of par, as against 4.2 per cent of par in 1850. See Table 28, chap. vii.

sion which prepared monthly price lists of commodities entering foreign trade.[4] These price lists were officially recognized as binding in the calculation of customs duties. Partly in order to insure greater efficiency in administering the tariff, and partly also in order to guard against contraband, Rosas inclined toward restricting overseas trade to Buenos Aires.

Port dues (*derechos de puerto*) were imposed upon all vessels entering the ports of the province. Distinction was usually made between ocean-going vessels and those engaged in coastal trade. Ocean-going ships were subject to higher taxes. The rates were revised from time to time to allow for change in the value of currency, but such revisions were infrequent. Revenues from this source were nominal. Only in three years out of sixteen, between 1835 and 1850, did this tax produce more than 1 per cent of total revenues. In the remaining thirteen years the income from this source fluctuated between 0.2 and 0.9 per cent of the total.[5]

The license tax (*derecho de patentes*) and the stamp duty (*papel sellado*) were usually combined in the yearly accounts of the treasury. Yet these taxes were distinct, both as to administration and incidence. The license tax was a fee exacted by the government from commercial and industrial enterprises. The tax was graduated according to the nature of the business. The early schedules recognized as many as eleven classes, and the tax ranged from 3 to 60 pesos per year.[6] In 1830 the number of categories was reduced to six, and the new rates amounted to from 20 to 200 pesos per year.[7] Eight years later the rates were once more revised. The new schedule called for eight classes, of which the lowest applied exclusively to vehicles engaged in interprovincial commerce. The remaining categories referred to business establishments and the fees ranged from 40 to 400 pesos.[8] These rates were retained until the end of 1844. In 1845 the license tax was considerably expanded. For the first time professions were made subject to the tax. The new law retained the distinction between estab-

---

[4] Law, August 13, 1842 (cf. *Recopilación* . . . p. 62). The price lists were published every month in the *Gaceta Mercantil*.

[5] See Tables 34 and 35.

[6] See above, chap. iii, p. 48; and also *Archivo General*, Ant. C.21–A.9–no. 7.

[7] Law, September 21, 1829 (RO–1203, L–8, no. –9).

[8] Law, November 23, 1838 (RO–1269, L–17, no. –11). Strictly speaking there were ten categories. Art. 9 of the law provided that stores selling wines and liquors must obtain special licenses, and art. 10 imposed double taxes upon jewelers and comb factories.

lishments located in the capital and those situated in the country. And the city of Buenos Aires was divided into two zones, one comprising the center of the city, where higher rates prevailed. The maximum rate was again raised to 500 pesos per year.[9] With only very slight changes in 1848 and 1850 this schedule remained in force until the end of Rosas' administration.[10]

The stamp duty (*papel sellado*) was, strictly speaking, a fee exacted for the use of paper bearing the provincial seal. The use of such paper was mandatory in contracts, legal acts, petitions, permits, and other documents, and the fee was determined by law in each case. The schedule which was in force when Rosas assumed the governorship of the province in 1835 was enacted in 1823. It provided that all contracts, monetary obligations, letters of exchange, powers of attorney, and other legal instruments involving definite sums be executed on official paper. The schedule recognized six categories, the lowest corresponding to transactions involving sums from 20 to 500 pesos, for which the fee was set at one-half peso. For transactions over 15,000 pesos the fee amounted to 15 pesos. Labor contracts were subject to a tax of one-half peso, petitions to government, and courts were required to use stamped paper of one peso; all documents and legal instruments which did not specify a definite sum were to use stamped paper of three pesos; while property titles, powers of attorney, and foreign passports paid fifteen pesos in stamp duty.[11] This schedule was renewed from year to year until 1838. In June of that year the fees were doubled and with slight modifications in 1848 and 1851 the new schedule continued in force until the fall of Rosas.[12]

Revenue from these two sources was relatively small. Normally both taxes produced between 2½ to 4½ per cent of the total revenue, a proportion too insignificant to influence materially the financial position of the treasury.[13] Pedro de Angelis complained in 1833 that "the greater the number of business enterprises, of properties, and of merchants, the smaller the revenue from a tax which is supposed to

---

[9] Law, December 26, 1844 (RO–1656, L–23, no. –12).

[10] Laws, December 29, 1847 (RO–1816, L–26, no. –12), and December 25, 1850 (RO–1980, L–29, no. –12).

[11] Law, January 24, 1833 (RO–413, L–12, no. –1).

[12] The doubling of stamp duties was effected by decree of June 26, 1838 (RO–1246, L–17, no. –6). For changes see laws, December 29, 1847 (RO–1771, L–25, no. –12) and December 26, 1850 (RO–1980, L–26, no. –12).

[13] See Tables 34 and 35. The blockade years were, of course, exceptions.

fall upon all classes." [14]   De Angelis pointed out that although all commercial and industrial enterprises were subject to the tax many businesses were not specified in the schedules, and for this reason escaped the tax altogether.   Moreover, in spite of currency depreciation, rates had not been changed since the tax was first introduced in 1823.   So it was that while in 1824 the license and stamp duties produced 118,907 silver pesos, equivalent to 832,000 pesos paper, revenues from these sources barely exceeded 400,000 paper pesos in 1835.   In a message to the Junta de Representantes covering his first full year in office Rosas described the administration of the license tax in terms no less emphatic than those used by Pedro de Angelis.   He reported, however, that the government had already taken appropriate measures to improve collection, and that revenues from this source increased considerably.[15]   A year later Rosas announced further improvement, but admitted that much still remained to be done.[16]   In 1839, it is true, income from these sources was just about double that for 1837, but this apparently phenomenal increase was evidently caused by factors other than more rigorous and efficient administration.   In the first place, 1839 rates were considerably higher than those in effect two years before.   And, secondly, currency depreciation so reduced the burden of the taxes that evasion became much less profitable.   The fact remains that in normal years of the fifth decade both taxes produced an even smaller proportion of provincial revenues than in the late thirties.

The property tax (*contribución directa*) was no less disappointing as a source of revenue.   Introduced during the administration of Martín Rodríguez in 1822, the *contribución directa* was expected to eventually become the backbone of the province's fiscal system.   It was hoped, that, as national wealth increased, revenues from this source would be

---

[14] Pedro de Angelis, *op. cit.*, pp. 115–116. In 1822 the stamp tax produced 74,789 silver pesos which at the time of de Angelis' writing was equivalent to 523,000 paper pesos. In 1833 the license tax and the stamp duty, together, brought in about 405,000 paper pesos. It was this circumstance which caused de Angelis to remark: "Los tributos marchan, pues, en razon inversa de los progresos del país.   Cuanto mas se complican sus relaciones sociales; cuanto mas se dilata la esfera de acción de su comercio é industria; cuanto mas se aumenta el número de sus establecimientos, de sus propriedades, de sus comerciantes, tanto menor es el producto de un impuesto, que abraza á todas las clases."

[15] Mabragaña I, 337 (Message, January 1, 1837).

[16] Mabragaña I, 369 (Message, December 27, 1837). "La última visita de patentes ha demostrado los progresos en punto a obediencia y subordinación.   Los multados han sido muy pocos.   Los ingresos de esta contribución han crecido; sin embargo, aun resta que hacer mucho para el puntual cumplimiento de la ley."

sufficient to make the provincial treasury relatively independent of foreign trade. It was hoped also that the *contribución directa* would make it possible for the government to pursue a more liberal tariff policy, and in this manner contribute to the prosperity of the province.[17] None of these expectations ever materialized. In his *Memoria* Pedro de Angelis stressed the fact that the *contribución directa* was producing much less revenue than the old *diezmo,* in spite of the fact that the country's wealth increased very considerably after 1821, the year when the *diezmo* was abolished. De Angelis ascribed the failure of the *contribución directa* to several causes. To begin with, the rates were too moderate, i.e., they were too low in view of the manner in which the law operated. The fact that the law made no provision for currency depreciation worked to the disadvantage of the treasury. Property owners were wholly within their right to value their property for purposes of taxation in terms of gold and pay the tax, calculated on a percentage basis, in paper money. So it was that the Sociedad Rural paid only 540 pesos paper on an *estancia* with nearly 19,000 heads of cattle. The tax on capital invested in the cattle alone should have been at least four times the sum the Sociedad actually paid. In the city the situation was not much better. A block of houses paid 110 paper pesos simply because the original investment was calculated at 55,000 gold pesos. Yet the annual yield from this property might well exceed the original investment. It was not surprising, therefore, that the *contribución directa* produced so little. For under these conditions the tax was "an insult to the good faith and dignity of the government." [18] Secondly, the rate structure of the *contribución directa* was not always sound. The law, it will be remembered, made a distinction between capital invested in commodities shipped to Buenos Aires on consignment and that invested in commodities bought outright. The tax in the former case was 4 pro mille, while in the latter 8 pro mille. It was to be expected that in order to avoid paying the higher rate merchants would declare their commodities to have been imported on consignment. This was even more difficult to prevent since the taxpayer's declaration was the sole basis for the administration and collection of the tax.

[17] The tax was levied upon all business property at the following rates: Farmers paid 2 *pro mille;* cattle breeders, 4 *pro mille;* manufacturers, 6 *pro mille;* merchants, 8 *pro mille* on own capital, and 4 *pro mille* on consigned merchandise. See *supra,* chap. iii. The schedule remained essentially unchanged throughout the period under discussion.

[18] Angelis, *Memoria,* pp. 89, *et seq.*

The circumstance that neither the treasury nor the tax administration had any reliable information concerning the values of properties subject to the *contribución directa* was particularly damaging to the interests of the Treasury.   As the Comisión de Cuentas put it: "so long as there is no census the tax is illusory." [19]   It was, indeed, too much to expect that the taxpayer would not underestimate the value of his property.   The government had no way of verifying the taxpayers' declarations, even though it might well doubt their veracity.   When in 1838 the Collector General was charged with the administration of the *contribución directa* he confessed complete inability to cope with the problem because of lack of pertinent information concerning the property subject to the tax.[20]   The Comisión de Cuentas suggested the organization of a special office where a record of all real estate could be kept.   Such an office would also gather all pertinent information relating to capital invested in commerce and industry.

The advice of the Comisión de Cuentas was, of course, sound and quite practicable.   But the legislature failed to act on the Commission's suggestion.   In January 1835 the provincial legislature postponed consideration of the problem until the following session.[21]   But the government, sorely pressed for funds, could not wait, and ordered collection of the tax on the basis of the 1834 schedule.[22]   It was not until 1838 that the rates were revised, and this only temporarily.   By a decree of May 28, 1838 the *contribución directa* was doubled.   Rosas justified this drastic increase by the severe drop in customs revenues. He expressed hope that the taxpayers would consider the difficult position of the treasury and would not attempt to evade the tax by making false declarations.[23]   That the taxpayers had not been as consci-

---

[19] *Diario de Sesiones,* Session 481 (December 29, 1834).   Report of the Comisión de Cuentas.

[20] *Archivo General,* Ant. C.23–A.5–no. 5 (Legajo no. 2).   *El Colector General al Señor Ministro de Hacienda* (julio 5 de 1838).

[21] Law, January 21, 1835 (RO–780, L–14, no. –1).   Art. 1 of the law retained the old rate upon *capitales a consignación.*   The remainder of the schedule was temporarily suspended until the new legislature considered the problem (art. 2).   If, however, the new legislature took no action within four months the 1834 rates were to be automatically reestablished.

[22] Mabragaña I, 302 (Message, December 31, 1835).

[23] RO–1239, L–17, no. –5.   The preamble said in part that the increase was necessary "para llenar en parte el vacío que ha dejado en las rentas públicas la cesación de la entrada marítima á causa del injusto bloqueo que sufre el país; y esperando el Gobierno que los contribuyentes, penetrandose de las necesidades públicas, harán las declaraciones de sus capitales con la mas escrupulosa exactitud."

entious as the government desired was an open secret. In his message to the fourteenth session of the Junta Rosas remarked somewhat sarcastically that the declarations of the taxpayers reveal one hundredth part of the wealth of the province.[24] Rosas blamed the law for this state of affairs. The law, argued Rosas, made no provision for an equitable and objective evaluation of taxable wealth. This omission was not only injurious to the treasury but it was also unjust to the taxpayer, for "nothing was more cruel and inhuman than to compel an individual to give an account of his private wealth." [25] Had this law, continued Rosas, been more in accord with the concepts of justice, had it been based upon principles of liberalism and equality, the tax would have been more productive of revenue, and might also encourage economy and frugality, the true sources of public and private wealth.[26]

The provincial legislature received Rosas' remonstrances rather indifferently. It failed to act either in 1837 or in 1838, and was apparently satisfied to leave the question of enforcement to the government. It was only when by his decree of May 28, 1838 Rosas showed his determination to obtain higher revenue from the *contribución directa* that the legislature decided to consider the problem. In his budget for 1839 Rosas estimated the income from property taxes at 3,000,000 pesos,[27] and the Junta was confronted with two alternatives. It could follow Rosas' initiative and raise the rates, or else it could devise a more efficient system of enforcing and administering the tax. The Junta quite understandably chose the second alternative. Early in 1839 it enacted a new law of *contribución directa*.[28]

The law of April 12, 1839 retained the original rates established in 1823. These rates, the Junta believed, were sufficiently high and were capable of producing the income desired by the government. Higher rates were dangerous, for they discouraged economic activity in the province. The fact that no serious objections had been raised in the preceding seventeen years was an indication that the rates were considered fair by the taxpayers.[29] At the same time the Junta sup-

---

[24] Mabragaña I, 338 (Message, January 1, 1837). "Si por ellas (declaraciones) se calculase la riqueza efectiva de esta provincia, quedaría reducida a la centésima parte."

[25] Mabragaña I, 338 and 369 (Messages, January 1 and December 27, 1837).

[26] Mabragaña I, 269 (Message, December 27, 1837).

[27] Mabragaña I, 401–402 (Message, December 27, 1838).

[28] Law, April 12, 1839 (RO–1311, L–18, no. –4).

[29] *Diario de Sesiones*, Session 635 (April 5, 1839). Speeches by deputies Baldomiro García and Garrigós.

pressed article 5 of the old law, which exempted small properties (2,000 pesos in the case of married persons, and 1,000 pesos in the case of unmarried persons) from the tax.[30] Nor was the Junta willing to concede any privileges to capital invested in bonds of the Fondo Público or treasury bills. The tax was thus made universal, and upon this universality the legislature based its hopes for increased revenue.

The question of rates was settled in the first article of the law. The remaining thirty articles dealt with the problem of administration. The most important provisions concerned the method of valuation of taxable properties. Special commissions, called the Comisión Reguladora de los Capitales, were set up in each district.[31] The Comisión Reguladora was composed of the justice of the peace and the *alcaldes*. The commission's duty was to determine the value of property subject to tax, to notify the taxpayer of its findings, and to make a detailed report to the Colecturía General. When the Collector General determined the amount due from each taxpayer the justices of the peace were required to make collections and remit the collected sums to the Treasury. Protests and other claims could be lodged before commissions composed of the nearest justice of the peace, one taxpayer named by the complainant, one taxpayer named by the justice of the peace, and two *alcaldes*. In certain cases the method of administering the tax was simplified. So, for example, commodities imported on consignment were to pay the tax of 4 pro mille at the time of payment of customs duties, while the tax of 2 pro mille on bonds and treasury bills were deducted by the Administración de Crédito Público and the Treasury at the time of interest payments. So also ships were assessed by a commission composed of the commander of the port and two ship masters appointed by the Colecturía General. The law made no distinction between holders of land in emphyteusis and owners of landed property. For purposes of the *contribución directa* tenants were considered owners of the land.

---

[30] Deputy Garrigós who reported the bill from the Financial Commission gave two reasons for this innovation. One was that exemptions of small capital opened the way to abuses of the law. The other was more general. Said Garrigós: "Es un principio establecido entre los economistas que los contribuyentes por pequeñas porciones son los que proporcionan mayores sumas, porque estas diminutas cotizaciones de contribución siendo muy numerosas dan un producto excesivo en razon de su número; y esto contribuirá a elevarla a la altura que ha determinado la ley."

[31] The city was divided into eleven districts, the province into thirty-nine districts. Cf. *Archivo General*, Ant. C.23–A.8–no. 6.

The most important innovation was, of course, the establishment of Comisiones Reguladoras de los Capitales. In the opinion of the legislature a detailed register of taxable wealth was essential if the tax was to function properly. The register would not only list the various properties subject to taxation, but would also note their value, permitting thus more exact assessment. Property owners were no longer the sole judges of their taxable wealth. This very important function was entrusted to the Comisión Reguladora. The difficulty was that the commissions were not always qualified to determine the value of taxable property. Yet the legislature did not think it necessary to leave this to experts. Deputy Garrigós, who spoke in the name of the Financial Commission, explained the attitude of the Junta as follows: "So it is that the bill does not call for expert assessors; it is enough that these assessors be residents of the district, able to judge and value property in an equitable manner; for those minute analyses which the experts might make would be embarrassing and would be a source of disgusting quarrels." [32] The deputies readily accepted the argument. Indeed, nothing could be more acceptable to the landowners. By leaving assessment in the hands of local officials the legislature very largely removed the threat of effective administration of the tax, for the justices of the peace as well as the *alcaldes* could be relied upon to show particular consideration for the interests of the *estanciero* class. So it was that the law of April 12, 1839 was once more rendered nugatory, but this time under the cloak of reform. The federalist party missed an excellent opportunity to demonstrate its sense of statesmanship.

The Financial Commission argued that a revenue of 3,000,000 pesos from the *contribución directa* was quite feasible. In fact deputy Garrigós contended that it was reasonable to expect much higher returns than the government anticipated in its budget for 1839. He based his argument upon a more or less detailed estimate of the province's taxable wealth, which in his opinion amounted to over 600,-000,000 pesos, excluding capital invested in shipping and commodities imported on consignment.[33] Nevertheless, either because the commission's calculations of the national wealth were optimistic, or because the law of April 12 proved less effective than expected, revenue from this source was disappointingly small. In 1839 the tax brought in only 891,400 pesos, or less than one-third of the amount

[32] *Diario de Sesiones*, Session 635 (April 5, 1839). Speech by deputy Garrigós.
[33] *Ibid.* For a summary analysis of Garrigós' estimate see chap. x.

anticipated by Garrigós. In the following year, when Rosas, taught by bitter experience, pared his expectations to 1,500,000 pesos, the tax produced very little over 1,000,000 pesos. And in 1841 revenues from this source dropped again to 868,000 pesos. It was at this time that Rosas demanded a new revision of the system of assessment.[34] But the Junta refused to heed Rosas' request. When the question came up for discussion in the legislature deputy Lahitte, reporting the opinion of the Finance Commission, opposed revision on the ground that imposition of new and revision of old taxes should not be undertaken too hastily and that the time was not propitious for such action.[35] Rosas accepted the verdict of the legislature without protest, and concentrated instead upon more efficient administration of the tax. But even in this respect he was not completely successful. Nearly every year until the end of his administration he had cause to complain about tardiness on the part of taxpayers. A report of February 16, 1844 by Pedro Bernal, the Collector General, revealed that in certain districts property taxes had remained unpaid since 1840.[36] This condition was not at all exceptional. Property tax payments four and five years in arrears appeared with monotonous regularity until the very end of Rosas' administration.

In spite of the assurances voiced in the legislature during the discussion of the act of April 12, 1839 the *contribución directa* remained a minor source of income. Rosas could claim no greater success than his predecessors in making the property tax the mainstay of the fiscal system of the province. It is true that in the forties revenues from this tax averaged over 1,200,000 pesos a year as against less than 500,000 pesos before 1835, but it is also true that in the last decade of Rosas' administration the average value of the peso stood at about 5 per cent of par as against 14 per cent in 1831–1835.[37] In 1839 the Finance Committee of the legislature predicted an income of 3,000,000 pesos from the property tax, or about 27 per cent of total revenues.

[34] Mabragaña II, 31 (Message, December 27, 1841).

[35] *Diario de Sesiones,* Session 702 (February 15, 1842). "Cuando se trata de establecer imposiciones sobre los pueblos, ó de reformar las que hay establecidas, es necesario marchar con mucha cordura y discreción, pulsar las circunstancias de la sociedad y asechar el momento, la oportunidad de estas inovaciones: sin esto pueden frustrarse las mas sabias medidas y los cálculos mejor levantados."

[36] Cf. *Archivo General,* Ant. C.23–A.10–no. 4. *Relación de los partidos de Campaña que no han remitido los Registros de Contribución Directa correspondiente a los años que se expresan:*

[37] Cf. Tables 34, 35, 36, 37.

TABLE 34

REVENUES OF THE PROVINCE OF BUENOS AIRES: 1840–1850

	Customs and Port duties	Stamp duty and License tax	Capital tax (Contribución Directa)	Saladeros y corrales tax	Sales, rentals, interest, etc.	Total revenues
1840	5,492,325$ 7½	1,036,000$ 0	996,342$ 2	122,600$ 0	231,969$ 4½	7,879,237$ 4
1841	36,397,759$ 4	868,800$ 4	1,446,846$ 4	211,100$ 0	382,439$ 2½	39,306,945$ 6½
1842	31,413,459$ 6½	916,100$ 0	1,106,002$ 1	430,000$ 0	265,244$ 5½	34,130,806$ 5
1843	33,110,992$ 5	952,700$ 0	2,200,870$ 1½	215,000$ 0	357,458$ 0	36,837,020$ 6½
1844	29,250,362$ 2½	1,079,700$ 0	1,607,938$ 7	215,000$ 0	388,183$ 4	32,511,186$ 5½
1845	27,871,184$ 0½	1,542,400$ 0	1,438,484$ 0	138,000$ 0	472,952$ 4¼	31,463,020$ 4¾
1846	6,036,121$ 0½	1,074,200$ 0	967,739$ 3½		641,926$ 1	8,719,986$ 5
1847	15,025,900$ 1	1,298,202$ 2	1,164,042$ 7	108,000$ 0	385,490$ 1½	17,977,635$ 3½
1848	28,807,864$ 0½	1,420,190$ 0	1,326,558$ 5½	158,000$ 0	547,872$ 3½	32,060,285$ 1½
1849	48,007,826$ 2	1,665,360$ 0	1,818,814$ 1¼		377,906$ 4¼	51,869,906$ 7½
1850	57,944,483$ 2½	1,782,780$ 0	1,941,897$ 2	158,000$ 0	400,645$ 7½	62,227,806$ 4

Yet in 1850, when total revenues reached the unprecedented figure of 62,000,000 pesos, the *contribución directa* brought very little over 3 per cent of the total. The failure of Rosas and his party becomes all the more apparent when it is considered that the bulk of the property tax revenues was paid by commerce. In 1849, for example, capital invested in commodities imported on consignment was alone responsible for 56 per cent of revenues obtained from the *contribución directa*. To this must be added also the contribution of native capital invested in foreign and domestic commerce. If, therefore, proper allowance is made for industrial and agricultural capital as well as real estate, the share contributed by landowners and cattle breeders appears very small indeed. At their door, then, must the blame be laid for the niggardly results of the law of April 12, 1839.

TABLE 35

REVENUES OF THE PROVINCE OF BUENOS AIRES: 1840–1850
(Percentages of Total)

	Customs and Port Duties	Stamp and Lic. Tax	Contri- bución directa	Saladeros and Corrales	Sales rent. inter.	Total
1840	69.71	13.15	12.64	1.56	2.94	100.00
1841	92.60	2.21	3.68	0.54	0.97	100.00
1842	92.04	2.68	3.24	1.26	0.78	100.00
1843	89.88	2.59	5.98	0.58	0.97	100.00
1844	89.89	3.32	4.94	0.66	1.19	100.00
1845	88.59	4.90	4.57	0.44	1.50	100.00
1846	69.22	12.32	11.10		7.36	100.00
1847	83.58	7.21	6.47	0.60	2.14	100.00
1848	89.85	4.43	4.13	0.49	1.09	100.00
1849	92.55	3.21	3.51		0.73	100.00
1850	93.11	2.88	3.12	0.25	0.64	100.00

The cattle tax (*derecho de saladeros y corrales*) had its origin in the financial reforms launched in 1829 by Juan José Viamonte. The original rates of 1 peso per head of cattle sold for domestic consumption and 1½ pesos upon cattle slaughtered for export were replaced in 1833 by a uniform rate of 4 reales per head.[38] For reasons which are not quite clear the government preferred to farm out the administration and collection of this tax. It should be noted that the rate remained unchanged throughout Rosas' administration. In 1836 revenue from

[38] *Diario de Sesiones*, Sessions 208 (August 13, 1830), 251 (November 14, 1831), 307 (February 1, 1833), and 373 (December 26, 1833). Also, RO–538, L–12, no. –12; RO–566, L–13, no. –1.

TABLE 36

EXPENDITURES OF THE PROVINCE OF BUENOS AIRES: 1840–1850

	Junta de Represen-tantes	Ministerio de Gobierno	Ministerio de Rel. Exter.	Ministerio de Guerra	Ministerio de Hacienda			Total Expenditures
					General Expenses	Service of long term debt	Treasury bills and direct oblig.	
1840	47,297$ 0	1,443,055$ 3	1,398,624$ 6¼	23,832,896$ 4	1,691,694$ 0	3,055,198$ 7	17,047,398$ 0¾	48,516,164$ 5
1841	45,888$ 0	2,062,224$ 0½	1,001,694$ 3¾	29,641,432$ 1¼	1,563,831$ 4¾	3,755,198$ 2	3,614,360$ 2½	41,684,628$ 6¾
1842	40,435$ 0	1,745,251$ 5½	669,541$ 5½	23,008,011$ 0	2,474,702$ 7½	3,755,198$ 2	4,626,411$ 2¼	36,319,551$ 2¾
1843	41,199$ 0	2,151,187$ 7	802,934$ 5½	18,643,854$ 4¾	3,211,502$ 0	3,755,198$ 2	6,535,982$ 0¼	35,156,859$ 1½
1844	41,688$ 1	2,455,048$ 4¾	788,433$ 5¾	20,934,642$ 5¼	2,710,280$ 7½	3,755,198$ 2	3,659,522$ 3	34,339,814$ 5¼
1845	40,859$ 2½	2,087,444$ 6½	1,289,946$ 2	18,535,948$ 1½	2,878,352$ 0	3,755,198$ 2	5,289,617$ 2	33,877,366$ 0½
1846	43,638$ 1	2,178,071$ 5½	1,819,319$ 2	15,493,177$ 5½	1,949,699$ 2¼	3,755,198$ 2	6,087,763$ 4¼	31,326,869$ 2½
1847	38,983$ 3	2,814,403$ 0½	1,776,006$ 0¼	22,638,334$ 1	2,100,712$ 1	3,755,200$ 0	5,950,991$ 7¼	39,074,632$ 5
1848	38,026$ 0	2,489,133$ 5¼	1,750,624$ 6¾	20,995,696$ 6½	2,203,786$ 4½	3,755,200$ 0	6,455,293$ 3¾	37,667,761$ 2¾
1849	38,095$ 4	4,075,554$ 0	1,574,708$ 2	28,197,810$ 3½	2,273,659$ 2½	3,755,200$ 0	8,477,085$ 3	48,192,112$ 7
1850	42,005$ 2	5,887,439$ 7½	1,247,734$ 1	27,937,331$ 5¾	4,702,039$ 2¼	3,755,200$ 0	12,444,201$ 4	56,015,951$ 6½

this source amounted to 115,000 pesos.   In 1850, when the total revenue was about six times larger, the *saladero* tax produced only 158,000 pesos.

Little need be said of other minor imposts.   The light tax (*alumbrado*), the fee for registration of cattle brands (*marcas*), market fees (*mercado*), bridge and highway tolls (*pontazgo, peage*), night police (*serenos*), and several others, were each of small consequence.   The method of administration and collection of these imposts varied.   Some were administered directly by the government, and others were supervised by the police.

TABLE 37

EXPENDITURES OF THE PROVINCE OF BUENOS AIRES: 1840–1850
(Percentages of Total)

	J.R.	Gobierno	Rel. Ext.	Guerra	Gnl. Exp.	Hacienda Long T. Dbt.	Tr. bills	Total
1840	0.10	3.00	2.80	49.10	3.50	6.30	35.20	100.0
1841	0.11	4.95	2.40	71.11	3.75	9.01	8.67	100.0
1842	0.11	4.80	1.84	63.35	6.81	10.34	12.75	100.0
1843	0.12	6.12	2.28	53.05	9.14	10.69	18.60	100.0
1844	0.12	7.15	2.30	60.95	7.89	10.93	10.66	100.0
1845	0.12	6.16	3.81	54.72	8.50	11.08	15.61	100.0
1846	0.14	6.95	5.81	49.45	6.22	11.99	19.44	100.0
1847	0.10	7.20	4.54	57.94	5.38	9.61	15.23	100.0
1848	0.10	6.60	4.65	55.71	5.85	9.96	17.13	100.0
1849	0.08	8.42	3.25	58.27	4.70	7.76	17.52	100.0
1850	0.08	10.51	2.23	49.87	8.39	6.70	21.22	100.0

Revenues from sources other than taxation were scant.   As stockholder of Banco Nacional the government was entitled to a share of the Bank's earnings.   This source of income disappeared, of course, after the dissolution of the bank in 1836.   Some income was derived from land and real estate which the government owned in Buenos Aires and other cities and towns.   Some of these properties were leased to private operators, while others were administered directly by the government.   Considerable sums were also realized from the sale of hides.   In some years as much as 675,000 pesos was obtained from this source.   The practice of collecting hides of cattle consumed in the army was inaugurated by Rosas in 1839.   In that year the treasury realized nearly 617,000 pesos.   But in 1845 this source produced not more than 320,000 pesos, and in the following year only 141,483 pesos.   Thereafter the treasury statements show no income whatever from this source.

From public lands the provincial government derived revenue in two ways. One was in the form of rentals on government-owned lands held in emphyteusis. This income was relatively modest. In 1835 and 1836, i.e., just before the original contracts expired, revenue on account of emphyteusis amounted in round figures to 152,000 and 198,000 pesos respectively. The revenue was drastically curtailed in 1837, primarily because many tenants (*enfiteutas*) availed themselves of the opportunity to buy the land outright.[39] Nevertheless, the provincial government had good reasons to complain about the manner in which emphyteusis was administered. Land, declared Rosas in his annual message, had been given in emphyteusis without proper formalities and measurements, provoking thus numerous complaints and quarrels. It was frequently impossible to determine the value of leased lands, and this prevented correct assessment of property taxes. Rosas proposed to remedy the situation by means of systematic surveys and even promised to prepare a rural code.[40] The code was never compiled, and the surveying of land holdings was under the best conditions a slow process. In the meantime Rosas insisted upon a more rigid observance of the prevailing emphyteusis law, and prompt payment of rentals. These were doubled early in 1838, i.e., after the original contracts expired.[41] However, the doubling of rentals had little effect on revenue. In 1839, the second year of the new rates, emphyteusis produced about 196,000 pesos, which was 2,000 pesos less than in 1836. In that year, according to some estimates, about 3,500 square leagues were held in emphyteusis, though it should be noted that most of the land thus held was of inferior value.[42] It is not possible to follow the history of emphyteusis revenues after 1839. Beginning with 1840 the reports of the provincial treasury contain no reference to this source of income. Whether emphyteusis rentals were merged with other revenues cannot be readily ascertained, but it may be safely assumed that emphyteusis continued to produce relatively insignificant sums.

Rather than extend the emphyteusis system and improve its ad-

---

[39] Law, May 10, 1836 in Joaquín M. Muzlera, *Tierras públicas. Recopilación de leyes, decretos y resoluciones de la provincia de Buenos Aires sobre tierras públicas, desde 1810 á 1895* (La Plata: 1896), t. 1, pp. 113–114.

[40] Mabragaña I, 332 (Message, January 1, 1837).

[41] Law, May 10, 1836; Law, May 28, 1838. Joaquín M. Muzlera, *op. cit.*

[42] *Diario de Sesiones*, Session 635 (April 5, 1839). Article 4 of Law of May 28, 1838 provided that emphyteusis contracts affecting land in certain specified areas could not be renewed.

ministration Rosas preferred to sell public land outright. He hoped
in this manner to obtain larger sums which in times of emergency
might be used to greater advantage. The first sale of land on a large
scale was sanctioned by the legislature on May 10, 1836. The government was authorized to dispose of 1,500 square leagues, part of
which was held in emphyteusis. The law fixed the price at 5,000
pesos per square league in territory north of Río Salado, at 4,000 pesos
in the area between the Río Salado and a line running from Sierra del
Volcán through Laguna Blanca and Fuerte Mayo to Fuerte Federación, and at 3,000 pesos in the remaining territory of the province.
Enfiteutas were given priority with respect to the land they leased, and
proceeds from the sale of land were to be used for the retirement of the
floating debt. In 1837 conditions concerning the sale of land were
formulated in a decree of July 27. Buyers were permitted to make
payments in three installments, if they bought the land before February 1838. For land bought between February 1838 and February
1839 one-third of the value must be paid in cash. And after February
1839 cash had to be paid at the time of the sale. At the end of 1838
Rosas admitted that a large portion of the 1,500 square leagues still
remained unsold. He expected, however, to obtain 1,000,000 pesos
from this source in 1839.[43] Actually the sale yielded 1,062,000 pesos
in 1839. But in 1840 the treasury received only 101,000 pesos, and
thereafter the treasury reported no income from this source.

2

After the fall of the Rivadavia regime budgeting became a lost art.
The laws of September 5, 1821 and of December 19, 1822 were disregarded rather consistently in the years following the Revolution of
Lavalle. At first the legislature insisted upon retaining control over
expenditures by voting global appropriations for each fiscal year. But
as the government never observed this limitation the practice was
gradually abandoned, and by the time Rosas began his second term
the legislature made no attempt to regain control of public expenditures. Invested with dictatorial powers (*suma del poder público*),
Rosas had ample authority to conduct the financial affairs of the province without consulting the provincial assembly. And the Junta was
fully prepared to accept the leadership of the executive, the more

[43] Mabragaña I, 396 (Message, December 27, 1838).

readily since Rosas could be relied upon to exercise extreme caution in matters of taxation.

The estimates of expenditure which Rosas included in his annual messages to the Junta were not, strictly speaking, budgets. They in no way curtailed the government's freedom of action, and it was tacitly understood by both the executive and legislative branches that should expenditures transcend the estimates the government would not be required to have the legislature's approval. At no time after 1835 had the legislature considered the province's expenditures in any detail. Its activities in this field were confined to more or less perfunctory approvals of the corresponding portions of the annual messages. And it was only when the government having found itself in financial difficulties demanded new appropriations that the legislature was permitted to discuss the financial problems of the province. Even then the legislature dared not inquire into the government's needs too closely, and confined itself usually to giving approval to whatever measures Rosas deemed necessary and appropriate.

The province's expenditures were classified under five headings. Under the heading Junta de Representantes were grouped all expenses relating to the administration and functioning of the legislative assembly. These expenditures were comparatively insignificant. In 1839 expenditures connected with the functioning of the Junta amounted to slightly over 51,000 pesos, or about 0.18 per cent of the total. In 1850, when the total expenditures rose to 56,000,000 pesos, as compared to 28,000,000 pesos in 1839, the legislature consumed only 42,000 pesos, or less than 0.1 per cent of the total. In none of the intervening years did expenditures of the Junta rise above 48,000 pesos, and in three successive years (1847–1849) they dropped below 40,000 pesos. Whatever the causes of the financial difficulties of the Rosas regime, none can be ascribed to the provincial legislature. The remaining four groups of expenditures corresponded to the four administrative departments of the government. Least important from the point of view of expenditures was the Ministry of Foreign Affairs (*Ministerio de Relaciones Exteriores*). In 1839 this department was responsible for 3.6 per cent of the total expenditures, and although at times the proportion rose above 4.5 per cent it frequently fell below 3 per cent. Much of the increase was due to currency depreciation, since all the expenditures in this department went into salaries, and a good portion of these had to be paid in foreign exchange or specie.

The Ministry of Government (*Ministerio de Gobierno*) ranked next to the Foreign Office in point of expenditures. This department, whose functions were numerous and varied, was also the first to suffer from economies introduced by Rosas. Expenditures of this Ministry ranged between 1,228,000 pesos in 1839 to 5,887,000 pesos in 1850, but for the most part stayed below 3,000,000 pesos. Here, too, currency depreciation helped to boost the budget. But the main reason for the comparatively low budget of this department was the fact that Rosas curtailed the activities of the Ministry of Government to a minimum. He closed the University of Buenos Aires, and reduced or altogether abolished subsidies to other educational institutions as well as to hospitals and the Sociedad de Beneficencia.[44] He likewise reduced the staff of the Ministry, though he could not avoid the necessity of increasing salaries to meet the rising cost of living.[45] It should also be noted that the Ministry of Government was in charge of the police which consumed a considerable portion of the Ministry's budget. Then, too, much of the expenditures of the Ministry of Government were discretional funds, used for political rather than administrative purposes.

By far the largest proportion of the government's expenditures originated in the Ministry of War (*Ministerio de Guerra*). This was perhaps inevitable. It was inevitable that the regime established by Rosas, uncompromising and absolutist, should have provoked violent reaction within the province and abroad. It was inevitable also that the national policies of Rosas should have encountered stubborn resistance in the other provinces of the Confederation as well as in the conterminous states which once recognized the authority of the viceroy of Buenos Aires. The result was that rebellion and foreign wars continued intermittently throughout Rosas' administration. The conflict with France, the revolution in the southern districts of the province, the war against the Bolivian dictator Santa Cruz, the intervention in Uruguay, and the Anglo-French blockade—all these conflicts imposed heavy burdens upon the provincial treasury. Rosas was compelled to maintain at all times a relatively large standing army in order to de-

---

[44] *Notas* to: Rector de la Universidad de Buenos Aires (April 27, 1838); Administrador del Hospital General de Mugeres (April 28, 1838); Comisión Administradora del Hospital General de Hombres (April 28, 1838); Administrador General de Vacunas (April 30, 1838); Inspector General de Escuelas (April 27, 1838); Presidente de la Sociedad de Beneficencia (April 27, 1838); Inspector General de Escuelas (April 27, 1838). Cf. *Recopilación de las leyes y decretos. . . .*

[45] Cf. *Recopilación de leyes y decretos* . . . Decree, May 10, 1832.

fend the regime against direct or indirect attacks of the unitaries, and in order, also, to extend help in men, money, and material to his allies in other provinces and abroad.

The war department's share in the provincial budget varied from year to year, depending upon the intensity of military operations. In 1836, a relatively peaceful year, military expenses amounted to 4,-000,000 pesos, or 27 per cent of total. But in 1839, the first full year of the French blockade, military expenditures rose to 11,000,000 pesos, in the following year to 23,000,000, and in 1840 to more than 29,-000,000 pesos. In that last year more than 71 per cent of total expenditures were accounted for by the war department. Thereafter, military expenditures were somewhat reduced, though they never fell below 49 per cent of the total.[46]

The Ministry of Finance (*Ministerio de Hacienda*) was responsible for the remaining expenditures. These included not only administration and collection of revenues but also the servicing of the public debt through the Caja de Administración del Crédito Público, payments of direct obligations and treasury bills. These last payments made up a very considerable portion of the treasury budget. The servicing of Fondos Públicos became stabilized after 1849 at 3,755,200 pesos, for after the loan of March 28, 1840 Rosas did not have recourse to bond issues. The amount of treasury bills that fell due each year fluctuated slightly from year to year, always well under 1,000,000 pesos. But payments on account of direct obligations varied widely. In 1840 the government paid on this account over 16,000,000 pesos, or about 33 per cent of the total expenditures, while in the following two years such payments fell to about 2,500,000 and 3,500,000 pesos. The average expenditure during the forties was close to 5,000,000 pesos per year.[47]

In spite of all his efforts Rosas never succeeded in meeting expenditures out of ordinary revenues. By means of strict economy and careful accounting he managed to reduce expenditures in certain departments, but these savings were altogether too small to affect the treasury's balance sheet. Military expenditures and payments on account of the public debt could not be easily reduced, and for this reason mainly the balancing of the budget depended largely upon Rosas' ability to increase revenues. But revenues from sources other than customs duties were disappointingly small, and Rosas was singularly

[46] See Table 37.
[47] See Tables 36, 37.

reluctant to impose new taxes.   Deficits were, therefore, unavoidable and the government was at all times grappling with financial difficulties.

3

To meet the ever mounting deficits Rosas followed the line of least resistance.   He realized only too well that a serious effort to attain financial equilibrium by way of adjusting the tax pattern to the actual cost of administration would arouse strong opposition among the powerful *estancieros*.   On the other hand, it was evident that the credit of the province was not yet wholly exhausted, and that for a time, at least, the government could mobilize considerable funds floating idly in the Buenos Aires market.   At the end of 1835 the long term debt of the province stood at less than 20,000,000 pesos even though in the preceding year new bonds to the amount of 8,000,000 pesos were thrown upon the market.   In fact, bond prices were steadily improving during 1835 and 1836, reflecting the market's confidence in both the stability of the Rosas regime and its ability to cope with the financial situation.   The time seemed advantageous for a new issue of Fondos Públicos.   In January of 1837 the government was authorized by law to issue 17,000,000 pesos in bonds, the largest operation in the history of the Fondos Públicos.[48]   The government refrained from disposing of the whole issue at once, and a large portion of the bonds was used as a basis for currency expansion.   By law of March 11, 1837 the Casa de Moneda was authorized to accept 7,000,000 in bonds as security against an issue of 4,200,000 pesos in currency.[49]   The government decided to sell the remaining bonds in the open market. Rosas argued that the money market was far from saturated and that amortization was sufficiently rapid to stimulate a sustained rise of bond prices.   It was reasonable to assume that the treasury would have no difficulty in placing the newly created issue at 60 per cent of par.[50]

[48] Law, January 30, 1837 (RO–1130, L–16, no. –2).

[49] RO–1143, L–16, no. –3.   Of the new currency 3,200,000 pesos were to be placed at the disposal of the treasury immediately, and the remaining 1,000,000 pesos in July 1837. The government reserved the right to sell the bonds deposited in the Casa de Moneda, and while the bonds remained unsold the interest was to be used for amortization of privately held Fondos Públicos.

[50] Mabragaña I, 374 (Message, December 27, 1837).   "Pudiera sin embargo temerse que la venta de los 8,000,000 pesos en Fondos Públicos no fuese realizable.   Mas, cómo alimentar esta sospecha cuando según se verá en el estado, aun vendidos los 8,000,000 de Fondos solo habría en circulación 27,000,000, y estos tienen un capital amortizable de

However, the government's optimism was ill founded. As soon as it became known that a new issue of bonds was contemplated the bond market became thoroughly demoralized. Demand for Fondos Públicos disappeared entirely as early as December of 1836, and it was not until the latter part of the following March [51] that trading in Fondos Públicos was again resumed. But now the prices were far below those demanded by the Treasury. In March of 1837 the bonds were quoted at 45 per cent of par and, although prices improved somewhat in the following months, the recovery was slow. Bond prices reached 60 per cent of par only in September of 1839. By this time the government had already disposed of the issue of March 1837 and was contemplating another long term loan. Indeed in March of 1840 it asked authorization for a new issue of Fondos Públicos to the amount of 10,000,000 pesos. On recommendation of the Finance Committee the legislature granted the government's request by law of March 28, 1840.[52] The Finance Committee emphasized that the government should not throw the whole issue on the market at once, and that the bonds should not be offered at less than 60 per cent of par. This latter condition was not difficult to safeguard. In view of the promptness with which the long term loans had been serviced the market for Fondos Públicos showed unusual firmness. Upon the passage of the law of March 28, 1840 bond prices dropped 5 points to 55 per cent, but recovered to 60 per cent in May of that year. And in October, after the lifting of the French blockade, bond prices rose still further, reaching a peak of 71 per cent in November.

The loan of March 28, 1840 was the last bond issue under Rosas. At the end of 1840 the long term internal debt of the province amounted to somewhat over 36,000,000 pesos, a sum that was not excessive considering the depreciation of the peso. This indebtedness was being rapidly reduced. In 1846 it fell to 18,700,000 pesos and by 1850 not

---

1,500,000 pesos m/n, que irá aumentando en los años sucesivos con notable rapidez? Podrá escaparse a los especuladores el conocimiento de que hoy se retiran de esa misma circulación, como 3,000,000 pesos en Fondos Públicos, y que con tan fuerte amortización la deuda debe extinguirse prontamente y el valor de los fondos tomar un incremento considerable? No es pues, presumible que esta cantidad de fondos no produce la suma que ha sido calculada."

[51] That is after 7,000,000 pesos worth of bonds had been deposited in the Casa de Moneda.

[52] *Diario de Sesiones*, Session 666 (March 28, 1840).

more than 13,750,000 of Fondos Públicos were still outstanding.[53]   It is not surprising, therefore, that bond prices continued to improve, reaching par in September of 1846, and selling at a premium in December of that year.

The reasons which induced Rosas to avoid having recourse to long term borrowing are not quite clear.   Nowhere in his official utterances did Rosas explain this break with the traditional method of financing. It may be that he considered the loans too costly, in view of the circumstance that the treasury had seldom been able to dispose of the bonds at less than 40 per cent discount.   The fact is that every new issue of Fondos Públicos, except the last, invariably created considerable nervousness in the Buenos Aires money market, and the treasury had to be extremely cautious in selling bonds.   Nor were the moneyed classes very receptive to continued bond issues.   The attitude of the *porteño* investors was clearly revealed in the report of the Finance Committee on the loan of 1840.   Speaking for the Committee deputy Garrigós emphasized that since the majority of merchants sympathized with the unitaries and would not, therefore, invest in bonds, the burden of the loan would fall mainly upon federalists, or rather the *hacendados* who alone were financially able to support the loan.   But the federalists, argued Garrigós, could not carry the whole burden of the province's long term debt, and it would not be just to force one group of citizens to furnish the needed funds.   For it was precisely this class (the *hacendados*) which was already helping the government in every possible way.   Long term borrowing was even more unnecessary in the opinion of the Finance Committee since the government had at its disposal a much more effective method of financing, namely the issue of paper money.[54]

This attitude of the powerful *estanciero* class could not be disregarded.   Through the Finance Committee it warned the government that further loans would not be forthcoming and that inflation was preferable to borrowing.   The position of the Finance Committee in the matter of long term borrowing was still stronger since on at least two previous occasions the government resorted to the printing press. In March of 1837 the government, hard pressed for ready funds and unable to float the 17,000,000 loan recently approved, requested au-

[53] This includes bonds held by benevolent and religious societies as well as unredeemed bonds.   See Tables 38–40.

[54] *Diario de Sesiones*, Session 666 (March 28, 1840).   Speech by deputy Garrigós.

TABLE 38

The Long Term Public Debt (Fondos Públicos) of the Province of
Buenos Aires, 1840–1850

Year	Total amortization	Amortized during the year	Outstanding
1840	15,743,730$ 3¾	2,335,651$ 1¼	36,280,578$ 3
1841	18,079,381$ 5	2,628,360$ 2½	33,625,348$ 0¾
1846	32,721,920$ 1¼	2,899,868$ 4	18,738,201$ 2¾
1847	35,589,569$ 7¾	1,008,642$ 2½	17,761,787$ 6¼
1848	36,614,675$ 6¾	226,155$ 2½	17,519,169$ 4
1849	37,067,864$ 5	2,427,835$ 1¾	14,864,300$ 1½
1850	39,490,829$ 5¾	1,113,450$ 6½	13,750,849$ 3

Sources: See Table 39.

TABLE 39

Amortization of the 4 Per Cent Loan (Fondos Públicos) of the
Province of Buenos Aires, 1840–1850

Year	Total amortization	Amortized during the year	Unredeemed and held by pious societies	In circulation	Total outstanding
1840	599,686$ 2¼	651$ 2¼	151,759$ 6½	1,247,902$ 5	1,399,622$ 3½
1841	600,337$ 4½	3,996$ 2	151,759$ 6½	1,243,996$ 3	1,305,756$ 1½
1846	685,863$ 7½	87,728$ 4	157,321$ 1¼	1,069,076$ 3¼	1,226,397$ 4½
1847	773,602$ 3½	31,344$ 6½	157,321$ 1¼	1,037,731$ 4¾	1,195,052$ 6½
1848	804,947$ 2	41,120$ 7¾	157,321$ 1¼	996,610$ 5	1,153,931$ 6½
1849	846,068$ 1¾	104,856$ 2	157,321$ 1¼	891,754$ 3	1,049,075$ 4½
1850	950,924$ 3¾	65,760$ 6	157,321$ 1¼	825,993$ 5	983,314$ 6½

Sources: *British Packet and Argentine News*, January 9, 1841; *Registro Oficial*, Libro 20; *Archivo Americano*, Nueva Serie, I (1847), 164; II (1848), no. 6; IV (1849), no. 13, p. 145; V (1850), no. 19; VII (1851), no. 23, p. 198.

TABLE 40

Amortization of the 6 Per Cent Loan (Fondos Públicos) of the
Province of Buenos Aires, 1840–1850

Year	Total amortization	Amortized during the year	Unredeemed and held by pious societies	In circulation	Total outstanding
1840	15,144,044$ 1½	2,334,909$ 7	288,680$ 2¾	34,592,275$ 4¾	34,880,955$ 7½
1841	17,479,044$ 0½	2,621,334$ 6½	342,141$ 6¾	31,914,450$ 0½	32,256,591$ 7¼
1846	32,036,056$ 1¼	2,812,140$ 0	830,283$ 5½	16,661,520$ 0¾	17,811,803$ 6¼
1847	34,813,967$ 4¼	977,297$ 4	862,483$ 3½	15,704,251$ 2¼	16,366,734$ 7¾
1848	35,809,728$ 4¾	185,034$ 2¾	872,483$ 3½	15,492,734$ 0	16,365,237$ 3½
1849	36,221,796$ 3¼	2,322,978$ 7¾	876,483$ 5½	12,938,740$ 7½	13,813,224$ 5
1850	38,544,775$ 3	1,047,690$ 0½	876,483$ 5½	11,891,050$ 7	12,767,534$ 4½

Sources: See Table 39.

thority to issue 4,200,000 pesos in currency. The bill introduced on March 10, 1837 provoked some opposition. The deputies recalled the government's solemn promises to maintain the currency on an even keel. But the Minister of Finance argued that in the preceding eight years the amount of notes in circulation had been stationary, while the population as well as the area of the province had considerably increased. At the time of the Banco de Descuentos there were 3,000,000 silver pesos in circulation serving the industrial and commercial needs of the province. The present 15,000,000 paper pesos represented 2,-200,000 pesos in specie, a sum that was obviously inadequate. The Minister insisted therefore that an issue of 5,500,000 paper pesos could be safely undertaken "without causing the least disturbance in foreign exchange, but bringing prices to a level advantageous to commerce and industry." The minister assured the Junta that should the new issue of currency prove harmful the government was determined to retire it at the earliest opportunity. The measure, continued the Minister, was but a temporary expedient, intended to tide the treasury over until the market for Fondos Públicos improved.[55]   The argument of the Minister of Finance was further developed by deputies Mansilla, Garrigós, and Lahitte. Mansilla argued that the country was inadequately supplied with circulating media. Scarcity of money was the principal cause of the financial crisis, and it was also the main factor making for economic stagnation. The country could not absorb the bonds which the government intended to float for the simple reason that there was not enough money.[56]   This argument was ably seconded by Garrigós who emphasized that there were less than 100 pesos in circulation per inhabitant and that an increase such as the government contemplated could not materially alter prices. Scarcity of money was not due to lack of confidence, asserted Garrigós, but rather to continued expansion of the provincial economy. Since the inception of Rosas' administration large sums had been invested in land and cattle breeding. These activities caused a steady drain upon the monetary resources of the province. Shortage of circulating media was the inevitable conse-

---

[55] *Diario de Sesiones,* Session 568 (March 11, 1837).

[56] *Loc. cit.* "Tengo una razón muy fuerte (for supporting the measure) y es, que veo el tamaño de la población; veo la cantidad circulante, y veo que la imposibilidad de realizarse hoy el empréstito, es porque no hay capitales bastantes en cajas de los que debieran hacer el empréstito. . . ."

quence of the expansion of money economy to regions where primitive economy had been predominant until recently.[57]

The bill authorizing the Casa de Moneda to issue 4,200,000 pesos was enacted into law on March 11, 1837.[58] The government was to deposit 7,000,000 in bonds as guarantee of eventual retirement of currency, but if these bonds were sold the proceeds were to be used entirely for currency amortization. This latter provision of the law was eventually repealed,[59] so that the 4,200,000 paper pesos became an integral part of the country's monetary stock. The effect of this issue upon foreign exchange did not bear out the government's predictions. The price of gold in Buenos Aires rose from 117 pesos per ounce in February of 1827 to 146 pesos in August, and became stabilized for a brief period at about 130.[60] In his message to the legislature Rosas recognized the dangers of inflation and reiterated his determination to avoid having recourse to further paper money issues.[61]

It is quite possible that Rosas could have kept his word had it not been for the French blockade. The financial effects of the blockade were disastrous. Within a short period the treasury was despoiled of its largest source of revenue, while at the same time military expenditures grew apace. In urgent need of funds, the government thought of using the 7,000,000 in bonds deposited in the Casa de Moneda, but it soon realized that this sum was entirely insufficient to relieve the treasury. The problem was brought before the legislature. Not less than five separate bills were submitted for the Junta's consideration. Each of these bills called for currency expansion, but they differed in important details. The bill submitted by the government called for the creation of 12,575,000 pesos, of which 4,000,000 pesos were to be issued immediately and the remainder in seven monthly installments. It further provided that the Financial Commission of the Junta consider means to raise additional revenue to the amount of 1,225,000 pesos per month, and to strengthen the *contribución directa* so as to insure revenue of 3,000,000 pesos from this source. The Financial Commission drafted its own bill, which called for a total of 6,400,000 pesos of new currency. In support of the bill the commission argued that a

---

[57] *Loc. cit.*
[58] RO–1143, L–16, no. –3.
[59] Law, October 30, 1838 (RO–1262, L–17, no. –10).
[60] The prices are monthly averages. See Table 41.
[61] Mabragaña, I, 364/5 (Message, December 27, 1837).

TABLE 41

Average Monthly Prices of Six Per Cent Internal Bonds in the Buenos Aires Market for the Years 1829–1848

	Jan.	Feb.	March	Apr.	May	June	July	Aug.	Sept.	Oct.	Nov.	Dec.	Yearly Average
1829	53.00	55.75	59.50	62.00	60.50	60.00	56.00	52.00	55.00	58.00	60.00	61.00	57.73
1830	60.50	62.00	63.00	70.00	72.50	72.00	72.50	77.00	77.50	78.00	77.50	78.00	71.71
1831	79.50	75.50	57.00	61.00	63.50	55.50	55.00	56.00	56.50	58.00	57.50	56.50	60.93
1832	57.00	53.50	47.50	46.50	44.50	42.25	42.50	42.50	42.25	45.25	44.50	44.50	46.02
1833	45.25	43.75	43.75	43.00	42.00	43.25	45.50	44.50	47.00	51.00	55.00	52.50	46.35
1834	52.25	51.00	51.00	49.00	48.00	46.50	52.00	52.00	55.50	57.50	52.50	45.50	51.06
1835	43.75	40.00	41.00	43.25	46.25	52.50	56.50	65.00	59.50	61.00	62.25	62.00	52.75
1836	65.25	64.50	65.00	71.00	74.50	74.50	74.00	72.00	70.00	69.00	69.50	69.50	68.23
1837	64.00	59.00	54.00	49.00	57.75	57.75	57.50	53.50	52.50	47.75	50.50	53.50	54.73
1838	52.50	55.00	52.00	49.50	47.00	44.50	42.00	45.00	53.50	50.00	39.00	44.00	47.83
1839	48.00	49.50	49.00	51.00	50.00	56.00	56.00	56.50	59.50	50.00	60.00	58.00	54.46
1840	65.00	57.00	55.00	55.00	60.00	56.00	60.00	60.00	60.00	60.00	60.00	65.00	58.12
1841	68.00	57.50	61.00	61.00	60.00	60.00	61.00	60.50	60.00	60.00	67.00	66.00	61.83
1842	69.50	69.50	68.00	62.50	62.50	66.50	66.50	66.50	66.50	66.50	66.50	66.00	66.46
1843	66.50	66.50	66.50	66.50	66.00	66.00	66.00	65.00	65.00	65.00	65.00	66.00	65.86
1844	70.00	70.00	70.00	69.50	61.50	58.00	65.50	66.00	72.50	71.50	70.50	77.00	66.83
1845	82.50	80.00	80.00	80.00	80.00	80.00	80.00	78.00	76.00	76.00	76.00	76.00	78.71
1846	76.00	76.00	76.00	76.00	78.00	81.00	82.00	81.00	100.00	100.00	98.00	95.00	84.92
1847	95.00	97.50	97.00	96.00	99.00	100.00	100.00	100.00	100.00	100.00	100.00	95.00	98.29
1848	104.50	102.50	100.00	100.00	103.00	104.00	100.00	100.00	101.50	100.00	100.00	104.50	99.08

Source: *The British Packet and Argentine News.*

monthly subsidy of 800,000 pesos should be sufficient to cover the
deficit, especially since the government withdrew the Fondos Públicos
from the Casa de Moneda and could count in addition upon large revenues from the sale of public lands.[62]   The bill further called for eventual retirement of 6,400,000 pesos and obligated the government to
submit appropriate measures to the Junta within three months of the
enactment of the present legislation.   The bills introduced by deputies
Lucio Mansilla, Lahitte, and Garrigós were more elaborate.   Mansilla's
bill would authorize an issue of 22,000,000 pesos, of which 16,000,000
pesos were to be transferred to the treasury, and the remaining 6,-
000,000 pesos added to the capital of the Casa de Moneda.   The government was instructed to retire all treasury bills in circulation and was
further forbidden to borrow at interest without express authorization.
The bill provided also that the new currency be amortized with profits
of the Casa de Moneda and certain revenues earmarked for this purpose.   At the same time the bill recommended a cut of 50 per cent of
all salaries above 3,000 pesos per year for the duration of the blockade.
The cut was to be restored after the blockade plus interest at the rate
of 1 per cent per month adjusted quarterly.   The bill introduced by
Lahitte called for an issue of 20,000,000 pesos.   Of this sum 15,000,000
were to be used for the retirement of all short term obligations, reimbursement of voluntary loans, and payment of other current debts.
The remaining 5,000,000 pesos were to be employed in aiding industry
and commerce.   The government was enjoined from issuing treasury
bills in any form, and from contracting debts within the province or
abroad.   No new issues were to be authorized until the present one
was entirely amortized.   Profits accrued to the Casa de Moneda as a
result of discount operations were to be used for the retirement of currency.   Amortization of the present issue was to begin three months

---

[62] The Commission's calculations were based upon a monthly budget of 2,075,000
pesos, to be obtained from the following sources:

Customs revenues	200,000	pesos
Stamp duties and license fees	50,000	"
Other taxes, including *contribución directa*	100,000	"
7,000,000 in bonds at 60 per cent would produce		
4,200,000 pesos, or monthly	525,000	"
Sale of land ....'	400,000	"
New currency	800,000	"
	2,075,000	"

Cf. *Diario de Sesiones,* Session 622 (November 15, 1838).

after the end of the blockade at the rate of 2,000,000 pesos annually in equal monthly installments. The following funds were to be earmarked for currency amortization: profits from operations of the Casa de Moneda; proceeds from the sale of government-owned real estate in Buenos Aires; revenues from taxes levied upon inheritances, gifts, legacies, and similar revenues from all new taxes sanctioned by the legislature.

Still more elaborate was the plan submitted by deputy Garrigós. It consisted of three separate bills. The first bill called for an issue of 15,000,000 pesos to be delivered to the treasury in three installments of 8,000,000 pesos (December 1838), 4,000,000 pesos (January 1839), and 3,000,000 pesos (February 1839). The second bill provided for the establishment of a Caja de Amortización de Billetes de Banco, to be administered by a board composed of three deputies, two landowners, and two merchants, directly responsible to the Junta. It further prescribed the manner in which the new notes were to be retired. The third bill established the amortization fund. The following taxes were proposed: a tax of one peso upon each head of cattle slaughtered in the *saladeros;* a tax of one-half peso upon cattle slaughtered for domestic consumption; a special tax upon real estate and land; a surtax of one to three per cent upon imports. Revenues from these sources were to be turned over to the Caja de Amortización and used exclusively for the retirement of currency.[63]

Of the five bills the one drafted by the government was considered first. It was pointed out in support of the bill that currency expansion was both necessary and advantageous in view of the general shortage of money. Garrigós claimed that the quantity of money in circulation was far below the actual needs of the province. There were 19,500,000 pesos in circulation. A considerable portion of this total found its way into country districts and into other provinces, where it tended to remain. It was estimated that about 10,000,000 pesos were thus eliminated from the channels of foreign trade. Scarcity of money and high interest rates were, therefore, the result of an expanding economy, and at the same time one of the principal causes of financial difficulties of the treasury. The government was unable to float long term loans not so much because its credit was impaired, but rather because of the general condition of the Buenos Aires money market. The proposed issue of currency would not only solve the financial difficulties of the prov-

[63] For the texts of the bills see *Diario de Sesiones, loc. cit.*

ince, but would also bring to life industry and commerce, now all but strangled by the blockade. If any criticism could be made with respect to the government bill it was that the contemplated issue was not large enough. Deputy Irigoyen suggested that the proposed issue be increased by 4,000,000 pesos, to 16,575,000 pesos.

In view of the general approval of the government bill deputies Garrigós and Mansilla withdrew their proposals. The government bill as amended by Irigoyen was finally approved by the legislature on December 8, 1838.[64] The law was put into effect immediately. In December alone the Casa de Moneda turned over to the treasury 8,000,000 pesos in new notes, a sum sufficient to cover the most urgent needs of the treasury. The remainder of the issue was made available in seven monthly installments of 1,225,000 pesos each. Needless to say, the effect of this issue upon exchange was instantaneous. In November of 1838 when the question of currency expansion was still being debated in the Junta, the price of gold rose 27 points to 179 pesos per ounce and in the following February the peso sank to 6⅔ per cent of par.[65]

The act of December 8, 1838 was based upon the assumption that the conflict with France would be ended within seven months. However, these calculations proved wrong, and by August of 1839 the government was once again in a critical financial situation. The funds created by the law of December 8 were exhausted, and revenues were still far below expenditures. In September the government transferred to the treasury half the profits accumulated by the Casa de Moneda. At the same time it ordered renewal of all notes in circulation and appropriated all notes not exchanged on account of loss or wear and tear. It was estimated that 10 per cent of all notes in circulation would not be presented for exchange, and the treasury obtained in this manner some 3,000,000 pesos.[66] But this brought only temporary relief and early in 1839 it became apparent that the treasury was facing a huge deficit. At the request of the government the Financial Commission suggested a convocation of the legislature in order to consider the situation. In a lengthy report deputy Garrigós presented the reasons which induced the Commission to advocate further issue of paper money.

[64] RO–1275, L–17, no. –12.
[65] See Table 41.
[66] RO–1340, L–18, no. –9. In 1847 the loss on this account was calculated at 3,605,854 pesos. Cf. *Estado que manifiesta las entradas, salidas y existencias de los capitales que ha girado la Casa de Moneda en el año de 1847* in *Archivo General*, Ant. C.24–A.3–no. 3.

Since the majority of merchants were unitary sympathizers they refused to support the government. The burden of a new bond issue would therefore fall upon federalists, who in turn were unable to furnish the necessary funds. An issue of treasury bills was also unacceptable. Such an issue besides raising formidable difficulties of a technical nature would impose upon the government a financial burden that was almost insupportable. The Commission rejected also the suggestion of extensive sales of public land on the ground that proceeds from this source would fall short of the needs of the treasury. There remained therefore one expedient, namely, the printing press. The Commission was aware of the government's opposition to continued currency expansion, but it reminded the Junta that twice in the past three years recourse had been had to such measures and that the situation was as grave now as on previous occasions. The Commission recommended, however, that the current issue of paper money be gradual in order to minimize its effects upon commerce and prices.[67]

The legislative assembly enacted the bill introduced by the Finance Commission almost without discussion. The law directed the Casa de Moneda to issue 12,000,000 pesos in currency for the account of the treasury. It further authorized a new issue of 6 per cent bonds to the amount of 10,000,000 pesos. The government was directed not to sell these bonds at less than 60 per cent of par. The new issue caused a sharp drop in the gold value of the peso. In January of 1840 gold at the Buenos Aires market sold at 282 pesos per ounce, but after the passage of the law of March 28 the price of gold rose to 346 pesos in April and 514 pesos in July. In the following months the peso slowly recovered to 5 per cent of par. Speculation became particularly widespread and the government was forced to intervene in order to prevent complete collapse of the monetary system of the province. Rosas blamed the unitaries for taking advantage of the financial difficulties of the government and admitted that it had been necessary to take strong measures to stamp out this "ruinous game."[68]

It was not until 1846 that Rosas was once more forced to resort to the printing press. The Anglo-French blockade cut off the major por-

[67] *Diario de Sesiones,* Session 666 (March 28, 1840).

[68] Mabragaña, II, 12 (Message of December 27, 1840). "El agio calculado por los salvajes traidores unitarios como elemento hostil contra el gobierno, el comercio y la población, fué contenido por medidas enérgicas. La autoridad descargó vigorosamente sobre los colaboradores de este ruinoso juego el peso de la justicia pública."

tion of the province's revenues, and in January of the following year the legislature was asked to approve new issues of paper money. Deputy Torres reported the findings of the Finance Commission and estimated that the government needed at least 1,800,000 pesos per month to meet the most essential needs. But since this estimate was based on prevailing prices and since, also, prices were certain to rise, he recommended a monthly subsidy of 2,300,000 pesos. Reviewing all possible sources of revenue he concluded that none was likely to provide the necessary income. Nor was a loan feasible at this time.

In appraising the outcome of a loan [said the report], it is necessary . . . to remember the condition of the country, with its paralyzed commerce, and the consequences of this stagnation in all fields of economic endeavor, among all classes. The merchant and the cattle breeder, the real estate owner, and the farmer—all are affected by the depression. They own large funds invested in merchandise, in cattle, in real estate, but they have no cash, nor can they liquidate their holdings even at a sacrifice.[69]

The amount of money in circulation, continued Torres, was not excessive. Of the 50,000,000 pesos so far issued about 20,000,000 had been withdrawn, and the demand for currency expansion was general among commercial and industrial classes. It was feared in some quarters that the proposed issue would bring about a rise in the price of specie. But to this argument Torres had the following answer:

Well, gentlemen, let the price of specie rise. In the last few months it rose without there being expansion of currency, and we know well that this artificial rise in the price of specie is of different origin. It is the work either of a few interested individuals, or else a manifestation of the hostility of our enemies, who are still allowed to plot in our midst.

The Junta offered no opposition and the bill was speedily enacted into law. It called for a monthly issue of 2,300,000 pesos until three months after the end of the blockade.[70] However, the issue was suspended before the date specified by law. Less than a month after the cessation of the blockade Rosas suspended operation of the currency expansion program.[71]

In the thirty-two months during which the law of January 16, 1846 remained in effect the Casa de Moneda issued 73,600,000 pesos in new currency, more than doubling the amount of paper money in circulation.

[69] *Diario de Sesiones,* 759 (Session of January 16, 1846).
[70] Law, January 16, 1846 (RO–1721, L–25, no. –1).
[71] Decree, September 15, 1848. RO–1865, L–27, no. –9. The blockade was formally lifted on August 26, 1848.

No commentary on Rosas' monetary policy is more revealing than a comparison of the amount of money in circulation before and after the federalist regime. In May 1836 when the Casa de Moneda took over the functions of the Banco Nacional, whose charter Rosas refused to renew, the currency of the province amounted to 15,283,540 pesos in notes of the bank. At the close of 1851 the last full year of Rosas' administration, the quantity of paper money in circulation rose to 125,264,294 pesos. The regime was thus responsible for the issue of 109,980,854 pesos, in a period of slightly over eleven years. This, then, was the secret of Rosas' ability to avoid financial bankruptcy. Nor is it surprising that after some hesitation Rosas abandoned long term borrowing in favor of currency issues as a means of financing deficits. The latter method was much more effective, and it encountered much less opposition. Bonds had to be sold, a difficult task at

TABLE 42

CURRENCY ISSUED DURING THE ADMINISTRATION OF ROSAS

Notes of the Banco Nacional (May 30, 1836)		15,283,540 p.
Law, March 11, 1837	4,200,000	
Law, December 8, 1838	16,575,000	
Law, September 17, 1839 [a]	3,605,854	
Law, March 28, 1840	12,000,000	
Law, January 16, 1846	73,600,000	
Total		109,980,854 p.
Total issued at end of regime		125,264,294 p.

Sources: RO–1143, L–16, no. –3; RO–1257, L–17, no. –12; RO–1340, L–18, no. –9; RO–1392, L–19, no. –3; RO–1721, L–25, no. –1.
[a] Ten per cent of total currency in circulation officially ruled as lost.

best, and they had to be amortized. None of these handicaps characterized currency expansion. Its cost was minimal, paid for with profits from lending operations of the Casa de Moneda, and its availability was instantaneous. There were other advantages attached to currency expansion which long term borrowing could not possibly offer. Fiat money imposed no additional burden upon the treasury in the form of interest and amortization, and made it possible, moreover, to reduce the public indebtedness of the province at a rate which would have been impossible under conditions of stable money. And, finally, it enabled Rosas to maintain his administration without extending the burden of taxation to the rural sector of the provincial economy. It is true, of course, that continued expansion of currency adversely affected prices and that this in turn necessitated ever larger issues of paper money. But it is also true that this process was not entirely to the disadvantage of the treasury. For one thing, a large portion of the treasury's expenditures consisted of salaries and wages, which usually lagged behind the general level of prices. And, secondly, currency expansion coincided with periods of economic stagnation when commodity prices were slow to respond to the growth of quantity of money in circulation.

CHAPTER IX

THE TARIFF: ISSUES AND POLICIES

Las circunstancias del país, sus necesidades reales, sus exigencias perentorias ó imperiosas han formado los principios de una política singular para circunstancias las más singulares, por no decir únicas . . . de una política cimentada en la experiencia adquirida durante veinte y seis años de sacudimientos radicales, en el conocimiento exacto de los sucesos y de los hombres, y en la formal y provechosa observancia no de soñados idealismos de una teórica absoluta, siempre inaplicable á la organización y estado especial de cada sociedad, sino de esas reglas que subministra en el seno mismo de las revoluciones el estudio práctico y discernido del cúmulo de causas, del Estado, y por consiguiente dan la medida de sus necesidades y de sus exigencias.—*Gaceta Mercantil*, no. 3937, July 25, 1836.

PERHAPS NO OTHER QUESTION of economic policy presented greater difficulties or aroused more bitter controversies than the tariff. Even before the fall of the unitary regime the tariff was one of the most controversial issues of the day. The tariff policies formulated during the twenties satisfied no one, and proponents of free trade as well as advocates of protection pressed for a solution of the problem with increasing vigor.

The problem was admittedly complicated. The tariff was not only an instrument of economic policy, but also the most important source of revenue. And because the nation's foreign trade centered in the port of Buenos Aires other provinces demanded a share in the formulation of tariff policies. Thus the tariff became simultaneously a provincial and a national issue, and to this extent it assumed political connotations which the *porteño* government could not disregard. The fiscal aspect of the problem though comparatively simple was none the less important. It was clear by now (1829) that neither the *contribución directa* nor the emphyteusis could be counted upon to provide sufficient revenue. The administration was, therefore, in no position to dispense with the income derived from foreign trade. With its eye upon the treasury the government was opposed to both free trade and outright protection. It endeavored to maintain a middle course, one that would reconcile the interests of the treasury with those of the economy of the province.

It was not at all an easy matter to determine what constituted the best interests of the provincial economy. In the twenty years since the abolition of colonial restrictions "free" trade proved to be a double-edged weapon. It could not be disputed that "free" trade released the dormant resources of the *pampa* to an extent unknown before. But at the same time it inflicted heavy damage upon those sectors of the economy which under the protection of colonial laws achieved a fair degree of stability. While it was generally conceded that return to the colonial system of trade restrictions was neither possible nor desirable, there was no lack of complaint in Buenos Aires and in the provinces against the liberal commercial policies of the Rivadavia administration. And as the effects of these policies became more widespread and their implications more clearly understood the trend toward protectionism became broader and also more persistent.

Opposition to Rivadavia's policy of "free" trade centered mainly in the federalist party, which alone was willing to champion the cause of domestic industry and agriculture. But the extent to which the federalist leaders were prepared to defend protectionism varied widely from province to province and from region to region. In Buenos Aires there was no unanimity in the federalist ranks on the issue of protection vs. "free" trade. The leaders, who were particularly sensitive to the immediate needs of the *estancieros* and *saladeristas,* were not enthusiastic about protection. Dependent entirely upon foreign trade they were unwilling to restrict the flow of goods through Buenos Aires. Low duties made for low cost of living, and this in turn helped to keep the cost of production at a level consistent with prices paid for hides and meat in overseas markets. The quarrel of the cattle breeders with the unitaries on matters of commercial policy did not involve the principle of "free" trade, but rather the manner in which it was applied.[1] They demanded lower export duties on hides and meat, and advocated a more liberal policy with respect to importations of salt and consumers' goods. But at the same time they refused to lend support to unitary tariff policies which in their opinion were based upon a profound misconception of the economic potential of the country. Unlike the unitaries the federalist leaders were conscious of a strong protectionist sentiment among the artisans, the farmers, and the small merchants who were less concerned with the political aspects of the constitutional problem than with its economic implications. And while the leading fed-

---

[1] This explains the singular silence maintained by *porteño* federalist leaders in the Constituent Congress and in the press on questions of protection, although there were several occasions on which the issue of protection vs. free trade could be properly raised.

eralists were careful not to commit themselves too explicitly they never failed to make political capital out of the economic plight of the middle classes and the farmers.   Thus an impression was created that the federalist party favored a protectionist commercial policy.

The demand for protection was not confined to the industrial and agricultural classes of Buenos Aires alone.   In the Interior as well as in the Litoral the demand for a more stringent commercial policy was even more outspoken and also more general than in Buenos Aires.   In some provinces protectionism was almost synonymous with federalism, and the failure of Rosas to raise import duties during his first administration was in many quarters interpreted as an outright betrayal of the federalist cause.   These provinces insisted that the problem of tariff policies could not be adequately solved except on a national basis. Formulation and enforcement of tariff policies, argued the provinces, should be vested in a national government, but until such government was established Buenos Aires should consider the economic desiderata of the provinces.

There was thus an important difference between the position of the industrial and agricultural classes in Buenos Aires and that of their brethren in the provinces.   As producers of a very considerable proportion of goods consumed in the country the provinces fought for a general increase in duties.   They could not be satisfied with partial revisions of the Rivadavia schedule.   Theirs was a demand for protection pure and simple, for a policy that would not only safeguard the existing industries but would also insure the growth and development of new industries.   The *porteños* took a different view of the problem. As consumers of the manufactures and produce of the Interior they were unwilling to shut off foreign imports and to strengthen thereby the hand of the provinces in the Buenos Aires market.   If the *porteños* demanded protection it was only under condition that higher duties apply solely to commodities already produced within the province.   Consequently the protectionist sentiment in Buenos Aires was much milder, its scope narrower, and its aims more specific.

It was due primarily to this lack of unanimity that Rosas and his collaborators succeeded for a time in sidetracking the tariff issue.   Indeed, except for two or three minor concessions to protectionists, the changes effected by Rosas during his first administration were designed solely to benefit the cattle breeder and the meat producer.

The administration of Juan José Viamonte introduced no major changes in the tariff schedule.   The surcharges of 2 to 10 per cent upon overseas imports were intended to be temporary, and did not foreshadow a change in economic policies.[2] In the months which followed Viamonte's short-lived administration the time was hardly propitious for a thorough reëxamination of the tariff problem. The new regime was not strong enough to attempt solution of a problem as complicated and as controversial as the tariff. The question of consolidating the federalist regime was the paramount issue of the day. The tariff could wait. It was not until October of 1831 that the Junta de Representantes sanctioned the tariff provisions of the decrees of September 18, 1829 and of January 7, 1831.[3] The decree of September 18, 1829 dealt with surcharges upon all imports, and the changes of January 7, 1831 referred solely to flour on which the duty was virtually nullified by the depreciation of the peso.

The decree of January 7, 1831 deserves closer analysis. The new schedule called for a duty of 9 pesos when the price of domestic flour did not exceed 45 pesos per quintal; when flour sold at 45 to 60 pesos per quintal the duty was reduced to 7 pesos; and, finally, imported flour was subject to a duty of 5 pesos per quintal, when domestic prices rose above 60 pesos.[4] The revision of flour duties was motivated by the circumstance that agricultural industries were "in danger of being totally abandoned for lack of sufficient incentive." [5] But it is doubtful whether the measure solved the problem of domestic agriculture. To begin with, the new rates were not more protective than those established by the tariffs of 1822 and 1824. In the early tariffs the duty on flour imports ranged from 66 per cent to 10 per cent *ad valorem.*[6] Now the tax amounted to 20 per cent when the domestic price was 45 pesos per quintal, and only to 8½ per cent when flour sold above 60 pesos. The government, moreover, failed to take any action whatever with respect to importations of wheat and other grains. Wheat continued to pay import duties according to the schedule of 1824, and as currency depreciated the duty became hardly more than nominal.[7] The conclusion seems inescapable that if anyone did benefit from the decree of January 7, 1831 it was the miller rather than the farmer.

---

[2] Cf. chap. iii, pp. 69–75. The surcharges were never revoked, and were finally merged with basic rates.

[3] RO–256, L–10, no. –10 (October 4, 1831).

[4] Decree, January 7, 1831 (*Registro Oficial*, no. –1, pp. 19–20). Also *Gaceta Mercantil*, no. 2091 (January 10, 1831).

[5] *Ibid.*

[6] Cf. chap. iii, pp. 70–71.

[7] For rates on wheat imports, see chap. iii, p. 71.

In 1834 the farmers publicly protested against the shabby treatment accorded them by the provincial government, and demanded that something be done to make agriculture more profitable.[8] But it was not until early in 1835 that the Finance Commission of the Junta took official cognizance of the difficulties facing domestic agriculture.[9]

Industry, and especially the hide and meat industry and hat manufacture, was treated with much greater consideration. In extending the 1831 tariff to the following year the government suggested important changes. It sought a reduction of duties upon salt to 1 peso per fanega, and it also proposed that the tax upon cattle brought to the city be lowered to 4 reales per head. At the same time the government demanded that the rate on foreign hats be increased to 13 pesos per hat.[10] The proposed reduction of salt duties is significant, especially when it is considered that the treasury was at the time in serious financial difficulties, and that the new duty threatened the prosperity of domestic salt industry. It is true that salt prices did not rise in proportion to currency depreciation. A duty of 2 pesos per fanega amounted, therefore, to 20 per cent and at times as much as 30 per cent *ad valorem*. But it is also true that precisely because salt did not participate in the general rise of prices the old duty could not be considered particularly burdensome to the hide and meat industries. It is noteworthy, too, that of all the tariff increases promulgated by Viamonte in 1829, that affecting salt was the only one which Rosas proposed to abolish.[11]

[8] Cf., for example, the letter signed "Unos labradores" in the *Gaceta Mercantil*, no. 3346 (July 28, 1834).

[9] Cf. *Diario de Sesiones*, Session of January 9, 1835 (no. 485), report by deputy Anchorena; *ibid.*, bill reported by the Finance Commission.

[10] Cf. RO–267, L–10, no. –11 (November 14, 1831). Before 1832 foreign salt paid 2 pesos per fanega, cattle from other provinces paid one peso per head, and the import duty on hats was 9 pesos per hat. See chap. iii, pp. 70 ff.

[11] Monthly average prices of foreign salt (in pesos per fanega on board ship) appear in the following table:

	1830	1831	1832	1833
January	13.60	7.00	9.87	10.56
February	14.00	8.75	10.50	12.87
March	18.60	9.75	10.50	13.30
April	21.50	10.70	7.31	13.50
May	25.75	9.81	7.94	13.75
June	14.40	10.00	8.50	13.80
July	12.60	10.01	9.25	13.50
August	12.50	7.31	15.40	14.40
September	12.25	7.50	16.12	18.00
October	11.15	7.45	16.10	17.25
November	12.25	8.50	11.31	11.80
December	8.25	9.40	10.70	10.25

The Finance Commission of the Junta urged approval of the government bill on the ground that meat producers in Buenos Aires were facing severe competition from Montevideo and Rio Grande do Sul, Brazil.
The commission argued also that a reduction of salt duties would stimulate expansion of the salt industry in Patagones.[12] Needless to say,
these arguments fell upon willing ears. The legislature had always
been dissatisfied with the salt tax and eagerly approved the government
bill.

The proposal to raise the duty on foreign-manufactured hats caused
protracted discussions in the legislature. Protectionists seized upon
this opportunity to voice their grievances and to raise the issue of tariff
revision. Deputy Pedro Aguirre demanded to know why the hat industry was singled out for protection, while "other products which
could be manufactured in the country and which deserved similar consideration" were not mentioned in the bill. He cited clothes, shoes,
furniture, and other products of carpentry as commodities which
merited protection, and he pointed out that the tariff as it stood was
discriminatory and did not solve the economic problem facing domestic industry.[13] The *rapporteur* of the Finance Commission believed that the government's position was justified not only because the
specific duty in force had been rendered nugatory by currency depreciation, but also because the hat industry was the only one to use domestic
raw materials and native labor. "The country," argued deputy Baldomero García, "demands above all that the hat industry be accorded special consideration, partly because the industry is thoroughly native, and
partly because many young individuals entered this promising trade and
are now without work." [14]

The demand that protection be extended to other domestic industries
remained unheeded. Both the government and the legislature were
not at this time prepared to sponsor a drastic revision of the time
honored policy of relatively moderate duties. However, early in 1833
the government proposed certain modifications in the tariff schedule.
The changes referred to exports of hides of unborn calves (*cueros de
nonato*) and to salt imports from Patagonia. The government called

---

[12] Cf. *Diario de Sesiones*, Session 251 (November 14, 1831). Report of the Financial
Commission by Felipe Senillosa.

[13] *Diario de Sesiones*, Session 251 (November 14, 1831).

[14] Cf. *Diario de Sesiones*, Session 251 (November 14, 1831), speech by Baldomero
García. See also speeches by Felipe Senillosa and Nicolás Anchorena.

for a reduction of export duties on calf hides to 2 reales per hide. Such reduction was thought to be justified on the ground that in view of the recent fall of prices the duty in force became excessive. The legislature readily accepted the government's point of view and approved the change without debate. But the provision which referred to salt duties provoked extended discussion. The legislature took a more radical view of the question than the government. The bill, as introduced by the government, provided for the abolition of the *contribución directa* on capital invested in salt imported from Patagonia. But the Finance Commission considered this measure inadequate and recommended abolition of duties on salt imported from Patagonia in national bottoms and reimbursement of duties on re-exports to Bahía Blanca to the amount of the value of the salt brought to Buenos Aires. The Junta approved the recommendations of the Finance Commission.[15]

In the tariff of 1834 two changes of consequence were approved. One referred to taxes imposed upon reloading from overseas ships into river boats. The tax was abolished altogether. As deputy Felipe Senillosa explained, the purpose of this measure was to attract river trade to Buenos Aires. Until then free reloading was limited to ocean-going vessels, so that river boats preferred to trade by way of Montevideo, where they could dispose of their cargo and obtain return shipments. Existing regulations, argued Senillosa, were no longer justifiable either economically or financially, and the government bill was but a recognition of new development in river commerce. The second change related to the tariff schedule proper. The Finance Commission proposed that the 10 per cent surcharge on imports subject to 30 per cent duty be reduced to 5 per cent, so that the total duty upon commodities within this category would amount to 35 per cent. Deputy Senillosa, who reported the bill out of the Finance Commission, indicated that this change presaged further reductions of surcharges, if not their abolition. Should this reduction result in a larger volume of trade the repeal of all additional duties instituted by Juan José Viamonte would then be advisable. The Junta approved the bill without changes, but in the course of discussion fear was expressed that repeal of reloading taxes might adversely affect food prices in Buenos Aires.[16]

---

[15] Law, March 1, 1833 (RO–429, L–12, no. –3). Cf. *Diario de Sesiones*, Sessions 306, 311, 312, 314 (January 28, February 7, 11, March 1, 1833).

[16] Law, December 26, 1833 (RO–537, L–12, no. –12). See also *Diario de Sesiones*, Session 373 (December 26, 1833).

In 1835 the provincial legislature voted several amendments to the general tariff schedule. At this time the Junta attempted to meet the problems created by currency depreciation and to eliminate certain inconsistencies which had accumulated in the past decade or so. To begin with, the old duty on wheat was revised. The new schedule provided for a minimum duty of 5 pesos per quintal when the internal price stood over 60 pesos, and for a maximum rate of 9 pesos when wheat sold below 45 pesos per quintal. When wheat prices fluctuated between 45 and 60 pesos the duty was fixed at 7 pesos per quintal.[17] It is doubtful whether these rates afforded adequate protection to wheat growers. Even at its highest the duty could not assure the farmer a reasonable profit. It was calculated in the Junta that in order to cover cost of production the farmer must be able to get for his wheat 4 silver pesos per quintal, or 28 paper pesos at the prevailing rate of exchange. But with foreign wheat selling in Buenos Aires at 11 pesos paper per quintal the duty of 9 pesos did little to improve the farmer's lot.[18] Opponents of higher duties countered these arguments with the assertion that the consumer deserved as much protection as the producer. If the cost of production of wheat was high it was largely because labor was scarce, and the most effective means of helping the farmer was to provide him with cheap labor. This in turn was not possible unless cost of living was maintained at the lowest possible level. Besides, continued the argument, the farmer should be taught to adopt improved methods of cultivation, and in the meantime agriculture should be relieved of the many taxes and fees with which it had been burdened in the past.[19]

By article 4 of the new tariff law import duties on raw hides, ostrich feathers, horns and horn tips, wool, crude and clean tallow, horsehair, and jerked beef were abolished, provided that these commodities were water-borne. The reason for this change was clearly stated by deputy Anchorena. It was desired, namely, to stimulate import of these commodities from the riparian provinces. The measure was aimed at Montevideo which competed with Buenos Aires for the Paraná and Uruguay river trade.

In an effort to stimulate national shipping the legislature approved a

[17] Article 2 of Law of January 14, 1835.

[18] The average price for January was somewhat higher, and it stood at about 19 pesos paper per fanega during the remainder of that year. Cf. *infra,* Table 43, chap. x.

[19] Cf. *Diario de Sesiones,* Sessions 485–487 (January 7, 10, 14, 1835).

tax of 15 per cent plus additional 2 per cent upon lumber imported in foreign bottoms. It was thought that this measure would force lumber traders to utilize national vessels, and that this would contribute to the development of a national merchant marine. Some doubt was expressed in the legislature as to the efficacy of the law, and it was suggested that vessels flying the Argentine flag be required to carry crews of Argentine citizens, but this amendment failed to gain sufficient support. The remaining provisions of the 1835 tariff were of minor importance. One revised the basis upon which the duty on wine from overseas ports was to be calculated (article 8). Another ordered that Uruguayan vessels touching Buenos Aires be accorded the same treatment as *porteño* vessels received in Montevideo. And, finally, it reaffirmed the abolition of duties on reloading of commodities, and extended the meaning of article 2 of the 1834 tariff to include interior ports (*puertos de cabo adentro*).

2

At the beginning of the debate on the 1835 tariff Nicolás Anchorena, leader of the federalist party, characterized the commercial policy pursued by Buenos Aires as one which reconciled the fiscal and economic interests of the province. The tariff of 1821 and the principles which it embodied were still sound and should, therefore, be preserved. Although changes in various instances had been necessary, and might be usefully introduced in the future, there was nothing in the experience of the preceding decade and a half which rendered the commercial policies of the Rodríguez administration inconsistent with the economic needs of the province. Foreign commerce, continued Anchorena, should be given all possible encouragement, not only because it provided the bulk of the province's revenue, but also because the prosperity of the country depended largely upon free access to foreign markets. Just as the province could not hope to prosper without exporting, so also must it import in order to utilize properly its reserves of labor and capital. Prohibition or even protection would, therefore, work to the disadvantage of the province, even though a policy of restriction might conceivably benefit certain industries.

Anchorena was no doubt on solid ground when he emphasized the importance of foreign commerce; and he did not exaggerate the treasury's dependence upon customs duties. Nevertheless, his claim that the tariff policies of the Rodríguez administration succeeded in reconciling the economic and fiscal interests of the province was unwarranted. If the experience of the fifteen years following 1821 proved anything at all it was precisely that the economic principles which underlay those policies were inapplicable to many sectors of the economy of Buenos Aires and of the country at large. The policy which Anchorena and the majority in the legislature championed was not, therefore, the one most suitable to the needs of the country; nor was it even in accord with the principles which Rivadavia laid down in the early twenties. For the changes introduced into the tariff after the advent of Rosas had shifted the balance of economic benefits in favor of that group of which Anchorena and Rosas were the foremost representatives. To speak, therefore, of the tariff of 1835 as one that served the interests of the province and the country was to identify the welfare of limited local groups with that of the nation. Rarely was the policy of the *porteño* legislature less representative of the needs of the province and the country in the period immediately following the first election of Rosas. Incomparably closer to the broad masses of the electorate were those few deputies who, like Baldomero García, could not be satisfied with partial revisions of specific tariff rates, which were also, from the point of view of the provinces, irrelevant. They demanded instead a thorough reëxamination of the whole tariff question, a reëxamination that would take into account the economic postulates of the provinces, on the one hand, and the industrial interests of Buenos Aires, on the other. This demand was not new. It resounded throughout the land long before the advent of Rosas, and was on more than one occasion echoed by the federalist parties in Buenos Aires as well as in the provinces.

In this sense the tariff question was distinctly a national issue, intimately related to the problem of national organization. That the tariff policies of Buenos Aires directly affected the welfare of the provinces could no longer be denied even by the most extreme isolationists. And it is not surprising that the question of protection raised in the *porteño* legislature in the years between 1829 and 1835 should have provoked one of the most bitter discussions both in the press and in diplomatic correspondence.

This public discussion, outspoken and direct, revealed, as no other controversy of the period did, the irrepressible conflict between Buenos Aires and the provinces, a conflict which rendered fruitless all efforts toward the solution of the constitutional problem. It disclosed, furthermore, the specific character of *porteño* federalism, its essentially isolationist nature, and its propensity toward political domination over the sister provinces. And it also determined the scope of the ensuing struggle between Buenos Aires and the provinces as well as the terms upon which a lasting peace could be secured some thirty years later.

The controversy came into the open early in 1832, when during the sessions of the Comisión Representativa in Santa Fe, Juan Facundo Quiroga intercepted confidential letters sent out by Manuel Leiva and Juan Bautista Marín to the governors of Catamarca and La Rioja.[20] But long before the Leiva incident the question had been discussed at great length around the conference table. As early as 1830 Pedro Ferré, who at the time led the protectionist movement in the Litoral, demanded that Rosas agree to a revision of the tariff policies of Buenos Aires.[21] The question was raised once again and on a much broader basis during the preliminary discussions of the tripartite treaty. It was on this occasion that Pedro Ferré insisted that the tariff problem be placed on the agenda. It was also at this time that José María Roxas y Patrón, the *porteño* delegate, submitted a lengthy memorandum in which the Buenos Aires government stated its position.[22] Without going into the theoretical aspects of the tariff question Roxas developed the thesis that prohibitive or protective duties were impractical and even dangerous. If industry demonstrates its ability to prosper without protection, then high duties are manifestly unfair to both consumers and manufacturers. And if, on the other hand, the country has no industries, or cannot successfully compete against foreign manufacturers, then protection is unjust, because it restricts consumption. Prohibition would encourage interprovincial wars, since each province would endeavor to defend its native industries against outside competition.

---

[20] For a more detailed discussion of the Leiva incident see *supra,* chap. vi.

[21] Cf. Pedro Ferré, *Memoria del brigadier general Pedro Ferré* (Buenos Aires: 1921), "Es de advertir que ya instruido yo de su meditado plan (to utilize the tariff as an instrument of control of the provinces), y de que según el no consentiría jamás en la prosperidad de los pueblos protegiendo su industria por medio de una nueva economía política, y siendo esto uno de los encargos principales que yo tenía de mi gobierno, de acuerdo con los demás me resistía a las pretensiones de Rosas mientras no cediese al justo reclamo de los pueblos sobre el particular" (p. 52).

[22] The text of the memorandum may be found in *Memoria del brigadier general Pedro Ferré, octubre de 1821 a diciembre de 1842* (Buenos Aires: 1921), pp. 366–371.

Santa Fe would not admit lumber, cotton, and linen from Corrientes, for these commodities are grown and produced in her territory. Corrientes would refuse to import brandies from San Juan and Mendoza, and fruit from Paraguay. Buenos Aires, too, would follow suit, for in the newly acquired territories in the south and on the shores of Patagonia, there will in time rise its industries. The same is true of grain from Entre Ríos, for Buenos Aires produces grain in abundance.[23]

But even if an economic war did not materialize it was very doubtful whether protection or prohibition was desirable. There could be no doubt, argued Roxas, that a policy such as Corrientes advocated would result in a general increase of prices on goods of prime necessity. Buenos Aires, Santa Fe, and Entre Ríos were agricultural economies, and even in Corrientes cattle breeding predominated. But the welfare of the pastoral industry depended on the one hand upon cheap land and cheap money, and, on the other, upon continued demand for hides in foreign markets. Prohibition or protection was certain to undermine the prosperity of the pastoral industry, not only because it would cause the cost of living to rise, but also because it would adversely affect the export trade of the country. The argument that protection would insure prosperity to those who did not depend upon cattle breeding must be rejected, if only because these classes formed a relatively small minority of the population. It should be remembered, furthermore, that native industry was incapable of meeting the internal demand for manufactured goods. So, for example, Corrientes, San Juan, Mendoza, and Tucumán could not meet the nation's demand for sugar and wine at prices as reasonable as those offered by Brazil and Cuba and Spain. The same was true of other provinces and of other commodities. If, therefore, the provinces insisted upon exclusion of foreign goods they should be prepared to face contraction of internal markets and the ultimate deterioration of the many industries which had sprung up since the opening of Buenos Aires to overseas commerce.

Thus protection, and to a still greater degree prohibition, would injure rather than benefit the broad masses of the population, and public opinion would soon force out of office any government which dared to restrict foreign commerce. Governments must not sacrifice present interests for the sake of some future benefits. They should, on the contrary, foster in every way possible the welfare and prosperity of the present generation. And while it cannot be denied that in many provinces industry had been in a state of stagnation, this was because the country never enjoyed peace long enough to permit a more rational ex-

[23] *Op. cit.*, p. 369.

ploitation of the available resources.   But once the constitutional
issue is solved and a federal government established, native industry
will again enter the broad highway of prosperity.   And in the meantime commerce should be encouraged, rather than hindered, for nature
itself "had disposed that no country may possess all that a civilized
nation needs."

Pedro Ferré refused to accept the argument.   In a reply to Roxas,
comendable for its conciseness and clarity, Ferré reiterated the protectionist position.[24]   Free competition, reasoned Ferré, was fatal to the
welfare of the country.   The few industries which survived the shock
of the Revolution of 1810 could not possibly continue in a market where
prices were determined by the cost of production in foreign countries.
Capital invested in domestic industries perished, and the demand for
native labor decreased sharply.   As it was, the country consumed more
than it produced, and the result was continued drainage upon its monetary stock.   The ultimate result of this process was poverty and
misery.   If it was true that free trade destroyed domestic industry,
existing or nascent, then a thorough revision of the tariff policies of the
Buenos Aires government became imperative.   Importation of commodities which could be produced at home should, therefore, be subjected to much higher duties, or entirely prohibited.   Such a measure
was drastic, no doubt, but no other measure could save the provinces of
the Interior and the Litoral from utter ruin.[25]

In one respect the discussion proved inconclusive.   Buenos Aires
refused to yield, and Corrientes, unable to secure effective support
from Santa Fe and Entre Ríos, withdrew from the conference.   The
treaty of 1831 was concluded without Corrientes.   When, however,
the Comisión Representativa was organized in Santa Fe, Corrientes
adhered to the treaty.   Once more Pedro Ferré attempted to force the
hand of Buenos Aires; only this time the discussion could no longer be
confined to the precincts of the Comisión.   The publication of Leiva's

---

[24] Cf. *Memoria, Anexo, III, F.,* pp. 371–376.

[25] Ferré's economic program was not confined solely to the tariff question.   While he
demanded a revision of the tariff, he insisted also upon opening of the Paraná and Uruguay ports to overseas trade.   The fact that Buenos Aires monopolized the country's foreign trade was one of the causes of the economic degradation of the Interior, argued
Ferré.   It was unjust to force the Interior provinces to trade with overseas markets
through Buenos Aires, when excellent ports, such as Santa Fe or Paraná, on the Paraná
River, were readily available.   These ports were natural points of contact with foreign
markets for the Litoral and the Interior, and it was only fair that these territories be allowed to make use of the advantages offered by nature.

and Marín's letters brought the issue into the open. Ferré refused to repudiate Leiva's actions and appealed to public opinion. In a circular letter to provincial governors [26] he reiterated his position. The economic policy of Buenos Aires, Ferré insisted, was bringing the country to its grave. If the country was to regain economic prosperity it was essential to remove every obstacle in the path of domestic industry. Importation of commodities produced in the country should be prohibited, and foreign trade should be encouraged by the opening of river ports to overseas vessels.[27]

In Buenos Aires the circular caused a storm of indignation both in government circles and in the press. The challenge could not be left unanswered, especially since Ferré appealed to the anti-*porteño* sentiment, always latent in the Interior. Ferré could not be accused of unitarism and it was all the more important to refute his argument. Protests against Ferré's attack appeared in the Buenos Aires press shortly after the publication of the famous circular and the answer of the governor of Corrientes concerning the activities of Manuel Leiva. Two of these deserve closer examination. One is a series of four letters published in the *Gaceta Mercantil* and signed by "El Cosmopolita," [28] and the other is an article in *El Lucero* of Buenos Aires.[29] "El Cosmopolita" began his argument by stating that the raising of the issue of protection endangered the peace and welfare of the country. Such discussions could not but fan anew the smoldering fires of intersectional rivalries. The highly complicated problem of revenues and tariffs should be left to the decision of a competent National Congress. Judged on its merits, continued "El Cosmopolita," Ferré's argument

[26] For text of letter see Francisco Centeno, *Epistolario de los generales Ferré y Paz* (Buenos Aires: 1923).

[27] The circular continued: "Habilitado, por exemplo, el puerto de Santa Fe se disminuirán las distancias que los artículos de comercio del país tienen que correr hasta llegar al mercado de Buenos Aires por supuesto se ahorrarán gastos de conducción, prohibida la introducción de vinos, aguardiente, tejidos y demás artículos que proporciona nuestro feraz territorio las producciones de este adquirirán la debida importancia y en igual sentido a proporción todos los ramos de industria nacional que se crearan, aun entrarán el valor de sus productos, asegurando la subsistencia de numerosas familias, sin que pueda dudarse, que este es un bien positivo y duradero para la república." *Ibid.*, p. 35.

[28] Nos. 2547–2550 (August 9–12, 1832). Also in "Relaciones Interprovinciales. La Liga Litoral, 1829–1833, Apéndice 2," no. 18, pp. 183–191. (Unpublished, in the Instituto de Investigaciones Históricas, Buenos Aires.)

[29] (Acusaciones formuladas en) *El Lucero* (contra el gobernador de Corrientes, D. Pedro Ferré, al juzgar éste la conducta de Buenos Aires), in "Relaciones Interprovinciales, Apéndice 2," no. 19, pp. 192–214.

was weak and inconclusive. Foreign trade offered two advantages which the country could not afford to forego. In the first place, free trade gave the country a better choice of markets, and, secondly, foreign commerce was the most important source of revenues. It was true that customs revenues were contingent upon the volume of foreign trade, but it was also true that neither domestic industry nor internal commerce could be relied upon to produce substantial revenues. Moreover, it was not at all certain whether expansion of domestic industry under the shelter of high duties was desirable. A general rise in real costs of production would inevitably accompany such expansion, and this in turn would nullify the very benefits which protection was intended to produce. Restriction of imports would place certain groups in a privileged position, and it would be manifestly unjust that farmers and artisans be allowed to grow rich at the expense of consumers. Besides it was improbable that protection could be made effective. High duties were certain to encourage contraband trade, and consumers accustomed to commodities of superior quality at reasonable prices would be only too glad to coöperate with smugglers.

El Lucero attacked the issue more specifically. It began by discounting Ferré's contention that the economic plight of the provinces was due primarily to free trade. Producers of wine and *aguardiente* in San Juan and Mendoza, for example, had no cause for complaint in view of the 40 per cent duty upon imports of these commodities from Spain. *Aguardiente* from Spain of 25° sold in Buenos Aires for 620 pesos per *pipa*. Since the duty amounted to 248 pesos the importer received only 372 pesos per *pipa*. *Aguardiente* from San Juan of the same alcoholic content sold in Buenos Aires at 450 pesos per *pipa*, but it paid no import duty whatever. Thus, San Juan producers received 74 pesos more per *pipa* than their Spanish competitors. Again, Malaga wine fetched in Buenos Aires 480 pesos per *pipa*, including a duty of 192 pesos. Mendoza wine sold in Buenos Aires at 400 pesos, giving the domestic producer an advantage of 112 pesos per *pipa*. Olive growers of the Interior enjoyed similar advantages under a duty of 24 per cent upon overseas imports. It cannot be said, stated *El Lucero*, that the provincial government treated domestic producers unfairly. On this account the record of Buenos Aires was much better than that of Corrientes, whose policy of stringent protection was directed as much against the Argentine provinces as it was against foreign countries.[30]

---

[30] *El Lucero* refers here to the famous laws of January 4, 1831. One of these ordered confiscation of all *aguardiente* imported into the province.

But more important than measures taken to safeguard the interests of specific industries was the much broader question as to whether restriction of foreign trade could be expected to encourage expansion of national economy. Ferré claimed that free trade caused a severe drain upon the country's wealth, yet curiously enough protectionist Corrientes showed an unfavorable balance of trade in five out of six years ending with 1830.[31] To argue as Ferré seemed to do that this would not happen had the other provinces followed in the steps of Corrientes was to beg the question. And if it was true that poverty and misery reigned supreme in Corrientes, it was reasonable to assume that prohibition was contrary to the best interests of the country. The disadvantages of protection, continued *El Lucero,* should be obvious to all. Once foreign commodities were barred from internal markets there would be no incentive to improve methods of production. It was, furthermore, likely, that domestic producers would endeavor to raise prices to the limit permitted by the tariff. Thirdly, economic isolation would tend to perpetuate rather than eliminate the country's industrial inferiority. Fourthly, high tariffs would inevitably result in extensive smuggling. And, finally, it was manifestly unjust to deprive the population of its right to buy in the cheapest market.

El Lucero's argument did not remain unanswered. In a lengthy pamphlet published anonymously,[32] the followers of Ferré denied that they advocated mercantilism. They insisted, however, that in Argentina the issue of protection was inseparable from the question of foreign domination of the country's economic life.

> The government of Corrientes, it cannot be repeated too often, neither condemns nor opposes foreign commerce; it merely advocates certain restrictions to which foreign trade should be subjected. Such restriction the nation has the right to impose in order that foreign trade might not destroy the prosperity which it is supposed to foster.

---

[31] *Value of Foreign Trade of the Province of Corrientes: 1825–1830*

	1825	1826	1827	1828	1829	1830
Imports........	357,624	391,075	385,411	196,801	626,448	462,934
Exports........	172,238	258,371	286,879	206,549	411,549	241,967
Bal. of tr........	−185,386	−132,702	−98,532	9,748	−215,245	−220,967

Cf. "Relaciones Interprovinciales," *loc. cit.*, p. 201. In 1828 communication between Buenos Aires and Corrientes was interrupted. This probably accounted for the favorable balance of trade in that year.

[32] *Contestación al* Lucero, *ó los falsos y peligrosos principios en descubierto.* Cf. "Relaciones Interprovinciales," *loc. cit., Apéndice* 2, no. 24, pp. 251–300.

In the pre-revolutionary period, when colonial governments decided to open the country to foreign trade they took care to insure that such trade remain in native hands. After 1810 the government abandoned this policy and reduced the tariff. Since then the country's balance of trade had been consistently unfavorable, and at the same time native merchants had suffered irreparable losses. Both wholesale export trade and retail import commerce had passed into foreign hands. The conclusion seems inescapable, therefore, that the opening of the country to foreigners proved harmful on balance. Foreigners displaced natives not only in commerce but in industry and agriculture as well.

It is not possible that Buenos Aires should have sacrificed blood and wealth solely for the purpose of becoming a consumer of the produce and manufacture of foreign countries, for such status is degrading and does not correspond to the great potentialities which nature bestowed upon the country.

Protection [continued the anonymous author], was certain to solve many of the problems facing the country. It would open new fields of economic activity and would provide employment to labor of both sexes. Such at least had been the experience of Corrientes. This province used to import sugar; now sugar is grown and manufactured locally, and the province improved its balance of trade by nearly 80,000 pesos. Similar results might be expected in the provinces of Cuyo if importation of wines and liquors were prohibited altogether. It is erroneous to assume that protection breeds monopoly. The fact is that Argentina which had been under a regime of free trade for over twenty years is now controlled by a handful of foreigners. If protection was going to dislodge foreign merchants from their position of economic preëminence the country would have occasion to congratulate itself on making the first step toward regaining its economic independence. The nation [concluded the writer], has fought and has triumphed. It is now formed and exists. It must defend itself and improve its position. It is its own master and is free to regulate foreign commerce. It cannot continue without restricting foreign trade, since restriction alone would make industrial expansion possible; it must no longer endure the weight of a monopoly which strangles every attempt at industrialization.

The controversy reached an impasse. No additional discussion could further clarify the issue. In Buenos Aires the merchants and the *estancieros* defended the *status quo* as a matter of course. To yield to Ferré meant to renounce much of what the cattle breeders and meat producers gained since the Revolution, and especially since the advent of Rosas and the federalist party. It meant the loss of a large portion of overseas commerce; it meant also higher cost of living and increased costs of production. It implied furthermore a redistribution of the national dividend both within the province and throughout the country. Hence the opposition to any revision of the tariff policy; hence also the refusal to coöperate whole-heartedly with the provinces toward an adequate solution of the constitutional problem.

Strong though the position of the Buenos Aires government was on the tariff issue, it was not impregnable. Within Buenos Aires opinion on the issue of protection was by no means unanimous. A not inconsiderable part of the community was as much opposed to Rivadavia's policies of laissez faire as the provinces in the Interior and the Litoral. The Leiva incident and the discussion which followed helped to crystallize opinion in Buenos Aires, and *porteño* protectionists were not slow to take advantage of the situation. Even in the legislature protectionist sentiment was rapidly gaining in strength. Many representatives demanded that measures be taken to protect agriculture and industry. The tariff issue became more or less closely linked with anti-foreign sentiment. The movement aimed not only at the exclusion of foreign manufactures but also at curtailment of foreign capital and labor. Typical in this respect was the proposal that every business establishment in Buenos Aires be compelled to employ at least two Argentines, that foreigners be excluded from businesses employing only one person; and that professions such as *cartillero*, *repartidor de pan*, and *aguadero* be reserved to natives only.[33] Native manufacturers demanded special privileges, and urged the government to follow the example of the United States.[34]

Against the rising tide of protectionism free traders fought a hopeless battle. They endeavored to demonstrate the iniquity of protectionism and to convince the middle classes that a policy of restriction would end in disaster. The most eloquent representative of this group was Pedro de Angelis, the editor of *Gaceta Mercantil*, whose plea in defense of free trade epitomized the views and economic convictions of the federalist leaders.[35] In presenting his case for low tariffs de Angelis invoked both theory and statistics. He set forth the nature and principles of economic development in a series of propositions, arguing, after Adam Smith, that self-interest is the ultimate motive force of economic progress and welfare. Government interference with economic processes is contrary to the best interests of society and of individuals, be-

[33] Cf. Letter by "El Patriota" in *Gaceta Mercantil*, no. 2924 (February 23, 1833) and following issues.

[34] Typical in this connection is the petition of one Carlos María Huergo, manufacturer of *yerba mate* in Buenos Aires (*Archivo General*, Ant. C.2–A.10–no. 6).

[35] *Memoria sobre el estado de la hacienda pública, escrita por orden del Gobierno* (Buenos Aires: 1834). Chapter on *Aduanas*, pp. 180–219.

cause it substitutes artificial measures for the natural course of development. Such interference inevitably results in increased costs of production. But protection is especially harmful. It forces capital and labor into employments which are naturally less productive. Protection may succeed in fostering the establishment of new industries, but this sort of success is attainable only at the expense of other industries, which would otherwise prosper. Scarcity follows in the wake of protection, and this in turn leads to general impoverishment. For the more every individual is able to obtain for a given quantity of labor the more prosperous is the country. To force the nation to produce goods which can be easily obtained from abroad at much lower prices is to flaunt the principle of division of labor. Besides, industries which cannot meet foreign competitors and which cannot thrive unless protected by the government are harmful to the state. If protection succeeds in cutting imports, then exports will decrease proportionately. To this extent the growth of protected industries is a direct menace to the welfare of export industries.

The existing duties, far from being too moderate, were high enough to threaten complete cessation of imports of a large number of vital commodities. Importation of wine and liquors from either France or Spain was no longer considered profitable among importers. The same may be said of imports of brandy from Spain, or of oil from Seville, or of ready-made shoes from France.[36] A reduction of duties upon these

---

[36] Angelis gives the following example to substantiate his argument:

100 dozens of shoes packed in 4 trunks at 24 francs a dozen			Fr. 2.400
Packing, freight to board of ship and commission			325
			2.725
		Exchange: .75 fr. per peso	3.633
Sold in Buenos Aires at 55 pesos a dozen			$5.500
Less: Freight and hauling from ship to shore		35.4	
Duty: at 30 per cent on value of 5.000	$1.500		
Amortization at 5 per cent	255		
Contribución directa	20		
Storage	2	1.777.0	
Storage—1 per cent		55.0	
Commission and insurance 7½ per cent		412.4	2.280
			3.220

Profit and Loss Account

Cost of 100 dozen shoes	3.633 pesos
Net received	3.220 pesos
Loss	413 pesos

and other commodities of general consumption would not only stimulate commerce, but also benefit consumers.

The plea fell on deaf ears. To argue as de Angelis did that free trade benefited the community as a whole was to argue in abstract terms. The shoemakers were primarily concerned with the prosperity of the shoe industry rather than with the possibility of raising the average standard of living of the community. The same was true of other artisans, the farmers and wine and liquor producers in the Interior. The argument that increased imports encouraged larger exports seemed irrelevant to all those who did not depend upon foreign trade. And the circumstance that the most violent defenders of free trade were recruited mainly from among large scale merchants, cattle breeders, and meat producers, made the protectionists still more suspicious of the motives behind de Angelis' argument. Theoretical soundness of de Angelis' position, and it was fully in accord with the principles of the liberal school of political economy, was in itself not sufficient to stem the tide of protectionism. The federalist party once again needed popular support and it was willing to pay the price. It recognized that free trade had to be sacrificed on the altar of political expediency, and it preferred to make this sacrifice.

3

The tariff act of December 18, 1835 marked the turning point in the foreign trade policies of Buenos Aires.[37] For the first time since 1821 Buenos Aires openly defied the Rivadavian tradition. And for the first time also the government made a serious effort to adapt its tariff policy to the economic pattern of the province and the Interior.

In comprehensiveness and thoroughness the new tariff at least equaled the best efforts of the Rodríguez administration. The tariff law consisted of eight chapters (*capítulos*), each dealing with a particular phase of foreign trade. Chapter I (*De las entradas marítimas*) dealt with imports. The basic import duty was set at 17 per cent *ad valorem* on all commodities not otherwise provided for. Hides, horsehair, crude wool, crude tallow, horns, bones, jerked beef, ostrich feathers, and precious metals were placed on the free list.[38] A tax of 5 per cent was imposed upon plaster, coal, bricks, tin plates, steel, bronze, mercury, raw wool, paintings, printed matter, watches, jewelry,

[37] RO–982, L–14, no. –12.
[38] Article 2.

and agricultural implements.[39]   Silk, tar, rice, sackcloth, and arms were to pay 10 per cent import duty,[40] and sugar, coffee, cocoa, tea, *yerba mate,* cotton, wool, and foodstuffs were subject to a tax of 24 per cent.[41]   A relatively long list of commodities was placed under a 35 per cent duty.   Footwear, clothing, furniture, wine, brandy, liquors, tobacco, oil, certain leather goods, cheese, guitars, ink, mirrors, etc., were placed in this category.[42]   Beer, saddles, spaghetti and other flour products, as well as potatoes, were subject to a tax of 50 per cent *ad valorem.*[43]   Two commodities, hats and salt, were singled out for special treatment.   The import duty on these commodities was specific. Hats whether made of wool, fur, or silk were to pay 13 pesos paper (*moneda corriente*) each, and salt was subject to a tax of 1 peso per fanega.[44]   Carrying charges from ship to shore (*derecho de eslingaje*) was set at one-half peso per parcel (*bulto*), and allowance for waste on imported liquids was fixed at from 3 to 10 per cent.[45]

Chapter II of the tariff law dealt with commodities whose importation was either partly or entirely prohibited.   Among commodities included in this category were brass and tin plate wares, ornamental iron, iron and steel goods, all kinds of kitchen utensils, textiles, wood products, and others.   Prohibition affected also certain agricultural products.   Among the most important were maize, peas, beans and other vegetables, butter, and mustard.   Wheat was not permitted to enter the country when the domestic price fell below 50 pesos per fanega. And when the price rose above 50 pesos importation of wheat was to be regulated by means of special permits.[46]   The above provisions did not apply to flour brought to the Buenos Aires port for re-export to other provinces.[47]

Chapter III of the tariff act (*De la salida marítima*) established duties on overseas exports.   All exports not otherwise taxed were sub-

---

[39] Article 3.

[40] Article 4.

[41] Article 5.

[42] Articles 10 and 11.   The deduction amounted to 10 per cent on liquids from ports beyond the "line" (the equator), 6 per cent on cargo from ports below the "line," and 3 per cent on cargo from river ports (*de cabos adentro*).

[43] Article 6.

[44] Article 7.

[45] Article 9.

[46] Articles 2 and 3.

[47] Article 4.   Articles 5 to 8 of the chapter regulated the administration of articles 3 and 4.

ject to a duty of 4 per cent *ad valorem*.[48] Hides of all kinds, except those of unborn calves, were to pay 1 peso per unit.[49] Hides of unborn calves (*cueros de nonato*) were dutiable at the rate of 2 reales per unit.[50] Gold and silver paid 1 per cent export duty.[51] Grains, biscuits, salted meat exported in national bottoms, manufactured furs, flour, wool, and domestic manufactures were subject to no export duties.[52] A tax of 2 per cent was imposed on all re-exports, but certain imported commodities shipped to interior ports in small tonnage (river) boats required no special registration.[53]

Tariff rates relating to overland trade were defined in chapters IV (*De la entrada terrestre*) and V (*De la salida terrestre*). With few exceptions overland imports paid no duty.[54] The exceptions were *yerba mate* and tobacco from Paraguay, Corrientes, and Misiones which were taxed at the rate of 10 per cent *ad valorem;* [55] cigars were subject to a 20 per cent tax; [56] wood and coke transported in foreign bottoms were to pay 17 per cent.[57] Exports to other provinces of the Confederation were free of duty. The final chapter (*De la manera de calcular y recaudar los derechos*) regulated the assessment and collection of customs duties, and provided, in addition, that upward revisions of tariff rates were not to go into effect until 30 to 240 days after promulgation of the law.

Although the tariff act of 1835 did not meet all the demands of the protectionist party it did remove some of the more important sources of friction. In his message to the provincial legislature Rosas explained that the purpose of the new tariff law was to aid domestic agriculture and industry. Rosas argued that foreign competition was the principal obstacle to industrial and agricultural recovery and that the tariff "should result in progressive growth of foreign and domestic commerce as well as in higher revenues." [58]

[48] Article 5.
[49] Article 1.
[50] Article 2.
[51] Articles 3 and 4. Manufactured gold and silver paid 1 per cent of their market value, while gold and silver money paid 1 per cent in specie.
[52] Article 6.
[53] Articles 7 and 8.
[54] Article 4, Chapter IV.
[55] Article 1, Chapter IV.
[56] Article 2.
[57] Article 3.
[58] Mabragaña I, 304 (December 31, 1835).

The new tariff differed from the traditional pattern in more than one way. To begin with, most of the surtaxes introduced in September of 1829 by Juan José Viamonte were integrated with the basic rates. The basic rate of 17 per cent continued unchanged, but many important commodities which had been previously subject to this duty were now transferred to higher categories. The maximum duty was raised to 50 per cent. More significant still was the establishment of two new categories. One comprised commodities which paid no import duties, and the other included manufactures whose importation was altogether prohibited. There was no contradiction in this. Free importation applied only to commodities in the production of which the province excelled. None of these commodities were normally imported to Buenos Aires, except for re-export, and to this extent abolition of import or transit duties directly benefited provincial commerce and shipping. Abolition of import duties involved, of course, the loss of certain revenues, but this loss was not large, and it could be easily made up through increased income from stamp duties, the *contribución directa,* and other internal taxes. The introduction of the list of prohibited commodities marked a sharp break with the traditional policies of the post-revolutionary period. For the first time it was officially recognized that expansion of foreign trade did not always and necessarily coincide with the economic interests of the nation. For the first time, also, the government expressed direct concern in the welfare of the middle classes. The measure revealed that Rosas seriously believed in the possibility of developing domestic production of manufactured commodities on a scale sufficient to meet internal demand. The program was modest, but precisely for this reason it seemed practicable and realizable. It was reasonable to assume that given time domestic industries would become strong enough to withstand foreign competition, and protection would in time become superfluous. Compared with the advantages of a balanced economy the price which the country was asked to pay in the form of higher living costs seemed small and well worth paying.

Apart from its long range potentialities the new tariff offered immediate advantages of economic as well as political order. In the first place agriculture, so consistently neglected in the preceding decade, was now assured of a reasonable profit. This was of the utmost importance, for grain growing threatened to disappear altogether from the province.[59] The new tariff with its provision for total prohibition of grain imports when the domestic price of wheat fell below 50 pesos per fanega brought new hope to farmers. The *porteño* federalist party kept its promise, and the farmers were quick to show their appreciation by giving enthusiastic support to the Rosas administration.[60]

The new agricultural policy favored not only *porteño* farmers, but also grain growers in other provinces. In the Interior foreign competition was less severe because of the prohibitive cost of overland transportation from Buenos Aires. Nevertheless, a free market in Buenos Aires exercised a depressing influence upon agricultural prices in the provinces. It is not surprising, therefore, that the provinces as far removed from the port as Mendoza heartily acclaimed the tariff of 1835.[61] Nor is it surprising that these provinces were anxious to see the Rosas administration continue in power. Immediate prosperity resulting from higher grain prices overshadowed the more distant dangers of dictatorship.

The government, too, had reasons to be gratified with the change in its agricultural policy. One year after the promulgation of the new tariff law Rosas called the attention of the provincial legislature to the rapid expansion of grain growing in the province. There was a notable increase in the area under cultivation, and agriculture became more diversified. Grains other than wheat were being sown in greater quantities than ever before, and the country was no longer dependent upon uncertainties of weather or upon foreign importations.[62]

[59] Characteristic in this connection is the following excerpt from a letter written in 1834 by the administrator of the government-owned farm "Chacarita": "Tengo el honor de comunicar a Vs. haber comprado a Dn. Diego Prado un lomo de ladrillo y la armazón de un galpón que se hallan edificados en este establecimiento en la cantidad de 300 pesos. El objeto que he tenido en vista al hacer esta compra, ha sido dedicarme a la elaboración de adobe lo que presenta mas ventajas que las siembras que se ha hecho en el espacio de 3 o 4 años. La agricultura, Sr. Ministro, demanda gastos enormes y sin la mas remota esperanza de utilizar algo. . . ." Cf. *Archivo General*, Ant. C.22–A.10–no. –6.

[60] The following note carried by the *British Packet and Argentine News* on February 6, 1836 (vol. 10, no. 494) may serve as an example of the impression which the new tariff created among the farmers of the province: "An address dated second instant has been presented to the government from the inhabitants of the township Cañuelas, thanking His Excellency the Governor for the protection he has granted to national industry, by the decree prohibiting the importation of foreign wheat and flour, except under certain conditions." It may be added that Cañuelas was not alone in expressing its gratitude and satisfaction.

[61] "An advance in wheat," reported the *British Packet and Argentine News*, "was the immediate consequence, and great activity has been infused in the agricultural and grazing branches of industry." February 6, 1836, vol. 10, no. 494.

[62] Mabragaña I, 326 (Message, January 1, 1837).

To domestic industry the new tariff promised even greater benefits than to agriculture. The handicraft industry of Buenos Aires was accorded a degree of protection which it never enjoyed before. The same was true, also, of the wine and liquor industries in the provinces of Cuyo and Tucumán, the textile and food industries of Córdoba and Santiago del Estero, and sheep grazing in the provinces of the Litoral. By liberalizing the regulations concerning the use of the Buenos Aires port Rosas stimulated commercial relations between Buenos Aires and the river ports and improved thereby the position of the litoral provinces in overseas markets.

The political implications of the new tariff were no less far reaching. Rosas could now count upon the undivided support of the middle classes in Buenos Aires, and his prestige beyond the provincial boundaries was enormously heightened. In the eyes of the provinces Rosas became the most Argentine of all *porteño* governors, the only governor in fact who placed the economic interests of the nation above those of foreign merchants. The Buenos Aires government revealed itself as a national government, and Rosas became the recognized leader of the nation.

How long Rosas could maintain his position of unchallenged supremacy depended among other things upon the efficacy of the new tariff policy. At this time it was still a matter of speculation whether the new tariff was capable of solving the fundamental problems facing the nation. Could the new commercial policy withstand the acid test of economic reality? Did the new tariff create a sufficiently broad basis for a permanent economic *rapprochement* between Buenos Aires and the provinces? Again, were the *porteños* prepared to endure the hardships which the new policy implied? And, if so, was Rosas able to continue this policy of economic nationalism? Time alone could answer these questions, and as the years wore on the answer was more and more clearly negative.

4

The history of the tariff in the decade and a half following the act of December 18, 1835 is relatively simple. The first major revision of the schedule occurred in the middle of 1837,[63] when additional duties of

[63] On a previous occasion (March 4, 1836) the tariff schedule was amended to meet evasion of duties on overseas goods brought to Buenos Aires by way of river ports. The decree provided that overseas imports brought to Buenos Aires in river vessels were subject to a surtax of 25 per cent of the normal duty. Cf. RO–1010, L–15, no. –3. This measure was aimed against Montevideo which often served as the relaying point for overseas commerce.

2 and 4 per cent were decreed on all overseas imports subject to *ad valorem* duties of 10 per cent or more.[64] The 2 per cent additional duty applied to imports paying 10 per cent and 17 per cent, and commodities subject to 24 per cent or more paid a surtax of 4 per cent. The government justified these surtaxes by exigencies of war. Additional revenues were badly needed for the campaign against the Bolivian dictator Santa Cruz, and internal taxation, argued Rosas, could not be relied upon to produce the necessary funds. Foreign trade offered the easiest and speediest means of financing the war.[65]

The additional duties strengthened, no doubt, the protectionist features of the tariff of 1835, and domestic industry gained further advantage over its competitors. But this advantage was short-lived. In the early months of the following year the provincial government was forced to reverse its policy of high duties. The immediate cause for this reversal was the blockade instituted by the French fleet on March 23, 1838.[66] The blockade brought to a standstill the nation's foreign trade, and it deprived the provincial treasury of its most important source of revenues. The province was, moreover, threatened with a scarcity of wheat and flour. In order to minimize the devastating effects of the blockade Rosas made two important changes in the tariff. The first change related to wheat and flour. By a decree of May 1, 1838,[67] export of these commodities was prohibited altogether on the ground that wheat prices rose above 50 pesos per fanega,[68] and that as a result of the blockade foreign supplies were not readily available. Some four weeks later duties upon all imports were reduced by one third.[69] This decree as well as that relating to grain exports was to remain in force for the duration of the blockade. At the same time Rosas suspended the operation of the decree of March 4, 1836, the suspension to last until three months after the end of the blockade.[70]

---

[64] Decree, August 31, 1837 (RO–1173, L–16, no. –8).

[65] Cf. Preamble of decree of August 31, 1837; also, Mabragaña I, 368 (Message of December 27, 1837).

[66] For a detailed discussion of the events leading to the conflict with France and the political and diplomatic aspects of this and the Anglo-French blockades, see Ricardo Levene, *op. cit.*, vol. 2; Saldías, *op. cit.*, vols. 3–5; and especially the monograph by John F. Cady, *Foreign Intervention in the Rio de la Plata* (Philadelphia, University of Pennsylvania Press: 1929).

[67] RO–1237, L–17, no. –5.

[68] Wheat sold at 51.5 pesos per fanega in May of 1838, and rose to 89 pesos in September of that year. Cf. Table 43, chap. x.

[69] Decree, May 28, 1838 (RO–1241, L–17, no. –5).

[70] Decree, May 28, 1838 (RO–1240, L–17, no. –5).

This meant that foreign cargoes brought to Montevideo or any other river port and shipped thence to Buenos Aires were no longer subject to the penalty of 25 per cent of the normal duty.

The French fleet lifted the blockade of Buenos Aires on October 29, 1839 and normal intercourse with overseas markets was rapidly restored. It became obvious, however, that a return to the economic and commercial policies of the pre-war period was no longer possible. Before the blockade the provincial government could well afford to forego some of the revenues derived from customs duties. Now such policy was a luxury beyond the means of the harassed treasury.

The decision to modify the protectionist tariff of 1835 was motivated by economic as well as fiscal considerations. The blockade had demonstrated as no verbal argument could that domestic industry was unequal to the task of supplying the country's demand for manufactured goods. It is true, of course, that under normal conditions industry might have given a much better account of itself. It is obviously unfair to judge the vitality of the industry on the basis of its performance under blockade conditions, for the burden imposed upon the industry was clearly incommensurate with the country's resources in raw materials, capital, and technical equipment. The country was not prepared to become economically self-sufficient on short notice. That it withstood the blockade was not so much because of the industry's ability to supplant foreign manufacturers, but rather to the circumstance that the country's demand for industrial goods was highly elastic. Nevertheless, the blockade did create a widespread scarcity of manufactured goods, and Rosas had no alternative but to relinquish his relatively modest aspirations in the field of economic independence.

The new policy was launched quite inconspicuously. In December of 1841 the government instructed the Collector General to permit importation of commodities which by the tariff act of 1835 had not been allowed to enter the country.[71] Commodities which until then had been on the prohibited list were to be admitted on payment of 17 per cent duty.

The decision of December 31, 1841 closed an important chapter in the tariff history of Buenos Aires. It ended an experiment which had only moderate possibilities of success even under more favorable conditions. The *porteño* government was once again forced to abandon principles for the sake of expediency, to "betray" the economic inter-

---

[71] Cf. *Registro Nacional*, II, 422, no. 2786 (December 31, 1841).

ests of the middle classes in the province as well as in the Interior and the Litoral. By his tariff of 1835 Rosas had made an important step toward the formulation of an economic policy that was national in scope, laying thereby a foundation for a lasting economic union of the Argentine provinces under the aegis of Buenos Aires. Such policy was no longer practicable. Partly by design and partly by force of circumstances Buenos Aires once more set itself apart from the other provinces of the Confederation. In an effort to rehabilitate its own economy Buenos Aires forsook the needs and aspirations of the provinces. In this sense Rosas had become a prisoner of his own party's economic egoism.

Rosas emerged victorious from the conflict with France. He succeeded in preserving intact the sovereignty of Argentina. He successfully defended the principle of self-determination on the South American continent. At the end of the conflict his political prestige in Argentina and throughout the continent was greater than ever before. Nevertheless, it was a Pyrrhic victory that Rosas gained. His enhanced prestige could not compensate for the economic losses inflicted upon the industrial and agricultural classes of the province and in the Interior. Sooner or later the fact that Rosas was unable to establish a just equilibrium between the economic interests of Buenos Aires and the provinces was bound to be rediscovered by friends and foes alike. The provinces were bound to reconsider their attitude toward the Rosas regime in the light of Ferré's exhortations of a decade ago. From their point of view there was hardly any difference between Rosas and Rivadavia, between *porteño* federalism and unitarism. Rosas no less than Rivadavia became the representative of Buenos Aires, the defender of its special interests, willing and ready to sacrifice the most vital needs of the provinces. And to the *porteño* middle class Rosas revealed himself as the champion of the wealthy landowners, cattle breeders, and meat producers, who were the real beneficiaries of the federalist regime.

Rosas made no serious effort to restore the protectionist system of the pre-blockade period. In the four years following the French blockade the government did nothing to return to the policy of economic nationalism. For although the tariff rates of 1835 were reestablished, the prohibited list was abolished shortly after the cessation of the blockade. To make up for this "betrayal" of the protectionist cause the provincial legislature authorized the government to extend special privileges to new industries for periods up to ten years. But the legislature failed to define these privileges, and the government did not avail itself of this authority. It was on this occasion that the Junta, through its Comisión Financiera, voiced opposition to any measure which threatened to reduce the volume of foreign trade.[72] Abolition of the prohibited list was intended to be temporary, until such time when the stock of manufactured commodities could be replenished. But the list was never restored. In 1845 the conflict with France flared up anew, and this time France was joined by Great Britain. Once again Rosas was forced to relax foreign trade regulations and to lower tariff rates in order "to encourage the spirit of enterprise and to increase revenues."[73] As in the case of the French blockade, duties on foreign imports were reduced by one-third. And in addition imports of goods reloaded in Montevideo or other river ports were not penalized. In 1846 the government permitted exports in Uruguayan ships, provided that these ships brought cargo to Buenos Aires.[74]

It was not until 1848 that the Anglo-French blockade was lifted, and in June of that year normal tariff rates were reëstablished.[75] But now the efficacy of the tariff as a measure of protection was largely illusory. Deterioration of the province's monetary system and the general impoverishment of the provincial population reduced internal markets to such an extent that industrial expansion would be difficult even under more stringent protection than that accorded by the tariff act of 1835. Thus, far from encouraging industrial expansion, the tariff merely served to raise the cost of living to a level at which extension of domestic markets was no longer possible. The effect of inflation was to shift the burden of war upon the middle and lower classes, to reduce their standard of living, and to contract proportionately the demand for consumers' goods.

The provinces, too, felt the effect of the blockades. To begin with, the Buenos Aires market had difficulty in absorbing all the produce and manufactures offered by the provinces. The fact that imports from the provinces had to be paid for in specie made commercial intercourse between Buenos Aires and the provinces difficult and often

---

[72] Cf. *Diario de Sesiones,* Session, June 17, 1841 (XXVII, 693, *et passim*).

[73] Decree, November 21, 1845 (*Registro Nacional*—2834).

[74] Decree, May 21, 1846 (*Registro Nacional*—2840).

[75] Mabragaña II, 242 (Message, December 27, 1848).

unprofitable. For as the value of currency fell real income and pur-
chasing power of these classes which consumed the bulk of domestic
production decreased. And the fact that Rosas insisted upon preferential treatment of *porteño* trade in the markets of the Interior made
the provinces all the more impatient with Buenos Aires and its commercial policies. Illustrative in this connection are two almost identical decrees issued by the governments of Tucumán and Salta immediately after the Anglo-French fleet began its blockade of Buenos Aires.
The Tucumán government imposed a surtax of 20 per cent upon all
imports from Chile and Bolivia [76] on the ground that importations from
these countries caused a fall in domestic prices, that such importations
drained the country of specie, and that it was in Tucumán's interest to
encourage commercial intercourse with Buenos Aires. Salta imposed
a surtax of 25 per cent on all overseas produce entering through non-
national ports. Among the *considerandos* the following were characteristic: firstly, that foreign commerce through non-national ports was
contrary to national interest; secondly, that such commerce tended to
isolate the province from the rest of the country; thirdly, that provincial commerce should not be directed through ports which were outside
the jurisdiction of the national government; and, finally, that it was
dangerous to substitute foreign markets for national markets.[77] When
in 1852 the legislature of Tucumán considered annulment of the decree
of January 22, 1848, one deputy recalled that the surtax was instituted in order to conform to the "pernicious policies of the tyrant
Rosas, even though the tax inflicted hardship upon consumers of the
province." [78]

So, once again, the economic aspect of national organization came to
the forefront. Buenos Aires again appeared to have subordinated the
welfare of the provinces to its own economic interests. It was clear
now, more than ever before, that Rosas was no longer willing or perhaps able to pursue a truly federalist policy with respect to overseas
trade. That the *porteño* government continued to profess faith in federalist principles deceived no one. In matters affecting the economic
status of the provinces the actions of the Buenos Aires government
were no different from those one might expect from a unitary adminis-

---

[76] Decree, January 22, 1848. Cf. *Archivo Americano,* nueva serie, vol. 6, no. 20
(1850), pp. 110–113.

[77] Cf. *ibid.,* pp. 113–114.

[78] Cf. *Actas de la Sala de Representantes,* Session, May 19, 1852.

tration.   In fact, Rosas was far more dangerous than Rivadavia, for, unlike the latter, the former had the political and material resources to enforce the will of Buenos Aires, and so long as the political and economic hegemony of Buenos Aires remained unchallenged the provinces could expect no concessions from the *porteño* administration.   Indeed, the provinces could rightly question the sincerity of the *porteño* government in matters affecting their political autonomy.   And if these fears were not groundless, then federalism itself was in danger of being wiped off the face of the country.

CHAPTER X

THE ECONOMICS OF DICTATORSHIP

But of what avail would it be to augment the territorial property of the province if the remaining public wants were not satisfied?—Archivo Americano, no. 6, August 31, 1843.

IN SHAPING the economic policies of his administration Rosas seldom ventured beyond the relatively narrow confines of the immediate interests of the province and the class he represented. To him as to the majority of *porteño* federalist leaders the concept of national economy was impracticable and even dangerous. National economy presupposed a degree of political and economic integration of the provinces that was not readily attainable and, from the point of view of Buenos Aires, undesirable. Buenos Aires could well afford to pursue an independent course in the field of economic endeavor. So long as the province was capable of producing export commodities in sufficient quantities and at reasonable prices, it remained relatively immune to the difficulties and maladjustments which afflicted the Interior and the Litoral. It was in foreign markets that Buenos Aires could dispose of the produce of its pastoral industries, and it was also there that the province could most advantageously satisfy its demand for manufactures and foodstuffs. Ever since the opening of Buenos Aires to foreign trade the province had been drawn into the orbit of European and North American economy. And at the same time the bond between Buenos Aires and the Interior, never too strong, had grown progressively weaker. It was toward the east and across the Atlantic that the province of Buenos Aires looked for its livelihood, and having once found its place in the world market it was determined to keep it at all costs.

From the earliest days of independence foreign trade had been relied upon to solve the economic problems of the country. Mariano Moreno had formulated the economic aspirations of Buenos Aires in terms of direct commerce with overseas countries. In the ten years following the Revolution of 1810 the principle of "free trade" was extended, until in the early twenties it became the cornerstone of the

Rodríguez-Rivadavia regime. Just as foreign trade brought Buenos Aires into closer contact with the outside world, so also could it become instrumental in attracting into the country capital, technical equipment, and skilled labor. Rivadavia and the unitary party were quite conscious of the economic backwardness of the young republic. They knew that the country's resources were insufficient to overcome the initial obstacle which the colonial regime had placed before it. But they were confident that with the help of foreign capital and enterprise the country's economic structure could be rapidly modernized. That in this revitalized national economy Buenos Aires should play the leading role seemed axiomatic, for Buenos Aires was not only the sole link between the Interior and the outside world, but also the most important commercial and financial center in the country.

It was precisely this emphasis upon national rather than provincial economic development which caused the *porteño* cattle breeders and landowners to distrust the unitary economic program and policies. In the federalist view the unitaries did not show sufficient concern for the welfare of the pastoral industry. Yet this industry was the mainstay of the provincial economy. Without it Buenos Aires could not hope to maintain its position of leadership in the national economy, all the more so since the country's foreign commerce was almost wholly dependent upon the produce of the pampa. Preoccupation with the problem of economic and political integration of the country prevented the unitaries from devoting more attention to provincial industries. The *porteño* federalists were not going to repeat the mistake of their adversaries. They proclaimed the principle of economic and political autonomy of the provinces; they disclaimed any intention of interfering in the internal affairs of the other provinces, but at the same time insisted upon complete freedom in shaping the economic destiny of Buenos Aires.

That destiny lay in the continued prosperity of the pastoral industries, and no one was more clearly aware of this than Rosas. The central problem facing cattle breeding in the early thirties was the growing scarcity of free land. Ever since the opening of Buenos Aires to foreign trade pressure upon grazing land had been steadily increasing, so that after twenty years grazing was rapidly approaching the limits of profitable expansion. Rivadavia attempted to solve the land problem by releasing public lands through the system of emphyteusis, but the supply of such lands was limited, and the emphyteusis system did not always work to the advantage of the pastoral industry.[1] At the same time cattle breeders were pushing southward into Indian territory in search of cheap land. But occupation and settlement of territories beyond the frontier was difficult and costly. Sustained and orderly expansion in these regions could not be hoped for unless the government was willing and able to insure safety against Indian attacks.

Rosas and other leaders of the federalist party recognized the importance of territorial expansion and land settlement. In 1830 the deputy government composed of Anchorena, Balcarce, and García spoke of settlement of the new frontier as "the solid foundation of provincial wealth and prosperity," [2] and it assured the legislature that plans were being considered to meet the problem. Lack of funds prevented action at that time. In 1831 the provincial government reported that it had not been able to distribute the newly acquired territories in Bahía Blanca, Cruz de Guerra, and Federación, and it estimated the cost of settling these lands at about one million pesos.[3] But colonization entered a new phase with the promulgation of the law of June 9, 1832. The government set aside nearly 360 square leagues in the vicinity of the forts Federación, Argentina, Bahía Blanca, and Mayo. This land was to be distributed among veterans of wars against the unitaries, and also among cattle breeders who were especially hard hit by the recent drought.[4] The law further terminated all emphyteusis contracts in these areas and provided for indemnification of tenants on terms defined in the decree of September 19, 1829.[5]

In 1833 Rosas organized the famous campaign against the Indians. He enlisted the coöperation of Córdoba and of the provinces of Cuyo, and induced Juan Facundo Quiroga to assume command of the expedition. The plan called for a simultaneous attack on the Indians in three columns: one under Félix Aldao in the Andean region; another under Ruiz Huidoboro in the Pampa Central; and the third column, led by Rosas, was to operate in southern Buenos Aires. The campaign was only partially successful. The armies of Cuyo and Córdoba were forced to withdraw from the field without accomplishing the main ob-

[1] For a more detailed discussion of the emphyteusis system, see *supra,* chap. iv, pp. 96–99.

[2] Mabragaña I, 248 (Message, May 1830).

[3] Mabragaña I, 255 (Message, May 20, 1831).

[4] RO–354, L–11, no. –6.

[5] The government offered outright ownership of one or two lots in exchange for the lease held under emphyteusis.

jective of the campaign. Lack of financial support from the provincial governments is to be blamed for this failure.[6] But the *porteño* column under Rosas remained in the field. Within one year Rosas brought under military control vast territories until then inhabited by independent Indian tribes. The newly conquered area extended 200 leagues to the west as far as the Andes, and beyond the rivers Negro, Neuquén, and Lima, as far as Cape Horn, to the south.[7] The campaign put an end to the military power of numerous Indian tribes who had for many years preyed upon *porteño* commerce and industry.

Once control over conquered Indian territory was more or less secured, the *porteño* government proceeded to transfer large tracts into private hands. In September of 1834, shortly after the campaign was concluded, the provincial legislature authorized distribution of 50 square leagues among the commanding officers of the expeditionary force.[8] By law of May 10, 1836 the Junta de Representantes approved the sale of 1,500 square leagues of the public domain, whether unoccupied or held in emphyteusis.[9] Land held in emphyteusis could not be sold to non-tenants, and leaseholders could not be forced to buy the land they held in emphyteusis, but rentals were to be doubled at the expiration of the emphyteusis period, i.e., in January 1838. The law established three price categories. In the region north of the Salado river the price was set at 5,000 pesos per square league; 4,000 pesos per square league was to be charged in the area between Río Salado and a line running from Sierra del Volcán y Tandil through Laguna Blanca, through Fuerte Mayo to Fuerte Federación; and, finally, land south of this line was to be offered at 3,000 pesos per square league.

The economic significance of the law of May 10, 1836 cannot be exaggerated. At one stroke the law released for economic exploitation vast tracts of grazing land. By fixing prices at a relatively low level the legislature hoped to stimulate expansion of grazing areas which until then were considered hardly suitable for cattle breeding. And at

[6] R. J. Cárcano, *Juan Facundo Quiroga. Simulación, infidencia, tragedia.* (Buenos Aires: 1931.)

[7] The new boundary of the province ran from Melincué to the line of San Rafael in the north, along the Andes in the west, and as far as the straits of Magellan in the south. Cf. Adolfo Saldías, *op. cit.,* chap. xxii.

[8] Law, September 30, 1834 (RO–695, L–13, no. –9). This law was supplemented by a decree of November 15, 1834 (RO–755, L–13, no. –10). Under the terms of this decree Ángel Pacheco received a grant of 7 square leagues, the remaining 43 leagues were distributed among eleven colonels. (*Acuerdo* of January 30, 1835.)

[9] *Recopilación de las leyes y decretos promulgados en Buenos Aires desde 1° de enero hasta fin de diciembre de 1840* (Buenos Aires: 1841), p. 1383.

the same time the law foreshadowed eventual abolition of emphyteusis. The law of May 10, 1836 did not, it is true, cancel existing emphyteusis contracts, but it seriously weakened the fundamental principle of the emphyteusis system by offering public land for sale. Moreover, it allowed tenants to buy outright the land they held in emphyteusis. And, as if to make certain that tenants would avail themselves of the right to buy the land they leased, the legislature doubled the rent rates beginning with the new emphyteusis period. In July of 1837 the government took further steps to restrict the emphyteusis system. It decreed that lands returned to the state because of unpaid rentals would be withdrawn from emphyteusis and offered for sale.[10] By another decree the government prohibited subdivision of land held in emphyteusis. Tenants were permitted to buy the land they leased, but they had to exercize this privilege within two months from the date of promulgation of the decree. On January 16, 1838 the rights of certain categories of tenants were declared forfeited and the land was offered for sale to the highest bidder.[11]

At the time when emphyteusis contracts came up for renewal (January 1838) the government made further inroads into the system. By decree of May 28, 1838 renewals of emphyteusis contracts for a period of 10 years were announced, but rentals were raised 100 per cent payable half in currency and half in treasury bills. However, a large area comprising the most populated and economically the most valuable part of the province was not subject to the law of emphyteusis. All land in this area[12] that was held in emphyteusis reverted to the state and was subject to public sale in accordance with provisions of the law of May 10, 1836. The government justified its decision to limit emphyteusis to outlying areas of the province on the following grounds. First, the provincial treasury was financially embarrassed and was anxious to increase revenues; secondly, the government was convinced that private ownership was more conducive to the welfare of society and state; thirdly, there was increased demand for land as a result of expansion of grazing; and, finally, the price set by the law of May 10,

---

[10] Decree, July 27, 1837. Cf. *Recopilación*.

[11] Cf. *Recopilación* (*Acuerdo*).

[12] The area was defined in article 4 of the decree as follows: From Río de la Plata along the coast down to Lobería Grande, from which point the line ran through the Sierras del Volcán and Tandil to Azul and Tapalque, along the river Las Flores to its confluence with the Río Salado, thence to Cañada de Tío Antonio, Pergamino, and Arroyo Medio.

1836 was so reasonable that no hardship was involved in the requirement that tenants buy the land they held in emphyteusis.[13]

It is not possible to determine whether new emphyteusis contracts were made after 1838. Information on this score is very scant. The circumstance that no reference to emphyteusis is to be found in Rosas' messages to the provincial legislature or in the more important compilations of provincial laws leads one to believe that the practice of leasing land fell into disuse shortly after 1838. This should not be surprising, for as currency depreciated to less than 4 per cent of par the price of 3,000 or 4,000 pesos per square league was no longer a serious obstacle to land ownership. Emphyteusis died a natural although perhaps a lingering death.

The swing toward private ownership of land was motivated by financial reasons as much as by considerations of economic order. Both the provincial legislature and the government hoped to restore the province's financial equilibrium with the proceeds from the sale of public land. But these calculations proved to be erroneous. In the seven months following the promulgation of the law of May 10, 1836 only 400 square leagues were sold for a total sum of about 1,500,000 pesos.[14] After this first rush the demand for land slackened, and the government sought other means of stimulating land distribution. It could not reduce prices, which were fixed by law, but it did permit payment in treasury bills and even in cattle, up to 50 per cent of the value of land bought.[15] Yet, even these concessions failed to produce satisfactory results. In a message to the legislature Rosas admitted that large areas remained unoccupied in spite of the fact that land values had risen sharply.[16] The government's inability to distribute the public domain more quickly could be ascribed to technical as well as economic factors. Transfer of land titles was necessarily a slow and complicated process. Consummation of transfers frequently required the intervention of courts. The government tried to simplify the process of land acquisition by instituting systematic surveys of public lands. But such surveys consumed time, especially in the outlying districts. Even more important was the economic factor. Exploitation of land

---

[13] Cf. Preamble to decree of May 28, 1838, and also Mabragaña I, 395–396 (Message, December 27, 1838).

[14] Mabragaña, I, 332 (Message, January 1, 1837).

[15] Law, July 27, 1837. Articles 3 and 4.

[16] Mabragaña, I, 366 (Message, December 27, 1837).

in the province was confined primarily to cattle breeding and to a lesser extent sheep breeding. But grazing depended ultimately upon foreign markets. Unless, therefore, foreign demand for hides and jerked beef or wool increased very considerably the pastoral industry was bound to reach the limit of profitable expansion very soon. Accessibility to foreign markets played of necessity an important part in the fortunes of the industry. Therefore, when in 1838 and 1839 the French fleet closed the Buenos Aires port, the demand for land declined to a minimum.

Within two years of the passage of the law of May 10, 1836 it became clear that the government would not be able to sell all the land at its disposal. The province continued to be the largest single landowner, without however deriving any financial or economic benefit from the vast public domain. If these areas were to produce any income at all they had to be incorporated into the economy. And since the land could not be sold the government decided to give it away. The mutiny of Dolores and Monsalvo on October 29, 1839 provided the occasion for a wholesale transfer of public lands to private ownership. Anxious to check the revolt as speedily as possible the Junta de Representantes promised land grants to loyal troops. The grants were defined in the law of November 9, 1839,[17] and were put into effect in the middle of 1840 when Rosas ordered the Contaduría General to issue land certificates.

The decree of July 9, 1840 marked the culminating point of Rosas' land policy. From the viewpoint of the *estanciero* class that policy was highly successful. In a relatively short period Rosas had fully realized the most important postulates of the federalist economic program. He virtually abolished the system of emphyteusis; he extended the southern frontiers of the province; and he assured the pastoral industry of a plentiful supply of land at reasonable prices. On this score alone Rosas deserved well of the cattle breeder and meat and hide producers. No other social group derived greater benefits from the Rosas regime, nor was any other group more intimately interested in maintaining the regime intact.

---

[17] RO–1350, L–18, no. –11. Art. 5 of the law outlined the pattern of grants as follows: Generals, 6 square leagues; Colonels, 5 square leagues; Lt. Colonels, 4 square leagues; Majors, 2 square leagues; Captains, 1 square league; other officers, ¾ square league; noncommissioned officers, ½ square league; privates, ¼ square league.

2

Rosas' solicitude for the welfare of the pastoral industry contrasted sharply with his somewhat lukewarm attitude toward other sectors of the provincial economy. It would seem as if concern for this one industry exhausted the resources of the government, or else that Rosas and the federalist party were incapable of formulating an economic program and policy which envisaged a more balanced expansion of the provincial economy. The privileges accorded the pastoral industry had cost the treasury a good deal in revenues. Reduction or abolition of cattle taxes or of duties upon salt imports, for example, meant that other taxes, however burdensome, had to be retained and even increased. Excessive regard for the interests of the *estancieros* and the *saladeristas* forced the government to exercise extreme caution when it came to extending a helping hand to the farmer and the industrialist. Nor did Rosas and his collaborators succeed in reconciling the divergent tendencies in the provincial economy. Quite naturally, the federalist leaders tended to identify the interests of the grazing industry with those of the province. Their economic program was based on the theory that what was good for the *estanciero* class was good for the society as a whole, and therefore also for each of its component parts. This was perhaps inevitable, but it was equally inevitable that political leaders of the Rosas regime should have become accustomed to view the economic issues of the day in a false perspective. It was unavoidable, also, that their policies should have been tinged with a strong admixture of opportunism.

The *estancieros* had realized most of their economic postulates even before Rosas began his second term in office. Henceforth his main objective was to guard against any radical changes in the established order, to maintain and to strengthen, if possible, the economic and political *status quo*. Both the government and the legislature were reluctant to strike out new paths of economic thought, and whenever the administration was forced under pressure to venture beyond the relatively narrow confines of the established economic pattern it did so half-heartedly and without conviction. The federalist leaders had little faith in the efficacy of protection. Nor were they certain that the province could eventually dispense with foreign importations of grain and flour. But they realized that a policy of economic nationalism demanded sacrifices in the form of higher living costs, increased cost of production, and possibly lower profits. The cattle breeders and meat and hide exporters were not prepared to make such sacrifices, and it was not until further resistance to the demand for protection became politically dangerous that Rosas agreed to revise the tariff policies of Buenos Aires. His conversion to protectionism was superficial, however, and he abandoned the new policy even before it could be thoroughly tested.

The agricultural policies of the Rosas administration revealed most clearly the federalist party's failure to rise above the limited scope of class interest, and its inability to solve the contradictions which slowly undermined the regime. Before Rosas successive *porteño* governments grappled with the problem of grain production without success. Not even the administration of Rodríguez, so anxious to develop the vast resources of the country, succeeded in lifting domestic agriculture to the level of economic respectability. In those years of exuberant progress the government entertained grandiose ideas. Plans were laid to populate the pampa, to expand the area under grain cultivation, and to make the province and the country agriculturally self-sustaining. With only slight regard for the financial and economic condition of the province the administration embarked upon a policy of subsidized immigration. But the government grossly overestimated its own resources and the economic capacity of the provincial economy. It relied too much upon the dynamic force of free enterprise and the availability of fertile soil. These two factors were deemed sufficient to insure lasting prosperity to agriculture just as they insured the continued expansion of cattle breeding. But the unitary leaders overlooked the fact that domestic agriculture had none of the advantages which grazing enjoyed. To begin with, agriculture called for proportionately larger investments of labor, which was notoriously scarce and expensive. Secondly, methods of cultivation were primitive, and the yield was low in spite of the excellent quality of the soil. In order to increase the yield the farmer would have to employ more capital in the form of machinery and agricultural implements. Thirdly, the high cost of transportation forced the farmer to move closer to cities, where, of course, land prices were higher. And, finally, unlike the cattle breeder, the farmer had to contend with foreign competition which was often ruinous.

This latter factor was of paramount importance. The domestic market was limited, and because foreign wheat and flour were usually of superior quality domestic farmers had small chance to survive. The primary problem facing the government was, therefore, not one of increasing the number of grain growers, but rather one of assuring the farmer a reasonable return by means of adequate protection of internal markets. But neither Rodríguez nor his successors viewed the problem in these terms. Protection as an instrument of economic policy was unacceptable on general grounds. It was especially distasteful in relation to agriculture, for a policy orientated toward higher wheat and flour prices was politically unpopular.

So it was that agriculture continued to occupy a minor position in the expanding economy of the province. So far from making any progress it deteriorated until grain-growing threatened to become a lost art. The result was that even moderately unfavorable weather conditions caused serious shortages of grain and flour. So, for example, in 1829 the provincial government was obliged to purchase some 1,500 barrels of flour at 97 pesos per barrel, for distribution among bakers, "who in the quality and size of their bread will not take advantage of the present fluctuating state of the market." [18]   There was no question that the farmer might take advantage of high wheat prices, for by the time his crop reached the market foreign imports would depress prices to a level which barely covered cost of production.

No wonder, then, that the farmer became embittered and disillusioned, and that he lost all confidence in the regime of economic liberalism so steadfastly championed by the unitaries. Nor is it any wonder that in the struggle for power between the unitaries and the federalists the farmer joined the federalist camp without hesitation. He followed Rosas not only because he mistrusted the unitaries but also and primarily because he hoped that a federalist administration would show greater sympathy for his economic difficulties. The federalist party always professed concern for the economic integrity of the native population and it opposed the unitary program of europeanization of the national economy, and although federalist leaders never came out openly for protection they did decry the damaging effect of foreign competition. To the farmer, therefore, as well as to the artisans, a federalist regime held out a promise of better days.

One of the first acts of the Rosas administration was to dismiss the Immigration Commission (Comisión de Inmigración) established in

[18] *British Packet and Argentine News*, vol. IV, no. 164 (October 10, 1829).

1824. Rosas justified this step on the ground that the commission failed to accomplish anything tangible, and that the results achieved did not warrant the outlay.[19]   But after this initial act of what seemed to be a forerunner of a new agricultural policy there followed prolonged silence.   It may be that the government postponed examination of the agricultural problem until more propitious times.   The country was suffering from a severe drought,[20] and there was little that the government could do to assist the farmer.   At the same time it became necessary to keep wheat and flour prices under control, in order to prevent social and political unrest.

In January of 1831 the government revised import duties on flour, but left the 1826 duties on wheat imports unchanged.[21]   Apparently the administration was not satisfied with the harvest outlook and decided to keep open the doors to foreign imports.   Indeed, toward the end of 1831 wheat prices rose steadily.   This upward movement of wheat prices continued throughout 1832.   In October of 1831 wheat sold at 32.4 pesos per fanega, and in November of 1832 the price rose to 51.1 pesos.   In December of that year wheat sold at 72.7 pesos per fanega.[22]   Early in 1833 wheat prices declined sharply to about 32 pesos per fanega, and in 1834 they fluctuated between 20 and 30 pesos, although the harvest was not very promising.[23]   In 1835 prices declined still further, to about 19 pesos per fanega, except in January when wheat sold as low as 13 pesos.   The sharp rise from 13 pesos in January to about 20 pesos in February was in all probability due to the revision of wheat duties.[24]   The new tariff did not solve the problem of domestic agriculture as a whole, since it assured profitability

---

[19] Decree, August 20, 1830 (RO, L–9, no. 9, pp. 5–6).

[20] "The drought which has prevailed this season has been of infinite detriment to the estancias; many of the proprietors have ordered the cattle upon their estates to be killed from the want of water and grass to subsist them." *British Packet and Argentine News* (May 8, 1830), vol. IV, no. 194.

[21] See above, chap. iii, pp. 71 ff., and chap. ix, p. 221.

[22] See below, Table 43.

[23] *Ibid.*, the *Diario de la Tarde* had the following to say concerning the harvest outlook for 1834: "Tenemos entendido que el gobierno ha pedido á los jueces de campaña le informen sobre el estado de la próxima cosecha, sin duda con el objeto de anticipar las disposiciones convenientes.   Ignoramos el resultado de aquella demanda, pero hemos oido asegurar particularmente, que la cosecha no será tan abundante como se esperó hasta mediados de noviembre, porque algunos incidentes que sobrevinieron han desmejorado la calidad de los granos, y ocasionado la pérdida de muchos sembrados." (January 4, 1834, no. 780.)

[24] See above, chap. ix, p. 225.

TABLE 43
WHEAT PRICES IN THE BUENOS AIRES MARKET: 1831–1851
(in pesos per fanega)

	Jan.	Feb.	Mar.	Apr.	May	June	July	Aug.	Sept.	Oct.	Nov.	Dec.
1831	31.2				41.7	42.5	41.6	39.0		22.5	28.0	72.7
1832	70.0		31.8								51.1	30.0
1833	20.9	23.5	30.6	27.5	26.0	27.6	28.5	22.3	22.4			12.7
1834	13.4	19.8	20.0	19.0	18.7	17.3		19.7	19.4			
1835		23.0	22.3	20.7	18.9	20.4		21.7	21.4	23.5	21.5	
1836												
1837												
1838	28.0	33.0	33.3	44.0	51.5	55.5	58.0	69.0	89.0			
1839	41.6	68.0	79.5	82.1	83.6	92.4	99.0	103.5	100.9	104.6	119.0	91.7
1840	53.3	73.0	72.9	86.0		79.2	83.3	102.0	103.5	81.5		72.2
1841												
1842	159.3	133.9	142.1	168.4	162.0	189.8	200.0	254.8	330.0	344.0	342.8	225.0
1843	276.4	272.5	286.5	286.5	304.0	309.0	314.0	294.0	239.0	197.0	212.5	146.2
1844	143.6	121.0	112.4	101.8	120.6	114.5	84.3	81.2	105.2	98.5	72.2	84.6
1845	77.6	70.1	77.4	86.0	103.0	123.4	137.0	163.3	135.3	136.6	138.5	111.0
1846	85.0	91.1	116.8	150.0	184.4	164.0	170.6	148.0	155.0	174.0	184.0	160.2
1847	161.0	170.3	176.0	195.7	186.0	188.0	204.6	207.2	259.0	285.0	240.0	162.3
1848	157.0	154.0	144.0	147.0	153.0	142.5	131.6	131.0	114.0	105.0	129.0	102.0
1849	88.2	76.0	67.5	68.6	65.0	57.5	47.6	57.0	66.6	71.5	79.0	66.0
1850	45.0	47.2	49.6	53.3	51.4	48.0	53.5	60.0	35.0	72.5	90.0	80.0
1851	81.6	109.0		96.6	79.0					120.0	144.0	127.0

only to the economically stronger farms, but it did stabilize the internal wheat market. In the following year the government reaffirmed its policy of stabilized wheat prices. As the Collector General of Customs put it the tariff of December 18, 1835 [25] was intended to "extend effective protection to domestic agriculture, which until then had been rapidly deteriorating" and also to protect the population against possible scarcity of wheat and flour.[26] Prohibition of wheat importation did not materially affect prices in either 1836 or in 1837. In these two years harvests were so abundant that the province exported both wheat and flour to other provinces and abroad. In 1836 overseas exports of wheat and flour were valued at 192,633 pesos, and in 1837 and 1838 exports to foreign markets amounted to 506,894 pesos and 438,706 pesos respectively. At the same time the province exported wheat and flour to the Interior to the amount of 404,606 pesos in 1837 and 273,622 pesos in 1838.[27] These exports, it is true, played but a nominal part in the province's foreign trade. Nevertheless, the very fact that domestic agriculture was capable of producing a surplus was looked upon as a significant advance in the economic development of the province. The government was quick to note the growing strength of agriculture and spoke of farming as the new and rapidly growing source of prosperity.[28]

These hopes did not materialize. In 1838 the French fleet blockaded the port of Buenos Aires, causing virtual cessation of foreign commerce. Prices in Buenos Aires began to rise quite rapidly, and wheat fully participated in this movement. In March of 1838 wheat sold at 33 pesos per fanega, and in September of that year the price of wheat reached 89 pesos. The government at first prohibited exportation of wheat and flour to the Interior, but rescinded this order when it became clear early in 1839 that the crop would more than cover the province's needs. Permits to export wheat to the provinces were granted quite liberally throughout 1839, 1840, and 1841 even though wheat

[25] See above, chap. ix, p. 238.

[26] *Archivo General*, Ant. C.23–A.5–no. 5, Legajo 2. "Dos objetos se propuso la ley vigente de aduana. . . . El uno fué prestar una protección eficaz a la agricultura del país que iba en decadencia progresiva por no poder competir con el estrangero en la venta de aquellos artículos. Y el otro no exponer a la población a la carencia de ellos, por cualquier accidente, o a que los comprase a un precio exorbitante por su escasez."

[27] *Registro Oficial*, L–16, no. –10; L–17, no. –5; L–18, no. –3; L–18, no. –5. See Table 44.

[28] Cf. *Gaceta Mercantil*, January 22, 1838 (no. 4385). "Así este ramo que antes estaba en la mayor nulidad ha tomado un incremento que aumenta con rapidez."

prices rose at times above 100 pesos per fanega.[29] But exports ceased in 1842. Wheat rose sharply from 159 pesos in January to 344 pesos per fanega in October of 1842. These scarcity prices persisted throughout 1843. Relief came in 1844 when abundant harvests once again assured adequate supplies for domestic consumption. In the second half of 1845, when Buenos Aires was for the second time closed to foreign trade, wheat again became scarce. High prices were maintained during 1846 and 1847, but early in 1848, as the blockade became less effective and the threat of North American competition became more likely, prices subsided until in 1849 they fluctuated between 80 pesos (in January) and 48 pesos (July). With some exceptions these prices continued throughout 1850.

Little is known about the condition of the *porteño* farmer during the last decade of Rosas' administration. To judge by the debates in the provincial legislature and the annual reports to the Junta, agriculture hardly existed in Buenos Aires. In the early years of his second administration Rosas was wont to view the future of agriculture with a good deal of optimism. He relied upon protection to make agriculture strong and prosperous.[30] But protection was not always tenable; nor was it as efficacious as had been originally believed. And having failed to find the proper solution of the agricultural problem Rosas became more reticent and also less specific in his public utterances. Not even when it became quite obvious that protection was no longer advisable did Rosas or the Junta suggest the need for a reformulation of agricultural policies. Had protection succeeded in stabilizing agriculture as a profitable field of economic activity, Rosas and his party might have reëxamined their conception of the economic future of the province. But as agriculture showed no signs of economic virility the federalist leaders were loath to sacrifice resources and political prestige for

[29] Cf. *Archivo General* Ant. C.23–A.6–no. 4; Ant. C.23–A.7–no. 1; and Ant. C.23–A.7–no. 2.

[30] It may be well to quote in this connection the opinion of the Collector General of Customs, who often spoke the mind of the government. Said the Collector: "Muy noble fué el objeto que tuvo la ley en vista (tariff act of 1835) para prohibir la importación de granos y harinas cual era el fomento de la agricultura y labranza de la provincia: en la certidumbre de que ella poseía en sí misma los medios y recursos necesarios para proveer superabundantemente el mercado de aquellos artículos que su consumo diario y permanente hace ya una necesidad de ellos. Lo contrario sería haberla sencionado para hostilizar la población igualmente acreedora a que se le proteja haciendola carecer de unas producciones de cuyo uso no puede ya prescindir, y que suplen en gran parte la falta de otros alimentos." January 18, 1842. *Archivo General*, Ant. C.23–A.8–no. 6.

the sake of what they considered to be an economic mirage. After all, the farmers formed but an insignificant part of the provincial society; they were economically weak and politically inarticulate.

3

In January of 1836 the shoemakers of Buenos Aires petitioned the government to prohibit importation of foreign-made shoes. Foreign producers, complained the shoemakers, sell their manufactures at extremely low prices

either because raw material in Europe is cheap, or because salaries are low due to excessive supply of labor, or because they use all kinds of machinery that is unknown here; we cannot imitate foreign methods of production; nor can we compete against foreign manufacturers without facing immediate ruin, for we lack all the necessary factors which might reduce our cost of production.[31]

This statement was true not only of the shoe industry, but of *porteño* industry in general.[32] The tariff of 1835 bears evidence that the Rosas administration recognized the plight of domestic producers, and it acceded to the widespread demands for effective protection. It is not easy to determine whether Rosas' revision of the tariff was intended as the cornerstone of a new economic policy or whether it was dictated by reasons of political expediency. In his messages Rosas spoke of the importance of protection, and expressed hope that the new tariff would stimulate industrial expansion. But these utterances did not always reflect the true opinions of Rosas and his collaborators. These were political writings designed to defend the acts of the government and did not necessarily reveal the administration's innermost plans and convictions. References to industry and industrial policies in these messages were hardly more than routine remarks. And toward the end of his administration Rosas rarely broached the subject of industrial and economic policies. This taciturnity on the subject of economic policies contrasted sharply with his loquacity on political and military questions. The conclusion seems therefore inescapable that Rosas had no clearly defined industrial program to begin with, and that after his first attempt at protection had broken down under the strain of the French blockade he failed to develop a consistent long range policy. Nor were the federalist leaders sufficiently interested to press for a more or less precise definition of the government's attitude toward in-

---

[31] Cf. *Archivo General*, Ant. C.23–A.2–no. 2.

[32] That the shoemakers assumed the role of spokesmen for the industry was due to the circumstance that the tariff act of 1835 failed to place footwear on the prohibited list.

dustrial expansion. On this question, as on many others that did not directly affect the pastoral industry, Rosas preferred to follow the line of least resistance.

Rosas' opportunism in matters of industrial and commercial policies was not a question of choice. Like all cattle breeders and meat producers he was a free trader. A policy of laissez faire suited him best, not only because it was in accord with the interests of the pastoral industries, but also because it was a less expensive policy. Were Rosas and his collaborators free to follow their inclinations they would have continued the unitary policies of economic liberalism.[33] But Rosas was not free to shape the province's economic policies. Protection and economic nationalism were political debts, which had to be paid sooner or later. Rosas paid the debt, but he paid it under duress.

There was yet another factor which vitiated the federalist economic doctrine. Political dictatorship, such as the federalists established in March of 1835, invited government regulation of and intervention into fields of activity which under normal conditions would have remained beyond the scope of administrative supervision. Political absolutism bred economic paternalism. Entrepreneurs and industrialists often invited government intervention. Deprived of the protection of law and constitutional guarantees they hesitated to make business investments without the express approval of the government. For such approval provided the necessary modicum of security against sudden changes of policy. And precisely because the government exercised unlimited authority it came to be regarded as the dispenser of both economic justice and special privilege.

Political considerations, too, compelled the government to extend control over industry and commerce. When, for example, one Joaquín B. de Acuña wished to establish a manufactory of grease and tallow in Lomas de San Fernando the government required that no unitaries were to be employed in the enterprise.[34] The fact that the federalist regime was not kindly disposed toward foreigners was in itself a major obstacle to industrial development. Native capital preferred as a rule

---

[33] It should be recalled here that *porteño* federalist leaders did not object to economic liberalism as such. Federalist critique of Rivadavia's economic policy was directed mainly against forced europeanization of *porteño* economy through state intervention.

[34] Cf. *Archivo General*, Ant. C.23–A.10–no. 4 (December 13, 1844). "Se concede . . . el permiso . . . para establecer una fábrica de vapor de sebo y graza . . . con calidad precisa que la casa no podrá ser administrada ni servida por persona o personas salvages unitarios."

to seek employment in pastoral industries and commerce, where risks were normal and profits assured. In order to venture into untried fields of manufacture it needed the stimulus of guaranteed markets and protection against competition. So, for example, in 1837 one Hugo E. Fiddis was willing to erect a flour mill operated by steam if granted a ten-year monopoly.[35] In 1842, to cite another case, Pedro Lezica, a wealthy *porteño* merchant, proposed to erect a stearine and candle factory, provided the government guaranteed a bounty of 10 per cent on exports over a period of five years.[36] Lezica argued that while production of stearine was not new, the enterprise in Buenos Aires involved considerable risks in view of the fact that foreign manufacturers were strongly entrenched in the domestic market. The Collector General of Revenue refused to support Lezica's plea on the ground that privileges such as Lezica demanded bred monopolies, which stifled individual initiative and jeopardized the welfare of society. If there was a genuine demand for domestic manufactures, continued the Collector General, industry needed no extraordinary guarantees. And if, on the other hand, a new enterprise failed to take root it was because the enterprise was superfluous, and the capital invested in it should have been directed into other channels.[37]

It is quite possible that in the later years of his administration Rosas no longer believed in the efficacy of absolute protection as an instrument of economic policy. If after several years of stringent protection domestic industry could not overcome the initial handicap in the struggle for internal markets, the conclusion seemed inevitable that foreign manufacturers were simply better equipped to supply the needs of the province. Certainly the young industries argument lost all validity in the forties, after most of the native industry had enjoyed the most vigorous protection since 1836.[38] As the Collector General put it in a report dated October 4, 1843 "experience . . . had demonstrated that (prohibition) handicapped rather than stimulated the

---

[35] Cf. *Archivo General*, Ant. C.23–A.3–no. 1.

[36] Cf. *Archivo General*, Ant. C.23–A.8–no. 6.

[37] *Ibid.* "El empresario prosperará sin duda si el uso de esta manufactura conviene a los consumidores y los es útil que estos le protejan comprandole, es a lo que ha de aspirar, y le compraran si les es provechoso. Si así no suceda, de esta industria no necesita el País, es estemporánea, y el capital empleado en ella que lo dedique a otra clase de negocio."

[38] The French blockade was as effective in keeping foreign competitors away from Buenos Aires as was the tariff act of December 18, 1835.

progress of industry and national wealth." [39] It was only natural for Rosas to feel that domestic industry forfeited whatever claim it had upon society. The federalist regime, Rosas could argue, had given native manufacturers and artisans the opportunity to gain a firm foothold in Buenos Aires. During the five years from 1836 to the end of the French blockade domestic industry should have been able to develop sufficient strength to meet foreign competition. The fact that it could not compete against foreign manufacturers was prima facie evidence of its low survival value. The French and Anglo-French blockades had demonstrated beyond doubt that domestic industry was unable to satisfy the needs of the province even under the most favorable conditions. Domestic manufacturers took advantage of rising prices, but did little or nothing to increase output or to improve the quality of production. However, the government could not afford to pursue a policy of scarcity any more than it could afford to curtail deliberately the flow of foreign commerce. For just as prohibition imposed undue burdens upon consumers, so curtailment of foreign trade undermined the financial stability of the treasury.

It has already been stated that Rosas had little understanding of the needs and problems of *porteño* industry. What in the words of an anonymous writer the province needed most was "skill and enterprise and capital, to call into operation our own resources." [40] None of these elements were abundant in the province. Loanable capital was chronically scarce in Buenos Aires in spite of Rosas' inflationary policies,[41]

[39] Cf. *Archivo General*, Ant. C.23–A.9–no. 4. The report of the Collector General referred to a petition submitted by Juan Pablo Granca and Vicente Risoto, manufacturers of starch. The petitioners asked for revision of the decree of December 21, 1841, which removed foreign starch from the prohibited list.

[40] Cf. "Reflections on the Present Situation and Future Prospects of Buenos Aires" in *British Packet and Argentine News*, vol. XIII, no. 654 (March 2, 1839).

[41] The following are yearly averages of Buenos Aires discount rates per month quoted in the *British Packet and Argentine News* on the third Friday of each month:

1829	2.031	1839	1.376
1830	2.739	1840	1.250
1831	2.167	1841	1.489
1832	1.906	1842	1.542
1833	2.031	1843	1.625
1834	2.250	1844	1.844
1835	1.790	1845	2.010
1836	1.750	1846	2.146
1837	1.750	1847	1.479
1838	1.854		

and skill and enterprise were equally scarce in a country without industrial tradition. These factors of production had to be sought overseas, but the Rosas regime far from stimulating the inflow of foreign capital and labor had pursued a consistent anti-foreign policy. Then, too, civil wars and the unpredictability of personal rule provided an effective barrier against foreign investments in Argentina.

Scarcity of labor was another obstacle to industrial development. Complaints that wages were high were common throughout Rosas' administration. Rosas attempted to solve the problem of labor supply by increasing the number of working days in the year. In November of 1832 the number of holidays in addition to Sundays was reduced to ten, including one half-holiday.[42] Sixteen years later further reduction of holidays was found necessary "since any interruption of work in field or factory was very costly in view of the fact that wages were high and labor scarce."[43] It was argued in Buenos Aires that labor was not scarce, but that the cost of living was too low. "Labourers are not scarce in our country," claimed the *Archivo Americano*, "if wages are high, it rather proceeds from the facility of obtaining subsistence, from the abundance with which the principal necessities of life are provided for."[44] No doubt there was a good deal of truth in the assertion of the *Archivo Americano*, for the cost of living at subsistence level was very low indeed.[45] But whatever the reason, the

[42] RO–383, L–11, no. –11. Among the *considerandos* the following are of interest: "Que las pasiones sofocadas con el trabajo entre semana, se ensanchan criminalmente en los días festivos, con notable degradación de la sana moral; Que las artes, el comercio y la agricultura que son el alma de los Estados, padecen un enorme quebranto con la multiplicidad de días festivos."

[43] Cf. Decree, January 2, 1849.

[44] Cf. *Archivo Americano* (April 30, 1845), II, 229. See also *Gaceta Mercantil* (February 15, 1839), no. 4694.

[45] The following account of living expenses for three *peones* in 1838 is instructive. The account bears the following title: Razon del gasto que deven haser los tres peones que deven quedar permanentemente en el camino de la boca del Riachuelo en los 24 días de trabajo del mes:

Por carne media arroba en cada día de los espresados 24 a 1 p.	24$
Por pan—4 rs. a 2 r en los mismos 24 días	7$ 4
Por 2 rs diarios de leña en los dhos 24 días	6$
Por sal en los mismos 24 días un quartillo el día	$ 6
Por sevolla un real en uno de los 24 días	6$
Suma	44$ 2

Cf. *Archivo General*, Ant. C.23–A.5–no. 5–Legajo 2.

supply of labor in Buenos Aires was normally insufficient to meet the demand, and on occasions this shortage was quite serious. So, for example, in October of 1831 the government partially revoked the law of February 4, 1831 which prohibited the importation of slaves. This revision was thought justified on the ground that domestic labor was scarce.[46]   Again, in 1843 the Collector General, unable to secure laborers for work on the Martín García island, suggested that soldiers be hired to do the work.[47]   It would appear from this and other evidence that shortage of labor was not a temporary phenomenon brought about by artificial fall in the prices of foodstuffs, such as might result from a blockade. It was rather a chronic condition, caused partly by the fact that the economy grew much faster than population, and partly by the circumstance that a large proportion of the able-bodied population was more or less permanently immobilized in the army. The solution of the problem lay not in higher food prices, as the *Archivo Americano* seemed to suggest, but in opening the country to immigration from abroad. This point Rosas refused to concede.

4

The failure of *porteño* industry to win a more prominent place in the provincial economy was not unduly disturbing to Rosas and the federalist party. To his critics Rosas could answer with a good deal of justification that Buenos Aires was simply not slated to become an industrial economy, and that in other fields of economic endeavor marked progress had been achieved. He could point to the expansion of the pastoral industry, to the growth of the hide and meat industries, and he could refer to the expanding volume of overseas commerce. It is true that these achievements were all in a field in which Buenos Aires had always excelled. But in the eyes of *porteño* federalists this circumstance did not lessen the importance of Rosas' accomplishments. If anything it added prestige to Rosas' administration as the first to gauge correctly the economic potentialities of the province. For Rosas had fulfilled the economic destiny of the province. He had removed the last remaining barriers to the expansion of the province's basic industry, had broadened its scope, had given it new fields to conquer.

Rosas did not venture beyond the established frontiers. He lacked the imagination and daring of Rivadavia. He was a practical man,

[46] Cf. *Gaceta Mercantil*, October 28, 1831.
[47] Cf. *Archivo General*, Ant. C.23–A.9–no. 3.

not a doctrinaire; a business man above all. The economic greatness of Buenos Aires, its wealth and its strength, derived from the soil, and it was there also that it was to find security in the future. Buenos Aires did not raise the standard of economic revolt against the Metropolis in the name of industrialization on the European pattern. Economic revolution, which preceded by many years the Cabildo Abierto of May 25, 1810, germinated in the country, on the pastures of the pampa, among cattle breeders. And it was in the *campaña* that the revolution was destined to continue its work of social and economic transformation. In this sense Rosas and the federalists were the guardians of revolutionary tradition. They, and not the unitaries, expressed the true economic interests of the province, and by the same token they were also the stanchest defenders of the economic *status quo*.

Indeed, during the twenty-two years of almost uninterrupted federalist rule the economy of the country changed but little. In Buenos Aires cattle breeding retained its position of preëminence, and the province continued to depend upon foreign countries for most of the manufactures it consumed. The province's foreign commerce reflected this condition most clearly. As in the past, cattle breeding provided by far the largest proportion of the province's exportable produce.

Unfortunately it has not been possible to secure complete data on the foreign trade of Buenos Aires. Beginning with 1836 the *porteño* government began publishing in the *Registro Oficial* detailed reports on the province's foreign commerce, but it abandoned this practice in 1840 as an economy measure. The period covered by this series extends from July 1835 to June 1840. However, the figures for 1838, 1839, and the first half of 1840 are not serviceable, primarily because during these years Buenos Aires had been under a blockade. For the last three and a half years of the Rosas administration (July 1848–December 1851) we have the compilation prepared by Woodbine Parish. This compilation is not as comprehensive or as accurate as the Collector General's report. To begin with, Parish expresses the value of *porteño* exports in pounds sterling, rather than paper pesos. Secondly, the figures given by Parish are based upon average prices. In order to obtain the value of hide exports Parish multiplied the number of hides exported in each year by 10 shillings. But hide prices were far from stable. In January of 1850, for example, ox hides sold at 35.5 paper pesos, while in June of that year the price rose to 42.75 paper pesos, and in May of 1851 the price reached 48.5 paper pesos. Then, too, the gold value of *porteño* currency fluctuated rather widely from month to month, and from year to year. In 1850 the average price of one ounce of gold was 247 paper pesos, and 10 shillings would indicate a price of 36.25 paper pesos. In reality, however, hide prices in 1850 were about 10 per cent higher, the average being 40.37 paper pesos.[48] Similar reservations are in order with respect to the other commodities which Buenos Aires exported.

The characteristic feature of the province's export trade is the preponderance of hide exports. In 1836 and 1837, the last normal years before the French blockade, hides of all kinds accounted for 68.4 and 64.2 per cent of the total value of *porteño* exports. In the last two years of Rosas' administration the value of hide exports amounted to 65 per cent in 1850 and 64.9 per cent in 1851. The above figures do not fully reflect the importance of cattle breeding in *porteño* export trade. A more accurate picture of the position of the cattle breeding industry will be obtained if exports of meat, horsehair, and horns were added to hide exports. This would raise the contribution of cattle breeding to *porteño* exports to 82.8 per cent in 1836, 76.1 per cent in 1837, 78.5 per cent in 1850, and 78 per cent in 1851. Two changes in the pattern of *porteño* exports should be mentioned. One was the increase in relative importance of tallow and wool. It reflected on the one hand the expansion of sheep breeding in Buenos Aires and the

[48] The difference varied from year to year and from month to month, as will be seen from the following table. Monthly average prices of salted ox hides, based upon quotations in the *British Packet and Argentine News*, are noted in column I. In column II are entered values of the price quoted by Woodbine Parish in terms of paper pesos at current rates of exchange. (See Table 49.)

	1848		1849		1850		1851	
	I	II	I	II	I	II	I	II
Jan.	46.50	57.75	44.00	51.00	35.50	36.50	42.50	33.75
Feb.	43.50	41.00	39.00	35.75	36.50	37.25	40.50	
March	43.50	48.00	38.00	47.65	38.00	36.75	43.00	36.00
April	43.50	52.25	41.00	46.20	39.00	38.00	43.50	38.75
May	39.50	53.00	43.00	48.00	41.50	37.50	48.50	40.75
June	45.50	54.00	42.50	44.00	42.75	36.25		
July	45.50	49.75	39.00	43.50	42.25	34.12		
Aug.	46.50	47.00	40.50	43.25	42.50	33.50		
Sept.	43.50	50.00	40.50	42.00	39.50	35.00		
Oct.	41.75	51.75	41.50	41.62	42.50	35.15		
Nov.	40.00	51.75	39.00	40.50	40.50	34.25		
Dec.	45.50	51.75	37.50	38.00	44.00	33.07		
Avge.	43.73	52.00	40.46	45.00	40.37	36.25		

TABLE 44

Value of the Principal Commodities Exported From Buenos Aires

1835 (first half), 1836, 1837, 1838, 1839, 1840 (first half), 1848 (second half), 1849, 1850, and 1851

	1835 Second half Paper $	1836 Paper $	1837 Paper $	1838 Paper $	1839 Paper $	1840 First half Paper $	1848 Second half Gold $	1849 Gold $	1850 Gold $	1851 Gold $
Hides.........	8,859,410	17,280,915	20,200,586	9,186,016	891,636	257,587	2,922,545	7,856,255	6,450,740	6,899,820
Horsehair.....	467,211	974,206	1,328,186	844,491	111,348	29,230	186,600	444,100	505,900	462,300
Meat........	660,701	2,391,911	2,302,909	2,289,707	106,720		418,870	1,119,935	781,460	863,745
Horns.......	105,999	252,301	120,904	50,283			25,080	54,175	52,715	65,035
Tallow.......	113,873	545,595	971,053	2,007,940	379,415	106,072	1,213,460	1,840,820	1,045,150	1,203,995
Sole leather...	21,561	95,120	93,775	144,366	106,720	40,000				
Wool........	365,004	1,913,592	3,498,477	3,298,688	461,670	6,250	681,800	1,335,400	1,055,000	1,096,000
Maize.......	3,240	6,930	8,870	40,377	17,565					
Wheat and flour...	35,060	172,623	506,894	438,706						
Other........	483,065	1,476,285	1,938,465	851,651	1,200,407	237,482	9,705	38,420	26,800	42,630
Total....	11,115,059	25,264,934	31,436,634	19,371,090	3,848,518	736,621	5,458,020	12,689,105	9,917,565	10,633,525

Sources: *Registro Oficial:* L-15, nos. 7, 11; L-16, nos. 6, 10; L-17, no. 5; L-18, nos. 3, 5; L-19, no. 5; L-20, no. 9, Woodbine Parish, *Buenos Ayres and the provinces of the Rio de la Plata* (London: 1852), p. 354.

TABLE 45

VALUE OF BUENOS AIRES OVERSEAS IMPORTS: 1837–1839

	1837 Paper pesos	%	1838 Paper pesos	%	1839 Paper pesos	%
Textiles	13,178,172	31.5	5,421,815	32.8	4,326,403	31.4
Beverages	3,292,746	7.9	1,697,225	10.3	1,691,385	12.3
Sugar	2,841,778	6.9	1,453,517	8.7	2,219,883	16.1
Yerba mate	2,437,480	5.8	924,258	5.6	2,169,285	15.7
Tobacco	803,416	1.9	748,790	4.5	1,122,541	8.2
Salt	767,290	1.8	746,762	4.5	85,420	0.6
Iron and tin	315,736	0.7	110,393	0.7	113,600	0.8
Other com.	18,176,154	43.5	5,435,293	32.9	2,059,592	14.9
Total	41,812,772	100.0	16,517,853	100.0	13,788,109	100.0

Sources: *Registro Oficial:* L–16, no. 10; L–17, no. 5; L–18, no. 3, 5; L–18, no. 12; L–19, no. 5.

TABLE 46

VALUE OF OVERLAND COMMERCE OF BUENOS AIRES: 1837–1839
(Overland Imports)

	1837 Paper pesos	%	1838 Paper pesos	%	1839 Paper pesos	%
Hides	6,982,864	45.4	3,586,999	40.0	1,387,205	20.0
Horsehair	770,876	5.0	336,780	3.8	267,520	3.9
Wool	722,904	4.7	399,631	4.5	376,492	5.4
Tallow	777,078	5.1	296,657	3.3	41,495	0.6
Sole leather	462,283	3.0	464,390	5.2	780,009	11.2
Meat	1,167,765	7.6	376,443	4.2	3,500	
Tobacco	489,049	3.2	188,478	2.1	672,953	9.7
Yerba mate	893,903	5.8	1,060,903	11.8	1,118,450	16.1
Beverages	204,222	1.3	517,979	5.8	649,896	9.4
Ponchos	252,156	1.6	257,221	2.1	344,562	5.2
Wheat and flour	205,313	1.3	128,670	1.4	28,580	0.4
Other com.	2,454,257	16.0	1,340,982	15.0	1,275,009	18.3
Total	15,382,670	100.0	8,955,133	100.0	6,945,671	100.0

Sources: See Table 45.

TABLE 47

VALUE OF OVERLAND COMMERCE OF BUENOS AIRES: 1837–1839
(Overland Exports)

	1837 Paper pesos	%	1838 Paper pesos	%	1839 Paper pesos	%
Textiles	6,090,481	47.0	3,510,980	45.4	1,774,139	32.1
Yerba mate	334,010	2.6	423,311	5.5	292,751	5.1
Tobacco	183,710	1.4	83,978	1.1	156,167	2.8
Sugar	523,140	4.0	324,275	4.2	103,935	1.9
Flour and wheat	404,606	3.1	273,622	3.5	579,698	10.5
Ponchos	208,949	1.6	118,566	1.5	64,242	1.2
Other com.	5,236,196	40.3	3,003,227	38.8	2,557,357	46.2
Total	12,981,092	100.0	7,737,959	100.0	5,528,289	100.0

Sources: See Table 45.

Litoral provinces, and on the other the rapid improvements in methods of production. The second change to be noted is the disappearance of grain and flour from the list of exportable commodities. The gains made by agriculture in the late thirties were apparently lost in the succeeding years. Agricultural greatness of Argentina was still a thing of the future.

TABLE 48

VALUE OF EXPORTS OF BUENOS AIRES IN CERTAIN YEARS IN PER CENT OF TOTAL

	1836	1837	1838	1839	1848	1849	1850	1851
Hides	68.4	64.2	47.4	23.2	53.5	61.9	65.0	64.9
Horsehair	3.9	4.2	4.3	2.9	3.4	3.5	5.1	4.4
Meat	9.5	7.3	11.8	2.8	7.7	8.8	7.9	8.1
Horns	1.0	0.4	0.4		0.5	0.4	0.5	0.6
Tallow	2.1	3.1	10.4	9.8	22.2	14.5	10.5	11.3
Sole leather	0.4	0.3	0.7	4.9				
Wool	7.6	11.1	17.0	12.0	12.5	10.6	10.6	10.3
Maize			0.2	0.5				
Wheat	0.7	1.6	2.3					
Other com.	6.4	7.8	5.5	43.9	0.2	0.3	0.3	0.4
Total	100.0	100.0	100.0	100.0	100.0	100.0	100.0	100.0

Information concerning overseas imports is even more sketchy than export statistics. The *Registro Oficial* did not begin to publish data on this phase of the province's foreign trade until 1837. The period covered extends only over 3½ years, of which 2½ were blockade years. Parish was unable to obtain any information on Buenos Aires imports except that available in the exporting countries of Europe and North America. But data from these sources make no distinction between Buenos Aires, Montevideo, and other ports of the River Plate, and cannot, therefore, be accepted. What these data do indicate is the pattern of *porteño* imports, since the economies of Buenos Aires and the other River Plate regions were very much alike.

The pattern of Buenos Aires imports changed but little during Rosas' administration. As in the early years of independence the bulk of the province's imports consisted of manufactures, liquors, tobacco, and certain foodstuffs. In 1837, the last normal year before the French blockade, textiles alone were responsible for nearly 31 per cent of the province's imports. Nearly 8 per cent of total imports were accounted for by liquor and wine, and tobacco and *yerba mate* formed 7.7 per cent of total. The province imported sugar in considerable quantities,

TABLE 49

MONTHLY AND YEARLY AVERAGE PRICES PAID FOR ONE OUNCE OF GOLD ON THE BUENOS AIRES STOCK EXCHANGE

	Jan.	Feb.	March	April	May	June	July	Aug.	Sept.	Oct.	Nov.	Dec.	Yearly Aver.
1835	118 3/8	119 1/20	120 1/2	119 6/8	119	118	117 3/4	118	—	117 3/4	118	118 5/8	118 5/8
1836	119 1/4	120	121 1/2	121 1/4	120 3/8	119 6/8	118 1/8	116 5/8	116 3/4	137 3/8	117 3/8	116 3/4	118 3/4
1837	116 7/8	117	120 1/5	123 3/8	124 7/8	131 5/6	133 3/8	146 1/8	144	143 1/8	138	132 1/4	130 7/8
1838	130	129 3/4	136 1/3	150 3/4	146	146 3/8	143 1/8	139 3/4	133 2/3	152 1/4	179	177	147
1839	211 1/4	253	251 5/8	239 1/3	227 1/2	246	243 1/2	243 2/3	265 4/5	280 2/3	292	293	254
1840	282	291	298 1/8	346 5/8	349 3/8	381 1/8	514 3/4	490 3/4	434 5/8	429 1/4	328	343	374 1/16
1841	350 1/3	336 3/8	322 5/8	306 3/4	298 3/8	303 1/2	301 5/8	—	303	296	283 1/8	287 1/2	353 1/2
1842	293 1/2	291 1/4	284 3/4	276	278 1/2	254 1/3	265 3/8	274 2/3	268 5/8	272 1/2	284 1/16	284 1/2	277 1/4
1843	282	276	270	264 1/2	271 1/3	269 3/4	265 5/8	261 5/8	265 1/2	257	253 7/8	245	265 1/4
1844	244 3/4	241 1/4	225 7/8	218 1/8	222	220	222 1/3	233	222 1/4	218	217 1/4	206 3/4	224 1/4
1845	196 2/3	109	229	250 1/2	225 3/8	208	228 1/8	246 1/8	252	273	314 3/4	362 1/4	248 3/4
1846	398 2/3	374 1/4	374 1/3	374 5/8	384 3/4	414 5/8	317 3/8	274 1/4	380 1/3	380 1/3	342 1/2	329	362 1/2
1847	325 7/8	316 7/8	328 7/8	311 3/4	293 3/4	310 1/5	381 7/8	364 1/3	390	395 1/3	393 5/8	397 3/8	350 3/4
1848	393 1/2	279 2/3	326 1/4	349	361 2/3	365 2/3	339 1/8	330 3/8	340 1/4	352 3/8	352 1/8	350 1/4	353 1/3
1849	347 1/2	243 1/2	334 2/3	314 1/5	336 2/3	299 1/5	296	294 7/8	286 1/2	283	276 1/4	258 2/3	306
1850	249	254 1/2	250 1/2	258 1/2	255 1/2	247 1/2	232 1/2	227 1/4	238 1/2	239	233	225	247
1851	230 1/2	—	244	264 1/2	277	283 1/4	296 1/2	380 1/2	352 1/2	319 3/4	331 1/4	315 1/4	299
1852	—	—	—	—	273 1/2	278 1/4	286 1/3	283 2/3	262 1/4	261 1/16	274 1/4	274 1/2	274 1/4

Source: Pedro Agote, *Informe del Presidente del Crédito Público . . . sobre la Deuda Pública, Bancos y Emisiones de Papel Moneda y Acuñación de Monedas de la República Argentina* (Buenos Aires: 1881), I, 126–127.

largely from Brazil, and salt which competed with domestic salt works in Patagonia. Importation of iron and tin for use of native handicraft industry was less than 1 per cent of total. The remainder of imports was accounted for by non-textile manufactures, machinery, and utensils of all kinds.

As in the years before Rosas Buenos Aires continued to be the intermediary between the Interior and Litoral provinces, on the one hand, and the overseas markets, on the other. A not inconsiderable proportion of the commodities imported from overseas found its way to provincial markets. In 1837, for example, nearly 40 per cent of the textiles brought to Buenos Aires was re-exported to the Interior, and of other manufactures over 25 per cent was distributed in the hinterland. To the Interior Buenos Aires exported also considerable quantities of sugar, *yerba mate,* tobacco, and even wheat and flour. In exchange for these commodities, largely overseas manufactures, the provinces sent to Buenos Aires hides, meat, wool and tallow for re-export, as well as goods destined for the *porteño* market. Among the latter the most important were foodstuffs, liquors and wine, fruit, tobacco, and *yerba mate,* and some coarse textiles. The pattern as well as the value of commerce with the Interior for the three years from 1837 to 1839 is shown in Tables 46 and 47.

While the commerce of Buenos Aires changed but little structurally, it grew in volume and value during the years of the Rosas regime. Lack of data makes detailed examination impossible, but sufficient information is available to show the general trend. So, for example, while in 1837 Buenos Aires exported 823,635 ox hides, in 1851 the number of hides sold abroad rose to 2,601,140. Similar increase is to be noted in the export of meat, from 178,877 quintals in 1837 to 431,873 quintals in 1851. Wool and tallow exports grew even more rapidly. In 1829 Buenos Aires sold abroad 30,334 arrobas. Export of wool rose from 164,706 arrobas in 1837, to 201,312 arrobas in 1843,[49] and to about 640,000 arrobas in 1851.[50] The growth of tallow exports was as spectacular. In 1829 the country exported 21,757 arrobas; in 1837 this export increased almost fivefold to 100,249 arrobas. And toward the end of the regime about 600 thousand arrobas left the port of Buenos Aires for overseas markets.

The growth of the volume of *porteño* overseas commerce was re-

[49] Cf. *Archivo Americano* III, 25 (March 12, 1846), p. 13.
[50] Woodbine Parish, *loc. cit.*

flected in the number of merchant ships entering the port of Buenos Aires. It will be noticed from the compilation presented below that the number of ships arriving at Buenos Aires each year between 1829 and 1837 was well under 300. But after the end of the French blockade shipping in the Buenos Aires port almost doubled. In the fourteen months from November 1, 1840 to December 31, 1841, not less than 642 entered the port. And although in 1842 the number of incoming vessels fell to 400 the decrease was temporary, for in each of the two following years over 500 ships were registered in Buenos Aires.

TABLE 50

FOREIGN MERCHANT VESSELS WHICH HAVE ARRIVED AT THE PORT OF BUENOS AIRES

	American	British	French	Brazilian	Sardinian	Other	Total
1829	97	78	28	15	15	12	245
1830	83	73	16	38	23	24	257
1831	77	44	10	42	20	14	207
1832	55	48	22	44	26	18	213
1833	91	74	17	47	30	35	294
1834	67	61	10	43	43	43	261
1835	51	54	14	42	23	29	213
1836	37	49	19	39	21	35	200
1837	40	61	24	42	20	41	228
1838	20	18	6	8	2	16	70 to Mar. 28, 1838
1841	106	178	56	87	49	166	642 Beg. Nov. 1840
1842	62	82	41	60	44	117	406
1843	75	127	54	64	69	186	575
1844	88	100	38	56	47	185	512

Sources: *British Packet and Argentine News*, nos. 363, 386, 438, 489, 620, 802, 856, 912, 960.

Value of *porteño* commerce both foreign and interprovincial is not an infallible index of economic development. The fact that the price of gold rose from about 77 pesos per ounce in 1829 to 306 pesos in 1849 suggests that comparison of absolute totals is deceptive and often meaningless. In 1849 the Minister of Finance suggested publication of an editorial which would stress the threefold increase in provincial commerce since 1837.[51] On formal grounds the statement could not be controverted, as will readily appear from the table below. But the impression which the Minister sought to convey, namely that capital invested in trade had trebled in the course of twelve years was false.

[51] Cf. *Archivo General*, Ant. C.24–A.4–no. 6. The suggested article was to say in part: "Con solo fijar la atención que en el año de 1837 la importación marítima era de 40 millones y de 10 la terrestre, siendo equivalente al valor de la exportación, y el giro anual en aquel año de 100,000,000 de pesos comparado este capital con el que representan en el año corriente las importaciones y exportaciones se ve que ha triplicado."

It was false simply because the unit of value used in 1849 was not the same as that used in 1837. In fact it was nearly 60 per cent smaller and, expressed in terms of 1837 pesos, the commerce in 1849 appears much less prosperous than the editorial implied. A much truer picture of the development of *porteño* commerce would be had if the values were expressed in terms of gold. Taking the average price of

TABLE 51

VALUE OF BUENOS AIRES COMMERCE IN SPECIFIED YEARS

Year	Import	Export	Total
1829	36,836,704	25,561,940	62,398,644
1837	57,195,442	44,417,726	101,613,168
1838	25,472,986	27,109,049	52,582,035 blockade year
1839	20,733,780	9,376,807	30,110,587 blockade year
1849	139,962,448	152,634,646	292,597,094

gold as the basis of comparison we find that the value of commerce in 1829 was 13,416,913 pesos, in 1837 it amounted to 13,282,767 pesos, and that in 1849 it rose to 16,255,394 pesos. It should be stated, however, that even gold is not quite a satisfactory standard, primarily because it takes no account of changes in price relations. It not only assumes that all prices moved uniformly upward as the peso depreciated, but it postulates also that gold prices had remained stable throughout the twenty years. Both assumptions are unwarranted. Gold prices did not remain stable. Nor did currency depreciation uniformly affect paper prices. Foreign commodities, for example, rose in proportion to the rise of gold. Prices of certain export commodities, too, followed more or less closely the rate of exchange. But wages lagged behind the general price level, and domestic products destined for internal markets did not always respond to depreciation, or at least not to the same extent. In view of these considerations it would be hazardous to accept money values alone as an adequate index of commercial expansion.

One thing appears to be certain. It is clear, namely, that the claim of the Minister in the report cited above was grossly exaggerated. Undoubtedly the provincial economy expanded in the course of the twenty years of federalist rule. But it is also true that progress was not as spectacular as the report seemed to imply. Quite the contrary, disturbances of varying intensity, recessions and crises, were frequent visitors on the shores of La Plata. And it was only because of the remarkable recuperative powers latent in the economy that at the end of the regime the province could boast sizable gains in the economic field.

No more than a simple chronological record of the fluctuating fortunes of the provincial economy can be attempted here. In 1830 the *British Packet and Argentine News* reported that "in the country districts of this province a drought has prevailed, and the loss of cattle on some of the *estancias* has been immense." [52] Conditions must have improved shortly thereafter for we hear no complaints in the following year. In fact, toward the close of 1832 "the aspect which the country presented in the south and southwest part of the province of Buenos Aires (was) of the most flattering description." [53] But prosperity of the cattle industry depended not only upon favorable weather but also upon the condition of the Buenos Aires market. *Porteño* commerce, always sensitive to political changes, suffered heavily after Rosas' first term had run its course, and especially when it became evident that Balcarce's tenure of office was rather uncertain. Early in 1834 the *Diario de la Tarde* demanded that measures be taken to revive commerce which had been stagnant for some time,[54] and nearly two years later the *British Packet and Argentine News* complained of "want of confidence in the commercial world occasioned by the failure of the house of Lezica," [55] one of the most important commercial firms in Buenos Aires. The effect of the failure of Lezica wore off gradually and as the federalist regime consolidated its position the country not only regained economic equilibrium but made rapid gains in commerce and industry.

Prosperity was brought to an abrupt end by the French blockade in March of 1838. The blockade lasted nearly three years, and although never fully effective it inflicted severe damage upon the provincial economy. Prices of export commodities fell off sharply. Hardly any business was done during 1839 when the French fleet was particularly active and, after the blockade, recovery was slow and difficult, impeded to no small extent by the expedition of Juan Lavalle and the rebellion in the southern districts of the province. Economic stability was further impeded by the government's policy of open and consistent inflation.

[52] October 23, 1830 (vol. V, no. 218).
[53] *British Packet and Argentine News* (November 24, 1832), vol. VII, no. 327.
[54] January 28, 1834, no. 799.
[55] October 10, 1835, vol. X, no. 477.

No sooner had the provincial economy adapted itself to new monetary conditions than the *porteño* government became once again involved in a conflict with European powers. As early as January of 1845 commerce in Buenos Aires was severely hit by violent fluctuations in the rate of exchange.[56] In September of that year Buenos Aires was closed to foreign commerce by the Franco-British fleet. The blockade wrought havoc with *porteño* business. Foreign exchange and gold commanded scarcity rates and prices of imported commodities followed suit. The rise of prices was nominal, for buyers were difficult to find.[57] At the same time prices of export commodities failed to respond to the rising rate of exchange.[58] Conditions improved toward the end of 1846, when prospects of ending the conflict became brighter with the arrival of the British plenipotentiary in Buenos Aires, and after the British fleet withdrew from the River Plate the blockade was little more than nominal. Nevertheless, economic activity remained at a low ebb. In a report for 1848 the Casa de Moneda complained that "poor business during the major part of the year was responsible for low discount operations."[59] It was not until 1849 that provincial economy was once again on the road to recovery.

It is claimed that the blockade did little harm to the province and the country at large, and that since the Confederation was nearly self-sufficient in foodstuffs it was a hopeless task to starve Buenos Aires into submission. No doubt, there is a good deal of truth in these contentions. No one understood this more clearly than Rosas. The blockade, Rosas argued, might cause some inconvenience, but it did not deprive the country of prime necessities. Foodstuffs were so abundant that regardless of the duration of the blockade the country could hold out indefinitely.[60] The blockade, moreover, could never become really

---

[56] In a letter to C. Murrieta of London the *porteño* merchant Martínez de Hoz described conditions in Buenos Aires in the following words: "Con motivo de una gran desmoralización en los cambios en esta se halla la plaza sumamente abatida y de consiguiente las transasiones que se hasen son forsadas . . ." (January 20, 1845).

[57] Martínez de Hoz to J. Vieira Barbosa of Rio de Janeiro (October 11, 1845). A month later (November 28, 1845) Martínez de Hoz wrote to one J. A. Eguren of Arroyo Azul: "La plaza se halla hoy como nunca se ha visto, pues a mas de los altos precios a que se hallan los efectos de importancia la desconfianza se ha aumentado hasta el estremo."

[58] ". . . siguemos en igual estado de bloqueo y de consiguiente los comestibles y demas artículos subiendo como es natural y los frutos del país en poca demanda. . . ." Martínez de Hoz to Guillermo Ormachea of Salta (May 23, 1846).

[59] Cf. *Archivo General*, Ant. C.24–A.5–no. 5 (January 14, 1849).

[60] Cf. *Archivo General*, Ant. C.29–A.3–no. 6. Letter signed by Rosas. Address or date unknown since the first page of the letter is missing.

effective, both because the blockading fleet was inadequate to patrol the very extensive coastline, and because the Paraná river remained under Rosas' control.

Nevertheless, it cannot be maintained that the country came through the ordeal unscathed. Victory was won at a heavy sacrifice, which strained to the breaking point the economic and social structure of the province. Were the economic effects of the blockade evenly distributed among the component parts of the body politic, the province might have absorbed the shock with relative ease. But as a matter of fact the extent of damage inflicted upon the population varied from group to group and from class to class. Furthermore, while some classes suffered only temporary losses, others were forced to relinquish outright a part of the share of the national income. The *hacendados*, for example, did not fare badly. No doubt they were hit hard by the blockade, but as soon as hostilities were over they not only recouped their losses but reaped additional benefits in the form of increased herds accumulated during the period of enforced inactivity. Paradoxically enough the *estancieros* grew richer precisely because the province was temporarily cut off from overseas markets. Inflation did not seriously affect their economic position since their capital was invested in commodities and land. The merchants were much more vulnerable. They lost trade and they were forced to assume risks which usually accompany inflation. But they speedily adapted themselves to the new economic environment and without undue effort regained their place in the provincial economy after hostilities were over. The real sufferers were the middle and lower classes. The small merchants and artisans in the city, the farmers in the country districts, the government officials and the laborers bore the brunt of the struggle in defense of the country's political integrity. It was because these classes were willing to reduce their standard of living to bare necessities that the government could view with relative complacency the closing of the port of Buenos Aires. The reward for this sacrifice was impoverishment, accentuated by rising prices and diminishing real incomes.

The ultimate effect of the blockades was to redistribute the national wealth in such a way as to enhance economic and social inequality. The rich grew richer, often at the expense of the lower classes. And as this inequality solidified after the blockade it endangered the stability of the political regime. The French and British fleets failed to force capitulation, but they did upset the social economic balance of the province.　They sowed seeds of discontent among that inarticulate and passive mass of the *porteño* population which had always stanchly supported Rosas and patiently waited for the promised reward.　None came, and when the decisive hour struck the population turned its back upon the Restorer of the Laws.

CHAPTER XI

THE ECONOMIC ASPECTS OF THE FALL OF ROSAS

Oíd, mortales el grito sagrado
Libertad! Libertad! Libertad!
Oíd el ruido de rotas cadenas
Poned en trono a la noble igualdad.

THE BRILLIANT SUCCESSES of Rosas in the field of diplomacy could not compensate the country for his failure to solve the outstanding problems which had agitated the provinces ever since the dissolution of the Constituent Congress. The tripartite treaty of January 4, 1831 held out to the provinces the promise of internal peace and the hope of economic stability and progress. Neither was fulfilled, for Buenos Aires was not yet prepared to yield its position of economic and political preeminence in the Confederation. Had the provinces been in a position to risk an open break with Buenos Aires, had they been willing to follow the leadership of Ferré, Leiva, and Marín, Rosas and Buenos Aires might have been more attentive to the pleas and entreaties of the *provincianos*. But economic exhaustion in some provinces, political shortsightedness in others, and divided councils in the anti-*porteño* camp prevented common action at an opportune moment.

Rosas withdrew from the Comisión Representativa as soon as he perceived that the Comisión might become the spokesman of provincial interests rather than an instrument of *porteño* diplomacy. Indeed, almost from the very beginning the Comisión had demonstrated a degree of independence that threatened to undermine *porteño* hegemony. It had demonstrated also that many provinces took federalism quite seriously and accepted the tripartite treaty at its face value. Clearly this was not what Rosas bargained for, and rather than meet all the provinces at a round table on equal terms Buenos Aires preferred to deal with each province separately. While this latter method was the more tortuous, it was, nevertheless, the more effective in safeguarding *porteño* supremacy.

Rosas claimed that he had no intention of repudiating the treaty of 1831. He extolled the Pact and considered its provisions binding upon Buenos Aires, but he argued also that the treaty could not be put to the test of practical politics until the country enjoyed "unquestioned peace" (*plena tranquilidad*) and order. But who was to decide what constituted peace and order? Who was to determine whether peace and order had been reëstablished? And were peace and order attainable without a central authority to enforce them? For it must not be forgotten that interprovincial rivalry was extremely intense, that the unitaries were still very active. It was precisely the implementation of the treaty of 1831 that offered the best hope for the pacification of the country. No wonder, then, that men like Pedro Ferré and Manuel Leiva rejected the invocation of the "peace" clause as a diplomatic stratagem designed to befuddle the basic issues and to conceal in this manner the real intentions of the Buenos Aires government. Nor is it any wonder that these leaders accused Rosas of bad faith and insisted that Buenos Aires would not willingly abide by the terms of the tripartite treaty.

By forcing the dissolution of the Comisión Representativa Rosas at one stroke removed the constitutional problem from the realm of practical politics. But he also sowed the seeds of dissatisfaction which twenty years later were to blossom into open rebellion. The Comisión Representativa was not an ordinary committee. Called upon to put into practice the provisions of the treaty of 1831 it embodied the hopes and aspirations of the provinces; it carried the promise of rendering political and economic justice and of safeguarding the principles of home rule. Rosas shattered these hopes and aspirations. Instead of home rule he gave the provinces political tutelage, and for economic justice he substituted financial and other subsidies. By dissolving the Comisión Representativa the *porteño* government assumed heavy obligations of political and economic order. Buenos Aires was quite willing and even anxious to take responsibility for the conduct of foreign affairs and of peace and war; but it refused to accept responsibility for the economic and social welfare of the country. Therein lay the tragic inconsistency of the system which Rosas so patiently built and so stubbornly defended.

The position of the *porteño* federalists was from the very beginning contradictory. They defended the autonomy of Buenos Aires to the point of refusing to participate in any real effort to solve the constitutional problem. They insisted upon home rule and strict non-intervention in the internal affairs of the provinces. But they demanded also that provincial governments conform to the pattern approved by

Buenos Aires. Because of its material resources and political prestige the Buenos Aires government could and did exert pressure upon the provinces. It was vitally interested in the political struggles within the provinces and did not hesitate to tip the scales in order to insure victory of factions which accepted without reservations the *porteño* conception of federalism. And as the federalist regime in Buenos Aires became securely entrenched Rosas insisted not only upon uniformity of political organization but also upon uniformity of political opinion throughout the land.

The provinces had hoped that once in power Rosas would clear the way to such a reconsideration of the constitutional problem as would result in the formulation of a truly national economic policy. But the provinces had hoped in vain. Rosas could no more satisfy the economic postulates of the provinces than he could accede to the establishment of a national government. The *porteño* government refused to consider nationalization of customs revenues on the ground that these originated in the city of Buenos Aires. It refused to permit trade with overseas markets through ports other than Buenos Aires. It at all times opposed the opening of the Paraná river to foreign vessels. So in addition to exercising control over the political destinies of the provinces Buenos Aires assumed the role of the arbiter of their economic fortunes as well.

It is true that on the question of protection Rosas was less inflexible. The tariff of 1836 embodied a number of protectionist features and seemed to fulfill some of the provincial desiderata. But Rosas' conversion to protectionist policies was short-lived. Protectionism never had the wholehearted approval of the ruling classes of Buenos Aires, and was speedily abandoned when the blockade of 1838–1840 had caused a shortage of manufactures.

The iniquity of the economic system instituted and defended by Buenos Aires became especially oppressive during the blockades, for the incidence of trade disruption was uniformly severe in the provinces, and especially in the Litoral. Of course, the struggle against France in the thirties, and against France and Great Britain in the forties, was a national struggle. Rosas had the right to call upon the whole nation to contribute to the defense of the country's political integrity. But from the point of view of provincial economic interests the struggle was costly and victory meaningless. The provinces gained nothing. After the termination of the conflicts their economic and political condition was as precarious as ever. It made little difference to the provinces whether Buenos Aires or some foreign power controlled the La Plata estuary. In fact, during the second blockade the riparian provinces were inclined to side with the blockaders, not only in order to shorten the agony of commercial isolation but also in order to break *porteño* monopoly of Argentina's foreign commerce.

In Buenos Aires, too, Rosas failed to achieve that integration of economic interests which was so essential to political and social stability. The *idée maitresse* of *porteño* federalist ideology was to free the dynamic forces of provincial economy from the dead weight of the backward and impoverished areas of the young Confederation. Federalism was to free the province from the tyranny of an overbearing and distant national government. It was to establish a local government, intimately acquainted with the needs and problems of an expanding provincial economy. It was to be a government closely associated with the population, a democratic government, determined to defend the people's birthright against the greed of native speculators and foreign financiers. Economic autonomy, the cornerstone of the federalist doctrine, was a meaningful slogan to all classes of the provincial population. It implied not only political democracy but economic and social justice as well. It promised to improve the lot of the lower and middle classes by retaining a larger proportion of the national income within provincial boundaries. And it offered new hope to the rural classes, who had been so consistently neglected by the unitary regime during the twenties. For was not Rosas himself raised in the *campaña?* Was he not the foremost landowner and industrialist in the province?

Whether Rosas ever intended to live up to the expectations aroused by the federalists during the period of their struggle for power is, of course, impossible to say. If he had such intentions he made no serious effort to put them to the test of practical politics, or else he was simply unable to control the forces which his party had brought into being. The failure of his first administration to launch a broad program of economic and social amelioration was perhaps justified, for the country had just passed through a period of profound unrest and civil war. Political consolidation of the new regime and rehabilitation of the treasury monopolized the attention and energies of the government. Rosas met the difficulties of his first term with skill and courage, and could with clear conscience demand a sweeping mandate two years later.

For two years after Rosas began his second administration the province enjoyed stability undisturbed by internal disorders and foreign wars. Economic recovery accompanied political stability, and the government did everything in its power to contribute to the progressive expansion of the provincial economy. Incorporation of the newly conquered territories into the economic system of the province provided a broad foundation for the growth and diversification of pastoral industries. The new tariff opened promising possibilities for local industry, and the policy of stable currency went a long way toward restoration of confidence among merchants of the city. Indeed, it seemed as if the province was at long last to enter a period of sustained prosperity.

Had Rosas been able to refrain from venturing beyond the realm of purely provincial interests, continued prosperity in Buenos Aires would have been assured. But isolation, whether political or economic, from the rest of the country was, of course, impossible. Buenos Aires could not remain indifferent to the political life of the provinces; nor could it shirk the responsibility for the conduct of the country's foreign affairs without endangering its position of political and economic preëminence. That preëminence was in part conditioned upon the ability of the *porteño* governments to maintain the political *status quo*. This in turn meant constant vigilance and frequent use of military force against recalcitrant *caudillos* and against nonconformist provinces. So it was that barely two years after the beginning of his second administration Rosas became involved in a series of foreign and internal conflicts which gradually rendered nugatory the gains derived from economic isolation. Such was the price of leadership.

No doubt, Buenos Aires was prepared to pay handsomely in money and effort for the advantages it secured under the system established by Rosas. But it could not pay indefinitely. For as the difficulties of maintaining the *status quo* mounted, a point was reached at which the cost of supporting the Rosas regime outweighed the advantages it offered. When this point had been reached Rosas and his policy had outlived their usefulness. However, as long as Rosas' government remained essentially a provincial government it served a useful purpose and was economically justified. But when by force of circumstances the *porteño* government assumed the functions of a national government it not only forsook the interests of Buenos Aires but it also fanned the flames of bitter resentment in the Interior and the Litoral. In this precisely consisted the tragic failure of Rosas.

Rosas failed because he succeeded too well. He succeeded in imposing upon the country the *porteño* brand of federalism, a political system to which the provinces could not be reconciled. The provinces accepted federalism because they opposed the centralizing tendencies of the unitary doctrine and because they desired an equitable share of the economic benefits at the disposal of the nation. Federalism swept the country on the wave of indignation against the economic and financial monopoly of Buenos Aires. It was a rallying cry against the transformation of the Interior and the Litoral into a happy hunting ground for foreign speculators and merchants-capitalists. But, above all, it was a plea for a more equitable distribution of the burden of readjustment to a new post-revolutionary politico-economic environment, and a demand for a balanced national economy. This was precisely what Rosas and his party would not concede. So it was that Rosas, the foremost executor of Dorrego's political testament, became the most important single obstacle to the realization of that testament.

The revolt which forced Rosas to leave the shores of La Plata was led by Justo José Urquiza, a *provinciano* and a federalist par excellence. Eight days after the battle of Caseros the provisional governor of Buenos Aires, Vicente Fidel López, referred to the fallen dictator as the savage unitary Juan Manuel Rosas. The epithet was not wholly unjustified, for in a sense Rosas and federalism had parted ways long before Caseros.

BIBLIOGRAPHY

A. Manuscript Sources and Archival Material

A LARGE PART of the decoumentary material examined in the preparation of this study was found in the Archivo General de la Nación, Buenos Aires. The holdings of the Archivo General de la Nación were found to be classified according to the branch of government where the documents were filed. The documents are arranged more or less chronologically in *legajos*. *Legajos* bearing the general titles of *Hacienda, Gobierno,* and *Varia* were found to be particularly rich in material pertinent to the subject matter of this study.

In some provincial archives documentary material was found to be arranged in strict chronological order bound into volumes. In the Archivo del Gobierno de la Provincia de Córdoba volumes 91 to 219 referred to the period discussed in this study, and in the Archivo Histórico de la Provincia de Tucumán documents relating to the years 1820 to 1853 were found to be assembled in volumes 66 to 125.

Material for this study was gathered in the following public and private archives:

Archivo General de la Nación, Buenos Aires
Archivo del Gobierno de la Provincia de Córdoba, Córdoba
Archivo Histórico de la Provincia de Entre Ríos, Paraná, Entre Ríos
Archivo del Gobierno, Santa Fe, Santa Fe
Archivo Histórico de la Provincia de Tucumán, Tucumán
Instituto de Investigaciones Históricas, Facultad de Filosofía y Letras, Universidad de Buenos Aires, Buenos Aires
A. Martínez de Hoz, Buenos Aires (private archives)
Julio Irazusta, Gualeguaychú, Entre Ríos (private archives)

B. Official Publications, Compilations, Newspapers, etc.

ONLY the more important publications are listed below. Many of the publications consulted were found in the Biblioteca Nacional, Buenos Aires, and the libraries of the Museo Mitre, Buenos Aires, the Banco Tornquist, Buenos Aires, the Universidad de La Plata, La Plata, the Harvard College Library and the Harvard Law School Library, and the Library of Congress.

Archivo de la Honorable Cámara de Diputados de la Provincia de Córdoba, 6 vols. (Córdoba: 1912–1914).

Archivo Histórico de la Provincia de Tucumán. Actas de la Sala de Representantes desde 1823 hasta 1852, xlix, 375 pp. (Tucumán: 1917).

Compilación de leyes, decretos, acuerdos de la Excelentísima Cámara de Justicia y demás disposiciones de caracter público dictadas en la Provincia de Córdoba desde 1810 á 1870 (Córdoba: 1870).

Mabragaña, Heraclio (ed.), *Los mensajes. Historia del desenvolvimiento de la nación argentina, redactada cronológicamente por sus gobernantes, 1810–1910. Publicación autorizada por la Comisión Nacional del Centenario,* 6 vols. (Buenos Aires: 1910).

Ravignani, Emilio (ed.), *Asambleas constituyentes argentinas, seguidas de los textos constitucionales, legislativos y pactos interprovinciales que organizaron políticamente la nación, fuentes seleccionadas, coordinadas y anotadas en cumplimiento de la ley 11.857,* 6 vols. (Buenos Aires: Jacobo Peuser, ltda., 1937–1939).

Recopilación de leyes y decretos promulgados en Buenos Aires desde el 25 de mayo de 1810 hasta fin de diciembre de 1835 (Buenos Aires: 1836).

Recopilación de leyes, decretos y acuerdos de la Provincia de Entre-Ríos desde 1821 á 1873, 15 vols. (Uruguay: 1875–1880).

Registro Oficial. Salta. (8 numbers, November 30, 1828 to October 1831.)

Registro Oficial. Salta. (Nos. 1–4; 6–13 for 1832. Nos. 1–5 for 1833.)

Registro Oficial de la Provincia de Buenos Aires, 1821–1851 (Buenos Aires).

Registro Oficial de la Provincia de Corrientes, correspondiente á los años 1825 á 1839, 2 vols. (Corrientes).

Registro Oficial de la Provincia de Corrientes. Segundo tomo. Años 1826–1830. Publicación oficial (Corrientes: 1925).

Registro Oficial de la Provincia de Corrientes, año 1841 (Corrientes: 1886).

Registro Oficial de la Provincia de Corrientes, años 1843, 1845, 1847, 1849, 4 vols. (Corrientes: 1886).

Registro Oficial de la Provinicia de San Juan, años 1825–1829 (July 1825–August 1829).

Registro Oficial de la Provincia de San Juan, año 1832.

Diario de Sesiones de la Junta de Representantes de la Provincia de Buenos Aires, 1827–1851 (Buenos Aires).

Registro Estadístico de la Provincia de Buenos Aires, 1821–1823 (Buenos Aires).

The British Packet and Argentine News (Buenos Aires: 1829–1852). (Weekly.)

Gaceta Mercantil (Buenos Aires: 1830–1852). (Daily.)

Relaciones Interprovinciales: La Liga Litoral (Collection of articles in *porteño* and provincial newspapers, 1829–1833. Unpublished, in the Instituo de Investigaciones Históricas).

Frías, U. S. (compiler), *Trabajos legislativos de las primeras asambleas argentinas desde la Junta de 1811 hasta la dissolución del Congreso en 1827,* 3 vols. (Buenos Aires: 1882).

Fuente, Diego de la (ed.), *Primer censo de la República Argentina, 1869* (Buenos Aires: 1872).

Archivo Americano y Espíritu de la Prensa del Mundo, Primera época: 1843–1847, 4 vols.; *Segunda época: 1847–1851,* 8 vols. Edited by Pedro de Angelis (Buenos Aires: 1843–1851).

Semanario de Agricultura Industria y Comercio. Reimpresión facsimilar publicada por la Junta de Historia y Numismática Americana, vol. 1, 1802–1803; vol. 2, 1803–1804; vol. 3, 1804–1805 (Buenos Aires: 1928–1937).

El Argos de Buenos Aires. Reimpresión facsimilar dirigida por los señores Antonio Dellepiane, Mariano de Vedia y Mitre y Rómulo Zavala, y prologada por el señor Arturo Capdevila, 3 vols. (Buenos Aires: 1931–1939).

Diario de la Tarde (Buenos Aires: scattered numbers, 1833–1835).

C. SECONDARY SOURCES: GENERAL WORKS, SPECIAL STUDIES, TRAVELERS' ACCOUNTS, MONOGRAPHS, ETC.

PUBLICATIONS dealing with purely political or military aspects have as a rule been excluded from the bibliography listed below.

Agote, Pedro de, *Informe del presidente del crédito público sobre la deuda pública, bancos y emisiones de papel moneda y acuñación de monedas de la República Argentina,* 5 vols. (Buenos Aires: 1881–1888).

Álvarez, Juan, *Ensayo sobre la historia de Santa Fe* (Buenos Aires: 1910).

————, *Estudio sobre las guerras civiles argentinas*, 291 pp. (Buenos Aires: 1914).

————, *Historia de Rosario*, 658 pp. (Buenos Aires: 1943).

————, *Temas de historia económica argentina*, 237 pp. (Buenos Aires: 1929).

Anchorena, Juan José Cristobal de, *Dictamen sobre el establecimiento de una compañía general del comercio en las Provincias Unidas de la Plata*, n. p. (1818).

Andree, Karl, *Buenos Aires und die argentinischen Provinzen*, xx, 426 pp. (Leipzig: 1856).

Andrews, Joseph, *Journey from Buenos Ayres through the provinces of Córdova, Tucumán and Salta to Potosí, thence by the deserts of Coranja to Arica, and subsequently, to Santiago de Chili and Coquimbo, undertaken on behalf of the Chilian and Peruvian Association, in the years 1825–1826*, 2 vols. (London: 1827).

Angelis, Pedro de, *Memoria sobre el estado de la hacienda pública escrita por orden del gobierno*, 219 pp. (Buenos Aires: 1834).

Antola, Carlos G., *El colectivismo agrario de Rivadavia*, vi, 174 pp. (Buenos Aires: 1919).

Anuario de historia argentina (Buenos Aires, Sociedad de Historia Argentina: 1941–).

Apuntes sobre la Provincia de Entre Ríos (Gualeguaychú, Entre Ríos: 1851).

Arenales, José Ildefonso, *Noticias históricas y descripciones sobre el gran país del Chaco y río Bermejo con observaciones relativas á un plan de navegación y colonización que se propone*, v, 421 pp. (Buenos Aires: 1833).

Ayarragaray, Lucas, *La anarquía argentina y el caudillismo*, viii, 353 pp. (Buenos Aires: 1904).

Azara, Félix de, *Viajes por la América meridional, por D. Félix de Azara, comisario y comandante de los límites españoles en el Paraguay desde 1781 hasta 1801. Publicados con arreglo a los manuscritos del autor, con una noticia sobre su vida y sus escritos por C. A. Walckenaer, enriquecidos con notas por G. Cuvier. Traducida del francés por Francisco de las Barras de Aragón*, 2 vols. (Madrid: 1923).

Banco y Casa de Moneda, Buenos Aires. *Colección de leyes y decretos* (Buenos Aires: 1857).

Barreda Laos, Felipe, *General Tomás Guido*, 387 pp. (Buenos Aires: 1942).

Bassi, Ángel C., *El tirano Rosas*, 461 pp. (Buenos Aires: 1942).

Beaumont, J. A. B., *Travels in Buenos Ayres and the adjacent provinces of the Rio de la Plata*, xii, 270 pp. (London: 1828).

Bilbao, Manuel, *Buenos Aires desde su fundación hasta nuestros días, especialmente el período comprendido en los siglos XVIII y XIX*, xii, 664 pp. (Buenos Aires: 1902).

————, *Historia de Rosas. Desde 1810 hasta 1852* (Buenos Aires: 1868).

————, *Vindicación y memorias de don Antonino Reyes* (Buenos Aires: 1883).

Blondel, J. J., *Almanaque político y de comercio de la ciudad de Buenos Aires*, 4 vols.; 1826, 1830, 1834, 1836 (Buenos Aires).

Brossard, Alfredo de, *Rosas visto por un diplomático francés*, 372 pp. (Buenos Aires: 1942).

Buenos Ayres et le Paraguay; ou histoire, moeurs, usages des habitants (Paris: 1823).

Busaniche, José, *Estanislao López y el federalismo del Litoral* (Buenos Aires).

Caldcleugh, Alexander, *Travels in South America, during the years 1819–20–21; containing an account of the present state of Brazil, Buenos Ayres, and Chile*, 2 vols. (London: 1825).

Capdevila, Arturo, *Rivadavia y el españolismo liberal de la revolución argentina*, 268 pp. (Buenos Aires: 1931).

Carbia, Rómulo de, *Gravámenes al comercio colonial en el Río de la Plata* (Buenos Aires: 1916).

Cárcano, Miguel A., *Evolución histórica del régimen de la tierra pública, 1810–1916*, xxiv, 593 pp. (Buenos Aires: 1917).

Cárcano, Ramón J., *Historia de los medios de comunicación y transporte en la República Argentina*, 2 vols. (Buenos Aires: 1893).

——, *Juan Facundo Quiroga; simulación, infidencia, tragedia*, Tercera edición, 382 pp. (Buenos Aires: 1931).

Carlés, M., "Antecedentes económicos de la constitución argentina" (*Revista de Derecho, Historia y Letras*, vol. 46, 1913).

Carranza, Ángel Justiniano, *El general Lavalle ante la justicia póstuma*, 225 pp. (Buenos Aires: 1941).

——, *La revolución del 39 en el sur de Buenos Aires*, xxii, 431 pp. (Buenos Aires: 1880).

Carranza, Arturo B., *La cuestión capital de la República, 1826 a 1887 (antecedentes, proyectos de leyes)*, 4 vols. (Buenos Aires: 1926–1929).

Carrasco, Eudoro, *Anales de la ciudad del Rosario de Santa Fe, 1527–1865*, 674 pp. (Buenos Aires: 1897).

Carrillo, Joaquín, *Jujui, provincia federal arjentina. Apuntes de su historia civil*, 534 pp. (Buenos Aires: 1877).

Casarino, Nicolás, *El Banco de la Provincia de Buenos Aires en su primer centenario, 1822–1922*, 351 pp. (Buenos Aires: 1922).

Castro Esteves, Ramón de, *Rosas ante la historia. Prólogo de* Enrique de Gandía, 164 pp. (Buenos Aires: 1931).

Cervera, Manuel M., *Historia de la ciudad y provincia de Santa Fe, 1573–1853*, 2 vols. (Santa Fe: 1908).

Coni, Emilio A., *Rivadavia y su obra colonizadora* (Buenos Aires: 1924).

——, *La verdad sobre la enfiteusis de Rivadavia*, 226 pp. (Buenos Aires: 1927).

Cortes Funes, Gerónimo, "La enfiteusis como instrumento de colonización" (*Revista Argentina de Ciencias Políticas*, vol. 22, 1921).

Cuestión del día: Banco Nacional (Buenos Aires: 1825).

Dictamen de la Comisión de Hacienda sobre los proyectos presentados por el gobierno con el objeto de reglar el sistema de hacienda de la Provincia (Buenos Aires: 1827).

Documentos relativos á la formación de un Banco Nacional en las Provincias Unidas de Sud América (Buenos Aires: 1824).

Dorrego y el federalismo argentino. Con introducción del Dr. Antonio Dellepiane (Buenos Aires: n.d.).

Echeverría, Esteban, *Obras completas*, 5 vols. (Buenos Aires: 1870–1874).

Estrada, José Manuel, *La política liberal bajo la tiranía de Rosas* (Buenos Aires: 1917).

Ferré, Pedro, *Memoria del brigadier general Pedro Ferré*, 991 pp. (Buenos Aires: 1921).

"Las finanzas en la época de Rosas" (*Revista Nacional*, vol. 1, 1886).

A five years' residence in Buenos Ayres during the years 1820–1825. By an Englishman. Second edition, viii, 176 pp. (London: 1827).

Flairoto, Matilda T., *Mariano Moreno. Estudio de su personalidad y de su obra*, 620 pp. (Buenos Aires: 1916).

Font Ezcurra, Ricardo, *La unidad nacional*, 253 pp. (Buenos Aires: 1938).

Gálvez, Jaime, *Rosas y la libre navegación de los Ríos*, 263 pp. (Buenos Aires: 1944).

García, Juan Agustín, *La ciudad indiana*, xiv, 375 pp. (Buenos Aires: 1909).

García Mérou, Martín, *Ensayo sobre Echeverría*, 251 pp. (Buenos Aires: 1894).

Gibson, E., *The history and the present day sheep breeding industry in the Argentine Republic* (Buenos Aires: 1893).

Gómez, Hernán F., *Historia de la Provincia de Corrientes* (Corrientes: 1929).

Gondra, Enrique, "Apuntes de historia económica" (*Revista de Ciencias Económicas*, año vii, nos. 87–88, 1920).

Gondra, Luis Roque, *Las ideas económicas de Manuel Belgrano*, 357 pp. (Buenos Aires: 1923).

González, Joaquín V., *Estudios de historia argentina* (Buenos Aires: 1930).

Gónzalez Arrilli, B., *Lavalle, paladín de la libertad* (Buenos Aires: 1942).

———, *La tiranía y la libertad. Juan Manuel de Rozas según 127 autores*, 640 pp. (Buenos Aires: 1943).

González Calderón, Juan A., "La renuncia de Rivadavia" (*La Prensa*, Buenos Aires, 28 de junio de 1927).

Groussac, Paul, *Las Bases de Alberdi y el desarrollo constitucional* (Buenos Aires: 1918).

Haigh, Samuel. *Sketches of Buenos Ayres and Chile*, xviii, 316 pp. (London: 1829).

Hansen, Emilio, *La moneda argentina, estudio histórico*, 555 pp. (Buenos Aires: 1916).

Head, S. B., *Reports relating to the failure of the Rio Plata Mining Association, formed under an authority signed by his Excellency Don B. Rivadavia* (London: 1827).

Heras, Carlos, "Confiscaciones y embargos durante el gobierno de Rosas" (*Humanidades*, La Plata, vol. 20, 1929).

Ibarguren, Carlos, *Juan Manuel de Rosas. Su vida, su tiempo y su drama*. Tercera edición, 468 pp. (Buenos Aires: 1930).

Ingenieros, José, *La evolución de las ideas argentinas*, 2 vols. (Buenos Aires: 1918–1920).

Irazusta, Julio, *Vida política de Juan Manuel de Rosas a través de su correspondencia* (Buenos Aires: 1941–1943).

Isabelle, Arsène, *Voyage à Buenos Aires et à Porto Alegre, par la Banda Oriental, les Misiones d'Uruguay et la province de Rio Grande do Sul* (Havre: 1835).

King, John Anthony, *Twenty four years in the Argentine Republic*, 324 pp. (London: 1846).

L., C., *Relation d'un voyage fait recemment dans les provinces de la Plata* (Paris: 1818).

Lagrange, Francisco, *Sarmiento y su época*, 141 pp. (Córdoba: 1918).

Lamas, Andrés, *La época de Rosas* (Buenos Aires: 1910).

———, *Estudio histórico y científico del Banco de la Provincia de Buenos Aires*, 205 pp. (Buenos Aires: 1886).

———, *La obra económica de Bernardino Rivadavia*, xxiii, 143 pp. (Buenos Aires: 1917).

———, *Rivadavia, su obra política y cultural*, 366 pp. (Buenos Aires: 1915).

Laplaza, Francisco P., *Rosas y la unidad nacional*, 35 pp. (Santa Fe: 1942).

Levene, Ricardo, "La anarquía de 1820 en Buenos Aires" (*Boletin de la Junta de Historia y Numismática Americana*, vol. viii, pp. 159–168).

———, *Ensayo histórico sobre la Revolución de Mayo y Mariano Moreno. Contribución al estudio de los aspectos político, jurídico y económico de la Revolución de 1810*, 2 vols. (Buenos Aires: 1920–1921).

———, *Investigaciones acerca de la historia económica del virreinato del Plata*, 2 vols. (La Plata: 1927–1928).

———, *Lecciones de historia argentina*, 2 vols. (Buenos Aires: 1913).

——— (ed.), *Historia de la nación argentina, desde sus orígenes hasta la organización definitiva en 1862*. Vol. IX. *Historia de las provincias*, 762 pp. (Buenos Aires: 1941).

López, Vicente Fidel. *Historia de la República Argentina, su origen, su revolución y su desarrollo político hasta 1852*, 10 vols. (Buenos Aires: 1883–1893).

MacCann, William, *Two thousand miles' ride through the Argentine Provinces*, 2 vols. (London: 1853).

Mannequin, Théodore, *Les provinces Argentines et Buénos Aires depuis leur independance jusqu'à nos jours. Étude historique et économique au point de vue de l'état actuel des choses dans les contrées*, 48 pp. (Paris: 1856).

Marbais du Graty, Alfred Louis Hubert Ghislain, *La Confédération Argentine*, xii, 371 pp. (Paris: 1858).

Martin de Moussy, J. A. V., *Description géographique et statistique de la Confédération Argentine*, 3 vols. (Paris: 1860–1873).

Martínez Paz, Enrique, *La formación histórica de la provincia de Córdoba*, 292 pp. (Córdoba: 1941).

Molinari, Diego Luis, *La "Representación de los hacendados" de Mariano Moreno* (Buenos Aires: 1914).

Moreno, Manuel, *Vida y memorias del doctor Don Mariano Moreno*, 277 pp. (Buenos Aires: 1918).

Moreno, Mariano, *Escritos políticos y económicos; ordenados y con prólogo por Norberto Piñero*, 370 pp. (Buenos Aires: 1915).

Núñez, Ignacio, *Noticias históricas, políticas y estadísticas de las Provincias Unidas del Río de la Plata con un apéndice sobre la usurpación de Montevideo por los gobiernos portugués y brasilero* (Londres: 1825).

Oddone, Jacinto, *El factor económico en nuestras luchas civiles*, 376 pp. (Buenos Aires: 1937).

Orgaz, R. Arturo, *Las ideas sociales de Echeverría* (Córdoba: 1912).

Palcos, Alberto, *Echeverría y la democracia argentina*, 224 pp. (Buenos Aires: 1941).

Parish, Woodbine, *Buenos Ayres and the Provinces of the Río de la Plata, from their discovery and conquest by the Spaniards to the establishment of their political independence. With some account of their present state, trade, debt, etc.; an appendix of historical and statistical documents; and a description of the geology and fossil monsters of the pampas*, 434 pp. (London: 1852).

Pelliza, Mariano A., *La dictadura de Rosas*, 309 pp. (Buenos Aires: 1917).

Piccirilli, Ricardo, *Rivadavia y su tiempo*, 2 vols. (Buenos Aires: 1943).

Piñero, Norberto, "La disolución del Banco Nacional de 1826" (*Revista Argentina de Ciencias Políticas*, vol. 14, 1917).

Pont, José Marco del, *Moneda de Tucumán, 1820–1824* (Buenos Aires: 1915).

Poucel, Benjamin, *Les otages de Durazno; souvenirs de Rio de la Plata pendant l'intervention anglo-français de 1845 à 1851*, vii, 351 pp. (Paris: 1864).

Puiggrós, Rodolfo, *Rosas el Pequeño*, 382 pp. (Montevideo: 1944).

Quesada, Ernesto, *La época de Rosas. Su verdadero caracter histórico*, 392 pp. (Buenos Aires: 1898).

Ramos Mejía, J. M., *Rosas y su tiempo*, 3 vols. (Buenos Aires: 1907).

Ravignani, Emilio, *Historia constitucional de la República Argentina* (Buenos Aires: 1926).

——, "Primeras disidencias entre los federales triunfantes: elección de Juan Manuel de Rosas, 1829" (*Boletín de la Junta de Historia y Numismática Americana*, vol. ix, 1936).

"Relación de los viajes de monsieur Ascarate du Biscay al Río de la Plata y desde aquí por tierra hasta el Perú, con observaciones sobre estos países, etc." (*Revista de Buenos Aires*, t. xiii).

Rivarola, Rodolfo, "Ciclos de ideas-fuerzas en la historia argentina" (*Boletín de la Junta de Historia y Numismática Americana*, vol. viii).

Rivera Indarte, José, *Rosas y sus opositores*, 3 vols. (Buenos Aires: 1929).

Robertson, John Paris, and William P. Robertson, *Letters on South America, comprising travels on the banks of the Paraná and Río de la Plata* (London: 1843).

Rodney, Caesar Augustus, and John Graham, *The reports on the present state of the United Provinces of South America; drawn up by Messrs. C. A. Rodney and J. Graham, commissioners sent to Buenos Aires by the government of North America* and laid before the Congress of the United States; with their accompanying documents, occasional notes by the editor and an introductory discourse intended to present, with the reports and documents, a view of the present state of the country, and of progress of the independents, 358 pp. (London: 1819).

Rossi, Vicente, El gaucho, su origen y evolución, 127 pp. (La Plata: 1921).

Saldías, Adolfo, La evolución republicana durante la revolución argentina, 409 pp. (Madrid: 1919).

———, Rosas y su época. Segunda edición, 5 vols. (Buenos Aires: 1892).

Sarasketa, Victorino de, "El sistema rentístico argentino de 1810 á 1820" (Revista Argentina de Ciencias Políticas, vol. 15, 1917).

———, El régimen tributario colonial (La Plata: 1919).

Sarmiento, Domingo F., Obras completas, 52 vols. (Santiago: 1887–1902).

———, Contra Rosas (Buenos Aires: 1934).

———, Facundo (Buenos Aires: 1915).

Scarone, Arturo, El gaucho, xiii, 126 pp. (Montevideo: 1922).

Schleh, Emilio J., La industria azucarera en su primer centenario, 1821–1921, 444 pp. (Buenos Aires: 1921).

Schmidtmeyer, Peter, Travels into Chile over the Andes in the years 1820 and 1821 (London: 1824).

Silva, Carlos Alberto, El poder legislativo de la nación Argentina, vol. 2 (Buenos Aires: 1938).

Silva, J. Francisco V., "Federalismo del Norte y Centro en 1820" (Revista de la Universidad Nacional de Córdoba, año xviii, 1931).

———, "Formas federales de Tucumán y Córdoba en 1820" (Revista de la Universidad Nacional de Córdoba, año xviii, 1931).

Terry, José Antonio, "Contribución á la historia financiera de la República Argentina" (La Nación, Buenos Aires, 25 de Mayo de 1910).

Urien, Carlos María, Esteban Echeverría, ensayo crítico-histórico sobre su vida y obras con motivo de la erección de su estatua (Buenos Aires: 1905).

———, Impresiones y recuerdos; un contemporáneo el general Lucio Victorio Mansilla, 470 pp. (Buenos Aires: 1914).

Vedia, Agustín de, Banco Nacional (Buenos Aires: 1890).

Vedia y Mitre, Mariano de, De Rivadavia a Rosas (Buenos Aires: 1935).

Vergara, M. A., and J. Picchetti, "El cultivo y la elaboración de la caña de azucar en la jurisdicción de Jujuy. Datos históricos" (Boletín del Instituto de Investigaciones Históricas, años xi–xiii, tomo xvi, 1933, no. 55–57).

Vidal, E. E., Picturesque illustrations of Buenos Aires and Montevideo consisting of twenty four views: accompanied with descriptions of the scenery and of the costumes, manners, etc., of the inhabitants of those cities and their environs, xviii, 115 pp. (London: 1820).

Wilde, José A., Buenos Aires desde años atras, 350 pp. (Buenos Aires: 1881).

Zinny, Antonio, Historia de los gobernadores de las provincias argentinas. Edición reordenada, con un prólogo de Pedro Bonastre, 5 vols. (Buenos Aires: 1920–1921).

INDEX